15.00
T3-AKB-489

THE RISE OF SCOTLAND YARD

New Scotland Yard (South) *New Scotland Yard (Central)* *New Scotland Yard (North)*

METROPOLITAN POLICE HEADQUARTERS

THE RISE OF SCOTLAND YARD

A History of the Metropolitan Police

by

DOUGLAS G. BROWNE

JOINT AUTHOR OF "BERNARD SPILSBURY"
"FINGERPRINTS"
AUTHOR OF
"PRIVATE THOMAS ATKINS" "PLAN XVI"
"WHAT BECKONING GHOST"
"SERGEANT DEATH" ETC.

GREENWOOD PRESS, PUBLISHERS
WESTPORT, CONNECTICUT

Library of Congress Cataloging in Publication Data

Browne, Douglas Gordon, 1884-
The rise of Scotland Yard.

Reprint of the 1956 ed. published by Harrap, London.
Bibliography: p.
1. Great Britain. Metropolitan Police Office. Criminal Investigation Dept. I. Title.
[HV8198.L7B7 1973] 363.2'09421 73-6257
ISBN 0-8371-6898-8

First published in Great Britain 1956
by George G. Harrap & Co. Ltd.

Reprinted with the permission
of George G. Harrap & Company Ltd.

First Greenwood Reprinting 1973

Library of Congress Catalogue Card Number 73-6257

ISBN 0-8371-6898-8

Printed in the United States of America

PREFACE

SEVERAL years ago my friend Ralph Straus began a history of the Metropolitan Police. He had the generous help of the authorities at New Scotland Yard in being given access to the records without which such a work as he contemplated could not have been undertaken. This privilege was later extended to me, but I would like to make it clear to my readers that, unless otherwise stated, expressions of opinion are my own and must be accepted as such. As Ralph's health began to fail he found the double task of research and composition too much for him, and he asked me to help him with what had become the labour of writing. Before we had really got down to things together he went into hospital for the last time.

His completed text had brought the narrative only to the year 1850. A few pages of the chapter entitled "'King' Mayne" were in typescript, and he had left some notes for this and later chapters. More than a hundred years, therefore, remained to be covered when I took up the task.

Ralph had the instincts and patience of the scholar, and in his small, neat handwriting he had filled several foolscap books with notes on the early history of London's police, including the first twenty-one years of his main theme. He had collected a small library of printed works, some of them rare, dealing with his subject. Had he lived to finish the book, as no doubt he realized, he would have had to compress his valuable introductory chapters, going back to Saxon times. To cut and summarize so much conscientious work was a difficult undertaking for his successor; and, once accomplished, it merely raised another problem. Ralph's text had been retained, whenever possible, and at an early stage of the book there was an obvious change of style. With the agreement of all concerned, to achieve unity, I tackled these chapters once more, and put them in my own words.

In doing so, however, I have endeavoured, as throughout the book, to hold fast to Ralph's original design. He did not intend to write a chronicle of police work, except where this was necessary to illustrate his theme, which was the development of a unique but typically British institution against the national and political background of a hundred and twenty-five years. Here I am only his follower, and his is the credit of the design and of the foundation on which the finished structure has been raised.

D. G. B.

CONTENTS

Book One

THE OLD POLICE

Book Two

THE NEW POLICE

Book Three

THE MODERN POLICE

ILLUSTRATIONS

BOOK ONE

The Old Police

1

THE METROPOLIS: 1050 to 1600

Two British travellers, sheltering from the rain in a little estaminet in the Graisivaudan, fell into talk with the only other customer at the bar, an unshaven, genial specimen who apparently had no English. It somehow emerged, however, that one of the travellers wrote *romans policiers*, whereupon their interlocutor, with obvious pride in his knowledge, ejaculated, "Ah, Scotlan' Yarr'! Sherlock 'Olmes!" He had some English, after all, though these two names may well have been the beginning and end of it.

That they have become household words almost throughout the globe scarcely needs emphasizing, but the linking of them together in this way in a village on the Isère is a useful illustration of how equally world-wide, in the case of Scotland Yard, is the confusion between fact and fiction.[1] It may be that this is so because the confusion begins at home. Not only the untutored foreigner thinks of Scotland Yard almost solely in terms of crime, and a questionnaire on its functions in general might produce some surprising answers. There is, for example, the belief—held chiefly, perhaps, by Londoners—that it is the headquarters of all the police forces in the country. Of those who know better it may be hazarded that many have no very clear ideas about the constitution, powers, and limitations of the Metropolitan Police.

Powers and limitations are bound up with the constitution—that is to say, with the origins and history of the force. Now only one of many separate forces in the country, it is the prototype of them all, and it remains by far the largest; but it is not because of priority or size that its history is of particular interest. The police force specifically allotted to a capital, or to a vastly preponderant part of it which houses the

[1] A Scandinavian correspondent has recently requested Scotland Yard to forward him the autographs of Sir Arthur Conan Doyle and Mr Sherlock Holmes.

whole machinery of national government, must stand in a peculiar relation to authority, and must be affected by national affairs—in other words, by politics—to a degree happily unknown to provincial forces. There are, however, more cogent reasons why the annals of the Metropolitan Police have throughout its existence been interwoven with the mutations of public and Parliamentary feeling.

It is in one sense a political creation, and the position of its headquarters, on the doorstep of Parliament, is symbolic of the fact that the force is not locally independent in the way that provincial constabularies are. All are servants of the Crown, and subject to Parliament's supervision, but only the Metropolitan Police comes directly under Ministerial control. The "Police Authority" in the London Area is the Home Secretary. He advises the Crown on the appointment of the commanding officer, the Commissioner, and the latter's immediate subordinates. Until recently even promotions within the ranks required his formal consent. At the other end of the scale he "fixes the police rate in the Metropolitan boroughs and parishes, and through his financial officer, the Receiver for the Metropolitan Police District, collects the revenue and controls the expenditure of the force." The Commissioner's responsibility for internal matters, and for dealing with crime and maintaining order, is "subject always to his obtaining the approval of the Home Secretary to all his standing regulations, and to all important orders affecting the public."[1]

This state of affairs is the outcome of a long process of experiment in the theory and practice of maintaining law and order in British political conditions, and not only in London. But the problems of London, like Mr Weller's knowledge of it, have always been extensive and peculiar, because of its size and situation, and because it is the capital. The history of its police—using the word in the modern sense—is an important chapter in the history of the country.

2

The very term Metropolitan Police embodies the statement of a historical oddity—that in the case of London, alone among the world's capitals, the Metropolis is only a part of the whole, though now overwhelmingly the greater part. The word, to English people, means London outside the City. The most relevant instance of a distinction that goes back nine hundred years is the existence to-day, within the capital as a whole, of two separate and independent police forces. The

[1] Sir Edward Troup, *The Home Office* (Putnam, 1925).

City Police, under their own Commissioner, still control their original area of roughly one square mile, the area of Roman London, with a small and dwindling permanent population. The enormous shell in which this kernel is now embedded, a territory of some seven hundred square miles, three times the size of the Isle of Man, including one ancient county, one new one, and portions of four others, and inhabited by over eight million people, is the responsibility of the Metropolitan Police.

The germ of all this was a few acres of buildings grouped round the palace which Edward the Confessor erected beside his new minster on the site of Thorney Abbey. In these rural and marshy surroundings, two miles up the Thames from the City of London, the "City and Liberty of Westminster" continually expanded, until what had been a small manor belonging to the Abbey became the real political capital of the country. It was an untidy process. For more than eight centuries Westminster was a city rather by courtesy than by incorporation. During much of this period the neighbouring City of London controlled certain parishes outside its walls, including the transpontine suburb of Southwark, though for long this was in a class by itself.

The City had, as it has still, its own ways of keeping order. Its traditions, its wealth, its compactness, its walls, its division into wards, and its form of administration should have rendered this task relatively easy. It was a different matter with the mushroom growth of Westminster, a casual association of townships, parishes, and privileged places straggling in course of time from Fleet Street to Kensington, and from the Thames to Paddington and Marylebone. The problem of how to maintain 'the king's peace' in such a congeries differed only in degree from that which faced authority throughout the country. Normal police difficulties in the Middle Ages were indeed aggravated in Westminster by features peculiar to a mixed locality which accident had made populous and important.

'The king's peace' has come to signify no more than the absence of disorder. It seems to have originated in the special sanctity attaching at one time to the king's person and family. A breach of it was an act of disobedience to the monarch. Royal protection, however, having been extended to certain persons in return for their services, this protection gradually became general; the allegiance of the king's subjects entitled them in theory to peace and personal safety, guaranteed by him as Chief Magistrate. He delegated some of his magisterial powers to stewards, the shire-reeves or sheriffs, who were given charge of the various divisions of the kingdom (afterwards the counties), and who at first possessed considerable vice-regal powers, having their own courts of justice. In their police capacity they could muster an armed defence force, the *posse comitatus*, to deal with serious disorders. The system was never popular, and when the more localized court leets were instituted, each with a steward nominated by the lord of the manor, the sheriff's tourn, or circuit, was superseded. "The whole history of English Justice and Police," to quote Maitland, "might be brought under the Rubric, the Decline and Fall of the Sheriff."

In this way another police system, already at work, came fully into its own. The great landowner became responsible for the good behaviour of those legally dependent upon him. For their own protection these dependants were banded together into tens, or tythings, each tything having its headborough. Every ten tythings formed a hundred (later to have a territorial meaning), each again with its responsible head. Every member of a tything or hundred bore some measure of responsibility for the deeds of his fellows. The headboroughs, or aeldors, later to become aldermen, who took an oath to bring all offenders in their district to justice, may be looked upon as the earliest constables.

Such, in its simplest form, was the frank-pledge system, which largely depended on the still-extant assumption that every adult male subject of the Crown is a potential policeman. In rural districts it may have worked tolerably well, but in the towns it proved less satisfactory. Even in the City of London the burghers found it necessary to protect themselves by the formation of frith-guilds, mutual assurance societies which sometimes employed their own private police. This was not enough, and, the old manors and liberties of the City having given place to twenty-four wards, each with its alderman, these latter were required to act as police supervisors, with watchmen working under them. A separate "marching watch" was organized for emergencies—a forerunner of the much later "patroles." On the whole the City seems to have been in the van of a very general movement, during the thirteenth and fourteenth centuries, to improve the means of dealing with lawlessness, and to have taken an increasingly wide view of police work. Neither the City Fathers nor anyone else, of course, would then have used that term. The word 'police' was unknown to the Middle Ages. Even in its early meaning of 'policy' it is not found in England before the sixteenth century.

JOHN TOWNSEND, BOW STREET RUNNER
Model in the Black Museum at Scotland Yard.

SIR THOMAS DE VEIL

[*See pp.* 22–24.]

SIR JOHN FIELDING

"*Picture Post*" *Library*

[*See pp.* 28–43.]

PATRICK COLQUHOUN

"*Picture Post*" *Library*

[*See pp.* 47–50.]

CAPTAIN JOHN HARRIOTT

[*See pp.* 49–50.]

3

Endeavours to improve the police systems of the country after the Norman Conquest can be traced through a series of enactments, beginning in 1164 with measures laid down at Henry II's Assize of Clarendon. Richard I, in 1195, appointed by proclamation certain knights to "swear to the King" all men over fifteen to keep the peace. Later called Conservators of the Peace, these officials were to have a long and honourable future. In the meantime, an Assize at Arms held in 1181 had been in part a police measure. In 1285, in the reign of Edward I, came the Statute of Winchester; and in 1328 Edward III inaugurated something like a new era in police history.

The Assize of Clarendon, by which sheriffs were commanded to assist one another in the pursuit of "reputed felons," shows a feeling for the need of better collaboration among the various authorities; and from this famous council, most probably, springs a peculiarly English method of dealing with the absconding criminal—the raising of Hue and Cry. This, like the later Riot Act, automatically brought into operation a series of special regulations.

The Statute of Winchester laid down the principle that the policing of an area was the compulsory duty of its inhabitants, added to the number of officers appointed for the purpose, and confirmed an early decree detailing two constables in every hundred to make a half-yearly inspection of arms. This last feature emphasizes the semi-military character of the constable at that date. There were other enactments in the Statute relating to Hue and Cry, the closing of city gates at dusk, the maintenance of watches by boroughs, and the widening of main roads. A special *Statute Comitatis* of the same year, applying only to the City of London, elaborated a system in force there of night patrols and sentries, and so initiated the long-lasting organization of Watch and Ward, or squads functioning by day as well as by night. Imitated in other cities, this organization was the forerunner of the London Trained Bands.

Richard I's Conservators of the Peace had been "executive officers only."[1] It was Edward III who in 1328 enlarged the functions of these officials, giving them powers which were gradually extended until, by the end of the fourteenth century, they were firmly established as Justices of the Peace. Each had a clerk, and certain "lowe and lay ministers,"[2] the petty or parish constables, took the place as peace

[1] W. L. Melville Lee, *A History of Police in England* (Methuen, 1901). For all this period see the earlier chapters of this work.

[2] William Lambarde, *Eirenarcha: or of the Office of the Justices of the Peace* (1581).

officers of the old tythingmen. Like the justices, these men were unpaid, and were required to serve for a year. Their duty was to arrest malefactors or vagrants, and they took an oath which does not differ materially from that which the police constable takes to-day.

For two or three centuries this combination of justice and constable persisted without major changes. On the whole the system was popular. In small market towns the justice was a well-known figure, a local man of standing who, unlike his nominal superior, the sheriff, understood local feeling and custom. As an owner of property—he had to have an estate worth twenty pounds a year—he generally realized that privileges entail responsibilities. It was scarcely his fault if he seemed helpless or inefficient in some serious crisis, such as Wat Tyler's revolt; the lack of anything like a common police organization made uprisings on a large scale irresistible in their early stages.

It was a different story in the few cities and big towns. Here the reluctance of men of standing to enter the Commission of the Peace left an opening for a new urban type, "men of small substance," in Lambarde's words, "whose povertie made them both covetous and contemptible." Contriving to evade the property qualification, such men became magistrates in order to make money. Justice was bought and sold, and an Elizabethan could describe an urban magistrate of his day as "a living creature that for half a dozen chickens would dispense with a whole dozen of penal statutes." Corruption pervaded the whole machinery, and those annually called upon to act as constables preferred to hire worthless substitutes who, like Elbow in *Measure for Measure*, might function for years with the minimum of activity and usefulness. The watchmen were as bad, and are shown in plays of the time summoning as their assistants elderly paupers with just enough cunning to know that a young spark in trouble would readily pay to avoid punishment.

There were, of course, honourable exceptions among the magistracy. Corruption in the magistrate's house, or "office," as it was to become, was, in fact, to grow worse. The better class of justice did much good work, especially under the Tudors. The most barbarous punishments continued to be inflicted for trivial offences, but a number of statutes were then passed which were designed rather to prevent than to punish crime. One against unlawful assemblies was to develop into the Riot Act of 1715; another gave justices certain licensing powers in respect of alehouses, often the scenes of violence and vice, which until that date could be opened by anybody not a foreigner.

It was towards the end of this period that conditions in the Metropolis began to receive special attention, for during Elizabeth's reign important measures were taken for "the suppressing and rooting out of vice" in Westminster.

4

Until 1584 all police powers in Westminster were in the hands of the Abbey authorities. This system may have worked in the eleventh century, when Westminster, in size, was still a village; but in the course of the next five centuries it had become the Metropolis, of which Maitland says:

> This town, we must remember, was in the eye of the law no town; it had no legal being. . . . Geography and remote history had done their worst for the Metropolis; the Commissions of the Peace for Middlesex, Surrey, Kent and Essex converged on the disorderly mass, while separate commissions for Westminster and the Liberty of the Tower confounded confusion.[1]

Maitland was writing of a rather later date, but his description accurately describes the Metropolis as it was when Elizabeth came to the throne. This "collection of townships and manors, parishes and extra-parochial places, which owned no common ruler save King and Parliament," included, beyond the nucleus of Westminster itself, agglomerations of buildings about Charing Cross and along the Strand and Fleet Street to the City boundary; a thickly populated area running northward to Holborn and Smithfield; a perimeter of villages and hamlets from St Giles-in-the-Fields by way of Clerkenwell and Shoreditch to the river beyond the Liberties of the Tower; and possibly certain places on the south bank of the Thames, though Southwark, at this date, had recently been incorporated in the City as a ward. The maintenance of law and order in this considerable district was disputed between church authorities, county justices, and various public or semi-public bodies claiming special privileges and possessing private watches and the like. Westminster itself, with its slums almost touching royal palaces and noblemen's mansions, its influx of foreign workers, and the riff-raff pouring into it from the City and Southwark, was the worst hotbed of crime in the kingdom.

The coming of Elizabeth saw the Abbot of Westminster displaced by a Dean, who was instructed to draw up statutes for a new executive body. He delegated his police powers to an official called the High Steward.[2] It was not, however, until 1584, when Burghley, the Lord

[1] F. W. Maitland, *The English Citizen*.

[2] This office, which for long years was allowed to lapse, has recently been revived with the appointment of the Earl of Halifax.

High Treasurer, was appointed to this office, that a serious attempt was made to give the ever-growing Metropolis a comprehensive police system. Parliament passed an Act by which "the City and Borough" of Westminster was divided into twelve wards, each under the charge of an unpaid and annually elected officer called a burgess. Each burgess had an assistant, and the duties of these officers were almost identical with those performed by the City Aldermen and their deputies, as Peel was to be reminded when, two hundred and fifty years later, the state of the police of the Metropolis was yet again under consideration. But whereas in the City there was a degree of cohesion and a central authority, even a High Steward of Burghley's standing could not enforce such conditions on Westminster. There was too much jealousy between the various bodies still claiming jurisdiction. It was necessary, for instance, to pacify the Middlesex justices by requiring them to receive notice within twenty-four hours of any committal to prison by a burgess. In short, authority remained divided, and until the eighteenth century burgesses and justices continued to bicker about their respective responsibilities, and not only in police matters. They fought over the appointment of scavengers, and a common policy for all Westminster was seldom or never attained.

Side by side with the new burgesses and their assistants the old parochial officers, the constables, continued their unpaid duties. These must have become more onerous, but little is to be gleaned about them at this time. In 1572 Elizabeth's Parliament had passed an often-quoted Act "which provided a stricter punishment for beggars and inaugurated a compulsory poor-rate to aid the deserving poor,"[1] and this meant more work and responsibility for the constable, who could now be fined 6*s*. 8*d*., then no mean sum, for neglecting to arrest a sturdy beggar. It is no wonder that his office was the least popular of all parochial posts, or that he was usually well content to pay a deputy, who cannot often have been a man of the best type. Dogberry and Verges and the sleep-loving watchman in *Much Ado about Nothing* are no doubt fairly typical of their kind at the beginning of the seventeenth century.

[1] Frank Aydelotte, *Elizabethan Rogues and Vagabonds* (Clarendon Press, 1913).

2

THE TRADING JUSTICE AND THE BIRTH OF BOW STREET

ALTHOUGH the seventeenth century saw an extraordinary efflorescence of diarists and satirists, journalists and letter-writers, almost all practising in London, surprisingly little of interest about the policing of the Metropolis can be gathered from such sources. A bustling and intensely curious age was perhaps not likely to concern itself with reform of the commonplace, and many existing evils were taken for granted—among them the disgraceful and dangerous state of the London streets. These appear to have been worse than ever before, at least in the early part of the century, when corruption among urban justices, of which much is heard, also reached a new level of depravity. The reign of James I is distinguished by the appearance of the "basket justice," so-called because of the empty basket displayed in front of him for gifts in kind from petitioners and offenders. The prevalence of this traffic implies a general degeneration among officers of police from High Constables downward. No longer the man of standing in his district that he had been, the High Constable was often such a creature as Mr Busie in Henry Glapthorne's very poor comedy *Wit in a Constable*. Busie, whose name and profession are again linked together to-day, thus warns his men:

> . . . if a thiefe chance to passe through your watch,
> Let him depart in peace; for should you stay him,
> To purchase his redemption he'le impart
> Some of his stolne goods, and you're apt to take them,
> Which makes you accessary to his theft,
> And so fit food for Tiburne.

This turbulent century, nevertheless, saw the first attempt, not only in England, but in Europe, to enforce a uniform system of order throughout the country. Cromwell's grandiose scheme, however, was a police system only in the sense understood in the modern police state; its object was political, and it was purely military in character. England and Wales were divided into twelve divisions, each under a Major-General. It is a proof of the anxiety felt about the influence and behaviour of the City of London, once a bulwark of the Parliamentary cause, that its square mile formed one of these divisions. Westminster and Middlesex made up another. A subsidiary aim of this experiment was a move in the right direction, for it curtailed considerably the powers of hundreds of petty and privileged authorities which refused to work together. But as a method of restoring order and eradicating vice it was bound to fail under any conditions; in fact, the senior military officers, ignoring instructions to co-operate with the local justices, and encouraging an elaborate spying system, left memories of oppression which had not been forgotten in Peel's day.

More than twenty years of violent upheaval left little more than a mockery of police in the Metropolis when Charles II returned to Westminster in 1660. While, however, in the City of London, an Act of Common Council introduced in 1663 a new force of paid bellmen popularly known as "Charleys," certain developments during the rest of the century left their permanent mark on Westminster. Street lighting and paving were introduced in new and wider thoroughfares and squares, attention was given to sanitation, and turnpikes were established. Additional powers granted to magistrates are proof that they were still considered superior police officials; authority to swear in extra men at times of emergency produced the first special constables. Commissioners were appointed to regulate, among other things, the growing traffic in the Metropolis. By a coincidence, to be repeated a generation or two later, the office of this new body was in Scotland Yard, and its members were known as the Commissioners of Scotland Yard. So began the licensing of public vehicles, which, in the Metropolis, still partly remains with the police.

The beginning of the eighteenth century found petty justice, as administered in the Metropolis, still at a shamefully low level. At Middlesex and Westminster Sessions there would be some façade of respectability, but in the privacy of his own "office," usually a room in his house, the "trading justice," as he was now called, did a lucrative business. Even when nominally unpaid he might make as much as £1000 a year. There were honest exceptions, such as Lord de la Warr and Sir John Gonson in Westminster; but in general justice, clerk, and constable—Mr Constable, as he was invariably addressed, for was he not also unpaid?—were all involved in a disgraceful traffic which came to include actual conspiracy with thieves and receivers. It was in this atmosphere that Jonathan Wild was able to build up the largest criminal organization London had ever seen. With the connivance of certain justices, Wild, as a "thief-taker," planned the robberies he was paid to prevent or punish. He was so successful a broker for the recovery of stolen goods, if rewards were offered and no questions asked, that, besides warehouses for storing them, he leased offices near the Old Bailey where their return to their owners could be arranged. Accepted in many quarters as an official with special constabulary powers, he paid newspapers to refer to him as "Thief-taker General," and carried a silver-mounted staff as an emblem of his fictitious rank. In 1724 he is found petitioning to be made a freeman of the City.

The following year saw the collapse of this edifice of crime, and Wild was hanged at Tyburn. His career is an outstanding example of how organized corruption can flourish for years in a capital city lacking a regularly appointed and disciplined police force. It was still a recent memory when Henry Fielding formed his little band of special "police" officers in the seventeen-fifties; and these men were hampered in their good work because they inherited the hated name of "thief-takers," and in general were regarded as little better than Wild himself.

2

From time to time, during the reigns of William and Mary, Anne, and George I, honest efforts were made to improve the shocking conditions in the Metropolis to which writers from Butler to Swift bear vigorous witness. Some of these efforts were ill-conceived, and made matters worse. Such were the Parliamentary rewards in cases of felony introduced at the end of the seventeenth century. Designed to counter the plague of highwaymen, this scheme was widened to include coiners, counterfeiters, and other criminals. Many of these rewards, which ranged from forty pounds downward, included a judge's certificate exempting the holder, or his nominee, from any office in the ward or parish where the crime had been committed; and these Tyburn tickets, as they were called, naturally came on the market, and were presently fetching from ten pounds to fifty pounds. The rewards themselves, popularly known as "blood-money," were usually divided between prosecutor, witnesses, and police officers, and one evil result of the system was that constables and watchmen were tempted to ignore minor misdeeds, in the hope that the offenders would later commit felonies.

An experiment tried in 1707, though it could do no harm, was no more successful. The ward beadles of the Metropolis, who acted as superintendents of the nightly watch, were sworn in as constables and required to patrol the streets by day, to arrest vagrants and report on various matters, from newcomers in the lodging-houses to "ffilth or

Dirt at the Doors." Such little progress as was made in these pre-Bow Street days is to be found in the nightly watch itself, though Westminster in this respect remained far behind the City of London. The Ordinances of 1585 were brought up to date, and the numbers of each parish watch appreciably increased. Far too many of these men, however, were deputies, elderly and wretchedly paid.

The more reputable justices appointed committees from time to time to consider the problems of crime and disease, and a notable figure in this campaign was John Gonson, who later, in 1729, became Sir John and Chairman of the Westminster Bench. Gonson took energetic measures against disorderly houses, and can be seen, in the second plate of Hogarth's *Harlot's Progress*, marching with his men into a brothel. It is just possible that for some years he occupied the post of Court Justice. This was an appointment which went back at least to Elizabeth's reign. Court Justices were selected by the Government for confidential work for the State, such as the examination of spies, or of important personages involved in affairs which it was desired to keep secret. Sir Edmund Berry Godfrey, whose murder in 1678 remains one of the most fascinating of historical mysteries, was a Court Justice, and his successor was Sir John Reresby, of the *Travels and Memoirs*; Gonson may have been among those who followed Reresby. If so, he preceded in this confidential and privileged post another Westminster justice who was to make police history—Thomas de Veil.

3

Colonel de Veil, as he was known after being given command of a battalion of the Westminster Militia, was the son of a Huguenot cleric. He fought in Spain and Portugal under the Earl of Galway, another Huguenot. As a half-pay captain he set himself up as adviser to fellow-officers in his position, addressing his circulars from—of all places—Scotland Yard. As the scope of his business widened he made a study of the Law; and since he was able and energetic, honest, fair-minded, and something of a showman, it is not surprising that by 1729 he was in the Commission of the Peace for Westminster and Middlesex. He was then forty-five.

During the next eighteen years he not only succeeded in raising the status of the Metropolitan magistracy, but brought into being what was to become something like a Central Police Office for the Metropolis. In 1739 he came to live in Bow Street, and with the opening of his "Public Office" there a new era in police history begins.

There was an air of efficiency about his office unknown to any other in the Metropolis. Criminals found themselves being hounded with a vigour to which they were quite unaccustomed. Though Sir John Gonson continued to be Chairman of the Westminster Bench, de Veil was generally regarded as the chief magistrate in the Metropolis. He was the last Court Justice to be called by that name, for his successors in the post, all of whom were attached to the Bow Street office, were known as Principal Justices, and, later, Chief Magistrates, in Westminster.

It was de Veil who took the lead when, in 1736, the Westminster magistrates persuaded Parliament to bring in an unworkable Bill to regulate the sale of gin, and in consequence he had to face an infuriated mob which gathered before the house in which he then lived in "Thrift Street, Sohoe," the modern Frith Street. He was prominent in another scene in the Little Theatre in the Haymarket, where young Henry Fielding's political satires had so angered the Prime Minister, Walpole, that a Bill was passed requiring all plays, except those acted in theatres under royal patent, to be licensed by the Lord Chamberlain. This silenced Fielding, who took to the Law, a decision of importance for the future; the Government reopened the Little Theatre with a company of French players, who appeared on the stage between two files of Grenadiers, and after de Veil, who had the Riot Act in his pocket, in vain tried to make himself heard in the ensuing uproar,[1] this unusual first night came to an early end amid wild confusion.

This was in 1739, when de Veil, by moving to Bow Street, founded a tradition, and gave to the chief police office in the Metropolis a local habitation and a name, which have endured to this day. Bow Street was no longer the fashionable quarter it had been when Waller, Wycherley, Grinling Gibbons, and Kneller lived there. It had a bad reputation; but its houses were large, and de Veil, four times married, had a numerous family. He obtained a lease from the Duke of Bedford of No. 4, on the western side of the street. He was by now an ailing man; if he is the magistrate in a drawing by the younger Laroon, now in the Windsor Castle collection, by 1740 he was becoming dropsical. But he never lost his courage and resolution, as was shown when in 1744 he faced another angry crowd, this time of London

[1] Missiles were hurled about the theatre, and "various portable instruments that could make a disagreeable noise" were brought into action. Several ambassadors, who were present with their ladies, found that the traces of their coaches had been cut by the mob outside. Constables and watchmen were prudently elsewhere, and troops in the Haymarket apparently made no attempt to interfere.—*History of the Theatres of London and Dublin from 1730* (1761).

footmen, protesting against "unfair competition from other brothers of the cloth" imported from France. The footmen were joined in Bow Street by the usual mob, but de Veil, his family behind him, held them at bay with a pistol until the military arrived.

In the following year he did much useful work at the time of the alarm, approaching panic, caused by the march of Prince Charles Edward and his army to Derby. For his many and varied services de Veil received a knighthood in 1744, only to die before long in the midst of his labours.

In many respects in advance of his day, and certainly of most of his fellow-justices, de Veil possessed his own kind of integrity. He "traded," like the rest, but took only what he held to be fair profit, and he kept the most scrupulous accounts. He knew his law, and endeavoured to administer it with fairness. Though there is no evidence that he envisaged anything like a new police system, he strongly condemned much of what existed, and he realized the value of co-operation in preventive measures. He seems to have had real detective ability, solving many cases himself by a process of deduction from observed facts; and once at least he further anticipated the procedure and functions of later Bow Street officers, and of the modern C.I.D., by being called in to assist in a provincial murder case.

3

THE FIELDINGS

IT has often been said that de Veil's immediate successor at the Bow Street office was the author of *Tom Jones*. This is incorrect. The Westminster rate-books[1] show that after de Veil's death No. 4 Bow Street was almost at once taken over by an elderly justice named Thomas Burdus. Burdus, who had the help of his predecessor's clerk, Joshua Brogden, a captain in the Westminster Militia, of which de Veil had been colonel, seems to have taken his duties seriously; his death in the early summer of 1748 may have been hastened by shock or injuries suffered during a raid on a Strand coffee-house in the previous October. He was followed as Chairman of the Westminster Bench and Bow Street magistrate by Richard Lilly, a "Doctor of Physick," who did not live at No. 4. The justice-room and a small office there continued to be used by a fellow Middlesex and Westminster justice, John Poulson,[2] who took the lease of another house in Bow Street, on the opposite, or eastern, side. This fact almost certainly explains the contradictory statements as to the precise position of the first Bow Street office. Poulson, who was in his late seventies, seems soon to have relinquished his duties to two other justices, Thomas Ellis (or Ellys) and John Green, and he died in December 1748, a week or two after Henry Fielding took the oaths as Justice of the Peace for Westminster, and, already a sick man at forty-one, began his short but notable reign at Bow Street. Careless with money and often in debt, a playwright and satirist, a far from successful barrister, and the author of *Joseph Andrews*, in 1748 Henry Fielding had almost completed *Tom Jones*. His appointment to Bow Street seems to have been a political favour. Handicapped by his past, he was at once attacked in the public

[1] Acknowledgment of special indebtedness is due to Mr C. F. Osborne, Archivist to the City of Westminster, who was good enough to search both Middlesex and Westminster records, with the result that the true facts about the Bow Street house during 1747 and 1748 are here printed for the first time.

[2] This may have created a precedent. The justices at the Union Hall Public Office in Southwark later claimed that magistrates had sat continuously in that building since 1740; but de Veil had been at Bow Street a year earlier, and no other house is known to have been passed on from justice to justice until John Fielding persuaded some of his fellow-justices to establish regular offices where one of their number should always be found on duty.

prints. When *Tom Jones* conquered the town it made more ammunition for his political opponents. A partner, though not an active one, in the Universal Register Office, a business designed to bring buyers and sellers together, recently opened by his half-brother, John, he was even indirectly accused of trafficking in stolen goods.[1] Many of these attacks, the most vitriolic of which was to come from Smollett, the new magistrate could ignore, but he was at some pains to assure his patrons and friends that by refraining from plundering the poor, and by composing quarrels, he had soon reduced an income of "£500 a year of the dirtiest money on earth" to little more than £300, most of which went to pay Joshua Brogden, who was still clerk. In fact, the easygoing playwright and *bon viveur* appears as transformed, almost in a night, into a punctilious and active magistrate, who was shocked by the crime and misery of which he now gained first-hand knowledge, and no less by the way his predecessors had exploited this human frailty to fill their own pockets. In the justice-room itself, though Brogden was conscientious, there was much laxity. With astonishing energy, Henry Fielding applied himself to the double task of remedying abuses and devising constructive measures to deal with the general lawlessness in London. Within five years he had done so much that his work has been described as "the foundation stone of all subsequent legal and police reform."[2]

Some credit must go to Brogden, and to two men outside the Bow Street office—John Fielding and the then High Constable of Holborn, Saunders Welch. This pair acted as Henry Fielding's unofficial assistants. Welch, who had a grocery-shop in what is now Museum Street, laid down in his *Observations on the Office of Constable*, published in 1754, many principles and "Cautions" for the guidance of his own constables which could be applied to times long after his day. The state of the London streets, as then described, was if anything worse when Fielding took office; and the latter had been only a few months at Bow Street when he had to meet the first real test of his ability and firmness.

On the 29th of June, 1749, he delivered his famous *Charge to the Grand Jury*, in the most uncomfortable quarters, adjoining Old Palace Yard, where the Westminster Sessions were then held. A day or two later there were serious affrays in and about the Strand. It was the week-end, and Fielding was at his farm in Ealing. Fires were started, and a

[1] Memories of Jonathan Wild's brokerage transactions no doubt inspired such accusations.

[2] Charles Reith, *The Police Idea: its History and Evolution in England in the Eighteenth Century and After* (Oxford University Press, 1938).

house of call known as the Star was half demolished. Though Welch acted energetically, securing troops from the Tilt Yard, for two days the mob did very much as it pleased. Fielding returned to Bow Street on the Monday, read the Riot Act to a crowd outside the office, and summoned more troops; and by Tuesday morning all was quiet. But there was to be an unfortunate sequel.

Prisoners had been taken, but the ringleaders of the mob had got away. A man of doubtful character named Bosavern Penlez was convicted, it seems wrongly, and executed. There was an outcry, and Fielding justified his actions in a pamphlet, *A True State of the Case of Bosavern Penlez*, which is one of his most skilful productions, and which is still of interest because of the picture it gives of the actual riots, and its warning of what might happen under a Government which allowed such disturbances to gather head unchecked. This warning reiterated, but with the added force of the late alarming example, that uttered in the *Charge to the Grand Jury*. In between these pronouncements the Metropolis had suffered a foretaste of the "downright state of wild and savage barbarism" which the first predicted. Local resources had as usual proved worthless in a serious emergency. A call for the constables produced at first one man; Fielding's fellow-magistrates were afraid to act; and even when the Guards arrived they behaved, it was said, more like amused spectators than keepers of the peace.

But Fielding was not a mere prophet of woe, content to wait for higher authority to do something. He had a Plan. The *Charge to the Grand Jury*, the Penlez pamphlet, and *An Enquiry into the Causes of the Late Increase of Robbers* (published in January 1750/1) contain many proposals embodied in the *Plan* itself, which was drawn up in 1753 for the consideration of the Secretary of State, the Duke of Newcastle. Some of these proposals had been tentatively carried into effect—most notably an experiment perhaps inspired by the success of the mixed patrol of troops and selected peace officers employed on the last night of the Strand riots of 1749. Soon afterwards, with the assistance of Saunders Welch and probably of John Fielding, now unofficially helping his half-brother at Bow Street, the nucleus was formed of a permanent force of constables, "actuated by a truly public spirit against thieves," who would be willing to continue their duties after their year of office expired. Some six or seven householders of good repute, all except one ex-constables of Westminster who had not employed deputies, were selected to form what was in effect the first detective force in England.

"Mr Fielding's People," as they were called, later "The Bow Street Runners," were, to begin with, neither official nor in receipt of pay. They were entitled to a part of the rewards or "blood-money" offered for the apprehension of criminals. They wore no uniform,[1] though presumably they always carried the constable's staff. Attached to Bow Street, they came directly under the orders of the magistrate there. They made their presence felt at once, breaking up several gangs of thieves within a month or two; and so well had they been chosen that though the Recorder of London refused them what they considered their fair share of blood-money,[2] they continued their work. Early successes were perhaps partly due to the fact that few people were then aware of their existence. But though it was not until 1758 that details of the little force and its duties were made public, the secret was soon out, and for a time this historic experiment was hampered by the popular belief that the Bow Street men were merely thief-takers of the Jonathan Wild type under another name. Finally, for want of funds, "Mr Fielding's People" were for a time disbanded; but under his half-brother a similar staff of trained detectives was established, and as the "Runners"—a name which came into use about 1790—was officially recognized and paid. With the Runners and Constables attached to the other police offices created in 1792, it continued to exist for a few years independently of the new Metropolitan Police.

Henry Fielding did not live to see more than the introduction and promising beginnings of his Plan. It was left to his half-brother to publish the details of the novelist's last great work,[3] the foundation upon which John Fielding himself raised the structure that went far towards "moulding London to the form we now know."[4]

2

John Fielding's position at Bow Street had been regularized in 1750, four years before his half-brother's death, when he became a Westminster justice. When Henry died in Lisbon, John had recently been

[1] Nor did they at any later date, as stated by the Oxford English Dictionary, Mr Reith, and others. The only police officers to wear red waistcoats were the Horse (Mounted and Dismounted) Patrols of the early 1800's, and it was they who were nicknamed "Robin Redbreasts." The Runners were plain-clothes detectives, and to give them any sort of uniform would have been to destroy their usefulness.

[2] Fielding in vain endeavoured to get this fair share for his men, though he was opposed in general to the principle of official rewards. Experience seems to have modified this attitude later.

[3] John Fielding, *An Account of the Origin and Effects of a Police set on Foot by His Grace the Duke of Newcastle in the Year 1753, upon a Plan presented to his Grace by the Late Henry Fielding, Esq.* . . . (1758).

[4] Troup, *op. cit.*

raised to the Commission of the Peace for Middlesex. He reigned at Bow Street from 1754 to 1779, dying in the following year. Fourteen years younger than Henry, he was only thirty-three when he succeeded the former as Principal Metropolitan Justice; since he was nineteen or twenty, from what cause is uncertain, he had been stone blind. This affliction merely spurred on his ambition and sharpened his other senses, so that it was said of him that he was able to recognize the voice of any man who had once been brought up before him. He lacked his half-brother's tact and personal modesty, being rather too fond of calling attention to his own virtues and accomplishments. The inadequate sketch of his character and career by Sir Leslie Stephen in the *Dictionary of National Biography* is, however, ungenerous and unfair; some of the outstanding points of these are more happily emphasized by R. Leslie-Melville in a sentence from his biography:[1]

> As if forming the first organised detective force, investigating and trying cases nearly every day, running the Universal Register Office, and looking after his dead brother's family as well as his own were not enough to keep him busy, John Fielding had to play a leading part in the foundation of three charities which are still doing splendid work; the Marine Society, the Magdalen Hospital and the Royal Female Orphanage. . . . In short, he was in the forefront of the great philanthropic movement which distinguished the second half of the eighteenth century.

In addition to all this, as a police reformer John Fielding stands in the same class as his half-brother. His far longer career at Bow Street enabled him to perform more than the latter could attempt. He invested the justice-room with something of the formal dignity of a court of law. He prepared the way, by constant advocacy, for the creation of stipendiary magistrates, establishing, as a preliminary step, what he called Rotation Offices. He revived his brother's small detective force. He attempted, though unsuccessfully, to keep the drink traffic out of the hands of men who turned publican in order to run what were little better than common brothels; and as part of his general campaign for the prevention of crime he evolved schemes for the care of young prostitutes and of children from unsatisfactory homes, arranging, with the help of the philanthropist Jonas Hanway, for a number of poor boys to be sent to sea under favourable conditions. The Marine Society was formed to carry on this work. These interests alone place Fielding in the notable group who in social conscience and outlook were far ahead of their time.

While extending his activities to such small matters as the bad

[1] *The Life and Work of Sir John Fielding* (L. Williams, 1934).

lighting of Berkeley Square, at the other end of the scale he was responsible for at least one Act of Parliament, dealing with gaming in public houses, and, in his *Plan for Preventing Robberies within Twenty Miles of London*, for a comprehensive project for policing the Metropolis. An abstract of this new Plan, submitted in 1762, has been preserved.[1] If little more than a recapitulation of proposals already advocated, it drew these together into a system which, in general, anticipates those to be sponsored by Parliamentary Committees more than half a century later.

The head and forefront of the scheme, the first practical attempt to introduce the essential feature of any large reform of the existing police system, was the creation of what were called Rotation Offices, to be presided over by paid magistrates. These justices were to work in close co-operation with Bow Street, which retained its position as the "Police Center," where alone serious charges of felony could be heard. Five or six Rotation Offices were established in the Metropolis during the next few years; but, as Fielding had feared, the short-sighted opposition of the Treasury doomed them from the start. Except in one special case, stipendiary appointments were never seriously considered. The new justices were therefore too often of the old bad type. The mere cost of the upkeep of the offices themselves was deemed excessive, though to meet it Fielding proposed that all clerks' fees should go into a fund to be used for rent, wages, newspaper advertisements, and running expenses. Among these last it is interesting to find the fees of a solicitor specially appointed to serve the police; and other proposals have an equally modern flavour. Each Rotation Justice was to keep his own register of criminals, copies of which were to be furnished regularly to Bow Street. To render these records more comprehensive, the Secretary at War was to be asked for periodic lists of deserters from the Army. An official *Police Gazette*, containing all relevant information, should "be established by Law."

The existing police system was to be overhauled. The methods of the watch must be amended, and a Foot Patrole instituted to cover the fields outside the Metropolis on winter evenings. A crying need was a constant guard on the turnpikes and elsewhere to intercept criminals hoping to escape pursuit by crossing a parochial boundary; but this would mean a greatly increased force of paid officers, and Fielding seems to have felt that so expensive a remedy had no chance at that time. Instead, as the Seven Years War was then drawing to an end, he suggested that a regiment of light horse should be stationed in the

[1] Among the Liverpool Papers in the British Museum (B.M. Add. MSS. 38334, f. 75).

environs of the Metropolis—as a temporary measure, he added hopefully.

He did not get his light horse; but George Grenville, who was then (in 1763) First Lord of the Treasury, sanctioned the cost of a Horse Patrole of eight men, later increased to ten. The men, who did not wear uniform, were selected from constables and others who had worked for Fielding. Though there were then turnpikes within two or three miles of Charing Cross, the patrole had to cover a wide area. It was generally welcomed, and its usefulness was not denied; but after less than eighteen months the experiment was discontinued, at the instance, Fielding believed, of the First Secretary to the Treasury, Charles Jenkinson, Horace Walpole's "shrewd, timid, cautious and dark man," who afterwards became Earl of Liverpool. The Horse Patrole was not to be revived until 1805. The proposed Foot Patrole, however, came into being, and became a recognized feature of the police system.

Fielding's interest in street lighting was not limited to improving the amenities of Berkeley Square; better lighting of the Metropolis, especially in the outskirts, was urgently needed for the protection of citizens, and his insistence on this caused the provision of lamps to be put in hand on a large scale. He seems to have been the first to propose that lamps should be erected on posts on the outside of the footway, instead of being attached to house walls. In 1764 the Treasury granted £10,000 for the further lighting of Westminster, and a little later eighty-nine lamps were put up along the stretch of road of evil reputation between Hyde Park Corner and Kensington.

All this had the effect of making the more thoughtful section of the public alive to its obligations in police matters. The disappearance of the short-lived Horse Patrole coincided with the raising of several private patroles by local subscription. A wealthy Bayswater citizen raised one at his own expense. By 1767 such outlying villages as Islington and Highgate had one or more evening patroles on the roads leading into London, each consisting of "two stout young men . . . provided with thick white great coats, hangers, halberds and fire arms." Fielding's own thief-takers, gradually overcoming prejudice caused by association in the popular mind with Jonathan Wild and his successor Stephen M'Daniel (rumoured to be one of "Mr Fielding's People"), became generally recognized as a valuable nucleus of trained police, and were soon to receive that stamp of public approval, a familiar nickname.

3

It is fitting that the reign of the Fieldings at Bow Street, which covered thirty years, should see the word *police* coming into fairly common use, though still not always with the meaning it bears to-day. Imported into Scotland from France in 1714, when Commissioners of Police were appointed in Edinburgh, the word then stood for local government in its widest sense. For another fifty years it usually connoted civil *policy* or *polity*. In Corbyn Morris's *Proposals for a Better Regulation of the Police of this Metropolis* (1751) there is little or no reference to magisterial or constabulary work. Thirty years later *A Plan of Police* is the title given by Thomas Gilbert, M.P., to proposals for an economic scheme to deal with the poor, and Adam Smith uses the word to denote the general control of a trade in his essay on *The Police of Grain*. In 1792 Arthur Young writes of "the police of corn." Even more curiously, a series of reports in the *Daily Gazetteer* of 1767 on conditions in the transatlantic colonies is headed "The American Police." Exactly when the term was first employed to mean the civil regulation of an area and the men required for that purpose it is difficult to say. But it seems probable that John Fielding did much to popularize it in this sense. His commemoration of his brother's work, published in 1758, was entitled *An Account of the Origin and Effects of a Police set on Foot*, etc. After this came his regular advertisements of "wanted" men in the *Public Advertiser*; and three years later, in *Extracts from Such of the Penal Laws as particularly relate to the Peace and Good Order of this Metropolis*, he gave what he described as "The best definition I have ever met with of the Word itself . . . *Viz.*, that it is the Regulation and Government of a City or Country, as far as regards the Inhabitants." He goes on to point out that a police proper for England must differ both from that used by an arbitrary government and that of a republic, "being principally obtained by keeping up a Diligence and Activity of that noble Institution the Civil Power."

Though in 1763 a correspondent in the *Public Advertiser* held that the word was little understood "beyond the purlieus of Covent Garden," its currency in politer circles is suggested by the title of a pamphlet issued anonymously in that year by Sir William Mildmay. *The Police of France* shows that others besides the Fieldings were envisaging a professional and wholly civil protective and preventive force in no way under parochial control. Mildmay's theme was, in fact, the expediency of establishing an English Ministry of Police. His pamphlet made small impression on his contemporaries, but it was a sign of the times; and in the year of its publication events occurred in London which forced the Government to consider in earnest the whole question of preserving law and order in the Metropolis.

4

WILKES, PARLIAMENT, AND THE GORDON RIOTS

A MAN of pleasure, a wit, and a most unconventional politician, John Wilkes was M.P. for Aylesbury when he founded a paper called *The North Briton*, in opposition to the Government publication *The Briton.* No. 45 of *The North Briton*, appearing in April 1763, was held to contain a libel on the King; Wilkes and some of his printers were arrested, and the offending issue of his paper was ordered to be burnt by the common hangman. The general warrant under which the arrests were made was declared by Lord Chief Justice Pratt to be unconstitutional; nevertheless Wilkes was expelled from the House of Commons and outlawed. He was then re-elected by the voters of Middlesex. Heedless of warnings, the Government continued to handle the affair in the worst possible manner, and, the founder of *The North Briton* being immensely popular with the mob, besides having powerful friends in the City, he became the symbol of every sort of dissatisfaction with Ministers, from the Peace of Paris and the rule of the King's Friends to current industrial grievances. The result was a series of public demonstrations, disorders, and incidents humiliating to the Government, but thoroughly enjoyed by Wilkes, which was to go on for seven years.

The public burning of *The North Briton* had led to serious disturbances in the capital. The next outbreak of disorder, two years later, though caused by quite a different matter, revived the cry of "Wilkes and Liberty." A deputation of the weavers of Spitalfields, marching to present a petition to the King against the import of French silks, was accompanied by an unruly mob which for several days swarmed about the Metropolis from Westminster to Bloomsbury, and, indeed, much farther afield. Troops were called out, and after something like a battle in Bloomsbury Square, where the Duke of Bedford's house was attacked, the mob was dispersed; but this display of military force was yet another alarming illustration of the weakness of the civil power. A committee of the Lords, appointed to inquire into the behaviour of the London magistrates, made Sir John Fielding (as he now was) the chief scapegoat. Fielding had underestimated the danger, but the committee forgot how limited were his means of obtaining beforehand information of coming trouble, largely because so many of his proposals had been ignored.

In the next year or two troops were again used during demonstrations which took on the appearance of strikes.[1] Though some of the malcontents were arrested for attacking the soldiers with swords and sticks, they were almost invariably discharged by the magistrates. Fresh disturbances on a large scale occurred in 1768. They arose directly out of the affairs of Wilkes, and their significance could not be ignored.

Returning from Paris, more than ever a popular idol, Wilkes was made a freeman of the City, and in March 1768 he stood for Parliament as its member. He was defeated, but stood again for Middlesex, and was again at the top of the poll. That evening, March the 28th, cheering crowds wearing his blue cockade thronged Westminster. Houses had to be illuminated, and chariots on the road adorned with a "45." On the whole, rough work was limited to breaking unlighted windows; but noblemen were forced to play host to visitors of a kind never before seen in their saloons, and their wives had to leave their chairs to cry "Wilkes and Liberty." The general alarm was heightened by the fact that at a time when it was almost impossible to move in the Strand, Piccadilly, or Whitehall, not a constable was to be seen. The Guards were called out, but except in the Strand had little to do.

This time Fielding was in no way responsible for the complete absence of peace officers. They were elsewhere. Lord Weymouth, the new Secretary of State for the Northern Department, having ordered the Westminster constables to be kept in readiness, received news from Fielding which revealed strikingly the dangers of divided authority, and the magistrate's own helplessness in the matter. The Sheriff of Middlesex had commanded the High Constable of Westminster to bring his peace officers to Brentford, where there were dense crowds at the polling-booths; as a result, Fielding wrote: "I do not suppose there is one constable within the City and Liberty of Westminster."

He did not wish to call for troops, "lest it should provoke what it is intended to prevent," but he had to call for them when rioting broke out in the Strand. Though the immediate crisis passed, he must have felt that he was in an almost impossible position. "Instructions" from

[1] Or *were* real strikes, in the modern sense of the term, as when in 1766 the journeymen shoemakers struck for higher wages and held illegal meetings, peaceably dispersed by Saunders Welch.

Weymouth's office poured in upon him, but all they did was to make it clear that whatever happened no blame was to fall on the Secretary of State. Everybody knew, moreover, that there might be more trouble ahead. Wilkes, still an outlaw, had promised to appear at the Court of King's Bench on the 20th of April to submit to the laws of his country. On the 16th the magistrates of Westminster met to make their plans for possible disorder.

The 20th, as it happened, passed quietly. Lord Mansfield held that an outlaw could not be brought to trial until the sheriff had served him with a writ. On the 27th Wilkes was in court again, and it was while he was being removed in custody, bail having been refused, that he made all London laugh by what Weymouth called his "indecent contempt" for the civil power. Put into a coach with a guard, he was rescued by the mob which as usual was attending him, and while Fielding and other magistrates were chasing the coach, the outlaw turned up at King's Bench Prison, demanding admittance.

Weymouth was furious, and Robert Wood, the Under-Secretary of State, in a stiff note to Fielding, threatened the Westminster magistrates with dismissal should such a thing occur again. (Wood had more reason than most to detest Wilkes, who had obtained £1000 damages from him in the matter of the general warrant.) That some of Fielding's fellow-justices may have been Wilkeites is suggested by his observation, in his reply, that on any future occasion of the kind there might be "a difficulty of getting them together."

Within a week or two there were far worse happenings in Southwark. Crowds gathered daily there, outside the King's Bench Prison in St George's Fields, to cheer for Wilkes. Attempts at his rescue were feared, and troops were ordered to stand by; and on the 10th of May there was a clash with the mob during which the Guards fired, though there is no proof that the Riot Act was read. Some half a dozen people were killed, and a score of others, including a woman, more or less seriously injured. Even after something like order had been restored a young farmer named Allen was bayoneted and then shot dead. The soldier who fired the shot was highly commended by the Government for doing his duty and given thirty pounds, and when brought to trial for murder, on a coroner's warrant, he was acquitted.

This was the last occasion on which Wilkes was the prime cause of serious disorders. The "St George's Fields Massacre," following the ridicule he had brought upon the civil power, wrought in their different ways upon public opinion; and to this stimulus was added, in these later days of his campaign, a marked increase in the graver types of crime in London and its outskirts, a common result of war and rioting. Even official circles realized that something should be done. Here, where Fielding's views were known, he had his supporters; and one of these, Lord Rochford, succeeded Weymouth in the autumn of 1768. An important step forward was now taken by the appointment of a Parliamentary Committee to inquire into the recent robberies in and about the Cities of London and Westminster, and to consider more effectual methods to prevent such crimes in future.

2

This 1770 Committee was the first of many of its kind which were to be convoked to report on the state of the police of the Metropolis. The limitation is to be noticed; though the terms of reference included the City of London, the Committee's report made it clear that the aldermen and wealthy merchants of the City proper had been successful in excluding it from the inquiry. In 1770, as in 1829, they considered themselves representatives of a corporation apart, opposed to even the smallest measure of real co-operation.

The Committee being thus obliged to confine its attention to Westminster and its environs, Fielding was inevitably the chief witness. During his evidence he submitted two papers embodying his suggested reforms, but except on one point they contained little that he had not said before. This new recommendation was that an increased number of constables, appointed by magistrates, and not, as was the practice, by a leet jury, should work under one central authority, as in the City, thus ceasing to be officers of a parish.

The Committee accepted in principle the majority of Fielding's proposals, though on the question of a paid magistracy, which he raised once more, its members were silent. The only effective result of their deliberations seems to have been an Act which permitted the trial of an alleged receiver even though the thief concerned had not been apprehended.

It was at this inquiry that Fielding introduced a topic which had only recently come into prominence—the shocking state of the London prisons. Not even he seems to have realized the close interdependence of criminal-law reform and reform of the police. Peel was probably among the first to do so. But more humane ideas about penal methods and their effects were finding their way into print. A third English edition of Beccaria's *Essay on Crime and Punishment*, with a commentary attributed to Voltaire, was issued in 1770, and it may be supposed that Fielding was acquainted with this work. Both he and his brother had always maintained that ferocious sentences were not the best deterrents.

Fielding's position, already almost unassailable, was at least strengthened by the Committee's respectful acceptance of his views; and it was about this time that as a result of another of his schemes the Bow Street office began to win general, if not official, recognition throughout the country. For some time he had been advocating the establishment of a regular police bulletin. The Home Department procrastinated, but in 1771 an outrage in Chelsea ending in murder gave Fielding an opportunity to put at any rate a part of his plan in operation. A party of nine men raided a farmhouse in the King's Road, and in the course of a scuffle a labourer was fatally shot. The assailants were said to be Jews. Three men of that race were detained, but released, and though at Fielding's request the Government offered a reward of fifty pounds, for some weeks no further arrests were made. At length a man named Isaacs came forward to give king's evidence, and disclosed the names and descriptions of most of the gang, all Jews from Central Europe. The leader was Levi Weil, a medical man with a Leyden degree.

Fielding saw his chance. Handbills were printed giving particulars of the wanted men, and copies were sent to every postmaster in England, and to those in Edinburgh and Dublin. It was something entirely new in the history of criminal investigation in these islands. All over the country Jews were questioned, and in some cases arrested, and messages from some of the larger towns led to the dispatch of thief-takers or other Bow Street officers. One of these was Fielding's clerk, Nicholas Bond, afterwards a Bow Street justice; and it was he who brought back from Birmingham four of the gang. Two others were taken a day or two later. Weil was among the captives, and he and three more were hanged at Tyburn. This case is notable not only for the novel means employed to solve it, but as a forerunner, in its Jewish and Central European element, of the crimes in Tottenham and Houndsditch with which the City and Metropolitan Police were to deal nearly a hundred and fifty years later.

Fielding used his success to press his case with the new Secretary of State in charge of Home Affairs, Lord Suffolk, and, the authorities still hesitating, made another experiment on his own responsibility. In a letter to the county magistrates, afterwards printed in the newspapers and on widely distributed handbills, he announced that he would print a quarterly list of criminals wanted in London and believed to be in the country. A weekly bulletin would also be sent to magistrates free of charge "in which the advertisements relating to offences and offenders from our office will be printed in such a large type that when cut out of the paper and stuck up they will be very legible." So were established the *Quarterly Pursuit*, the *Weekly Pursuit*, and an occasional supplement, the *Extraordinary Pursuit*, all of which, Fielding suggested, should be exhibited on boards bearing the words "Weekly Hue and Cry." From these beginnings sprang the issue, in 1786, of the first number of the *Public Hue and Cry*, the creation of Fielding's successor at Bow Street, Sir Sampson Wright, and the direct precursor of the *Police Gazette*.

This means of "intercourse between the civil power in the country and in the metropolis" was welcomed by the provincial authorities. The annual cost of the bulletins, Fielding told Suffolk, could not exceed £400. Suffolk was sufficiently impressed to go further with the plan, and to obtain the King's approval. In this way a start was made, as Mr Leslie-Melville has pointed out, towards the creation of what may fairly be called a national detective office; and it was a fitting sequel to the labours and innovations of John Fielding, and of his assistants and immediate predecessors, that though the executive duties performed by them as Principal Magistrates in Westminster were eventually taken over by the Commissioners of Police, the official police bulletin under its several names continued for some considerable time to be issued from Bow Street.

3

Only a start, however, had been made. There was little hope of real improvement in the situation so long as there was no central police authority powerful enough to enforce a common set of regulations, as was proved by the failure of an Act of 1774, the outcome of an inquiry by yet one more Parliamentary Committee into the state of the nightly watch in Westminster. The Act included in its scope one or two of Westminster's neighbours, and as far as it went was a good one; but, moderate as its provisions were, they were largely ignored. A change of outlook, even a change of heart,[1] was needed among those in high places, and only a great shock could bring this about. One was at hand, and though when it came it was met with hesitation and half-measures, or none at all, its ultimate effects were profound.

The Wilkes riots and other disorders in London during the century

[1] The words are used in this connexion by Jonas Hanway in *The Defects of Police the Cause of Immorality*, published in 1775.

had been relatively minor and localized affairs. In 1780 the capital suddenly found itself faced with something like an insurrection, when for some days the City and Westminster were in the hands of a hysterical and drunken mob numbering many thousands, bent on pillage and destruction. Contemporary narratives of the Gordon Riots[1] are contradictory, but about the chief events of that dreadful week in June there is little dispute. A Catholic Disabilities Bill, passed in 1778, enraged the more fanatical anti-Catholics, and a Protestant Association was formed, under the presidency of Lord George Gordon, to obtain the repeal of the Act. Gordon, who was a Member of Parliament, remains rather an enigmatic figure, but he was ill-balanced and a most unsuitable leader. On Friday, June 2, 1780, he led the chief of several processions from St George's Fields to Westminster to present a monster petition against the Act. The House of Commons having refused to consider the petition, it found itself besieged by a yelling multitude from the slums, which had joined the processions. The lobby was invaded, and it is said that within a few hours there were fifty thousand people in and about Palace Yard, where peers and prelates were pelted and beaten. Horse and Foot Guards were sent for, and Samson Rainsforth, the ex-High Constable of Holborn, who underwent some rough treatment, managed to get word to Bow Street, from which some thief-takers arrived and effected a dozen arrests. For the time the bulk of the mob streamed elsewhere, but the trouble was only beginning. That night, in Lincoln's Inn and in Warwick Street, by Golden Square, the private chapels of the Sardinian and Bavarian Ministers went up in flames; and though the next day was fairly quiet, Sunday, the 4th, saw the outbreak in earnest of such a reign of lawlessness as even London had never known.

It lasted a week. The police were helpless, and were usually absent, as were most of the magistrates. Those who were seen gave no orders to the troops, who merely patrolled the streets without interfering with the mob. At Bow Street something was done to maintain its traditions, but John Fielding was on his death-bed in his Brompton house, and on the Tuesday the Chief Police Office itself was attacked and wrecked. A great portion of Sir John's official records, and many of Henry Fielding's manuscripts, were burnt in the street. It was on this day that Lord Mansfield and Mr Justice Hyde, among others, had their houses sacked or burnt, the former losing an irreplaceable library,

[1] An excellent modern account is *The Gordon Riots* (Oxford University Press, 1926), by J. Paul de Castro. That given by Dickens in *Barnaby Rudge*, though not history, is a vivid story written while the riots were almost within living memory.

and that Dance's newly erected prison at Newgate, built like a fortress, was stormed, fired, and gutted, most of the prisoners joining their rescuers. The following day, Wednesday, was the wildest of all—a day long remembered. The Old Bailey, the Sessions House next door, the Fleet Prison, and the King's Bench Prison were badly damaged. In Holborn a large distillery was set on fire, and as huge quantities of spirit poured into the street, men, women, and even children fought to get near the stream. They lapped up the liquor like animals, and many, too drunk to move when the flames reached them, perished horribly where they lay. How many private houses were burnt and sacked that day is not known, but the next dawn broke upon a still-smoking London that looked like a battlefield.

It was the King who put an end to these disgraceful scenes. Wedderburn, the Attorney-General, having given his opinion that since the magistrates had failed in their duty, this devolved on the troops, who were entitled to fire on their own responsibility, George III announced that if necessary he would ride out and give the order himself. Opposition from the Privy Council was overruled. Warning being received that the Bank of England was to be attacked that night, the Guards marched to Threadneedle Street (as they have marched every night since) with the new instructions; and when the mob arrived with its sticks and clubs it was dispersed by volleys. Scores, including spectators, were killed or wounded in the bloodiest scene of all. But it was the last.

It was not unnaturally suspected at the time that the Gordon Riots represented a serious attempt to overthrow an unpopular Government. Lords of the opposition were said to be involved, and there was even a rumour that the rebellious American colonies were prolonging the war then in progress because they had been assured that London and Westminster "were to be destroyed this summer." It may be, as Mr Reith suggests, that rich City merchants whose trade was suffering were among those working behind the scenes. Whatever the secret history of the riots may be, they have a permanent importance in police history, the whole future of which was to be influenced by the outbreak and its consequences. The outstanding feature of the week's events was the helplessness of all those in charge of the civil power, whether the Lord Mayor and aldermen or the Metropolitan justices. Authority, in Lecky's words, was completely paralysed.

The symptom was not new; the novelty, and the lesson, lay in the devastating scale of the outbreak. Behind mere ruffianism was revealed a growing strength of opinion against anything in the nature of military rule. Only a little while before, in the House of Commons, certain justices who had sent for troops at the time of an election were denounced as "reptiles," an epithet that has a modern flavour; and during the black week in June nervous magistrates remembered how one of their number had been put on his trial for murder because he issued an order to fire upon a crowd of Wilkes's supporters. For a justice merely to appear with troops might mean the loss of his property, and possibly his life, at the hands of the mob.

The few exceptions to the lamentable failure of the civil power made it only the more apparent. Wilkes himself, now a City magistrate, continued to sit, and he did his best to put some spirit into the trembling Lord Mayor. Though Fielding was dying and Saunders Welch was in Rome, at Bow Street Sampson Wright made his mark, and he was vigorously assisted by his junior colleague, William Addington. But for the rest, at any rate of the Westminster magistrates, Lord Mansfield, smarting under his loss, spoke scathingly of their "native imbecility." (It is interesting to find him describing the riots as an "insurrection.") The same language was used by many others. Few, however, pointed the moral. The *Public Advertiser* of June the 14th summed up the situation in a sentence: "The late riots were shocking in their effects, but should a vigilant and regular police be established, nothing of the kind can happen in the future." But of those whose word carried weight, only Lord Shelburne, in a speech in the House of Lords, urged the creation of such a force at the time. And Shelburne, a clever but unpredictable statesman, with ideas in front of his day, was not trusted. Only a few hours before he had protested against the use of military in any civil disturbance, and he was even suspected of being among those who had fomented the riots.

In short, though nearly everybody was in agreement that something drastic must be done, and done quickly, amid disagreement on every other point, and general confusion of counsel, nothing was done.

5

THE FIRST POLICE MAGISTRATES AND THE RIVER POLICE

THERE is no evidence that John Fielding was able by his voice or pen to inject some common sense into the confusion. His last official letter that survives is dated November the 24th, 1779; and though his name appeared on notices from Bow Street for nearly another year, this does not mean that he was attending there in person. He had been ill for months before he died, at the age of fifty-nine, on the 4th of September, 1780. Greatly admired as he was in his day, his reputation was for some time after under a cloud. But his transcendant merits as a magistrate, and still more as a reformer, are now recognized.

While he lay dying, and while it seemed that politicians and reformers alike failed to profit by the lesson of the Gordon Riots, the leaven was in fact working. Even in Whitehall there were those who at last were studying the problem in earnest. Two years later, with the resignation of North and the end of the American War, Shelburne was in power in the second Rockingham administration, as, in effect, the first Home Secretary in the modern sense. During his brief tenure of this post important steps were taken towards departmental reorganization; "the Home Office and the Foreign Office came into existence as separate departments."[1] But the new Minister for "Domestic Affairs and the Colonies," having succeeded Rockingham when the latter died, was soon after forced out of office, never to return.

There had been some progress in the meantime at Bow Street, where Sampson Wright obtained sanction for a new force, in addition to his half-dozen specially trained thief-takers, not yet generally known as Runners. The Foot Patrole (also called the Night Patrole) consisted of sixty-eight men, armed with cutlasses, but wearing no uniform. A part-time force, paid half a crown a night (the captains got five shillings), its numbers were to be materially increased as the scope of its duties widened.

The theorists were still at work, but only one calls for mention.

[1] Troup, *op. cit.*

Edward Sayer, a justice, in *Observations on the Police or Civil Government of Westminster*, published in 1784, proposed reforms which were to include a paid magistracy and the surrender by the Dean and Chapter to the Crown of their municipal rights. A species of militia, "always embodied," was to act as a watch. Sayer, like everybody else, shrank from the idea of a paid police force. Even a uniformed one was thought to be the thin edge of militarism; and a new Police Bill, introduced in 1786, during Pitt's first months as Prime Minister, again excluded any suggestion of full-time payment. Under the Bill, however, there were to be three paid "Commissioners," a title to be heard of in the future. A technical flaw caused the Bill's withdrawal, and it was not reintroduced. The City, in particular, would have nothing to do with it.

During the next pause in the slow movement for reform there was a gleam of light from Dublin, where in 1786 the authorities adapted some of the provisions of Pitt's unfortunate Bill and set up a small paid constabulary under three Commissioners of Police. But in the Metropolis things almost seemed to be getting worse again, for with the trading justice still there, and most of the Rotation Offices little better than justice-shops themselves, a new and sinister figure now appeared, the political 'boss,' whose methods foreshadowed those in vogue in New York sixty or seventy years later. The most powerful of these bosses was William Mainwaring, a banker, a justice who became Chairman of both the Middlesex and Westminster Benches,[1] and a Member of Parliament. For a quarter of a century this outwardly respectable personage was dealing in corruption behind the scenes, and exercising an evil influence on police matters that can hardly be overestimated. The shadiest of financiers, leagued with the brewers, and with his own nominees among the licensing justices, at the same time (and without the knowledge of his brother magistrates) he was in receipt of allowances from the Treasury, for the purpose, suggest the Webbs, of "keeping Middlesex quiet." He was much helped by his equally unscrupulous son, who was County Treasurer. Though he had done his best to hamper Pitt's abortive measure of 1785, six years later he is found called in to assist in preparing the so-called "Middlesex Justices Bill," an event of great importance in police history.[2]

The "Bill for the more effectual Administration of the Office of a Justice of the Peace in such parts of the County of Middlesex as lie in

[1] The records are not complete, but probably Mainwaring succeeded Sir John Fielding as Chairman of the Westminster Bench in (or before) 1780, and Sir John Hawkins, on the senior Bench, in the following year.

[2] For some light on Mainwaring's obscure activities see a pamphlet entitled *A Defence of the Police Bill, in Answers to a Charge delivered by W. Mainwaring, Esq., at the Sessions of the Peace held for the County of Middlesex in September, 1785.*

or near the Metropolis," is more shortly and correctly described as a Police Bill, as it was by the newspapers of the day. It is remarkable among such Bills of the period because it became law, the third reading being passed in both Houses in June 1792. It appointed seven public offices in the Metropolis, each with three magistrates, all of whom were to be salaried and constantly on duty.[1] Salaries were fixed at £400 a year. Each office was to have a small number of paid police officers, generally six. Originally given an experimental period of three years, the working of the Act was extended, and it was made permanent in 1812.

Here, at last, was a very definite step forward. The "Police Offices," as they were called from the first, with their salaried magistrates, were the forerunners of the Magistrates' Courts of to-day. The shade of Henry Fielding may well have rejoiced.

2

There were two of the new offices in Westminster, and in one of them the tradition has been carried on for a hundred and sixty years without a break, for it was in Great Marlborough Street, "at 26, W. end, the third door on the L. from Argyll-street."[2] On this site is the present Magistrates' Court. The second Westminster office was opened in Queen Square, now Queen Anne's Gate. This took the place of the Litchfield Street Rotation Office, closed soon after.

The Middlesex offices were at 54 Hatton Garden, 23 Worship Street (north of the present Finsbury Square; an old Rotation Office), in Lambeth (or Lambert) Street, Whitechapel, and at 157 Shadwell High Street. With the seventh Police Office a point was stretched; it was in Southwark, in Surrey, at Union Hall, the old Borough Rotation Office. Most of the premises of these establishments must have needed adapting to their new purposes, in or about 1792; and an interesting reference to them in this connexion has come to light among the papers of Benjamin Latrobe, the architect responsible for much of the design of the Capitol at Washington, D.C. Latrobe, who left England in 1795, describes himself as having been "Surveyor to the Police Offices."[3]

[1] As originally drafted, the Bill made provision for only one paid magistrate at each office. In the collection of the late Ralph Straus is a manuscript note prepared in the Solicitor-General's office in which it is said that this law officer's advisers "think that the body of the justices will ever be what they are, and that the addition of an appointed justice would not do much, as he would be overpowered by his colleagues."

[2] Lockie's *Topography of London* (1810).

[3] For this information thanks are due to Miss Dorothy Stroud, of Sir John Soane's Museum, and to Professor Talbot Hamlin, of the School of Architecture, Columbia University, New York, U.S.A., the author of a biography of Latrobe.

The police areas of which these seven offices were the headquarters were apportioned among the twenty-one new magistrates soon after their appointments. The list of these justices, selected by the Home Secretary, now Henry Dundas, included two Members of Parliament, an ex-Lord Mayor of London, City Councillors, three or four barristers, a clergyman, a former Provost of Glasgow, and the Poet Laureate, Henry Pye, who, if not much of a poet, was an ex-M.P. Some owed their place to political patronage, and Henry Mainwaring's intrigues may have accounted for one or two more; within a few years he was certainly able to introduce other creatures of his own kidney, as retirements occurred. Of the original twenty-one, the former Lord Provost of Glasgow, Patrick Colquhoun, at Queen Square, was to stand out from the rest.

The experiment, if of great promise, was not at first the success it should have been. For some time none of the new offices was to rise much above the status of a Rotation Office of the better sort, still less to become a serious rival to Bow Street. Another war was in progress, the struggle with revolutionary France which was to go on for a quarter of a century, and ensuing disorders in London, which included bread riots, were a severe test for the new magistrates and their police. The latter had not been brought into existence to deal with large crowds; the force was far too small, and was used up in protecting Ministers' houses and public buildings. Troops had to be sent for in the old way. In the old way, too, there was lack of co-operation between the new offices, and between them and Bow Street, which, with its Runners, its patroles, its Government work, and its extra premises recently taken at the Brown Bear opposite, remained its stately self, aloof from the doings of the upstarts. The latter met with every sort of obstruction from parish constables and their underlings, and the City of London officers, characteristically, refused to allow their new comrades of the Metropolis to intrude within the City boundaries.

After a difficult start, however, the Police Offices began to make their mark, especially those at Union Hall and in Shadwell. With no help from Bow Street, they tried to model themselves on that paragon, each having its quota of Runners, who in their local rôle[1] did much good work, though miserably low pay and the bad system of blood-money inevitably led to abuses. By 1796 most of the obvious misfits among the magistrates had departed, and it was clear that the new Act was in

[1] Bow Street contrived to enforce an unwritten rule of its own that no officers from other Police Offices should be sent into the country. The reason given was that the jurisdiction of Bow Street had no defined area. The rule was broken in exceptional cases, such as the Ratcliffe Highway murders in 1811.

no danger of being repealed. The war caused rearrangements of personnel, alike at Bow Street and in the seven offices, such novel duties as the distribution of food and the supervision of aliens and suspected spies (quite a modern touch) resulting in much extra work. According to Farrington, Sampson Wright's successor at Bow Street, Richard Ford, who came there from Shadwell, formed a special department which employed émigrés and other agents to collect information inside France. A man of exceptional ability, Ford now occupied a position that would make any modern police magistrate stare; he was made acting Under-Secretary of State and, leaving much of his Bow Street work to a colleague, William Addington, doubled the rest with his duties at the Home Office.

Ford and the man who followed him at Shadwell represent the best type of police magistrate of the time. John Nares came of a gifted and interesting family, being the son of a well-known judge, the nephew of a composer, and the grandfather of an Arctic explorer. But for poor health he must have risen high himself. On the other hand, the wrong type of justice was still to be found in the police magistracy. Such were Daniel Williams, a colonel of militia, at the Lambeth Street office, and his friend Joseph Merceron, the 'boss' of Bethnal Green. Both were Mainwaring's creatures, and, with Mainwaring himself at their backs, they introduced their confederates into such positions of responsibility as that of High Constable, and, of course, into the police force itself. Some of these men were wholly illiterate, and at least two police officers nominated by the Home Department on Mainwaring's recommendation were of known bad character. It says much for men like Ford and Nares that the existence of this jobbery on a considerable scale did no more than retard the growing respect for the work of the Police Offices. Another outstanding man of this type was Patrick Colquhoun.

3

Colquhoun was among the first of the "commercial diplomats" at this time laying the foundations of the unique trading position which Great Britain was to attain in the century to come. He was a man of immense energy, and, having settled in London in 1789, he immediately began to show that activity in public affairs which had raised him to distinction in Glasgow. His interest in the problems of the poor has caused him to be known as the Father of the Soup Kitchen; and as a pioneer in police development he stands on a par with the Fieldings and Robert Peel. His writings probably did more than anything else in his day to bring home to the public the difficulties confronting the creation of an efficient police force, and not less the need of one. His monumental *Treatise on the Police of the Metropolis* passed through seven editions in ten years, and in its final form (1806), at any rate, the book stands entirely by itself.

What Colquhoun proposed was what, in effect, Peel was to create a generation later—a central board of salaried Police Commissioners given wide powers in every part of the capital and responsible only to the Home Department; under them superintending officers for each district served by a Police Office who would command an increased force of police. A reformed and carefully selected watch, better paid and eligible for promotion into the regular police, would act as a sort of militia or reserve. Perhaps the most revolutionary features of the scheme were the inclusion in it of the City of London, and the provisions for finance. No one knew better than Colquhoun how great an outcry was raised by the smallest increase in a police rate. He looked well ahead of his time when he proposed that various municipal duties only indirectly, if at all, concerned with crime should be included among the functions of the police, and made to help in part to pay for the latter. He added a formidable list of dealers, from rag-and-bone merchants to persons using stamping-presses and rolling-mills, who should be licensed, like publicans. With all this, and the fees of the Police Offices, he hoped to produce an "aggregate collection" which would "go very far towards easing the resources of the County of the expenses of what the Select Committee of the House of Commons denominate a very inefficient system of Police."

The Committee (on Finance) referred to, appointed by Pitt in 1798, had, in its 28th Report, recommended Colquhoun's proposals to Parliament. It need scarcely be said that both inside and outside Parliament there was a bigger outcry than any increase in a police rate would raise. Every vested interest was up in arms, headed by the City. The suggested Board of Police Revenue was luridly described as "a new Engine of Power and Authority so enormous and extensive as to threaten a species of despotism and inquisition hitherto without a parallel in this country."[1] It had all been heard before, and was to be heard again. Whether, in a very emasculated form, the scheme had then any chance of being tried out in practice, it is impossible to say. The City, at any rate, would have kept out of it. Once more political events thrust police affairs into the background; a Bill based on

[1] *Observations on a Late Publication intituled, A Treatise on the Police of the Metropolis by P. Colquhoun, Esq.*, by a Citizen of London: but no Magistrate (1800).

Colquhoun's proposals was before the House of Commons when, in 1801, Pitt resigned. The new Prime Minister was Henry Addington, a distant relation of the Bow Street magistrate of that name. Some years later, as Lord Sidmouth, Addington was to introduce some small police reforms, as well as sterner measures, but when he first took office he had many other matters on his hands. The Bill was dropped.

It is not, therefore, as an earlier Peel that Colquhoun is celebrated in police history. His larger ideas survive only on paper. But three years before his Bill passed into oblivion he had helped to accomplish another project by which his name lives among people who have never heard of his Commissioners and his Board of Police Revenue. He had founded the first police force, in the modern sense, in the Metropolis—indeed, in the country—and it forms a part of the Metropolitan Police to-day.

In the earlier editions of his *Treatise* he had written of the plundering of the London Docks, where "lumpers," "glutmen," and "scuffle-hunters," with juvenile "mudlarks" in attendance, pillaged ships and warehouses at the orders of various receivers in league with ships' officers, and even with some of the Revenue Officers ashore. In later editions of the book specific plans for a Thames Police were put forward.

In 1797 these ideas came to the notice of a Captain John Harriott, at one time in the Navy, a man of enterprise and ingenuity, but no money-maker and pursued by ill-luck. When the *Treatise* fell into his hands he was working on an improved ship's pump and trying to persuade the Admiralty of the value of sea- and river-fencibles in time of threatened invasion. With this bent for marine matters, Colquhoun's tentative suggestions for a river police roused his interest, and he took a plan of his own to the Lord Mayor. Though the City was a great sufferer by pillaging at the docks, the Lord Mayor did not think that a river police was the concern of the City Fathers. It is said that an attempt by Harriott to interest the overworked Home Department was equally fruitless. He did, however, impress one of Colquhoun's fellow-magistrates, John Staples, of the Shadwell Police Office; and through Staples, Harriott and Colquhoun met. Having the ear of Dundas and other influential personages, Colquhoun pressed for the adoption of a scheme which he himself had advocated. With his prestige and energy behind it, the issue seems never to have been in doubt, a surprising instance of acquiescence by authority in a police measure as novel as it was useful.

On June the 26th, 1798, the immediate establishment was announced of a Marine Police Institution with headquarters at Wapping New

Stairs and a permanent staff of eighty, supplemented on paper by a large number of "occasionals." Harriott was Resident Justice, while Colquhoun, whose energy and tact had carried the measure through, was made honorary Superintending Magistrate, special arrangements being made to relieve him of some of his duties at Queen Square. Final features of the scheme were the creation of a small fleet of well-armed barges, manned by river constables or "perambulating surveyors"; Marine Police Guards on the quays and in the lighters, and ship-constables acting as searchers on board ships unloading; the swearing in of all master lumpers employed, and the formation of a register of those working under them, a precaution designed to exclude doubtful characters from the ranks of these occasionals. The cost of all this was originally estimated at £14,000 a year.

In a little while the results of this experiment were such that others besides the merchants who had sponsored it desired to be included in an expanded scheme. In 1800 a Thames Police Bill, the work for the most part of Colquhoun and Jeremy Bentham, was introduced into Parliament and passed without serious opposition. It provided for a Thames Police Office with the usual three stipendiaries, Harriott being the senior, and the existing permanent staff. Colquhoun retained his connexion with it as Receiver.[1] Harriott, with his knowledge of maritime affairs, was able to gather most of the executive duties of the office into his own hands. His efficient but perhaps rather autocratic rule at Wapping lasted until 1816. In 1810 he was accused of malversation of public funds, but at his trial in the Court of King's Bench he was honourably acquitted, except on a minor technical point for which he was fined. It was unfortunate that a coolness soon sprang up between him and Colquhoun, each of them, apparently, being inclined to take all the credit for a successful project to which, in fact, both had contributed a share.[2]

4

In the meantime there had been interesting developments at Bow Street, where the successful revival of a short-lived experiment of forty years back rounded off a decade of authentic progress in the policing of the Metropolis.

[1] According to official letters passing after his death between his son and the Home Department, Colquhoun does not seem to have kept very careful accounts.

[2] In Colquhoun's *Treatise on the Commerce and Police of the River Thames*, published as early as 1800, Harriott is not mentioned. During Harriott's own rather petulant evidence before the 1816 Committee he was asked if he were the founder of the Thames Police, and replied, "I was the original projector of it." So he was, but Colquhoun had propounded the idea before him.

It has been seen that Richard Ford was there, when he was not at the Home Office, with William Addington. Neither seems to have had overmuch time for judicial work. In 1800 Addington retired on a pension of £400, it was believed as a result of trouble with the City authorities. The Bow Street justices had taken part in an inquiry at the Bank of England, apparently in connexion with forged banknotes; Addington, at any rate, received anonymous letters about such forgeries, one of which is preserved at the Public Record Office. The City resented this interference, and advertised in *The Times* of April 23, 1800, a resolution passed on the previous day at a Court of Aldermen thanking the Lord Mayor for a sharp protest against the improper intrusion of Bow Street in an affair and at a place outside its jurisdiction. If forged notes were in question, they were the concern of everybody, and the Bank itself would seem to be the obvious venue for an inquiry; but the Bow Street magistrates had rushed in without observing proper etiquette. Addington ignored the Lord Mayor's rebuke, and *The Times* was soon announcing that he had been "superseded." The news was premature, but in December he resigned.

Ford was now Chief Magistrate at Bow Street. He is best remembered for his connexions with the theatre; his father, a doctor, was part-proprietor with Sheridan of Drury Lane, and Richard formed an association with Dorothy Jordan, the actress, who left him in 1790 for the Duke of Clarence, the future William IV. Ford later married a Miss Booth, probably of theatrical stock. It is for other reasons, however, that his short reign at Bow Street—he died, comparatively young, in 1806—is a notable period in its annals.

Besides enhancing its importance as a police centre, he re-created the ill-fated Mounted Patrole of 1763, with the active encouragement of a new Home Secretary, Charles Jenkinson, now Lord Hawkesbury. By February 1805 parties of the patrole were on the western roads out of London after nightfall. The new force was larger than the old one; in all, there were fifty-two men under two inspectors, a number that was to vary slightly from year to year because the annual sum of £5000 for maintenance had to take into account considerable fluctuations in the price of fodder and other requirements. The men were paid five shillings a night, or twenty-eight shillings a week, and apparently they were found quarters. They were the first police force in the Metropolis to wear what might properly be called a uniform. This comprised a black leather hat, a leather stock, a blue greatcoat with a sabre worn outside, blue trousers, white leather gloves, and Wellingtons with steel spurs. Beneath the greatcoat was the scarlet waistcoat which was to earn the force its nickname of "Redbreasts," often wrongly applied to the Runners. Each man carried also a pistol, a truncheon, and a pair of handcuffs. As he rode along his appointed stretch of road he would call out "Bow Street Patrole" to such carriages or horsemen as passed by.[1]

So began the second oldest police force—the River Police coming first by seven years—existing in the Metropolis to-day. From the start the revived Horse Patrole was a success. Sir Richard Ford, as he had become, selected married men over thirty-five who had served in the cavalry. He was an ardent horseman himself, and according to Farrington he allowed the force to use his own stables. For the next fifteen years there was little change in its composition or duties, though in 1813 its control was to pass from the Chief Magistrate into the Home Secretary's own hands. It was in time to be absorbed, as later was the River Police, into Peel's new disciplined force, as the Mounted Police.

[1] There has been some confusion in the books about police uniforms in use in the Metropolis before 1829. Some of the Fieldings' "people," and some of the private patroles in the suburbs, wore a livery. The one outward sign of authority of the Bow Street Runners was a short staff or baton, surmounted by a small gold crown. Scarlet waistcoats, if worn by them, were not part of any uniform; similarly, it is a mistake to speak of the Foot Patrole existing at the time under notice as the "Robin Redbreasts," for, though they wore a belted greatcoat probably cut to a common pattern, they were not a uniformed body.

BOOK TWO

The New Police

6

A LONDON PANIC

IN December 1811 there occurred in Ratcliffe Highway, Shadwell, the "horrid and unparalleled" murders immortalized by De Quincey in his *Murder considered as One of the Fine Arts*. They have a distinctive place in police history, for riots that threatened large parts of London with destruction did less than the crimes of John Williams to rouse the thoughtful section of the public to the urgent need of a complete overhaul of the police system.

In the timing of these crimes, as De Quincey may have felt, there seems to have been almost an element of design. Londoners were going through one of their periodical fits of alarm about the lawlessness of the capital, and not without reason. Robberies were still increasing in number, and during the past twelve months there had been a startling number of murders—no less than six in the Shadwell district alone[1]—which remained unsolved mysteries. Hardly a week passed without a plain-spoken article in one of the newspapers on the increase in crimes of violence, the corruption of the police, or the ineptitude of the magistrates. Sir Samuel Romilly had launched his Parliamentary campaign for a reform of the criminal code. It was a time, moreover, of strain and uneasiness throughout the country: the war in the Peninsula was not going too well, trouble was brewing with the United States, and growing unemployment in the Midlands led to serious disturbances, while the Luddite Riots spread to Yorkshire and Lancashire with a rapidity which suggested a widespread conspiracy. Spencer Perceval's Government was thought to be handling the trouble weakly, and the new Home Secretary, Richard Ryder, seems to have shown a lack of decision. The general, if vague, feeling of dissatisfaction might, however, have died down, as similar agitations had died down before;

[1] *Morning Chronicle*, December 13, 1811.

an impulse was needed to give it substance, and the appalling tragedies in Ratcliffe Highway supplied it.

2

No. 29 Ratcliffe Highway was at this time a hosier's shop kept by a young couple named Marr. They had a baby a few months old, and employed a girl, Margaret Jewell, and a boy of fourteen. Business had been brisk on the evening of Saturday, December 7, 1811, and it was almost midnight before Mr Marr prepared to shut his shop. His wife sent the girl out to buy some oysters, a barrelful of which, in those happy days, cost little more than a shilling.

Some twenty minutes later she returned empty-handed, the oyster-shops being closed. The shutters at No. 29 were now up; but she was surprised to see no light, and to find the shop-door locked. She knocked and rang, and while she waited footsteps sounded on the stairs. She heard the baby crying; and then the crying ceased. Again and again she knocked and rang in vain. All the neighbours were in bed, but on her way out she had seen the watchman, Olley, passing "with a person in charge," and, being now seriously alarmed, she decided to wait until he returned to call the hour.

The circumstances of this scene have a peculiar horror, and the vigil of Margaret Jewell, lingering fearfully in the dark, silent street at the door of that dreadful house, tapping and listening long after all within was silence too, reaches the heights of the macabre. Not until one o'clock did Olley come by again. In his turn he failed to get any reply to his knocking. The noise now roused one of the next-door neighbours, a pawnbroker named Murray, who from the back door of his own house tried to rouse somebody's attention in No. 29. A candle was burning in the window of Marr's store-room, and the door of this was ajar; and, the ominous silence continuing, Murray climbed the party fence and with considerable courage entered at the open door, calling Marr by name.

What he saw, by the light of the candle, so shocked and unnerved him that he could scarcely bring himself to walk to the front door. Out in the street Olley had sprung his rattle. Late though it was, within a very few minutes a small crowd had collected, and a second watchman arrived before the shaken Murray had got the front door open. A little later two Runners hurried up from the Shadwell office, which was near at hand, and a search of the house by the four officers revealed the full horror of the tragedy.

The whole household, except Margaret Jewell, had been slaughtered in the twenty minutes during which she was absent. The body of the shop-boy, the first to be seen by Murray, lay in the blood-spattered store-room. In the shop Mrs Marr, horribly slashed about the head, had been struck down near the street door; her husband, a jagged cut across his throat and his head battered in, was found behind the counter. The baby lay in its blood-soaked cradle in the basement kitchen, its throat cut to silence the crying Margaret Jewell had heard.

The investigation into this atrocity was followed by the greater part of London's population with the most painful anxiety, though this was nothing to the consequences of the sequel less than a fortnight later. From the newspaper reports and the hastily printed pamphlets of the time it is possible to trace most of the measures taken by the police. No single official supervised them, but no fewer than seventeen police magistrates, a score or more of Runners from at least four offices, and a "strong corps" of the Bow Street patrole were at one time or another engaged in the inquiry.

Though ordinarily there was little co-operation between Bow Street and the various offices, in the case of a spectacular crime in any London district every office lent what help it could,[1] and such aid was now the more welcome in Shadwell because the three magistrates there already had an epidemic of murder on their hands. Of some moral assistance was the widely held but mistaken belief that Bow Street had assumed control, the name of one of its justices, Aaron Graham, known as a clever investigator, being freely mentioned. Bow Street itself, however, was exceptionally busy at this time, particularly on a complicated case of fraud in which Benjamin Walsh, M.P. for Wootton Bassett, was implicated, and even with two extra magistrates (one of whom was a professor of music, Sir William Parsons, Master of the King's Band) was hard put to it to get through the work. Its full resources were not at once available for the Ratcliffe Highway inquiry, but early on Sunday, the day after the murders, the patrole and a Runner or two were sent to Shadwell. This party collected at least two of the local Runners, and was joined by Goff, from Union Hall, across the river, one of the few police officers outside Bow Street who then had more than a local reputation. John Harriott and one of his colleagues, Kinnard, arrived from the Thames office, and set their own officers to work searching for

[1] Giving evidence in 1816 before the Select Committee, the then Chief Magistrate, Sir Nathaniel Conant, said: "We never stop a moment in the case of a serious offence to the public: if a person at the farthest end of the neighbouring counties gave notice of a murder or any atrocious offence being committed, I should send one, two, or three officers immediately to the spot for information, and send others in all directions to search out the offenders, and no party would ever be applied to for the expense."

likely suspects in riverside lodgings and on ships in dock, a move inspired by the discovery in the Marrs' house of a ship-carpenter's ripping-chisel and a maul with blood and hair sticking to it.

In the beginning, nevertheless, the brunt of the business fell on the Shadwell magistrates—the venerable George Storey, who had been sitting there continuously since 1792, the resident justice, Edward Markland, also elderly, and the more youthful Robert Rainsford, who was to give some interesting evidence before the Select Committee of 1816. To them was joined an extra justice named Robert Capper. It was known that these last three had begun the inquiry, and the vast crowds that converged on Shadwell that Sunday morning to gaze at the Marrs' house or watch for developments outside the Police Office had the pleasure of seeing several men brought in for questioning. In greater style, but apparently impelled by the same morbid curiosity, the City Sheriffs came in their coach to visit the house; the City did not interest itself officially in the matter until the investigation was almost completed. That afternoon the first handbills were locally distributed, rewards of fifty pounds and twenty pounds being offered by the parish authorities of St George-in-the-East for information about three men, whose dress and general appearance were described. One of the three, seen near the Marrs' house on the previous night, wore "a light-coloured sort of Flushing coat," to be heard of again.

During the next few days, which drew crowds as large as ever to Ratcliffe Highway, public feeling continued to rise, until, in De Quincey's words, "the mere delirium of indignant horror in some" became the "delirium of panic in others." Though Ryder and his Under-Secretaries were giving most of their attention to riots in Nottingham, the Government felt it necessary to offer substantial rewards for the discovery of the murderer or murderers. The total, with those already promised locally, came to more than £700. The inquest provided little in the way of sensation, though it was shown that a maid recently dismissed by Mrs Marr had departed uttering threats of murder. It was felt that no woman could have perpetrated such a massacre, and in the meantime the men brought in daily for questioning were being allowed to go.

On the evening after the inquest the field of inquiry was widened. No fewer than nine men were examined that day; one of them, named Pugh, had been employed by Marr during the previous month to carry out some alterations at the shop, and he now told the magistrates that a certain Hart, a carpenter working for him, had borrowed a ripping-chisel from a neighbour. Hart was found, and proved his innocence;

the chisel, he said, he had left at No. 29; but the same night came news of yet another carpenter, also at one time employed by Pugh's firm, who was one of the wanted men described in the handbills. He was now reported as having been seen on the Portsmouth road.

Jobbing carpenters all over the country were brought in to account for themselves. The man seen on the Portsmouth road was run to earth at Peper Harrow, where Lord Middleton had detained him, and two Shadwell officers fetched him to London. All these suspected persons had to be released; nor could anything be proved against several Portuguese arrested by Whitechapel Runners. The exhibitionist is not new, though the word may be, and much time was wasted over silly people who 'confessed' to the murders, at the risk of their lives if the mob had caught them. One of them dragged yet another Police Office into the inquiry by giving himself up at Queen Square. On account of the state of alarm in London, Colquhoun and his junior colleague, Henry Fielding's son William,[1] dared not free the man immediately.

Among others who came under suspicion were Mrs Marr's brother, and also the brother of Marr. The former, a hackney-coach driver, was estranged from his family, and did not even know where his sister was living, but by a coincidence only really permissible in modern detective fiction he had driven a fare to Ratcliffe Highway on the night of the crime. As for the Marr brothers, there was said to be bad blood between them, and a lawsuit pending; and Aaron Graham, having undertaken, according to an admiring newspaper reporter, "the task of detecting those who committed the massacre of Mr Marr and family," had the other Marr arrested and locked in the strong-room at the Brown Bear,[2] whence he was later fetched to be interrogated at Graham's house in Queen Street, Lincoln's Inn Fields. The magistrate had acted on erroneous information, and Marr was set free; the dismissed servant had by this time come forward and cleared herself, and, though a

[1] William Fielding, after long practice at the Bar, was appointed to the Queen Square office in 1808. Colquhoun was then living in Hammersmith, and, Pye, the Poet Laureate, having resigned, Fielding applied for the latter's post as resident magistrate, being, as he said, "very lame." One of the extra justices at Bow Street, Richard Birnie, apparently one of Mainwaring's men, made a similar application. Ryder, the Home Secretary, gave the post to Fielding. (Public Record Office, H.O. 65. 1.)

[2] The Brown Bear, referred to in a previous chapter as being opposite the Bow Street office, was soon to lose its strong-room. A house next door to the office had just been leased for sixteen and a half years at an annual rent of ninety pounds, apparently at the instance of James Read, one of the justices, who suggested that if the two houses were knocked into one there would be room for "housing the Patrole at night when any disturbance was expected." It was not until September 1812, however, that the £1295 required for the necessary alterations, which included a new strong-room, or "prisoners' base," was authorized. (Public Record Office, H.O. 65. 1.)

number of other persons, many of them foreigners, were still being detained in connexion with the affair, the inquiry seemed to have come to a standstill.

Nearly a fortnight had gone by since the murders when the first really valuable clue was provided by Harriott at the Thames office. The bloodstained maul found in the Marrs' house was on view here. Shipwrights and old-iron merchants had failed to throw any light on it, but now Harriott caused it to be examined again, and discovered beneath the blood and dirt, faintly impressed in dots, the initials J.P.

The discovery, announced in the newspapers of Friday, the 20th of December, came just too late. On the previous evening the murderer had struck again.

3

The King's Arms, in New Gravel Lane, a turning off Ratcliffe Highway not far from St George's Church, was a respectable tavern much frequented by foreign seamen. The proprietor, Mr Williamson, being a strict manager, the house, according to De Quincey, was also popular with the better sort of citizens of Shadwell. Though Williamson always cleared his bar at eleven o'clock, the official closing hour, he left his front door ajar until midnight for the convenience of neighbours who wanted one more jugful of beer. He was a man of seventy, reputed to be rich, and living on the premises with him were his wife, a small granddaughter (or niece), a middle-aged female servant, and a young lodger, John Turner. Carpenters had already figured rather prominently in the local sensation, and Turner was another. He was to be involved more closely than he liked.

On that Thursday evening, the 19th, as he told the Shadwell magistrates, he had noticed an oddly dressed man with red hair and staring eyes "lurking" about the King's Arms. He spoke about this fellow to Williamson, who paid little attention. When the bar emptied at eleven o'clock Turner went up to bed, and was not yet fully asleep when he was roused by the bang of the front door. This noise was followed by groans and cries of the most alarming kind. He went to his bedroom door in time to hear a despairing cry of "Murder," whereupon, still in his shirt and nightcap, he ran barefooted downstairs until he could see into the small parlour of the inn. Like Murray the pawnbroker, a fortnight earlier, he was appalled by what he saw.

Near the fireplace lay the bodies of the servant and Mrs Williamson, the former terribly wounded in the head, her mistress covered with blood. Stooping over Mrs Williamson was a man in "a shaggy bearskin coat," whose face Turner could not see. The back view was enough; here was the "sort of Flushing coat" associated with the Marr murders. Here, too, no doubt, was the man with the staring eyes. As Turner stood "half paralysed" on the stairs the sinister figure moved out of sight, his shoes creaking and Mrs Williamson's keys chinking in his hand. The terrified carpenter crept back to his bedroom; if he was perhaps no hero he is scarcely to be blamed for thinking only of escape, for it was believed then, and stated in pamphlets widely read, that the massacre of the Marrs was the work of a gang. Turner, at any rate, set about tearing his sheets into strips and knotting these together to make a rope. This cannot have been the work of a moment, and his feelings, while he listened for the creaking shoes to come up the stairs, may be imagined. The last knot tied, he waited only to slip on "a Jersey coat," and then opened his window, which was over the street, and let himself down.

De Quincey's dramatic picture of a bare-legged figure dangling ten or twelve feet from the ground, too frightened to call out and not immediately seen because of a ground-mist rolling up from the river, is somewhat imaginative. Turner did cry out, and was heard and seen by a watchman, who caught him in his arms and immediately raised the alarm. A constable living opposite the inn came running across; other neighbours were roused and organized as an armed search-party. The door of the tavern was now, however, locked, and before it could be broken down, or the house surrounded, the murderer had escaped by a back window, and so across an empty site belonging to the London Docks Company, where he left some clear footprints in a patch of wet clay.

The Marrs' killer had taken fright before he found any store of money; this time—if it were the same man—thanks to Mrs Williamson's keys, he was better rewarded. And that it was the same man, or men, no one for a moment doubted, for the atrocity at the King's Arms bore many of the sickening hall-marks of the murders at the hosier's shop. The little girl, happily, was more fortunate than the Marrs' baby; she was found asleep and unharmed in her bedroom on the first floor; but both Mrs Williamson and the servant were dead, and Williamson's body was found in the cellar, where he had gone to draw a jug of beer. Beneath him was a ripping-hook, but all three victims had been killed by blows on the head from some weapon as murderous as the maul used on the Marrs.

At the moment of Turner's rescue two Shadwell officers happened to be in a house of call near by, and Mr Mallett, the chief clerk to the

Shadwell justices, was still at the Police Office. No justice being at hand, he assumed control. A picquet of militia stationed in the neighbourhood was called out, and armed parties of angry men began to patrol the streets, stopping carriages and questioning passers-by. As the morning came the news spread all over London, and with it rumours of other murders committed or threatened, as a result of which at least one of the many public houses in Ratcliffe Highway was given a special guard. A strong party of the Bow Street patrole arrived, under orders to co-operate with the Runners from the three local Police Offices.

Shadwell itself was in an uproar. A systematic search was being made for all who had been in the King's Arms on the previous evening, and for other habitués, the fact that Williamson had gone down to the cellar to draw beer after closing-time suggesting that the murderer was some one known to him. Four or five men were detained for examination, and, in addition, all who had been interrogated about the Marr murders were brought in. Everybody with traces of clay on his shoes or clothes was in danger of arrest or even of serious assault. De Quincey's "delirium of panic" was mounting and spreading fast.

Already, however, the net was closing about the man in the shaggy coat. At a Wapping public house, the Pear Tree, kept by one Vermilloe, two young artisans named Harris and Cutburn had been sharing a room with a seafaring man known as John Williams. The latter had roused Harris's curiosity by shaving off his whiskers, and by his odd behaviour generally. When the newspapers of the 20th gave details of the marked maul Harris recognized it as one belonging to a former lodger in the house, John Petersen, a Dane. It had been in a chestful of tools, all marked with Petersen's initials, which the latter had left in Vermilloe's charge. Petersen being now in Denmark, and Vermilloe a prisoner in Newgate for a twenty pounds debt, Harris searched the chest. The maul was missing.

Contemporary accounts of the affair become at this point more than usually vague and contradictory, but it seems probable that Harris conveyed his information to his landlord in Newgate, for it was Vermilloe who informed the justices. Robert Capper, the extra Shadwell justice, went to the prison and held his official examination there. John Williams had already been arrested, on Sunday, the 22nd, apparently at the Pear Tree, and much damaging circumstantial evidence against him was being pieced together.

Its main points were these. Williams had known the murdered Marr for some time, the pair having served on the same East Indiaman.

Three days before his arrest Williams had borrowed sixpence from Mrs Vermilloe, but when taken into custody he was wearing new clothes of good quality and had money in his pockets, and also a pawn-ticket for a pair of shoes which creaked. He had shown undue interest in a ripping-hook, apparently from Petersen's chest, which a watchman found near the Pear Tree shortly before the first murders. He had been seen with the carpenter Hart, who borrowed a chisel from Pugh, who in turn, by an odd chance, had it from Vermilloe. Twice in the past fortnight the women who washed his clothes had found blood on his shirt, and, finally, among his belongings, in the pocket of a waistcoat, was a bloodstained knife of a peculiar shape—such a knife, in the opinion of the surgeon who examined the bodies of the Marr household, as might have caused the throat-wounds.

Williams underwent two "long and rigid" interrogations. It was still thought that he might be one of a gang, and reports of other suspected persons, possibly his confederates, were still coming in from various parts of the country. Willans and Hewitt, the Shadwell officers who had arrested Williams, went to Marlborough to fetch a man, named Cahill, who lay under strong suspicion of having had a hand in the murders. All this was on the Sunday, the day of the arrest; and it was decided to hold a further examination of Williams on the following day.

Strongly guarded against the fury of the mob, he was taken to Cold-bath Fields House of Correction, and there placed in the re-examination cell "ironed on the right leg." When the turnkey went to rouse his prisoner at 7.30 the next morning he found him dead and cold. Williams had hanged himself in a determined manner from a beam so low that, in the words of the *Morning Post*, he must have been obliged "to sit down as it were to accomplish his purpose."

The public excitement did not immediately die down. It was kept alive by the interrogation of the suicide's associates, and of other suspects, all of whom, in the end, were discharged. Williams, as to whose guilt there was no real doubt, had done his dreadful work alone. To mark its peculiar atrocity, the Home Secretary, at the instigation of Robert Capper, authorized the Shadwell justices to stage a final scene as macabre as anything London had ever witnessed.

Fully dressed, "in a brown great coat lined with silk, a blue under-coat with yellow buttons, blue and white waistcoat, striped blue pantaloons, brown worsted stockings and shoes"—the new clothes Williams had worn when arrested—the body was attached by cords to a broad wooden slab or board. With it were fastened the maul and the ripping-hook found at the King's Arms. The board was mounted on a high open cart at such an angle that all those in the streets could see its ghastly burden. This singular hearse was driven slowly eastward, followed by magistrates, police officers, and a number of the Bow Street patrole. It paused outside the Marrs' house, and finally halted at the end of New Gravel Lane. There, as the great crowd stood silent and awed, the body was thrown into a hole in the ground and a stake driven through it before the grave was filled in.

At the Home Secretary's desire the maul and ripping-hook were sent, not to Shadwell or the Thames Police Office, but to Bow Street. On the other hand, John Harriott seems to have been the only police magistrate to receive from the Home Department any acknowledgment of the good work done on the case. The two young workmen, Harris and Cutburn, received substantial portions of the various rewards that had been offered.

7

A SECOND PARLIAMENTARY CAMPAIGN

THE people of London, whether well- or ill-informed, reacted to the Shadwell murders in the natural manner. There was an outcry against the magistracy and the police of the City and the Metropolis. The Shadwell and Bow Street justices were very sharply criticized. A complete reorganization of the nightly watch and the formation of an enlarged and 'unpolitical' police force were demanded. Parochial police schemes were introduced and enthusiastically supported. Wilder proposals, emanating from the newspapers, were that the Horse Guards should be used as a nightly patrole, and that "the most distinguished pugilists of good character," such as Tom Cribb, the champion of England, might be engaged as parochial watchmen.

The spectacle of a posse of large bruisers perambulating the streets at night might have its attractive features; an unimaginative Government, however, reacting in its own natural manner, shifted its responsibilities to yet another Select Committee. The Home Office, in these early months of the new year, 1812, had rather more than its usual share of trouble. The frame-breaking riots in Nottingham spread over the Midlands, assuming such proportions that the word 'rebellion' was used; two stipendiaries from the Great Marlborough Street office were dispatched to the scene of the disturbances to co-operate with the troops already sent there,[1] and a Bill was prepared making frame-breaking a capital offence. At the moment when the Home Secretary was about to set up his Select Committee he was much occupied with a scandal, the first of its kind, affecting the police force itself. George Skene, the chief clerk at the Queen Square office, who was rather loosely ranked as the first officer in the police, was convicted of forgery. Two days after Skene was condemned to death, then the punishment for his crime, Ryder moved in the House of Commons for a Select Committee to inquire into the state of the nightly watch.

[1] It seems probable that these magistrates, Conant and Baker, took with them men from their own office, not, as stated in the *Annual Register*, Bow Street Runners. Four years later, at the request of the Recorder of Leicester, five Runners attended the trial of some of the frame-breakers at the Leicester Assizes.

Though by this time the mass of Londoners had lost interest in the matter, the more thoughtful minority, including the police reformers, taking to heart the lesson of the Shadwell murders, were keeping it very much alive. In the Commons, however, it had now become a political question, and the appointment of the proposed Committee was bitterly attacked. Nevertheless it was duly constituted, among its members being Ryder himself, the ageing Sheridan, Sir Francis Burdett, a confirmed trouble-maker, and that brilliant, reckless, and ill-used figure Lord Cochrane. The evidence heard by the Committee was never printed, but a Report issued on April the 17th was radical enough to please even the reformers. None of the recommendations was entirely new; most of them, in a somewhat different form, had been embodied in the ill-fated Bill of 1785. One gave to the police magistrates and those at Bow Street superintending powers over all constables, beadles, and watchmen. Bow Street was to be a central bureau to which other officers were to send police information. Police officers were to have increased powers of arrest, and were to be rewarded by magistrates, though not by Parliament, for any special piece of good work, irrespective of a conviction. Preparations were put in hand for a Nightly Watch Regulation Bill, and Ryder saw to the enforcement of certain rules which had come to be generally ignored.

What would have become of this well-meant scheme can never be known. It went the way of so many others, though from a cause no one could have foreseen. On May the 11th, in the lobby of the House, where neither police officers nor patroles were on guard, the Prime Minister, Spencer Perceval, was shot dead by John Bellingham. Ryder, with some of his colleagues, was swept out of office, and most of his police reforms went with him.

2

The new, and purely Tory, administration, formed by Lord Liverpool, was to last for nearly fifteen years. Liverpool was at least interested in police matters; when Home Secretary, as Lord Hawkesbury, he had established the Horse Patrole. Ryder's successor at the Home Office, Lord Sidmouth, though in general inclined to leave well alone, shared some of his chief's views, and he at once put in hand a somewhat weakened version of the Nightly Watch Regulation Bill. Violent opposition, led by Burdett, Samuel Whitbread, and Brougham, caused it to be abandoned; and for nearly nine years no further serious attempt was made to forward any major measure of the kind.

Sidmouth, however, effected some minor improvements in the

"PEELERS"

SIR ROBERT PEEL
John Linnell.
By courtesy of the Director of the National Portrait Gallery

OLD SCOTLAND YARD, WHITEHALL PLACE

[*See p.* 80.]

existing system, such as the payment of small pensions to officers past their work, and in certain cases to their widows. With his encouragement the Bow Street *Hue and Cry and Police Gazette* was enlarged, and its circulation increased. At Bow Street, in this year (1814), it was discovered that three members of the patrole were also officers at Worship Street and drawing double pay; Sidmouth ordered them to resign one or other of their posts. A stop was also put to the practice by which Runners (who except at Bow Street were not necessarily whole-time officers) supplemented their weekly guinea by trading or even managing public houses, the licences of which were held in other names. When Sidmouth retired from office almost every Runner or member of a patrole was required to give his whole time to police work.

The year 1814 also saw the downfall of William Mainwaring. Threatened by financial disaster, he used his position as a Commissioner of Sewers to transfer the Commission's accounts from Drummond's Bank to his own; but the affairs of the latter were already involved past mending, and in November its failure was announced in the *London Gazette*. In spite of much plain speaking in the papers, it was some little time before Mainwaring felt compelled to resign his chairmanship of the Westminster Bench.

In the new Administration the Chief Secretary for Ireland was Robert Peel the younger, who in 1812 was only twenty-four; and two years later it was Ireland, already in the news in connexion with police reform, that saw a fresh development. Faced with the prospect of trouble over the question of Catholic Emancipation, Peel revived the Insurrection Act. Reorganization of the Dublin Police having brought no help to country districts, he also formed a force called the Peace Preservation Police, which was the forerunner of the Royal Irish Constabulary. In Dublin, fifteen years before London was to coin the word "Peelers," officers of the new force were known by that name.

3

The end of the prolonged war with France brought a widespread depression in England. Early in 1815 a new Corn Bill which, under certain conditions, prohibited the import of wheat, caused violent rioting in London. In Palace Yard there were scenes almost recalling those witnessed during the Gordon Riots. The Great Marlborough Street magistrate, Robert Baker, who brought about eighty Runners and patroles to reinforce the Westminster constables, thought it necessary to call for troops, and the Riot Act was read. In Westminster itself the huge mob seems to have been satisfied with shouting and booing, but in the meantime there were more serious disturbances elsewhere in London. The unpopular Eldon, the Lord Chancellor, who is said to have lost the Great Seal for a time, forgetting where he had buried it when his home at Encombe caught fire, had to fly from his London house in Bedford Square to the sanctuary of the British Museum, where a small military guard was then stationed. Eldon did not lack courage, and later ran after the rioters and arrested two. The Law came well out of the crisis, for Ellenborough, the Lord Chief Justice, faced the mob from his own doorstep and caused it to cheer him before moving elsewhere.

Nearly a score of large houses had suffered damage, and the Government offered a reward of £100 for the apprehension of leading rioters. Thirty men were in custody a week later,[1] but the agitation had quickly died down. There was much criticism of the measures taken to counter it. The delay of the High Bailiff of Westminster, not himself a magistrate, in getting in touch with those at Bow Street and Queen Square was a reminder that police and parish officers were still disinclined to work together.

Before the news of Waterloo reached London a Select Committee appointed to inquire into "the State of Mendicity in the Metropolis" called Conant and Colquhoun before it, among other witnesses, and may be regarded as a sort of curtain-raiser to the most elaborate investigation into the state of London's police that Parliament had as yet undertaken. The post-war depression continued, unaffected by the interlude of the Hundred Days, and discharged soldiers and sailors swelled the already numerous unemployed. In London there was a marked increase of burglary and shop-breaking; the Worship Street Runners were ordered to "scour" the streets at night, and other offices seem to have instituted more or less regular nightly patrols. Dissatisfaction with the existing state of things was reflected in the growing interest in police reform, coupled with penal reform, shown by Private Members of Parliament, notably by Michael Angelo Taylor, a close friend of Thomas Creevey and an advocate of the use of gas for street lighting and of the abolition of the pillory and by another of Creevey's associates, Henry Grey Bennet, a descendant of the Lord Arlington of the Cabal. It was Bennet who, in April 1816, moved for the appointment of a Select Committee to consider the whole question of the reform of London's police system. There must have been some laughter when one of Sidmouth's Under-Secretaries, his brother Hiley

[1] *Morning Chronicle*, March 17, 1815.

Addington, stated that the police magistrates, at their last meeting with Sidmouth himself, had pronounced that in their recollection the Metropolis had never been in a more tranquil state. It was known that many of these magistrates were strongly opposed to any detailed inquiry into the way they performed their duties. Addington, however, did not oppose the motion, and the Committee was at once set up, with Bennet in the chair.

Among the witnesses called before it were ten London magistrates and three of their clerks, Runners, and other police officers, four county magistrates, and such prominent figures as Romilly, Sir John Sylvester, the Recorder of London, Elizabeth Fry, and Robert Owen. There were many interesting revelations, and some discreditable. The most startling, perhaps, were provided by the Rev. Joshua King, of Bethnal Green, who thoroughly exposed the misdoings of two of Mainwaring's cronies among the justices, Joseph Merceron and Sir Daniel Williams. The evidence and proposals of another witness were no less instructive because they foreshadowed difficulties to be encountered by present and future police reformers, including Peel.

The High Bailiff of Westminster had come reluctantly into prominence during the recent Corn Bill riots. His post was purchased from the Dean like any other marketable commodity, and, its profits being considerable, the purchaser could afford a paid deputy to do most of what work there was. Any serious scheme of reform threatened anomalies of this kind, and William Tooke, the High Bailiff's deputy who came before the Select Committee, was the mouthpiece of various interests much concerned to preserve the status quo, or their part of it. In particular, it was obvious that sooner or later either parish constables or police officers would have to go, and as obviously the constables were most in danger of extinction. They were already being pushed to one side, as Tooke admitted when he informed the Committee that the eighty Westminster constables, unless called out to assist the magistrates during a disturbance, were instructed to leave all arrests for crimes to the police officers. To re-establish their waning powers, he suggested that Westminster would do well to copy the compact system of police, with its unity of control, then functioning in the City of London. Burgesses could act as aldermen, and three deputies could assist the High Constable. By this scheme Westminster's Court of Burgesses, under the High Steward (at this time Sidmouth himself), would recover some of its old-time importance, and a member of the Committee pointed the moral by asking if Mr Tooke wished to do away with the Police Offices, as, of course, he did. He could not say so, and the Committee seems to have remained unimpressed by his arguments.

Its chief business was the reform of the police, and under Bennet it probed far deeper than any previous Committee into the now common charges of incompetence and corruption. As it happened, the Minutes of Evidence given at the earlier sittings, hurriedly printed in July 1816, coincided with the disclosure of a scandal of the worst kind. George Vaughan, a member of the Foot Patrole, sometimes called a Bow Street Runner, copied the methods of Jonathan Wild, planning robberies and then arresting the culprits who had carried them out. With him in a brief but lucrative conspiracy were two ex-City police officers and a well-known thief. Vaughan would have got away with a sentence of five years' imprisonment had he not committed a robbery himself. For this crime he and a confederate were hanged. The trials aroused great interest, and with the newspapers printing long extracts from the Minutes of Evidence before the Select Committee, the City, at any rate, hastened to adopt improvements in its police system already repeatedly advocated. In instructions for a new uniform watch in all the wards, where the watchmen's boxes, so convenient for a comfortable doze, were to be abolished, there appears what seems to be the first mention in an official pronouncement of the use of a *dark* lantern.

In the Metropolis, Sidmouth was waiting for the Committee's Reports. Three were issued, the last, which touched on the dreadful state of the prisons, not appearing until the summer of 1818. In spite of Bennet's efforts, there was little new in them. That he and those with him who wished for drastic changes had met with powerful opposition is revealed in the statement that the Committee "would deprecate a severe system of police as inconsistent with the liberties of the people." The liberties of the people were to be in danger for another sixty or seventy years.

4

Sidmouth remained in office for three and a half years after the publication of the third and last Report of the Select Committee. He was to be succeeded as Home Secretary by Robert Peel. During these three and a half years many influences, direct and indirect, worked towards a realization of the police reformers' plans and hopes. Sidmouth himself, more by misguided measures at large than by further praiseworthy if minor improvements in the Metropolitan police system, did much to focus attention throughout the country on the need for drastic action against prevailing inefficiency and confusion of effort.

In successive years the "Peterloo Massacre" and the Cato Street Conspiracy luridly illuminated two aspects of the question—the danger inherent in the use of the military as a substitute for police, and the necessity of strengthening and unifying the police themselves. Political societies, often of a subversive nature, were raising novel problems for the Home Department; and Sidmouth's remedy, in addition to employing, like most of his predecessors, an army of spies, was to use a force of Yeomanry to maintain order. Lacking the discipline and detachment of regular troops—they were raised locally—the Yeomanry were largely responsible for the violent handling of unarmed mobs which culminated in the disastrous affray at St Peter's Field, in Manchester, when eleven men, women, and children were sabred or ridden down and several hundred others injured. When the whole truth came out the country was horrified, and the Government was rightly censured for its precipitate action in thanking the Manchester magistrates and the troops for the efficient measures taken. The scene of Napoleon's final defeat inspired the satirists to perpetuate the one-sided battle of the 16th of August, 1819, by the name of Peterloo.

The Cato Street Conspiracy in the following February was less ineptly handled. Informers betrayed the plot, and Government spies watched every move of Thistlewood, Ings, the Brighton butcher, and the other conspirators until they assembled for the last time in the Cato Street stable, on the night of Lord Harrowby's Cabinet dinner. Only then were warrants for their arrest dispatched to Bow Street, where, the Chief Magistrate, Conant, being ill, his colleague, Birnie, collected a strong party of Runners and constables. This posse was joined by a detachment of the Guards. Cato Street was an alley reached by an archway in John Street (now, to commemorate the dinner-party, Harrowby Street), off Edgware Road. The Guards marching to the wrong end of John Street, the peace officers, who were armed with pistols and cutlasses, rushed into the stable and up the ladder to the loft, where the plotters were preparing for their attack on Harrowby's house in Grosvenor Square. Thistlewood ran one of the patrole through the body before escaping. He was captured next day. Altogether eleven were taken; as many more got away.[1]

The plot had been a dangerous one; and in defeating it the reliance upon spies to the very last moment almost suggests a lack of trust in

[1] Some interesting details of the Cato Street Conspiracy are to be found in *The Diary of Henry Hobhouse (1820–1827)*, edited by Arthur Aspinall, and published in 1947.

the police. It appears that Birnie, at Bow Street, received no information or instructions until the warrants arrived. On the other hand, it seems that the sick Conant was held to be in some way to blame, and a fortnight later he resigned. Birnie, an ambitious man, who expected the succession, was bitterly chagrined when Robert Baker, from Great Marlborough Street, was brought in over his head.

There was trouble in London of another, and too familiar, kind a few months later, when Queen Caroline's return to England led to an outcrop of serious riots. Sidmouth and his friends had to defend his house. In the middle of this turmoil a wing of the Third Regiment of Guards, temporarily stationed in uncomfortable quarters in the Royal Mews at Charing Cross, and further dissatisfied by long hours of duty caused by the rioting and a Royal Drawing Room, refused to march to Portsmouth. A mob of course gathered at Charing Cross, and Sidmouth called out the Life Guards. The little attempt at mutiny was over within a few hours; but one result was a remarkable memorandum which the Duke of Wellington drew up for the Prime Minister. "In my opinion," said the Duke, after alluding to the incidents at Charing Cross, "the Government ought, without the loss of a moment's time, to adopt measures to form either a police in London or a military corps which should be of a different description from the regular military force, or both." This passage has led one or two of the Duke's biographers to bracket him with Peel as a creator of the Metropolitan Police.

The trial of Queen Caroline led to less trouble than had been expected. Her more irresponsible supporters soon lost enthusiasm for her cause. In readiness for trouble, a large body of troops was quartered in the capital, and Sidmouth brought in some of the Horse Patrole, the "Robin Redbreasts," now under the control of the Home Office. He may have made this experiment because he already had in mind an important change in the functions of this patrole. It had proved a most efficient force, and the chief task for which it had been formed was all but accomplished. Highwaymen were driven from the roads. At the end of 1820, accordingly, Sidmouth withdrew both the Horse Patrole and the less successful Foot Patrole from outlying parishes, concentrating them in the Metropolis, which was divided into sixteen police districts, forerunners of Peel's seventeen divisions; the outer area was policed by what was called the Horse Patrole Dismounted. This meant that while the numbers of the Foot Patrole remained the same, those of the Horse Patrole were augmented to nearly two hundred, of whom seventy-two were mounted. Some three hundred trained men in all were now available for night patrol duty in and around the Metropolis. Within a radius of twenty miles from Charing Cross doubtful characters might be stopped three or four times—by foot patrols and the Mounted and Dismounted Horse Patrole. By another innovation at this time Sidmouth again anticipated Peel by instituting a regular Day Patrole outside the City of London's boundaries. It was largely made up of men who attended nightly at the two Theatres Royal when required. Though then unavailable at Bow Street, they had been receiving double payment.

A Private Member's Bill passed in 1821 brought about other small improvements in the Metropolitan police system. There being no Police Office north of Oxford Street, the Shadwell office was closed, and its magistrates and staff were moved across London to Marylebone, where a mixed population was growing fast. The new office was in Marylebone Lane, which winds as it did then, and where a modern police station now stands. The Act also tightened regulations in all Police Offices, and in Sidmouth's last months as Home Secretary he enforced one of its clauses at the expense of two magistrates whom he considered negligent. For failing to attend, as instructed, at George IV's Coronation, George Mainwaring, the son of William, was so severely reprimanded that he resigned, and a Worship Street justice was in trouble for absenting himself before signing certain warrants sent specially to him from the Home Office.

Sidmouth was in Ireland with the King when yet another serious disturbance in London heralded the resignation, which was, in fact, the dismissal, of the new Chief Magistrate at Bow Street. In August Queen Caroline died suddenly in her house in Hammersmith. Her body had to be taken to Brunswick for burial, by way of Harwich. George IV being very unpopular, especially in the City, the Prime Minister, in his Home Secretary's absence, ordered the cortège to take a northerly route along the New Road, now Euston Road, and so round the City boundary into Essex, thus avoiding the more populous parts of the capital. Dislike of the King caused old feelings for Queen Caroline to be revived or exploited, and a great crowd in Kensington barricaded the lower end of Church Lane (the modern Church Street), up which the procession was to turn. Sir Robert Baker was sent for from Bow Street, but was trapped by the mob in Hyde Park. In the meantime Park Lane was barricaded, and when some of the small escort of Life Guards managed to break into the Park, and the cortège followed, it was only to find a larger and angrier mob at Tyburn, and further obstructions. As the Guards were hacking their way through a barrier some one gave the order to fire, and two men, one of whom was little more than a boy, were fatally wounded. The crowd was determined that the coffin should pass through the City, and after another stoppage, Baker, who was now in control, gave way. He had sent back the Life Guards, and, leading the procession himself to Temple Bar, there handed it over to the protection of the Lord Mayor and the City authorities. The mob having won its fight, there had been no more trouble.

But a scapegoat had to be found, and Baker was allowed to resign. It was as a superintendent of police that he had failed—he continued for some years to sit as a county justice—and this fact was not without its consequences. He was succeeded at Bow Street by Richard Birnie, who was immediately knighted.[1]

A fortnight later *The Times* emphasized some of the lessons of the affair. One had been becoming increasingly obvious since the days of the Major-Generals.

> If the civil power were increased, as it ought to be, in strength, there would be no pretext for the employment of soldiers in their modern and extraordinary character of police men. Fifty police officers on horseback would, in point of mere efficiency, be worth a whole regiment of dragoons. If none but the civil power appeared, there is not a decent individual among the King's subjects who would not eagerly assist them in the suppression of a riot, and in bringing the abettors of it to punishment.

If the events of another half-century and more were to show that *The Times* took a rather rosy view of the King's subjects, the root of the matter was in these words, written at a time when Sidmouth had decided to retire from an active political career, and when the question of his successor at the Home Office was about to be raised.

[1] A clever as well as a very ambitious man, Birnie never did anything for the police. The notice of him in the *Dictionary of National Biography*, mostly taken from an obituary notice in the *Gentleman's Magazine*, is far from accurate.

8

THE BIRTH OF SCOTLAND YARD

Robert Peel called himself a Tory, and Trevelyan has observed that he never knew he was not one. Perhaps he was what in those days was that very rare bird, later exemplified by Disraeli and Lord Randolph Churchill, the Tory Democrat, but the name had not then been invented. He has rightly been styled one of the greatest Home Secretaries; no other, indeed, has approached his accomplishment, within twenty years, of such measures as the amendment of the penal code, the creation of the Metropolitan Police, Catholic Emancipation, and the repeal of the Corn Laws, to say nothing of two important Bank Acts.

He moved slowly; and during his six years at the Irish Office he showed little sign of a liberal attitude towards social problems. Retiring temporarily from official politics in 1818, he became Home Secretary, in succession to Sidmouth, in January 1822. Within a month he was at work on police reform, but only in connexion with such minor matters as tightening discipline and an extension of the various patrols, as they may now be called, the final 'e' being often dropped in official documents about this time, though the earlier spelling is occasionally found in Victorian days. In March he moved for the appointment of a Select Committee to consider the state of the police, but, apart from one or two sensible recommendations, nothing, as usual, came of this. Peel, in his deliberate way, no doubt continued to turn the matter over in his mind, but it was put aside for some years while he concentrated on the closely related question of the reform of the criminal law. In the meantime two of the Select Committee's recommendations came into force: a head constable was appointed to each Police Office (he was in fact, if not in name, a police inspector), and a Daily Patrol was instituted, numbering twenty-seven men, who were required to "distribute themselves judiciously from 9 A.M. to 7 P.M., when they would be relieved by the night parties." These men wore the blue-and-red uniforms of the Horse Patrol. There were many ex-soldiers in the patrols, and Peel seems to have thought that a uniform might assist them "to be proud of their establishment." The old Foot Patrol continued to dress as it pleased. Patrols were becoming rather too numerous and confusing, but one and all were soon to be swept away.

If Peel's tidy mind was already moving in this direction, at this date he seems to have got no further than envisaging an amalgamation and enlargement of the patrols, and a closer connexion between them and the Runners. He must have realized that the latter, experts in their line, were not far removed from constituting a semi-private detective agency.[1] His earlier instructions strongly suggest that he was then working towards a unified force with its headquarters, for the time being, at Bow Street. Here the leases of No. 4 and the adjoining house had some five years to run, but neither was really convenient. There was nothing about their façade to suggest a public court; the Royal Arms in stone, with which Victorians were to become so familiar, had not yet been placed over the doorway; and it is clear from the Home Office papers that Peel was feeling that two narrow domestic buildings, not even of the same height, were no longer an appropriate home for the chief Police Office in the Metropolis. In April 1823 he had in view the erection of a new building, not necessarily in Bow Street. The project, however, was set aside, and 'Bow Street,' though moved across the way, remains. It was soon after this, in the summer of 1824, that police events far in the future were foreshadowed by the action of the Horse Patrol, which needed a headquarters of its own. Premises were found at No. 8 Cannon Row, almost on the site of New Scotland Yard.

Further developments, arising out of the report of the Select Committee of 1822, were encouragements to men of the Foot Patrol to look for promotion to the rank of police officer, and permission to patrolmen to go outside the London area if no Runner was immediately available when help in investigating some rural crime was applied for. The Runners are not likely to have approved of this. It was at this period that two Bow Street patrolmen, Henry Goddard and Nicholas Pearce, began successful careers; Pearce was to become the best-known detective in the Metropolitan Police in the 1840's, and eventually one of its most trusted superintendents, while Goddard, who was never in that force, is of interest for another reason. Taking up private-inquiry work, he left an account of his more

[1] The inquisitive reader may here be warned against a work entitled *Richmond; or, Scenes in the Life of a Bow Street Officer*. It is third-rate fiction, in which the Bow Street office is barely mentioned, nor has the anonymous author any apparent connexion with a man named Richmond who was then second clerk there.

dramatic cases in that rôle, and also what appears to be the only narrative of a Bow Street officer's duties with any claim to authenticity.[1]

2

During the next few years Peel was establishing that personal ascendancy in the House of Commons which raised his office to pre-eminence among Government departments. Another Committee considered the discipline of the police—or their indiscipline, if the view of Opposition journals is to be accepted. Crime was on the increase, and the Press itself was attacked for its sensational treatment of criminal matters, especially two notable cases which ended with trials and executions in 1824. One is now best remembered by a scrap of verse:

His throat they cut from ear to ear,
His brains they battered in:
His name was Mr William Weare,
He lived in Lyons Inn.

For this murder John Thurtell was hanged at Hertford in January. He had been arrested by a Bow Street Runner named Ruthven. Later in the year came the trial of Henry Fauntleroy, the banker; forgery being still a capital crime, he was also executed. In both cases the newspapers were charged with prejudicing the chances of the accused by publishing damaging details of their careers before they came up for trial. This latitude in dealing with criminal proceedings still *sub judice* was to reach its climax thirty years later with Palmer of Rugeley. Innocent alarm was also shown over the "injudicious" relations of Runners or patrolmen with undesirable characters, but it was beginning to be realized that informers played an inevitable and necessary part in most police inquiries.

In the winter of 1826 Peel was able once more to turn his mind to possible major changes in the police system. His scheme at this stage, as outlined to John Hobhouse, then Under-Secretary for Ireland, was simple enough, and owed something to both Colquhoun and the Fieldings. There was no mention of any new police corps, but a central authority was implied. The Metropolis, to a distance of ten miles from St Paul's, was to be treated as "one great city," divided for police purposes into six divisions, each with its office and justices. The

[1] This lengthy manuscript, written or dictated by Goddard in 1875–79, when he must have been a very old man, came into the hands of Chief Superintendent A. W. Rowlerson, of E Division, among other interesting material received in response to his appeal through *The Times* in 1949 for help in forming the Bow Street Museum, which is now in being.

police, presumably the amalgamated patrols, were to be managed and financed on a uniform plan. Peel remarked significantly that he doubted whether he would leave the police of the districts under the exclusive control of the justices—a hint of his future creation of Commissioners. The City of London was left severely alone; "I should be afraid to meddle with it."

Political events now intervened. In February 1827 Liverpool was struck down, and Canning succeeded him. Peel, on the Roman Catholic question, thought it necessary to resign. Canning died in August, and, after that "transient, embarrassed phantom," Lord Goderich, had held office for a few months, early in 1828, a very different character, the Duke of Wellington, became Prime Minister. Wellington's views about a police force for London have been quoted, and Peel, coming back as Home Secretary and Leader of the House, could expect full support from the Prime Minister for plans which in the meantime he had been developing along altogether new lines.

"What," he asked of Hobhouse, who had resigned his Under-Secretaryship, "am I to do with the police?" He was "not very sanguine" about the results of deliberations by a new Select Committee he set up, but in moving its appointment he used words which showed how his thoughts were crystallizing. "The time is come when . . . we may fairly pronounce that the country has outgrown her police institutions, and that the cheapest and safest course will be found in the introduction of a new mode of protection." The Committee's terms of reference were wide, and if witnesses told it little new, there was a quality in its Report distinguishing this from almost all previous ones. The Report reads as if Peel, then perhaps the most powerful man in the country, had been able to choose his own men to sit upon the Committee, and even to direct what questions should be put to witnesses. It need not be examined; the only clause in it that matters to-day was a proposal to create an "Office of Police," *under the Home Secretary*, which was to have control over all police establishments in the Metropolis. Details were to be worked out by Mr Secretary Peel and his advisers. Since it was taken for granted that the City of London was to remain unaffected,[1] the way was clear at last for a complete overhaul of the rest, and by far the major part, of the capital's police system.

[1] Not only Peel, but everybody since, except possibly Mayne, has been "afraid to meddle" with the City. In the middle of the enormous area over which the Home Secretary is the police authority the City's square mile remains outside his control, its own police authority, from the formation of its police force in 1839, being the Common Council, which, with the approval of the sovereign, appoints its own Commissioner who is responsible for the appointments and discipline of the force.

3

Intellectual honesty and moral courage are not perhaps in combination too common among professional politicians; it is a remarkable quality in Peel that he was able, after prolonged deliberation along some line of thought, to accept its logical conclusion and then to stand by it, regardless of consequences. He was to show this quality in an even higher degree in his repeal of the Corn Laws. He had no cause to worry unduly about the inevitable opposition to his reform of the Metropolitan police system, but this in itself was revolutionary. Such official papers or private letters as are available throw little light on the preparations for his great Police Bill, or at what stage—though it must have been an early one—he decided to create an entirely new police corps, with entirely new officials at the head of it. But evidently when the 1828 Committee issued its Report, leaving everything in his hands, his line of thought had not got beyond the old idea of the amalgamation of what existed. There is a vague hint of bigger things in a letter to Hobhouse in December that year. Then, within a few weeks, his mind was made up. There must be a clean cut with the past; patrols, Runners, watchmen, parish constables, beadles, the traditions and vested interests of centuries—all this must go; there must be one homogeneous force of police for the Metropolis, under discipline, with uniform dress and uniform pay for each rank, commanded from a central office whose orders would be obeyed at Bow Street or Southwark, in Highgate or in Camberwell. There was to be a genuine Metropolitan Police.

This is, of course, a simplification. The whole problem was a most intricate one, and Peel always made haste slowly. His famous Police Bill, as he admitted, gave him "great trouble." It is remarkable that he was able to give serious attention to it in that winter of 1828–29, for this was the time when, to the Cabinet's alarm, he was changing his views on the Catholic question. There was something like a political crisis. A Home Secretary with more than one major Bill on his hands felt compelled to resign his seat, and on standing again he was narrowly defeated. He was back in the House in the beginning of March 1829, and the Police Bill was pushed forward. No doubt much of the drafting was done by Peel's friend Gregson, a lawyer, and the Under-Secretaries, but it was Peel's driving force behind them that enabled him, on April the 15th, to rise in the House to propose the abandonment of an entire police system, and its supersession by one of a kind this country had never known.

Cautious as ever, Peel did not reveal in his speech the drastic changes he really contemplated. Except that the nightly watch, and the very name of watchmen, were to go, he seemed to presume a gradual process by which patrolmen, parish constables, and the rest were to be absorbed into a more uniform whole. But the proposed establishment, under the Home Secretary, of a controlling central office at Westminster, with three magistrates in charge—the title of Commissioner was not then used—was a guarantee that reform would be rapid and complete. No such officials, with such powers as they were to wield, would tolerate for a moment longer than was necessary the hodge-podge delivered into their hands. Moreover, at the end of his speech Peel proposed that after a first reading the Bill should be submitted (as it was) to the 1828 Committee for revision; and revision, by what amounted to a tribunal of his own nominees, meant the translation of the deliberately vague terms of most of the Bill into the concrete propositions he had been aiming at throughout.

Opposition to the Bill, even in its revised form, was surprisingly feeble. It passed through its committee stages, and was read for the third time on May the 25th. In the Lords, Wellington took pains to see that there were no avoidable delays. On July the 19th, five days before Parliament was prorogued, the Bill received the Royal Assent, and what was in fact a revolution in British domestic history had been effected with such quietness and dispatch that it was only later that many quarters most concerned were to realize fully what had happened.

Peel had already taken the first, and most important, step to implement the provisions of the Bill. It was a miraculously successful step. The final police authority for the Metropolis was now to be the Home Secretary; but at the start of such an experiment a great deal, if not everything, must depend on the men appointed to direct command of the new force. The idea of three magistrates at the central office was probably derived from the system in force at the existing Police Offices; but no doubt there were also cautionary lessons to be drawn from this arrangement, and the number of the new commanders was reduced to two. It must still have occurred to all concerned that to find two men who would be given equal powers, and very considerable powers at that, and who nevertheless would work amicably together over a period of years, was asking quite a lot of human nature. Yet it was done. The two supreme magistrates—it was now decided that they were to be styled Commissioners of the Metropolitan Police—were a middle-aged soldier of mixed Scottish and Irish stock, Colonel Charles Rowan, C.B., and a young Irish barrister, not yet thirty-three, named Richard Mayne. Happier choices could hardly have been made. Rowan and Mayne took an instant liking for one another, and in twenty-one years' association never, so far as appears, had any serious differences of opinion. What was more, though there was no precedent for the task they were called on to do, and though they were to be faced with problems which at times must have seemed almost beyond solution, they proceeded quietly and judiciously to build up a new police force more or less out of nothing. It may be doubted whether any other two men brought so unexpectedly together could have achieved what they did in the time; and credit must go to whoever it was, Peel or another, who did bring them together out of a considerable list of candidates for the joint post. As it can scarcely have been a lucky guess, somebody was a very good judge of character.

4

The two new Commissioners were given a room in the Home Office. Their work was lightened very considerably by an almost simultaneous appointment designed to safeguard still further Ministerial control of the new force. John Wray, another barrister, became Receiver for the Metropolitan Police. He was the first of a succession of able men who, side by side with the Commissioners, but quite independent of them, being, like them, appointed by Royal Warrant on the recommendation of the Home Secretary, have managed the force's finances. An acting chief clerk was also appointed, and a small staff was lent by the Home Office, pending the organization of a proper headquarters with its civilian element. This was to consist of civil servants within the force, which, as Sir John Moylan points out, is itself in a broad sense a branch of the Civil Service. The civil staff at Scotland Yard, however, is quite distinct from this. It now numbers about fifteen hundred.

No less urgent than the organization of headquarters was the finding of a permanent home for it. Where, precisely, was the "new Police Office in the City of Westminster" to be?

The whole world knows the answer. In the area covered by the old Palace of Whitehall was a small plot very generally known as "Scotland." Here, according to legend, lodgings were reserved for the Kings of Scotland when they came to pay annual homage to the Kings of England for lands possessed by the Scottish Crown south of the Tweed. There is a pleasant story that a part of Whitehall Court still stands on Scottish soil, an acre or so having been given by King Edgar of England, somewhere about 960, to Kenneth III of Scotland. At any rate, in 1829, as to-day, legend, and possibly history, was perpetuated by a narrow alley turning out of Whitehall on the east side. Only one small house now survives of the Great Scotland Yard of Peel's time. Before then, with the courts leading out of it, it had become a sort of residential 'close,' much favoured by eminent architects. Wren, Inigo Jones, and Vanbrugh had lived there. So had Milton. It was in Scotland Yard itself, as has been seen, that De Veil set up his first office. Then Government offices were housed in the area, to be removed in 1782, when a number of buildings were pulled down and a road was driven across what had been the garden of Northumberland House to connect Whitehall with the Strand. Alleys known as Middle Scotland Yard and Little Scotland Yard were merged during the Regency into a single street later called Whitehall Place; and here John Garden built a row of small houses which by 1820 was completed. It backed on to Great Scotland Yard. Garden himself seems to have lived for a few years in No. 4; then, in 1823, he leased the house to Charles Williams Wynn, at that date President of the Board of Control, whom Peel no doubt often visited there. Wynn moved out on his dismissal by Wellington in 1828, and after a short occupation by Sir Richard Vivian, the Inspector-General of Cavalry, No. 4 fell vacant. Peel at once seized upon it for his new police headquarters.

Alterations were put in hand. Servants' quarters at the back, extending to Great Scotland Yard, began to be converted into what was to be styled a "station-house." The watch was about to be disbanded, and the name watch-house was to disappear with it, and that of police station was yet in the future. A separate entrance was opened from the station-house to Great Scotland Yard; and here, in September 1829, was established the headquarters of the Central or Whitehall (A) Division of the new police.

The men of this division were soon speaking of their station by the name of the little street on which it faced. It was not much longer before even those who had business with the Commissioners or the Receiver at No. 4 Whitehall Place ceased to refer to it as "the Metropolitan Police Office"; and, Middle and Little Scotland Yard having vanished, the epithet 'Great' became redundant, and the whole headquarters was known, *tout court*, as Scotland Yard.

THE POLICE OFFICE IN BOW STREET

Early nineteenth century. Grace Collection, British Museum.

By courtesy of the Trustees of the British Museum

[*See p.* 89.]

THE LAST WATCHMAN

Photo R. B. Fleming

9

ORGANIZATION AND EARLY TROUBLES

PEEL'S Police Act was deliberately vague on many points, and ignored other urgent questions altogether. Those who drafted it, unlike some modern planners, had the sense to see that so novel an experiment must start experimentally. Many known problems, and others not yet foreseen, must be dealt with as they turned up. The empirical method was also politic, for opposition to the Bill would have been far more fierce had its opponents realized its implications. At an early stage, however, the physical framework in which the experiment was to operate had been mapped out in some detail. The Metropolitan District was to be divided into seventeen Police divisions, each with its own company of 165 men, or some 2800 in all. The limits of the District were roughly those of the Bow Street Foot Patrols, its radius varying from four to seven miles from Charing Cross. Between the two Commissioners, living in the rarefied atmosphere of 4 Whitehall Place, and the force they commanded there was a great gulf fixed, the highest of the four ranks in the police being that of superintendent. Each divisional company was in charge of one of these officers, who had under him four inspectors and sixteen sergeants. Each sergeant, again, had under him nine constables, of whom eight patrolled beats, leaving the ninth (sixteen in all) in reserve at the divisional station-house. The ranks of superintendent and inspector already existed, the one in the parochial police and the other in certain Bow Street patrols; the rank of sergeant was taken from the Army. Superintendents were to be paid £200 a year, inspectors £100; sergeants and constables drew weekly pay of 22*s.* 6*d.* and 21*s.* respectively, 2*s.* being deducted from the latter sum for free quarters. It will be seen that sergeants were then regarded as being little more than superior constables. All ranks were required to give their whole time to the service.

Peel laid down a ruling which has become a tradition in the Metropolitan Police—in his own words, it was to be filled up from below. At the start the senior ranks had to be completed by men accustomed to wield some authority, such as non-commissioned officers of the

Army; but there was to be no "officer class." He would not appoint gentlemen, Peel wrote, who "would refuse to associate with other persons holding the same offices who were not of equal rank," and who would "therefore degrade the latter in the eyes of the men. . . A sergeant of the Guards at £200 a year is a better man for my purpose than a captain of high military reputation if he would serve for nothing, or if I could give him a thousand a year."[1] One or two men who had held commissioned rank in the Army were brought into the police during the 1830's, but on the whole this rule was to be closely observed until the expansion of the force, and the creation of appointments higher than the rank of superintendent, resulted in most of these new posts being filled by importation from outside. Below these grades, apart from one short-lived experiment, the tradition of filling up from below has been maintained. In recent times, because of its bearing on the training of policemen to fit them for very responsible duties, the whole question has been raised again.

Peel's ruling was a perfectly natural one in 1829, not only because he was dealing with a force of around 3000 men, but because of the emphasis that had to be laid on its civilian and democratic character. This feature is now well understood, but when the Metropolitan Police was new, and for long after, talk of militarization and a "gendarmerie," which sounded very sinister, was constantly on the lips of people who should have known better, and in many cases did. So anxious were the authorities to allay what now seem ridiculous apprehensions that serious thought was given to the question, should the new police, or should they not, wear uniforms? The few score men of the Daily Patrol and the Horse Patrol, only seen in twos and threes, were one thing; a large force all dressed up, and positively drilled—for elementary drill there must be—might suggest terrible threats to liberty.

Giving evidence before a Select Committee in 1833, Colonel Rowan, accustomed all his life to uniforms, contented himself with the observation that "the advantages and disadvantages of the two systems were weighed; it was thought advisable that they should be in uniform." The die having been cast, the result was something of an anticlimax. It was felt, as the Colonel said, that the uniform should be "quiet," and the design adopted resembled a civilian livery, so quiet that except for his buttons and the lettering on his collar the new policeman was scarcely distinguishable from any other citizen. It was not apparent that his top hat was strengthened by a thick leather crown

[1] Peel to John Wilson Croker, October 10, 1829.

and stays of cane, and if he carried a rattle, his only weapon, a short truncheon, was hidden beneath the long tails of his coat. This was dark blue, with a low stiffened collar, a version of the stock, vestiges of which survived until very recently in the patent-leather tab sewn inside a policeman's winter tunic. The trousers were also of blue cloth, white trousers for summer wear being optional. The double-breasted greatcoat had a detachable cape for wet weather. A complete uniform of 1829 or the year after, less only the top-hat, which moths got at, hangs in a glass-fronted case in the so-called Black Museum at Scotland Yard. Army clothiers were invited to submit material for this costume, but the first contract went to a newcomer in Pall Mall East named Charles Hebbert.

The constable's truncheon was made of some very hard wood, such as lignum vitæ. It has undergone slight modification from time to time. This form of baton has long been a symbol of authority, whether for practical use or as a staff of office like that carried by the Bow Street Runners, and collections of truncheons are numerous. The London policeman's has no special peculiarity; but when the Criminal Investigation Department was formed its officers, being usually in plain clothes, were issued with a smaller version which was easily concealed.[1] An officer is supposed to use this weapon only in the last resort, and, having done so, he must report the fact on his return to his station.

Towards the end of 1829 the well-known blue-and-white striped armlet was added to the Metropolitan policeman's uniform. There had been complaints because officers in uniform, but actually off duty, had not responded to appeals by the public. The armlet indicates that a man is on duty, and is only worn then. It is worn by sergeants and constables; at first the former had it on the right arm, the latter on the left. Sergeants were later distinguished by the numerals on their collars, which ran from 1 to 16, and they then transferred the armlets to their left arms.

For constables and sergeants uniforms were an issue; superintendents and inspectors had to buy their own, which at first bore no badges of rank on the collar. Before long, lace was sewn on this.

There had been an idea of adding a cutlass to the policeman's normal equipment, but it was abandoned in deference to what was thought to be public opinion. Pistols, and later cutlasses, were, however, issued to police stations.

[1] The Women Police of to-day also carry a truncheon smaller than that in general use.

2

Applications for enrolment in the new force, except those from ex-officers, which were turned down out of hand, were reviewed on their merits and in conformity with a set of regulations almost certainly drawn up by Rowan, and, after 1830, only in the rarest cases disregarded. Constables must be under the age of thirty-five, and five foot seven or more in height. Though for inspectors and sergeants it was hoped to get many with previous police experience, the majority chosen seem to have been either in the Army or the Marines. Parishes recommending their watchmen for high rank, or any rank, appear usually to have been disappointed; on the other hand, in the rather hurried circumstances many men were accepted who soon proved to be unsuitable. The patrols, except the Horse Patrol, whose work lay beyond the limits of the Metropolitan District, though they continued for a time to function in their old way, were now technically under the Commissioners, and it was hoped to get a considerable proportion of the inspectors from their ranks, a hope not altogether fulfilled. The Runners, whether at Bow Street or elsewhere, on the whole kept jealously aloof from the new force, for which many of them, in any case, were too old. The Horse Patrol was in time to be absorbed as the Mounted Branch of the Metropolitan Police; the other patrolmen and Runners, as they retired, were replaced by regular policemen, and the names of these anachronisms vanished from London's police annals. In the persons of such men as Nicholas Pearce the best elements of the old force were carried forward into the new. The first superintendent of a division (F, the Paddington area) was Joseph Thomas, constable of St Paul's, Covent Garden. John Fisher, surgeon to the Foot Patrol since 1821, was appointed in the same capacity to the new police, and for a month or two must have been a very busy man, for hundreds of applicants were presenting themselves daily for medical examination.

Each successful applicant was presented with a small book, a result of much thought and discussion over two essential questions. How were recruits to be trained, and what were to be their instructions? Training was a very delicate matter. The men must be under strict discipline, to ensure the necessary high standard of behaviour, for the indiscipline of some of the police they were to supersede had been a scandal. They must be drilled, because some scores or hundreds of them might be required to hasten to a given point at short notice. But the mere words drill and discipline smacked of the Army and the Major-Generals, to say nothing of a *gendarmerie*. It was necessary to proceed with caution. The effects of discipline were mainly apparent in the cases of individuals dismissed for misconduct—a large number of men were so dismissed, chiefly for drunkenness, in the early months—but formed bodies being drilled were a public spectacle, and at once raised a clamour about militarization. It seems probable, from references to the subject in Police Orders, that some superintendents, perhaps too nervous of popular prejudice, turned a blind eye to slackness on parade; some, on the other hand, drilled their men more often and more conspicuously than was necessary. It is unlikely that Rowan was concerned about complaints that his insistence on drilling his "troops" at all was proof of an intention to create "a bodyguard for the Government," but he had to try to ensure that a sensible middle course was the rule.

A matter of more lasting importance was the compilation of the book of General Instructions for the Police. This was the joint work of the Commissioners, Mayne, probably, being largely responsible for the wording, and the fact that these Instructions have in principle never undergone material change is another tribute to the foresight and common sense of the pair. The book itself was divided into two parts, of which the second epitomized a number of the laws of the land with which, it was considered, every policeman should be acquainted. The first part is of considerable historical interest, because, while it introduced no new police theory, it elaborated the *preventive* idea in a manner allowing of little misunderstanding.

"The following general Instructions for the different ranks of the Police Force," it began,

> are not to be understood as containing rules of conduct applicable to every variety of circumstance that may occur in the performance of their duty; something must necessarily be left to the intelligence and discretion of individuals, and according to the degree in which they show themselves possessed of these qualities and to their zeal, activity and judgement on all occasions, will be their claim to future promotion and reward.

Then followed a much-quoted passage which emphasized and condensed the words of the Fieldings, Colquhoun, and Peel himself:

> It should be understood, at the outset, that the principal[1] object to be attained is "*the prevention of crime.*" To this great end every effort of the police is to be directed. The security of person and property, the preservation of public tranquillity and all the other objects of a Police Establishment will thus be better effected than by the detection and punishment of the offender after he has succeeded in committing the crime.

The frequency or infrequency of crime in a division, it was pointed

[1] The word was not printed in the first draft. It appears to have been Peel's own addition.

out, would be an index of efficiency. Detailed instructions on behaviour were included. Constables, in particular, were to form no false notions about their duties or powers; above all, "a perfect command of temper" was required of them. They were cautioned against drunkenness, and against accepting money from the public without the Commissioners' express permission. Among items of routine was the rather curious injunction to every constable to report to his sergeant whenever he had occasion to spring his rattle; the reason seems to have been that the rattle caused alarm and drew a crowd, thus possibly giving a criminal a chance to escape. But the circumstances envisaged by this order remain a little obscure.

If General Instructions are the policeman's vade-mecum, Police Orders are his day-to-day guide through the intricacies of a continually changing scene. The earliest orders are preserved at Scotland Yard in a folio book, the entries written in the laboured handwriting of clerks, or, more probably, for mis-spellings are frequent and sometimes comical, of the police sergeants specially attached to the Whitehall Division. From this volume can be obtained some idea of the events of the last few days of preparation, the first Order being dated Wednesday, September 17, 1829. Later volumes, also in manuscript, became very bulky, two or three years' Orders being bound together. In 1857 Orders began to be printed, and were bound annually, growing fatter every year until recent times, when for reasons of economy the daily issue became a bi-weekly one, and certain old-established items were excluded.

3

By the first days of August 1829 a good nucleus of the force was shaking down. Seventeen divisions could not be formed at once, with recruiting still going on and a shortage of equipment, but a start was made with the six[1] divisional areas nearest to Westminster on the north

[1] There has been some confusion about the number of divisions represented on the first patrols. The first printed Instructions gives the figure as five. Luckily there are preserved at Scotland Yard copies of the first and second proofs of these Instructions, both containing manuscript emendations and suggestions in various hands, Peel's included. Examination of these interesting sheets shows that it was not originally intended to make 4 Whitehall Place the headquarters of a division as well as the Commissioners' Office. It being found necessary to augment the small civilian staff by taking on men from the regular police, it was decided to form a Central Company, to patrol the immediate neighbourhood, with headquarters in the Scotland Yard station-house. This was the beginning of the Central or Whitehall (A) Division, from which has been evolved the present A Division, whose headquarters are at the head of Cannon Row. The book of Instructions was in print before this decision was made, but Police Orders make it clear that men from six companies, not five, as sometimes stated, took part in the first patrols, the sixth being formed from the Central Company. It was not until late in September that the further decision was made to expand this company into a division.

side of the Thames. After a series of parades in Old Palace Yard the men of these divisions assembled for what was called a dress parade on Saturday, September the 26th, in the grounds of the Foundling Hospital in Holborn. Still in their civilian clothes, the companies presented themselves, to the number of nearly a thousand men in all, at two-hourly intervals, starting with 'A' at 10 A.M. The Commissioners were present, and, the conditions of service having been read out, and assent obtained, though precisely in what way we are not told, the men were sworn-in by Rowan and Mayne in their capacity as magistrates. Each company was then formed into "Parties in regular order two deep," and by twos stepped out to receive parcels of uniform clothing from Hebbert and his men. This may have been no more than a final fitting, for the general distribution took place later, at another parade, on the Monday morning, when the men were informed where they would be lodged and fed. That evening the six divisional companies again paraded at their various stations to be shown their beats at night; and at 6 P.M. on Tuesday, September the 29th, from the still-unfinished station-house in Scotland Yard, and from five of the old watch-houses, the first parties of the Metropolitan Police marched out, as they do to this day, in single file and on the outer side of the pavement, and "proceeded" on duty.

A time-table of hours of duty and reliefs had been drawn up, but the system of having only four reliefs in the twenty-four hours was soon modified. Though the force was not expected to be complete before June 1830, at an early stage it was decided to split up most of the divisions into four sub-divisions, and these again into two sections, each of eight beats. Inspectors were in charge of sub-divisions. It says much for the Commissioners' organizing gifts that these arrangements were found to work without a hitch, and that in principle they are followed to-day. Probably they were largely Rowan's work.

A temporary building in Old Palace Yard was then the only place where candidates could be interviewed, selected men assembled, and uniforms and equipment issued. Hebbert, who worked night and day, set up a store which was soon bursting with hats, rattles, truncheons, and lamps, as well as clothing. While No. 4 Whitehall Place was soon ready for the Commissioners, the new station-house at the back was not habitable for some weeks, and in the meantime a survey of such existing watch-houses as it was thought might be converted to divisional or sub-divisional offices brought little but disillusion. Beadles and watchmen had too often been accommodated in what were described as "subterranean holes." The better watch-houses were inconveniently situated. Some consisted of a room or two in a house whose private tenants, not unnaturally, were reluctant to provide more space. Parish clerks who had not studied the Police Acts were scandalized to learn how much power was to be wrested from them, and were as obstructive as they could be.

It would seem that among the first five watch-houses considered fit to be taken over was a small, grim little building in Vine Street, on the north side of Piccadilly. Its successor was to be associated with Boat Race nights and other festivities. The watch-house in Covent Garden, by St Paul's Church, was also adapted at an early date, and was presently to cause the Receiver some perplexity. It stood in an open space very near to the church, and according to Superintendent Thomas of F Division, whose headquarters it became, was in every way convenient. Even through its underground cells a "free current of air" passed at all times, "to the great Advantage of the Prisoners confined there." Then a wooden structure was added to its side, and when a further addition was made to this the parishioners complained of what was delicately described as a "watering-place," which apparently enjoyed no purifying current of air, being erected by a path used by church-goers. It was declared, moreover, that the station-house stood on consecrated ground. The church authorities stepped in, with protests against, among other things, disturbances caused during Sunday-morning service by the shouts of prisoners recovering from drunken orgies. Superintendent Thomas begged Rowan to ignore these complaints, which had never been made when the building was a watch-house. But the "watering-place" had not been there then, and now no less a personage than the Bishop of London made a personal inspection of this "unsightly" annex and of the station-house and its cells, and endorsed the parishioners' grumbles.[1] The Commissioners asked Wray to investigate.

The latter agreed that the remonstrances were not groundless, and his search for an alternative station-house made more police history in Bow Street. Where the Brown Bear and a small court had been there was now an unoccupied site. It was large enough for a building to accommodate sixty men, which, if Thomas had to move, was what he wanted, to get his unmarried men under one roof, instead of their being scattered, as they were, in five houses. The Receiver also pointed out to the Home Secretary the advantage of a "Central Station, in which a large force may be assembled in every Public Disturbance . . . in a Neighbourhood abounding with the most desperate Characters."

[1] Public Record Office, H.O. 61. 5.

The Home Secretary gave his blessing, and Bow Street, in addition to its historic Public Office, was now to have its police station as well, only a few yards away from the present building opposite Covent Garden Theatre in which station and magistrates' courts are now housed together. The new station-house was not ready until 1832. It was thought very fine, unlike the old Public Office, which was extremely inconvenient. It may be noted in this connexion that, according to *The Times*, there had been an early plan to erect "a new range of buildings on a most extensive scale" in Chandos Street, to combine both Police Office and station. Robert Smirke was mentioned as the architect. Almost fifty years were to pass, however, before a more suitable Bow Street office, now become the Police Court, was raised on the opposite side of the street.

The question of quarters sent Wray and his staff exploring all London. No special provision had ever been made for watchmen, but casual methods would not do for the new police. For one thing, they must be kept together, or at least within easy call. Barracks—though the military word was not officially used—were required for single men, and lodgings for those who were married. By the time that all seventeen companies were at work nearly a hundred houses had been leased. At first the barest dormitories, with mess quarters, the next step was to make them reasonably comfortable, an aim variously attained according to the supervision exercised by senior officers. These dormitories were called section-houses, a name ever since retained, and applied to-day to the great hostels, like Macnaghten House in Judd Street, or Trenchard House in Soho, where single men under the rank of inspector are lodged in conditions that would have seemed palatial to the companies of 1829.

4

Peel expressed himself as well satisfied with the beginning that had been made. "I must say," he told Croker, "that it has been much better than I had expected." Prepared for personal attacks—his change of view on the Catholic question had gained him a number of enemies in whose eyes he could now do nothing right—he could laugh at the caricatures of himself, already numerous and sometimes scurrilous. One of the less obnoxious cartoons, entitled *Peeling a Charley*, which showed the Home Secretary stripping a watchman of his greatcoat, particularly amused him.[1] There were, of course, teething troubles,

[1] *The Private Letters of Sir Robert Peel* (Murray, 1920).

which began early, five men being dismissed for drunkenness after the first patrol. Resignations soon began, and became numerous; there were many complaints about the hours of duty,[1] and too much malingering, and the uniform was not popular. There were other causes for concern in the attitude of the common people, which ranged from sullen indifference to active dislike, and in the marked hostility of certain magistrates.

In all three lower ranks of the force there was a tendency to think that promotion would depend on the number of convictions secured. Drunkards and prostitutes were obvious prey, and so many of the latter were brought to the Hatton Garden office that one of the magistrates there, Allen Laing, was reported to have directed the police to "drive all such women into the City." Laing, who was later pilloried by Dickens and removed from office, denied that he had said anything of the sort; but police in the Piccadilly and Strand areas acted on the report, and numbers of "heroines of the pavement," as they were described, were escorted nightly to Temple Bar and even beyond, though Fleet Street was outside the Metropolitan District. Crowds gathered at Temple Bar to see the fun, which, of course, degenerated into scuffles in which City constables and watchmen, Metropolitan Police, and a jeering public all took part. The City authorities were naturally angered. What the *Standard* called "this whimsical war now raging between the police of London . . . and the Duke of Wellington's *gendarmerie*" went on for some days, until brought to an end by stern Police Orders.

It appears that the great majority of the new policemen were behaving very well, in circumstances novel and never easy. They were now the victims of physical attacks almost every day, and of accusations by newspapers which hitherto had been friendly. Among their enemies were the firemen, who complained of interference, and, what was more strange, the troops. Mr Reith seems to think that officers of high rank believed that "ill-feeling between troops and police should not be discouraged, because it would be of value in times of unrest"; but why this should be so is not clear, and he gives no authority for the assumption. What is apparent is that the troops, and their officers, resented the new-fangled police doing their duty in arresting drunken soldiers. After an affray in the middle of October outside a public house

[1] These were long by modern standards. Originally a man was expected to do twelve hours' duty in the twenty-four, in two equal periods. After it was decided to employ two-thirds instead of half the force at night, in a single relief, there were changes, and by 1832 the hours seem to have been nine at night, continuously, and ten during the day in two periods of varying lengths.

in York Street, Westminster, men of the 10th Hussars (the King's favourite regiment when he had been Prince Regent) were taken before the Queen Square magistrates, whereupon the Commissioners, anxious to patch up differences with the military, "requested that the men might be handed over to their officers to be dealt with, instead of being punished by the Civil Power." This friendly gesture, however, was not appreciated, and as the Commissioners did not like being snubbed, another incident of the kind in the following year led to the issue of instructions that all such military (or naval) offenders were to be taken before a magistrate.

By the spring of 1830 Rowan and Mayne must have been in a position to take stock of the general situation within the force. At 4 Whitehall Place, where the Colonel, a bachelor, had furnished chambers, the staff had been slightly augmented and the work subdivided. The station-house in Scotland Yard was in general use, but the superintendent, John May, was given separate quarters in Gardiner's (or Gardner's) Lane, off King Street, then one of the two southern continuations of Whitehall, the other being Parliament Street. For some little time this office was considered to be the headquarters of what was generally called the Home Division (A); later the division was to have its chief police station in King Street itself, from where this moved to Cannon Row about 1890. The Commissioners now had a chief clerk in the person of Charles Yardley, possibly the son of Samuel Yardley, for many years chief clerk at the Worship Street office. A Waterloo veteran, Yardley was to remain at Whitehall Place as long as Mayne himself. Another appointment of this time to be noted is that of Inspector Herring of B Company to superintendent, for before joining the new force Herring had been a Bow Street officer, and his promotion was the first of its kind.

According to an Abstract of Payments sent to the Home Office at the end of March 1830, six new divisions (G, H, K, L, M, and N) were functioning from February the 1st, and three more (P, S, and Sx, this last-named, it seems, a reserve of nineteen men, which ultimately became T) were in being a week later. During the next two months the appointment of two Army officers as superintendents must have caused some surprise, in view of Peel's known views about an "officer class" in the police. Captain Washington Carden became superintendent of S Division, with headquarters in Albany Street, Regent's Park, and about a month later Lieutenant William Hickman, possibly an ex-ranker, assumed charge of the Greenwich Company (R), which, together with V (Wandsworth) and a greatly enlarged Sx or T

(Kensington), was on duty for the first time on May the 10th. For Carden's appointment there was a rational explanation. Hitherto every complaint about a policeman's conduct, however trivial, had been investigated by the Commissioners themselves. Even anonymous letters were followed up when possible. There grew to be so many of these inquiries, each of which meant the appearance of at least one policeman at headquarters, and consequent adjustments in beat-duties, that the Commissioners asked Peel to forget his scruples for once, "a gentleman of his [Captain Carden's] standing" being wanted to relieve them of having to conduct all the preliminary investigations into "every little complaint."

By this date, May the 10th, the Metropolitan Police force was complete, with rather more than 3300 men in its ranks, and a very large number on its reserve list. The strength was thus considerably greater than that originally planned, and some of the companies were proportionately larger than the estimated 165 of all ranks. A Return sent to the Home Office on June 27, 1830, shows that the Stepney Division (K) had a company of 289 men. The Home Division (A) was the smallest, with 88. As new divisions were added considerable adjustments in divisional boundaries had to be made.

Having taken stock, the Commissioners might congratulate themselves. They were coming to be trusted by their men—according to some of the newspapers, Rowan was the better liked of the two—and discipline was improving. The increasing and usually undeserved unpopularity which the men had to endure fostered loyalty to one another and to their superiors. A genuine *esprit de corps* was growing. In official circles the good work being done was recognized; provincial towns had asked for advice and assistance from the Metropolis; a little later William Parlour, superintendent of the Stepney Division, was appointed head of Liverpool's new police, and even before all the seventeen divisions were formed the Gibraltar authorities asked for the services of two police sergeants, who were duly sent.

At the same time, the Commissioners had learnt much about the handicaps under which they and their men had to work. In spite of Peel's simplification of the criminal code, legal procedure was still full of anomalies. There was nothing in the nature of a Public Prosecutor's Department to advise the police, and only in very rare cases did the Home Office authorize legal aid to officers preparing prosecutions. These officers might have to face trained counsel or attorneys, possibly before a hostile magistrate or jury. If they failed to secure a conviction they might be called on to pay the court expenses, and, being unable to do so, could be sent, with monstrous injustice, to prison. Apart from such "costs against the police," there might be actions brought against them by acquitted parties for assault or the like, and further fines demanded.

Of these troublesome domestic matters the public knew little, and would have cared little had it known more; the growing discontent with the force, on various and generally unreasonable grounds, was now to be given its head by political events.

The Police Act laid down with some exactitude how money was to be obtained for the maintenance of the new force. As the latter took over each parish—there were eighty-eight at that time in the Metropolitan District—the old Watch Rate was taken over. The Commissioners were empowered to issue their warrant to the parish overseers demanding within forty days a sum determined by the amount of rateable property in the parish and at a rate of 8*d.* in the pound, either as a separate contribution or as part of the existing rate for the relief of the poor. At the beginning of October 1830 Rowan was able to inform Sir Robert Peel (he had now succeeded to his father's baronetcy) that no parish had refused to pay.

But this did not mean that all money due had been received, or that any had been obtained without the greatest difficulty. Every obstacle had been put in the Commissioners' way. Complaints poured in from the various vestries. Next came protest meetings, which received much attention in the Press. It was not, however, until after the death of George IV at the end of June, the overthrow of Charles X in Paris in July, and the assertion of independence by the Belgians that this sporadic agitation was merged into a political movement. The Radicals came into the open, fully realizing that an attack on the police was a most useful weapon. A new type of meeting was staged, the speakers, generally small traders or artisans of extreme views, inveighing against the undue powers of the Commissioners, their "secret" activities, and the "tyranny" which a reactionary Government was creating. Broadsheets or pamphlets were issued, or sold for a penny or two. One, now among the Home Office papers at the Public Record Office, has its special interest, for it was examined by Peel himself. Relatively mild in tone, it protested against the Commissioners' custom of investigating complaints about the police in private, and asked why Englishmen suffering from outrage and insult were referred to "this new POLICE COURT." Magistrates were being stripped of their power, and the sword of Justice was "placed in the hands of a MILITARY Man." All this must be ended; the people must institute a police system of their own under parochial appointment, with a central committee formed for "the Abolition of the NEW POLICE." This sheet had been handed to passers-by in the streets by "a man of gentlemanly exterior (although smoking a cigar)." The copy at the Record Office has a pencilled note in Peel's hand urging the preparation of a statement to the newspapers explaining the whole position with regard to the Police Rate: "We are run down by the Press when we have right completely on our side."

A whispering campaign was being directed at the alleged "espionage duties" of the police. In the previous September the *Standard* had spoken of the force as "professedly a corps of spies," and Popish (because Irish) spies at that. The only evidence produced of "Apostate" Peel's sinister intentions was an instruction to policemen to make themselves familiar with the neighbourhood in which they worked, a natural injunction which in similar terms had been issued to the Foot Patrole a generation back. The Radicals now fastened upon a further proof of "un-English" police methods. Contrary to general belief, even while Peel remained at the Home Office police on duty sometimes wore plain clothes—or "coloured clothes," as the term then went. A month after the *Standard's* accusations the sitting magistrate at Bow Street, in congratulating Sergeant Tyrrell on the arrest of three thieves in the Strand, observed, "I do not suppose he would ever have detected them if he had worn his uniform." No doubt almost from the first superintendents had been authorized to send out one or two picked men, generally sergeants, "in coloured clothes." This was the plainest common sense; the Runners had never worn uniform, and if the new police were to become as efficient at thief-catching as the old they must be allowed to work under similar conditions. Within thirteen years some of these plain-clothes men, having learned their job, were to form the nucleus of the Detective Office. Nothing, it is probable, would have been heard of them now, if their duties had not taken them to political meetings.

Henry Hunt and other prominent Radicals were staging huge meetings at the Rotunda in Blackfriars Road, and newly formed Working-class Associations were openly advocating a republic. There were rumours that arms were being collected. Sidmouth and his predecessors would have sent political spies to these gatherings, but Peel rightly decided that it was the business of the police to collect information that might lead to prosecutions. The superintendents chose their men with great care, and it was some time before the Radicals realized that there were chiels among them takin' notes. When they did there was a great to-do. At the same time, certain magistrates showed hostility to plain-clothes men who came before them to give evidence, Baker Sellon, senior magistrate at Hatton Garden, and W. H. A. White, at Queen Square, being particularly prominent. Such cases were widely reported, and accusations of espionage were made at what papers like the *Standard* and *Weekly Dispatch* called "respectable" meetings of protest. Public feeling in easily influenced quarters was worked up to a degree that might have led to trouble some months before the riots of November, if a tragedy, the first of its kind, had not brought about a temporary reaction.

P.C. John Long (G.43) was a man of excellent character and much experience, for he had been a watchman at St Luke's before entering the Metropolitan Police. Late on the evening of August 18, 1830, he was patrolling Gray's Inn Lane, now Gray's Inn Road, with another constable, John Newton. Seeing three men loitering in a suspicious manner, Long went to question them, following them as they walked away towards St Pancras burial-ground. Under the "dead" wall of this enclosure he was about to challenge them when one of the three leapt forward and plunged a knife into his heart.

Long died almost immediately, the knife still in the wound. Newton pursued the three men, and the murderer, identified by his brown coat and a scar on his cheek, ran into the arms of a private watchman, and was secured. He turned out to be a well-known criminal named Sapwell. The other two men were arrested later, but were ultimately released for want of evidence against them. Sapwell was hanged in the presence of a huge crowd, which, it is said from feelings of disgust at the crime, preserved absolute silence.

It was believed that Long had been marked for grave injury or assassination by a gang of burglars whom he had disturbed, possibly Sapwell and his confederates, who abandoned a number of house-breaking implements near the constable's body. The latter left a widow and five children; and, London being for a time shocked out of its antipathy or indifference to the police, a subscription list for the family was opened at more than one newspaper office. The three Bow Street magistrates gave their guineas, the police and the public subscribed, and letters in the Press showed for once a friendly and sympathetic attitude towards the force.

Meetings of protest against the Police Rate continued, however. Inhabitants of St James's, Piccadilly, were summoned for failing to pay it. *The Times*, in a long leading article in September, defended the rate, and treated as absurd the attacks on the police for being a military body.

> A military force supposes military weapons of some kind—the police have neither swords nor pistols to defend themselves; and recent circumstances suffice to prove that for the preservation of their own lives, to say nothing of the public, the bits of stick with which they are at present provided are anything but an adequate protection.[1] We ourselves have seen nothing of the police but exemplary courtesy, forbearance and propriety, great willingness to act and, when occasion calls for it, to refrain from acting. Overpaid, at a guinea a week each, no rational person can consider them.

These words are worth quoting, as a reminder that rational persons, or those not blinded by political prejudice and fears about the loss of parochial patronage, did exist at a time of which the impression is left that no one whatever saw anything good in London's police force.

If the words were timely they were soon forgotten, together with the tragedy of Long, as the political situation degenerated, and the police were again to become the "enemies of Liberty."

[1] After the murder of Long a number of policemen were permitted to carry both cutlasses and pistols; but in all such cases a special Police Order or Instructions to Superintendents was issued.

10

A DECADE OF CONSOLIDATION

PARLIAMENT reassembled on October the 26th in an atmosphere of tension. To menaces of revolutionary action were added agricultural riots in Kent and elsewhere, and the notorious but probably non-existent "Captain Swing" was spreading terror by threatening letters circulated in his name. On the 28th, and again on Monday, November the 1st, the new King and his Queen visited the theatre; all was quiet the first time, but at Covent Garden there was shouting and whistling from the gallery, and cries of "No new police!" Superintendent Thomas had stationed a number of his men near the theatre, but there were none inside. When the King and Queen left, their small mounted escort had difficulty in clearing a way for the royal carriage, and police reinforcements from Vine Street and Covent Garden had to be summoned to restore order in Pall Mall and Piccadilly, where the police on duty were being attacked.

The State opening of Parliament took place next day. The Commissioners made the most careful arrangements for what was their first real opportunity to show the public that the new police could handle excited crowds without help from the military. Men from almost every division were on duty in the streets, or held in reserve at the nearest station-houses and in Scotland Yard. Nevertheless there were scenes almost recalling the worst of the old days; criminal gangs and revolutionaries were mingled in tumultuous mobs which hustled the peers in their carriages and more than once all but overwhelmed the police. Handbills now openly advocated the use of knives. Policemen were injured in very ugly rushes as the gist of Wellington's speech became known.

The Duke had pronounced against any sort of reform; and as fuller news of his speech spread there were worse disturbances that evening. Two policemen who arrested pickpockets in St James's Street might have lost their lives but for the action of Lieutenant Hill, of the Horse Guards, who rode out from the Palace and helped the officers to escort their prisoners to Vine Street. Here a mob was breaking the windows of the station-house; tricolour flags were being waved. The handbills had done their work, and in Leicester Square, after cries of "Out with your knives!" P.C. James of A Division was struck down, to die of his wounds, the second Metropolitan policeman to give his life on duty.

The King and Queen were to have attended the Lord Mayor's Banquet on November the 9th, but on Peel's advice their visit was cancelled. The Home Secretary, giving his reasons for this step, read to the House of Commons extracts from some of the more outrageous handbills. "All London meets on Tuesday," began one of them, headed LIBERTY OR DEATH! "Come armed. We assure you from ocular evidence that 6000 cutlasses have been removed from the Tower, for the use of Peel's bloody gang." There were other sheets even more subversive in tone; it was now that some of them printed the story that the new police had been established in order to put Wellington on the throne.

Two could play at the rough game, however, and an odd combination seems to have initiated what unruly crowds were to find then, as they have found since, an unpleasant reply to rowdyism. The excellent Superintendent Thomas, of F Division, happened to be friendly with the Radical tailor, Francis Place. Thomas, apparently, was a man of liberal views, imbibed perhaps from other friends of his, Leigh Hunt and his brother John. But he was a policeman first, and Place was an unusual Radical for those times. "I advised Mr Thomas," he records,[1]

> not again to wait until his men were attacked and then, when they had been maltreated and bruised, to take a few vagabonds into custody; but when he saw a mob prepared to make an attack, to lead his men on and thrash those who composed the mob with their staves as long as any of them remained together; but to take none into custody; and that if this were done once or twice, there would be no more such mobs.

If Place was something of an optimist his advice was as admirable as it is surprising from such a quarter. Whether it was submitted to the Commissioners is not known; but on Lord Mayor's Day it was carried into effect. Thomas ordered the first baton charge, with excellent results.

The day before, "Orator" Hunt had presided at one of the now frequent meetings at the Rotunda. Sir Richard Birnie, from Bow Street, was in the audience, with at least one superintendent and some plainclothes officers. Trouble began after Hunt left; he was always careful with his words, and of his skin; no sooner had he gone than the tricolour was raised, and about a thousand men, shouting "Now for the

[1] Graham Wallas, *The Life of Francis Place* (Longmans, third edition, 1919).

West End!" and "Down with the Police!" marched out, and were joined by crowds waiting in Blackfriars Road. By way of Blackfriars Bridge and Waterloo Bridge the combined mob streamed to Whitehall. At the top of King Street it was met by the men of A Division. Reinforcements came from E Division, and from a new station-house in New Way, off Orchard Street, near the Abbey, and, seeing Royal Horse Guards also standing by, the rioters turned back. In small bands, however, hundreds remained in the streets all night; and early on the 9th, a Tuesday, there were signs of further trouble.

In the West End shops were closed and barricaded. By permission of the Benchers, police were in Gray's Inn Hall; other parties were held in reserve in the courtyard of Somerset House and near Hyde Park Corner. Thomas had a number of his men in the Strand, where a "Grand Illumination with Gas" had been widely advertised for Lord Mayor's Day. This was cancelled, and crowds assembling at dusk saw workmen dismantling gas-pipes. Some one raised a cry of "Fire," which was delightedly taken up, and to an excited mass of people now jamming Temple Bar was added a body of some three or four hundred roughs from the City, armed with sticks and cudgels made from wood torn from scaffolding in Chancery Lane, who forced their way through, crying "No Peel!" and "Down with the Raw Lobsters!" Turning into Catherine Street, this column drove back the first few police they met there; but at the head of the street now appeared sixty or seventy Lobsters in compact formation, their truncheons raised. A charge and a brief scuffle, and the little battle was over. A similar charge by a larger force of police at Hyde Park Corner, a little later, closed a notable occasion; for news of this dastardly behaviour seems to have spread rapidly, and by midnight all the "revolutionary armies" had disappeared.

Before all was over in the Strand, Superintendent Thomas's men, elated by their victory, went so far as to close the gate of Temple Bar. This brought out the City Marshal, with a posse of his own men, and the gates were reopened.

The effect of these small incidents was considerable. Next morning's *Courier* even expressed the view that the disturbances had proved a blessing in disguise, as they must have convinced the revolutionaries and rioters that they were "unequal to contend" with the new police. It was remarked that public peace had been restored without recourse to the military. From such sober quarters praise was showered on Peel. Some might have been given to the Commissioners, and Superintendent Thomas and Francis Place deserved honourable mention.

The Home Secretary had not long to enjoy these unaccustomed eulogies. Barely a week later Wellington resigned, and the founder of the Metropolitan Police ceased to be responsible for its well-being and efficiency.

2

The new Home Secretary, Lord Melbourne, was another type altogether. Nine years older than Peel, and now fifty-one, he was witty and charming, and, if affecting to be far more lazy than he was, by nature was always inclined to put off the evil day. He was a Whig, and since his party was last in office there had been many changes, not the least important being the reform of the police and its attachment to the department over which he was to preside. The Whigs regarded the new force with some suspicion, as a Tory invention; as Mr Reith observes, they needed, but feared, its success. Melbourne himself was too clear-headed and cynical to be a good partisan in the matter, but it was not to be expected that he would show any particular interest in his predecessor's creation. He had many other things on his hands; a greatly disturbed country, at the moment ravaged by cholera, was within two years to be plunged into the turmoil of the Reform Bill.

Peel's force, in any case, could now stand on its own legs. The vestries were still obstructive, and misunderstandings with magistrates were soon to be accentuated. Newspapers continued to abuse the police, the *Weekly Dispatch*, in particular, developing a campaign of vilification that was to go on for years. But the force had settled down. The whole of the Metropolitan district was now well policed throughout the twenty-four hours. There were ample reserves, and more candidates presented themselves every year. Outside bodies like the London Dock Company were applying for police services. Senior officers, with rare exceptions, had shown their fitness for their posts, and official returns revealed the high proportion of convictions for which the new police were responsible.[1] Wray, the Receiver, had done much to improve the station-houses and the men's lodgings. Nearly seventy old watch-houses had been taken over and properly adapted. These offices were now graded according to size, position, or general importance; divisional headquarters were as a rule known as stations, smaller and less busy ones as station-houses, and there were nine buildings where constables not regularly on duty could gather in an emergency which

[1] The Runners, now officially known as Constables of the Police Office, were still much relied upon in such cases of crime as jewel robberies and coining. Most crimes of violence, including murder, were almost as a matter of course now investigated by the regular police.

were called Detached Offices. These seem to have been given up within the next few years. The Commissioners already appear to have had in mind the erection of new stations to include, besides charge-room, cells, and other usual features, quarters for some of the single men, and perhaps accommodation for a superintendent or inspector as well.[1] More of the larger provincial towns were now considering remodelling their police forces on Metropolitan lines.

Easy-going though Melbourne was, the Commissioners found that the days of close relationship with the Home Office were ended. Unfortunately a change that was perhaps inevitable was accentuated by personal differences between Mayne and the Permanent Under-Secretary, March Phillipps. Hitherto on amicable terms, they now took a dislike to one another. Melbourne himself was thought to be vague and dilatory; he hated putting anything in writing, and still more to move in any matter that might involve Parliamentary action. An old vexed question, an arrest for an assault not committed in the presence of a policeman, caused more trouble before the Home Secretary could be persuaded to obtain an opinion from the Law Officers. Melbourne, again, and very rightly, disliked the idea of employing political spies; on the other hand, he was too tolerant with the new and often subversive "working-men's journals," only taking action when *The Poor Man's Guardian* and *The Republican* grossly insulted the King and advocated a British Republic to be achieved by force. He did not mind his private secretary, Tom Young, an ex-purser and journalist, acting as something very like a spy, and though the Commissioners do not mention Young in their official correspondence, they cannot have approved of his unilateral activities at a time when the confidential reports of their own superintendents were being regularly forwarded for the Home Secretary's inspection. That odd Radical Francis Place, who had once made Melbourne's breeches, was another of the latter's sources of information.[2]

The year 1831 opened stormily. There were riots in London after a Government defeat in Committee in April, and, Parliament having been prorogued and dissolved, the West End suffered a repetition of East End ruffianism. The Reformers had staged an "illumination," and unlighted houses had their windows broken. Peel's was among them, and an assault on Apsley House was called off only when it was learned that the Duchess of Wellington had just died there. More than 1100 police were in the streets, but there should have been more,

[1] Wray's reports to the Home Office give full details of all premises used by the police. (P.R.O., H.O. 61. 4, 5, and 6.)

[2] P.R.O., H.O. 61. 6.

and though baton charges were made, these tactics were less successful than they would have been under better direction and control. Superintendent Thomas, though a month before he had been stabbed and cudgelled, was conspicuously active.

In the new Parliament Melbourne was still Home Secretary, under the same Prime Minister, Earl Grey, and he was able to congratulate the force on its smart appearance at what was described as the "niggardly" Coronation of William IV in September. In the next month, however, there was further rioting on a big scale, and though this was expected, and the Commissioners made ample preparations, there were again blunders of execution. The police were not always where they were most badly needed. There were not enough at Hyde Park Corner, and this time the mob was able to wreak its vengeance upon Apsley House, smashing almost every window. Wellington never forgot the insult, and the heavy iron shutters he put up remained bolted until after his funeral more than twenty years later.

There was another scare in November. A mass meeting of extreme Reformers was advertised to take place on the 7th at White Conduit House, in Pentonville, which at one time had been a kind of minor Vauxhall. Rebuilt in 1829, the house now had an immense hall often used for political meetings. On the 5th Scotland Yard sent a circular letter to various vestry clerks suggesting the swearing in of special constables, whose enrolment and duties had just been clarified by a special Act. What response was forthcoming is not known, but news of these and other preparations by the police had so salutary an effect that the advertised meeting was abandoned. Had it been held, the tactics employed by the police might have been instructive; preventive measures in the case of a mass meeting previously advertised and held indoors could scarcely have included baton charges. Moreover, Melbourne decided to order two police magistrates, Frederick Roe and Allen Laing, to be present at the meeting, apparently the first of such occasions on which magistrates were officially in attendance. Roe, who was going to give much trouble in the future, took offence at the conduct of a superintendent, and complained in writing to Melbourne. He made the mistake of blaming the Commissioners for not consulting him beforehand, and even for failing to be at hand to receive him; and in a stiff correspondence with the Home Office which followed Mayne had the last word, observing that it was "no part of Mr Roe's duty to pronounce judgement on the Commissioners' conduct."[1] Melbourne, who thought that bishops died to vex him, may have felt that

[1] P.R.O., H.O. 61. 5.

Commissioners and magistrates were appointed for the same purpose. He refused to move in the matter, for it involved the question of who was to be in general charge of all police activities, the old magistracy or the new Commissioners, which only Parliament could decide; and eight years were to pass before it was legally settled in the Commissioners' favour.

One of the many police difficulties of this time, which Roe and others seized upon, was that certain of their duties, such as dealing with beggars and "street-nuisances" in general, could be performed only under the direction of special officers called Inspectors of Nuisances, appointed, in a Gilbertian manner, by the Office of Woods and Forests. The difficulty was partially overcome by appointing superintendents and inspectors to the post, without extra pay. Another source of vexation and acrimony between rival authorities was the use of the City as a refuge by rogues and vagabonds operating in the Metropolis; once on the other side of Temple Bar they could cock a snook at the Metropolitan policeman in pursuit of them. The City was obliged to take notice of this misuse of its privileges, and in April 1832 a new City Day Police of a hundred uniformed men was established more or less on Metropolitan lines. This force was to be expanded, seven years later, into the City Police which exists to-day.

In this April died Sir Richard Birnie, and Frederick Roe became Chief Magistrate at Bow Street in his place. As Roe was the most resolutely and vindictively opposed of all the Metropolitan magistrates to any enlargement of the Commissioners' powers, from the latters' point of view this was a disturbing appointment. Melbourne himself was not in favour of magisterial changes, because they meant political trouble, and if it had already been decided that in the fairly near future the Bow Street Horse Patrol was to be absorbed into the Metropolitan Police, he was no doubt the more anxious to placate Roe. But he was much to blame for promoting to the chief Metropolitan magistracy a man whose strained relations with Scotland Yard were notorious.

In one direction Melbourne was forced at this time to co-operate with the Commissioners. There was a long list of parishes in arrears with their Police Rates. Wray had already been obliged to ask for Treasury help, and had received a loan of £10,000. This had not been repaid, and the Receiver again appealed to the Home Secretary. Melbourne put pressure on St Pancras and Marylebone, both of which parishes had flatly refused to pay the final instalment of its rate. St Pancras paid up, but Marylebone was obdurate, and drew up a Memorial which a deputation took to the Home Office. Apparently the matter was allowed to rest there; the Treasury, at any rate, advanced the police a further £5000; but even Melbourne must have realized that the mutinous attitude of the parishes was bringing nearer the Parliamentary action from which he shrank.

3

Parliament, as it happened, was to be busy about police affairs in 1833, whether the Home Secretary liked it or not. Two Police Bills were uncontroversial,[1] as was the appointment of a Police Committee, intended to be permanent; but two Select Committees later set up were the outcome of events which made a great noise at the time.

The question of plain-clothes police acting as "spies" at political meetings flared into prominence with the case of Sergeant Popay. Though the Reformers and other subversive bodies were well aware that their proceedings were spied upon and reported, they were for long unable to obtain proof of this. Some time in April or early in May 1833 they learnt that a poor artist named Popay, a zealous and valued member of the National Union of the Working Classes, was, in fact, Police-Sergeant and acting Deputy-Inspector Popay, of P Division. One of his particular cronies in the Union had caught sight of him in the Park House Police Station. Popay, who must have been a plausible man, contrived to explain this awkward circumstance, but some members of the Union, including a prominent agitator named John Furzey, remained suspicious. Within a few days both Furzey and Popay were to figure in an affair which placed the latter's equivocal behaviour beyond doubt.

The extremists of the Union dragooned its Central Committee into authorizing a public meeting "to adopt preparatory measures for holding a National Convention, the only means of obtaining and securing the Rights of the People." It was to be held on May the 13th, at Coldbath Fields, a piece of waste land by the Clerkenwell House of Correction, where the Devil, according to Coleridge's poem, saw a solitary cell which "gave him a hint for improving his prisons in Hell."[2] This prison stood just to the east of the modern Farringdon Road, near Mount Pleasant. The usual preliminary bills were distributed, one of which called for the abolition of the Monarchy and the House of Lords; the Home Office thereupon issued a proclamation declaring the proposed demonstration illegal, and advising the public

[1] The first was for the most part a consolidating Bill, continuing for three years the more important innovations of the 1829 Act, with some useful amendments, particularly in relation to the Thames Police. The other was a Finance Bill.

[2] *The Devil's Thoughts.*

to keep away. The Commissioners saw Melbourne and March Phillipps, and Mayne, whose word may be accepted, maintained that they received verbal instructions to disperse the meeting and arrest the leaders if the latter made an attempt to address it. Unless this happened the police were not to interfere, or even show themselves. When, in defiance of the ban, the meeting took place there seem to have been some 600 police on hand. Rowan was there, in a private house near the Fields, and so was Sergeant Popay, one of several plain-clothes officers mingling with the crowd. Small and orderly at first, this was soon increased by noisy processions carrying not only banners but arms. A well-known agitator named Mee began to harangue the gathering; and as soon as Rowan was made aware of this he ordered Mee and other organizers to be arrested, and the crowd dispersed.

Of the typical conflict which ensued it need only be said that very few of the crowd, which included a number of the merely curious who had also ignored official warnings, suffered worse injuries than bruises. The police, who had to face a hail of brick-bats and stones, weighted cudgels, "folding daggers" (known as macaroni lances), and other knives of various sorts, themselves armed only with their truncheons, had two men seriously hurt and one killed, P.C. Robert Culley dying of knife-wounds in the abdomen. His murderer, though apparently known to many, was never brought to justice.

The really serious feature of this affray was the death of a policeman, but the excited state of the populace and the weakness of Ministers provoked a political storm in which the police were the defendants. The inquest on the body of poor Culley was disgraceful; the jury, mostly bakers from the Gray's Inn neighbourhood, defied the coroner and returned a verdict of "justifiable homicide." Their findings were later annulled, but they were made heroes, being escorted home by torchlight and, on the anniversary of their scandalous verdict, presented with medals and taken on a "marine excursion" in a new steam vessel up the Medway. It was true that all reasonable people were disgusted, for, Popay's acquaintance John Furzey being brought to trial at the Old Bailey on a charge of attempting to murder Sergeant Brooke, the police were able to tell their own story. Furzey was acquitted on a technical point, but newspapers opened appeals for help for the murdered Culley's widow. The Government granted her the unusually large gratuity of £200. Scarcely, however, had a reaction in favour of the police gathered weight than Furzey's own pertinacity brought to light the case of Sergeant Popay.

It was too good a chance for the most sober Radical to miss. Apparently on the advice of William Cobbett, now, at the age of seventy, at long last in Parliament, certain respectable artisans or small tradesmen drew up a petition against the employment of the police as spies and the payment of taxes to maintain them in this rôle. Cobbett presented the petition to the House of Commons, and so launched a campaign taken up with delight by the discontented of every kind. Melbourne was horrified, and the Government as a whole was weak; in addition to Popay's case, which perhaps called for Parliamentary inquiry, all the wild allegations about the affair in Coldbath Fields were allowed to be raked up again. Though the Police Committee referred to was in session, it was adjourned until the following year; and two special Select Committees were set up in its place. One dealt with Popay, the other with Coldbath Fields.

As a result of the first-named Special Committee's report, which censured Popay for "carrying concealment and deceit into the intercourse of private life," the sergeant was dismissed from the force. He seems to have been rather hardly treated. In laying it down that the use of police in plain clothes should be confined to detecting breaches of the law and preventing breaches of the peace, and that to go beyond this "was most abhorrent to the feeling of the people and most alien to the spirit of the constitution," the Committee did not, and could not, define at what precise point such duties as those upon which Popay was officially employed might be exceeded. The sergeant himself, who behaved very well throughout the inquiry into his conduct, denied that he had been enrolled as a member of the Union, and this accusation was not proved; but he seems to have realized that in going so far as to accept hospitality from those upon whom he was spying he was sailing near the wind. On the other hand, it may be remarked of the genuine members of the Union that while, like the fairies,

A tell-tale in their company
They never could endure,

they would certainly have taken a different ethical view had they been able to recruit or suborn some police officer in a position to warn them of coming events. And since the Committee's report printed an admission in evidence that the National Union was provided with arms, and that certain members had "exercised themselves in the use," the Union had no serious ground of complaint against any of the measures adopted to curtail its activities.

This was the view taken of police action at Coldbath Fields by the second Special Committee. Though Melbourne and March Phillipps shuffled over the verbal instructions given to the Commissioners, the latter were entirely exonerated from blame; the police had not "employed greater violence than was occasioned by the resistance they had met with." Much nonsense, of course, continued to be talked on this subject, and, in connexion with it, about the police themselves; it only deserves mention because of the height of absurdity reached when it was said of this civilian force, whose drill was limited to a few elementary movements, that it was "very well-trained in quasi-military duties on lines similar to those employed by Moore when training the light infantry at Shorncliffe." If this was read by Rowan, who had served under Moore, and who certainly knew a good deal about light-infantry training, he must have smiled.

4

During the next few years the Commissioners were to be much plagued by politics and magistrates. Old debates and controversies about matters which from the first were foregone conclusions make the most tedious reading; the more reasonable magistrates knew that the inexorable march of events was against them, and their struggles, under the embittered leadership of Sir Frederick Roe, have now only an academic interest. There could not much longer exist in the Metropolis two sets of police authorities, and two different police forces. The magistrates still had their Runners and other officers, whose duties were almost wholly detective, and whose anomalous position with regard to the Metropolitan Police was a constant nuisance; they still had certain executive police powers. Most of them resented the growing authority of the Commissioners, and they were not alone in this. Many politicians were, or professed to be, alarmed by it. Finally, there was still the question of the parishes, whose reluctance to pay the Police Rate was fomented by Roe himself and others.

A change of Ministry in 1834 added to the complexity of the situation. Melbourne became Prime Minister, and the new Home Secretary was his brother-in-law, Lord Duncannon. The latter was an ardent Reformer, but unfortunately was on very friendly terms with Roe, whose distrust of the growing powers of the police he apparently shared. An incident of a type to become only too familiar soon caused friction between him and the Commissioners. Trouble arising out of the arrest of a prostitute was complicated by the fact that her protector had a son in the police force; Roe got on the trail, and in the end two officers had to be dismissed. The Commissioners rightly complained of interference with their authority, and were rebuked by Duncannon; and then Roe, whose duties took him regularly to the Home Office, induced March Phillipps to write privately to Rowan on matters of general policy. The Police Committee adjourned in 1833 was now sitting again, and Roe and some of his fellow magistrates were employing as witnesses all their gifts of persuasion and argument towards reducing the powers of senior police officers. To this end, March Phillipps suggested that the salaries of superintendents should be cut on appointment by fifty pounds.

Mayne and Rowan appear to have been seriously worried. Their difficulties were relieved in an unexpected way; the King suddenly decided to dismiss Melbourne, and Duncannon went too. What was more, the new Prime Minister was to be Peel. He was in Rome, and the Duke of Wellington combined for a short time the offices of First Lord of the Treasury and Secretary of State, besides attending to business in other Ministries. If only for a few days, the Duke found himself head of a police force which he had helped materially to bring into being.

Under Peel, who kissed hands on February 9, 1835, Henry Goulburn was Home Secretary. Neither he nor his chief, however, was to have much time to make his presence felt; in April they were out, and Melbourne was again Prime Minister. And now the Home Office was to come under the control of a man to whom the police throughout the country were to owe a great deal. Lord John Russell's most important achievement was to prepare the way for compulsory education, but "the present generation," says his biographer, "may need to be reminded that during . . . [his] tenure of the Home Office he laid the foundation of another work which, in its ultimate results, has proved almost equally beneficial, by the formation of a rural police, by the regulation and improvement of prisons, by the better treatment of juvenile offenders, and by the gradual abolition of transportation."[1]

Like Peel, Russell moved slowly. But in his first twelve months at the Home Office he introduced his Municipal Corporations Bill, a measure which *inter alia* enabled various boroughs in England and Wales to establish their own police forces, and he laid down the principle that policemen seriously injured while on duty, or dangerously ill as a result of their work, were entitled to compensation. The Commissioners may have found him irritatingly stubborn in minor matters; for instance, they were still refused the official dress for which

[1] Spencer Walpole, *The Life of Lord John Russell* (Longmans, 1889).

they were asking; but at an early date he showed his appreciation of their work by urging provincial authorities to copy their methods. As a result applications poured in for the services of Metropolitan police officers, to assist local magistrates or in a few cases to help in the establishment of new constabulary forces.[1] Even the official dress was sanctioned in the end, just before Russell resigned from the Home Office in April 1839.

In spite of what Roe and other grumblers might say, the value of trained policemen was becoming so generally recognized that the Commissioners had to make a stand about this time against the constant requests for police services by private persons and organizations. To demands by railway companies and London theatres were added cries for help from public institutions like the Bank of England and the Stamp Office. These extra duties were most popular with the force, but they could not always be allowed. A beginning was made with Lord Eastnor, who in June 1835 was regretfully informed that he could not have the usual posse of police for the Reigate races.

The force, after all, still numbered considerably less than 4000 men, and, for the first and only time for many years to come, Mayne was worrying about the state of recruiting. The intellectual standard of recruits was disappointingly low, while the percentage of resignations and dismissals remained disappointingly high. As fewer men of the non-commissioned officer class were coming forward, Mayne actually suggested a temporary arrangement with the Army authorities by which all vacancies in the police should be filled by volunteers from cavalry regiments; a remarkable proposal which it is not surprising was turned down. The Army was associated with the police in another way when the latter's constant difficulties with the inefficient Fire Offices culminated in something like a pitched battle during a bad fire at the Millbank Penitentiary in October 1835; 400 police and a detachment of the Guards were required to restore order. Such was the misconduct of some of the Fire Companies that a newspaper proposed that police should be "put in command" at all large fires.

Once more, however, there was in office a Home Secretary who was not afraid of the idea of far-reaching reforms, and there was Peel, though in opposition, generally ready to support any Parliamentary action designed to improve the efficiency of the police. The recommendations of the Police Committee which had had to listen to Roe and his reactionaries were on the whole typically vague; but three

[1] If lent to provincial magistrates at time of threatened or actual disturbances, the London police, rather comically, had to be locally sworn in as special constables.

concrete proposals were made—the Horse Patrol should be incorporated in the Metropolitan force without delay, and the Thames Police in the near future, and, in view of the numerous resignations, provision for superannuation, allowances, and rewards for long service should be considered. In August 1836 Russell began to act upon these recommendations by introducing a short Bill which transferred the Horse Patrol to the newer police; and early in 1837 six inspectors and sixty-five men of the patrol took their horses with them to become Mounted Police. They were posted to one or other of the outer divisions.

The Home Secretary had now to leave the Metropolitan force for a time while he looked farther afield, and a Royal Commission began to deliberate "as to the best Means of Establishing an Efficient Constabulary Force in the Counties of England and Wales." Russell then turned back to the police affairs of the Metropolis, and at the end of March 1837 a Select Committee to review the whole tangled problem of the Police Offices and the stipendiary magistrates held its first session. Russell himself, in the meantime, startled and shocked the City by informing its authorities that in the opinion of the Government the City Police should be placed under the Commissioners, and the Committee then seriously discussed this most dangerous of all London's police questions. The City defied the Government, and again successfully; but in almost everything for which the Commissioners were fighting, and against which the Metropolitan magistrates, or, at any rate, Roe, were furiously contending, the Select Committee took a high hand. Its Report was published in the summer of 1838. Of its thirteen recommendations two were of paramount importance: firstly, the Thames Police and the old Westminster Constables should be placed with the Metropolitan Police under the central authority of the Home Office, and, secondly, the stipendiary magistrates should be called upon "to execute such duties only" as were "of a judicial character." Increased powers were necessarily given to the police, and for summary jurisdiction the various offices were to be regarded as police courts. Every reform that was anathema to Roe was recommended. If the Committee's proposal for the absorption of the City Police came to nothing, it is probable that after the reception of Russell's rather premature disclosure nothing was expected to come of it. As one legal commentator observed, an attempt to enforce such a step would have led to a contest "the consequences of which no human sagacity could have foreseen."[1]

The introduction of the necessary Police Bills was interrupted by a

[1] *The Police Guide*. The author was Richard Charnock, of the Inner Temple.

political crisis, but Russell introduced them in June 1839. The first, "for improving the Police in and near the Metropolis," enlarged the police district, took over the Thames Police, substituted policemen for the old Runners in offices, royal palaces, and other places where they had been specially employed, besides including clauses on such subjects as raising a Superannuation Fund, regulating the traffic, and increasing the salaries of the Commissioners. The second Bill dealt with the magistracy, and so did the third, "for regulating the Police Courts in the Metropolis," placing these, for financial purposes, under the Receiver. After all the earlier tumult and shouting the Bills met with little opposition, perhaps because Roe, given a knighthood, had taken his pension and disappeared from public view. With him heart went out of the dissentients. The Bills became law at the end of August.

In the meantime the Royal Commission on County Police had issued its report, which proposed a centralized police force for the whole country. This idea was rejected, and later in the year the so-called "Permissive Act" was passed, empowering the counties to establish paid police forces of their own if they so desired. So, within a decade of the creation of the Metropolitan Police, were effected the two further reforms which consolidated that force itself, and provided the entire country with a machinery for creating local forces modelled upon it.

The Commissioners began at once to give effect to their new powers. They held discussions with the magistrates of the police courts—the word 'office' was immediately dropped—where only police were in future to be in attendance. Three constables were to be permanently stationed at Bow Street, Hatton Garden, Lambeth Street, and Thames Police Courts; the others had two each. New "local courts" were opened at Greenwich and Deptford. New police divisions, one to take in the latter area, and another with Woolwich as its headquarters, were to be created next year. The Metropolitan District was enlarged, and another 600 men were asked for. Still more would be wanted, for the Admiralty was now considering with the Commissioners the advisability of handing over to the police the care of dockyards at Woolwich and Deptford; and this opened the wider question of the force policing all the dockyards in the country. The first dockyard divisions were formed early in 1841.

There was also a new appointment at Scotland Yard. Captain William Hay, another Peninsular and Waterloo veteran, became Inspecting Superintendent of the Metropolitan Police, to carry out supervisory duties in the enlarged police district which it was impossible for the

Commissioners themselves to perform. With the growing responsibilities and size of the force, and the difficulty of finding even senior superintendents with the required qualities, Peel's prejudice and ruling against the introduction from outside of the equivalent of an "officer class" was found to be, in certain circumstances, obstructive to efficiency; and Hay's appointment was to be the first of many of its kind.

While all this was happening in exalted quarters the lower ranks were going about their normal duties, and the Commissioners had to find time for theirs; and, to close these departmental annals on a lighter note, it may be added that in the autumn of 1840 a police station and the Commissioners' Office were alike briefly concerned with a social dilemma that had a flavour of the Middle Ages. The peerage had still not only its legal privileges, but it was held by many of its members, and by a large section of the public, to be in other respects a law unto itself. On the evening of September the 12th the inspector on duty at Wandsworth Police Station was considerably startled by the entry of a dapper, bewhiskered military gentleman who said he was Lord Cardigan, and that he had just shot a man in a duel on Wimbledon Common. Duelling might be a crime, but it was a recognized practice in polite circles, and even had a Code approved as recently as 1824 by no less a personage than the Duke of Wellington, who himself fought a duel a few years later; besides, in such a case, what did one do with an earl, and with this particular earl? Lord Cardigan was already notorious. He was even known to the inspector, who asked anxiously if his Lordship had shot a certain captain with whom he was on the worst possible terms. The Earl replied indignantly that he would not condescend to shoot one of his own officers. His victim, who happily was only wounded, had, in fact, been in Cardigan's regiment, but had now left the Army. The inspector pulled himself together and did his duty. He put the Earl under arrest, and then saw to it that he was immediately released on bail.[1]

[1] Cecil Woodham-Smith, *The Reason Why* (Constable, 1953).

POLICE GAZETTE; OR, HUE AND CRY.

Published by Authority.

No. 215.] SATURDAY, FEBRUARY 6, 1830.

Containing the Substance of all Informations received in Cases of Felonies, and Misdemeanors of an aggravated nature, and against Receivers of Stolen Goods, reputed Thieves and Offenders escaped from Custody, with the time, the place, and every particular circumstance marking the Offence. The Names of Persons charged, who are known but not in Custody, and of those who are not known, their Appearance, Dress, and every other mark of identity that can be described. The Names of Accomplices and Accessories, with every other particular which may lead to their Apprehension. The Names of all Persons brought before the Magistrates, charged with any of the Offences mentioned, and whether committed for Trial, Re-examination, or how otherwise disposed of. Also a Description of Property that has been Stolen, and particularly of Stolen Horses, with as much particularity as can be given, with every circumstance that may be useful for the purpose of Tracing and Recovering it.

ARSON AND WILFUL BURNING.

WHITEHALL, January 29th, 1830.

Whereas it hath been humbly represented unto the King, That, on the night of Saturday, the 9th day of January instant, a Seed Hay Rick, the property of Mr. Thomas Martin, of Compton, in the Parish of Enford, in the County of Wilts, was wilfully and maliciously set on Fire, by some evil-disposed Person or Persons unknown;

His Majesty, for the better apprehending and bringing to justice, the Persons concerned in the Felony before mentioned, is hereby pleased to promise His most gracious Pardon to any one of them (except the Person who actually set Fire to the said Rick) who shall discover his Accomplice or Accomplices therein, so that he, she, or they, may be apprehended and convicted thereof.

ROBERT PEEL.

And, as a further encouragement, a Reward of One Hundred Pounds is hereby offered to any Person (except as aforesaid) who shall discover the said Offender or Offenders, so that he, she, or they, may be apprehended and convicted of the said Offence.—Such Reward to be paid by the said Mr. Thomas Martin.

ROBBERY FROM THE PERSON.

On Thursday evening, the 4th instant, as Louisa Borden, of No. 5, Hatfield-street, Gray's-walk, Lambeth, was passing through Hyde Park, she was knocked down by a Soldier of the First Regiment of Guards, and robbed of two Shawls; one blue, and the other red and other colours.—The Soldier was of thin make, pale complexion, dark hair, and brown whiskers.

A most daring attempt at Robbery was committed on Wednesday night, the 27th ultimo, about half-past seven o'clock, in Peckham Lane. A poor woman living at New Cross, had been to Kensington, for relief, and was coming down the lane, with a child on her back, and it appears a woman was close behind her, who travels the country with Jewellery, and who is in the habit of stopping at the Red Cow, at Peckham, to take a little refreshment. When the poor woman with the child got down the lane a little way, she received a most dreadful blow on the head, with a stick; she put up her hand to save her head, and that is cut very much. The woman with the jewellery being close behind, ran back and screamed murder. The woman who was attacked, received several blows, when one of the party came up, and with an oath said, 'You are wrong'; from which it is evident they had been waiting for the woman with the jewellery.—One of the parties suspected of the above offence, was apprehended by one of the parish patrol, but it is believed the matter was compounded without going before a Magistrate.

HOUSE-BREAKING.

WHITEHALL, January 30th, 1830.

Whereas it hath been humbly represented unto the King, That, on the morning of Friday, the 22d day of January instant, between five and six o'clock, the Town House of the Hamlet of Mile End Old Town, situate in the Mile End Road, was burglariously entered by some Persons disguised, who proceeded into the Mistress's Chamber, and, threatening her with violence, took therefrom One Hundred and Twenty-five Pounds in Silver, a Butcher's Cheque for Seven Pounds Eight Shillings and Sixpence, and several other articles:

His Majesty, for the better apprehending and bringing to justice, the Persons concerned in the Felony before mentioned, is hereby pleased to promise His most gracious Pardon to any one of them who shall discover his Accomplice or Accomplices therein, so that he, she, or they, may be apprehended and convicted thereof.

ROBERT PEEL.

And, as a further encouragement, a Reward of Forty Pounds is hereby offered by the Churchwardens and Overseers of the above Hamlet, to any Person who shall discover the said Offender or Offenders, so that he, she, or they, may be apprehended and convicted of the said Offence.

On Tuesday, the 2nd instant, the Dwelling-house of Susannah Ogden, No. 117, Wardour-street, Soho, was broken and entered, and the following articles Stolen therefrom, viz.—Three Silver Tea-spoons, marked 'S. O. S.'; four ditto, 'T. I. G.'; one pair of Sugar-nippers, 'S. O. S.'; and one Table-spoon, not marked; also two new Silk Handkerchiefs, one of them marked 'O.' and the other 'T.'; one Black Silk Gown, one new Stuff ditto, two Table-cloths, one Umbrella, an old fashioned Silver Watch, one Mosaic Brooch, with the figure of a Dog; and one Red Silk Shawl.

On Wednesday morning, the 3rd instant, the House of Francis Atkins, No. 33, Trafalgar-square, Stepney, was entered by a Back Bed-room Window, and the following articles stolen therefrom:—One blue frock coat, one toilinet waistcoat with blue stripes, one white waistcoat, one pair of black trousers, twelve yards of Irish linen, two cotton gowns, one silk shawl, one worsted ditto, one pair of cotton stockings, and a child's red pattern frock.—The Thieves left behind a ladder and a piece of candle.

HENRY and RICHARD KEANS, of the Parish of Farleigh Wallop, in the County of Southampton, for whom warrants are issued, for breaking into a Shop, in the said Parish, on the 10th ultimo, have Absconded.—It is supposed HENRY will either enlist as a Marine, or offer himself as a Policeman. He is about twenty-four years of age, about five feet eight inches high, dark hair, and of pale complexion.—RICHARD is about five feet ten or eleven inches high, of dark complexion, black hair, stoops in his walk, good regular teeth, has a severe cut across the knuckle of the right hand, nearly separating the little finger, and is of Gipsy-like appearance; he had on a dirty round frock. They are Agricultural Labourers.

On Sunday night, the 31st ultimo, or early the following morning, the Premises of Mr. Scott, No. 43, Brompton-square, were broken and entered, and the following articles Stolen, viz.—Ten Table-spoons, sixteen Dessert-spoons, and twelve large Tea-spoons, not marked; five small Tea-spoons, one marked 'S. S.' and two 'F. R. M.', four Salt-spoons, two marked 'S. S.'; two Mustard-spoons, and one pair of Sugar-tongs, not marked; one Silver Watch, with 'W. H.' on the outside case; and one Razor.—Whoever will give information so that the Property may be obtained, shall receive Twenty Pounds Reward; or any person giving information of the offenders, shall, on their conviction, receive Five Pounds Reward, although the Property be not recovered.

On Tuesday night, the 2nd instant, or early on the following morning, the House of William Bayne, Esq., at New Grove, Mile End, was broken and entered, and the following articles were Stolen therefrom, viz.—A Drab Box Coat, with several capes; two Carriage Glasses; one dark Drab Coat; one pair of Boots; one white and pink striped Waistcoat; a Livery Hat, with Gold Band, made in Lombard-street; two Shoe-brushes, and a Carriage-brush; also a Spring Gun, and a Pig, which was killed in the Stable with a chopper.—The Thieves left behind a pair of shoes, made of carpet and drugget.—A Reward of Ten Pounds will be paid on conviction of the offender or offenders.

Whereas the House of Mr. R. Whiteaves, No 30, Fleet-street, was burglariously entered, on the night of the 31st of December, or early on the 1st of January, and the following Articles Stolen, viz.—One enamelled gold watch, nameless; one double-bottomed engine-turned gold chased dial, name 'R. Whiteaves, Fleet-street, No. 2948'; one single-case engine-turned jewelled gold lady's watch, gold dial, 'John Pearce, London, No. 138'; one single-case engine-turned lady's gold watch, gold dial, nameless; one engine-turned lady's gold watch, chased edges, and pendant, chased gold dial, jewelled, No. 8104; one engine-turned gold jewelled watch, gold dial, single case, nameless, No. 5033; one plain gold dome watch, jewelled, nameless; one enamelled gold watch, set with pearls back and front; one plain double-cased silver lever watch, capped and jewelled in four holes, hard dial, ruby pallets, going fusee, name 'R. Whiteaves, Fleet-street, No. 2920'; one double-bottomed silver horizontal watch, capped and jewelled in four holes, hard dial, steel wheel and seconds, 'R. Whiteaves, Fleet-street, No. 2943'; one double-bottomed box-cover silver hunter, hands set behind; one silver watch, 'John Lancaster, Prescot'; one silver double-bottomed watch, jewelled in four holes, duplex, going fusee, nameless; one double-bottomed silver watch, engine-turned, jewelled, 'No 8084, London'; one second-hand silver engine-turned horizontal watch, capped and jewelled in four holes, 'R. Cook, London, No. 166'; one silver double-bottomed watch, jewelled, with seconds, 'No. 374'; one plain gilt double-case watch, capped, 'R. Whiteaves, Fleet-street'; one double-circle gilt hunter; one gilt box and case in one, 'Joseph Littler'; one double-bottomed gilt watch, engine-turned, 'Hewett Clerkenwell, London, No. 176'; one gilt box and case in one, silver dial, 'R. White, London'; one double-bottomed gilt watch, with centre and seconds, capped and jewelled, name 'Gibson'; one plain gold French watch, nameless, No. 1360; one gilt watch, 'James Payne, Foster-lane, London, No. 2959'; one silver watch, jewelled, 'Austin and Co., Oxford-street, London, No. 4567'; one gilt watch, 'Nathaniel Hedge, Colchester'; one silver hunting watch, box-cover, jewelled, No. 814'; one gilt watch, capped and jewelled, patent centre and seconds, 'Jessop, London, No. 1905'; one Norraaco skin gilt watch, name 'T. Rogers, London, No. 372'; and one pair of engine-turned gold hunting cases.—Plate: one dozen pair fiddle-handled dessert-forks; one dozen ditto dessert-spoons; two gravy-spoons; one dozen plain tea-spoons; one dozen pair of fiddle-handled ditto; five table-spoons, plain; fifteen table ditto, tied in a bundle; two caddy-ladles, three dessert-spoons, plain; one half-pint can; two fish-slices; eight salt-spoons; four sugar-tongs; two pencil-cases; a small tea-pot; two antique table-spoons; five silver snuff-boxes; twenty gold seals, various gold keys, &c.; one lady's gold neckchain; two gentlemen's ditto, with camel leopard, &c.; several gold motto rings, and other articles of jewellery; a bag containing about nine ounces of English gold coins, various guineas and half-guineas, from James II. to George III. &c.; one three-pound piece of Charles I.; one sovereign of Elizabeth; one ditto of Edward VI.; one half-sovereign of Henry VIII.; one gold five-shilling piece of the Commonwealth; three or four foreign Nobles; one pattern of a seven-shilling-piece of George III.; one five-shilling-piece of James I. and Charles I. &c.; silver Greek coins, Macedon; Syracuse, Corinth, Roman coins, various; Olivers, broad, 1656; one angel of Henry VIII.; one ditto of Elizabeth; one guinea of George I.; one double-sovereign; one half ditto; one crown, one half ditto; one shilling; one sixpence; silver medals, various; one chased medal of Charles II. 1660; the Surrender of Guadaloupe, 1759; Frederick V. Paul and Mary, 1782; Prince of Orange Typographic Harlemum, Charles V.; Denmark and Norway, on the King's Recovery, by Dros; Tigurian Republick, 1761, Leopold 1825; one silver medal of Oliver on the Battle of Dunbar; one silver medal of the Duke of Wellington; one dollar struck by the Emperor's rebellious subjects; one medal of Luther; one chased ditto of William III.; one Jerom Napoleon; one medal of the Duke of Cumberland, 1745; a testoon of Clements XIII.; one Waterloo medal, 1815; two medals of James the Pretender; one ditto of Homespack Turin.—A Reward of One Hundred Pounds will be paid for the recovery of the Property, namely, Fifty Pounds on the recovery of the Watches; and Forty Pounds on recovery of the Plate, Coins, Seals and Chains, or in proportion for any part thereof, on application as above; and Ten Pounds on conviction of the offender or offenders.

PAGE FROM THE "POLICE GAZETTE" OF 1830

COLONEL SIR CHARLES ROWAN

By courtesy of the Marquess of Tweeddale

SIR RICHARD MAYNE

By courtesy of A. R. Heathcote, Esq.

11

A DETECTIVE OFFICE

In the summer of 1841 Melbourne resigned, and for the second time, but in circumstances very different from those of six years before, Peel became Prime Minister.

Sir James Graham succeeded Lord Normanby, who in the two years since Russell's resignation had been at the Home Office. Graham is almost forgotten, but Gladstone considered him to be "the greatest administrator of his time,"[1] and Lord Morley praises his sagacity and character. He was later made the scapegoat in the political storm caused by the disclosure that Mazzini's correspondence had been opened by Government order. Generally regarded as Peel's chief supporter, he shared the latter's interest in police matters, and is found discussing such routine details as the choice of a sergeant for confidential work outside London, and suggesting minor alterations in the uniform of the force. This was when, as the result of numerous complaints, Graham himself undertook inquiries into the quality of the cloth supplied by Hebbert, who in consequence lost his contract.

Graham had not been long in office, and was much preoccupied with the Chartist agitation, when events occurred which, like the Ratcliffe Highway murders, stimulated public interest in the question of police. They were to some extent responsible for the creation of a separate Detective Office at Scotland Yard, though this was no new idea. The Commissioners had been considering the establishment at least of a kind of detective reserve, either in the divisions or at Scotland Yard itself. In February 1840, after a serious jewel robbery in Welbeck Street, instructions were issued for the employment of "an active intelligent man in each Division" to trace the missing property.[2] A more elaborate experiment of the kind was to be attempted in 1844, but it was not altogether successful, and more than thirty years were to pass before the divisions were given their own full-time detectives. It appears, however, that one of the four special "mobile" inspectors at Scotland Yard who were only nominally attached to A Division

[1] Charles Whibley, *Political Portraits* (Macmillan, 1917).
[2] Police Orders, February 2, 1840.

was entrusted at least as early as 1840 with the duty of watching the activities of London's habitual criminals. This was Nicholas Pearce, already mentioned, and he was further given a roving commission as investigator in certain cases of murder or other serious crimes in the Metropolis. Having been transferred to headquarters from Marylebone, he played a prominent part in the inquiry into the murder of Lord William Russell in May 1840, if he was not actually in charge of the case, and he shared in the very considerable rewards offered. There is reason to suppose, though the records are silent on the point, that Pearce had the assistance of a sergeant named Thornton in E Division. By 1842 the pair of them seem to have become a kind of flying squad in miniature.

These two detectives, though unconnected with any of the divisions most directly concerned, are found engaged in such work, and reporting every few hours to the Commissioners, during the investigation into the first of two sensational murders in the spring of 1842. This case is often referred to as being the "cause" of the creation of a detective department.

2

About 8.30 on the evening of Wednesday, April 6, 1842, a four-wheeled pony-chaise pulled up at a tailor's shop in Wandsworth High Street. The driver, Daniel Good, who had his small son with him, was a middle-aged Irishman and the servant of Mr Shiell, a well-to-do retired West India merchant living at Roehampton. Good was known to Mr Collingbourne, the tailor, who allowed him to take a pair of black knee-breeches on credit; but as he was leaving he was seen by the shop-assistant to slip a pair of trousers under his coat. Followed to his chaise by Collingbourne and the assistant, he indignantly denied the theft and drove off.

A policeman was fetched, P.C. Gardner of V Division, which included Wandsworth, Putney, and part of Chelsea. Taking with him the shop-assistant and another youth employed next door, Gardner went to Roehampton, then a small village a mile or two from Putney, and at Mr Shiell's house was told that Good was probably at the stables, another quarter of a mile away. When found there Good again denied the theft, but offered to pay for the breeches. This was a mistake, for it must have strengthened Gardner's determination to search the premises. He discovered nothing to concern him in the coach-house, where the pony-chaise was standing; when, however, he proposed to look further Good raised objections. The policeman insisted, and Mr

Shiell's head gardener and bailiff, a man named Oughton, now appearing on the scene, the whole party of five entered the stables themselves. In a corner stall were some trusses of hay, which Good began to shift about; Gardner stopped him, removed a truss or two himself, and by the light of a candle saw what at first he took for a plucked goose. One of the shop-boys thought it was a dead pig. Another candle was lighted, but before the object could be examined events took a new turn. Good rushed out of the stables and locked the door behind him.

While attempts were being made to break it open Gardner cleared away more trusses and revealed the mutilated torso of a woman. The door was forced, and one of the youths was sent to the Police Office at Putney. Good's little boy had come down from a room over the stables, and was put in the charge of Oughton. Another policeman arrived, and rode off on a pony to fetch his superintendent from Wandsworth. This officer, Thomas Bicknell, came about midnight, bringing with him an inspector, a sergeant named Palmer, and a surgeon. Palmer noticed an obnoxious smell, and in the fireplace of the harness-room discovered the charred remains of a head and limbs.

Oughton, the bailiff, in the meantime, had learnt from Good's son that he was living with a woman whom he called mother, in a basement-kitchen in South Street, off Manchester Square. Superintendent Bicknell was so little interested in this piece of news that when, a little later, he drew up his preliminary report, or route-paper,[1] to be sent to Wandsworth for circulation throughout the divisions, he did not mention it. He seems to have delayed writing his report while he hunted for more remains and likely weapons—an axe and a hand-saw with traces of flesh on them were later recovered—and apparently he ignored some useful information acquired by P.C. Gardner. The bailiff's son had joined the grim party, and gave Gardner the names of two or three women who had recently been in Good's company.

This came out at the inquest, opened on Friday, the 8th, and adjourned, Bicknell having cut a poor figure. The police of A, C, D, and R Divisions were now busy, and during these days the newspapers

[1] Few details of the route-paper system have been preserved. From Rowan's evidence before the Select Committee of 1838 it appears that these reports contained a brief account of a crime, with any particulars known about the suspected criminal or other information likely to lead to his arrest. They were intended to be circulated to divisions at the earliest possible moment, presumably by dispatch-riders, every division at this time having its mounted men. Each station marked on the back of a route-paper the time at which it was received, and the Commissioners, having examined it to see that it had been properly circulated, decided whether the information given should be included in the next Daily Report. From some of the newspaper criticisms it would seem that the inspector or sergeant in charge at a station was expected without delay to send out the reserve, who would acquaint all men on beat duty with the news.

were able to tell their readers much about Good's movements both before and after the discovery in the stable, and, by the Monday, something about Good himself. He was still missing, but, said the *Morning Post*, "as he is well known, there are hopes that he will speedily be taken."

Among those to whom he was well known, it now appeared, were the police. His reputation was of the worst; in addition to several minor convictions for theft, he had been sentenced some years before to seven years' transportation, though this was commuted to two years' imprisonment. Once, in a fit of ungovernable rage, he had torn out a horse's tongue. He was married, and as on another occasion he had nearly caused his wife's death by setting fire to her bed, the idea of murder may not have been new to him. Mrs Good was now living in Bethnal Green, where her husband was well known. The woman at South Street, Jane Jones (or Sparks), whom the little boy called his mother, had been passing as Good's wife, while at Roehampton he posed as a widower, and was courting a girl named Rose Butcher, to whom, on the morning of the 6th, he had given some dresses which he said had belonged to his dead wife. With the freedom of the time, all this, and more, was revealed by the newspapers. The whereabouts of the real Mrs Good, or "Old Molly Good," as she was generally called, was disclosed by the *Morning Chronicle*, which added that on the Saturday she had been questioned by Inspector Pearce, accompanied by a local sergeant. On the Thursday and Friday, the days immediately after the discovery of the Roehampton remains, Good had been with her. She had last seen him in a coffee-house, where he made some excuse to leave her.

"Old Molly Good," as was to appear, knew more about her husband's affairs than she admitted at this interview; but its real interest lies in a feature of which so little was made at the time that during the rest of the inquiry Pearce's name was hardly mentioned, except when he was giving evidence. Here, however, at an early stage of a murder investigation, a Scotland Yard inspector is found, if not in charge of the case, actively assisting the local divisional police.

Good himself, whose guilt was by now taken for granted by Press and public, was still missing when at the resumed inquest the dead woman was identified as Jane Jones. A few days later the wanted man was recognized at Tonbridge by an ex-policeman of V Division. He appeared at Bow Street on April the 18th. His wife and a man named Gamble were also in the dock, Gamble having been found in possession of some of Jane Jones's belongings, which he obtained from Mrs

Good. This pair, committed for receiving, were acquitted; but there was no hope for Good. Having been tried and found guilty, he was hanged in the presence of a crowd larger, it was said, than any seen on a like occasion since the execution of Fauntleroy the banker.

Long before this—indeed, before Good's arrest—certain newspapers had been criticizing severely the handling of the case by the police. There was some justice in such criticisms of Superintendent Bicknell, and perhaps in those made by the *Morning Chronicle* of a sergeant in D Division, who, it was stated, had traced Good to Spitalfields on the day after the discovery of the crime, but then, instead of informing the police of that district (H Division), had told all and sundry that he was looking for Good, and so given the latter warning. The *Chronicle* was on the war-path again a few days later: "There is a feeling generally expressed against the police authorities for not using such diligence as must have had, under the circumstances, the effect of placing the monster in their custody." *The Times* expressed this feeling next day, complaining that a police force of 3800 men, maintained at heavy cost, had not, after ten days, been able to lay their hands on a man who had "already crossed their path" many times; and the *Weekly Dispatch*, as hostile as ever towards the police, pronounced its conduct of the case to be "marked with a looseness and want of decision which proves that unless a decided change is made in the present system, it is idle to expect that it can be an efficient detective force."

When the police were still to some extent on trial talk of this kind was more damaging than it would be now. In this instance it was not even altogether fair. Good was at large for less than a fortnight; and Inspector Pearce and his sergeant, when giving evidence at Bow Street, had shown that in that time they had cleared up almost every point of importance. They had traced Good's movements, hour by hour, from the moment of his escape from the stables at Roehampton until, thirty-six hours later, he left his wife in the coffee-house, and they collected witnesses who identified almost every article of clothing the murdered woman had possessed, even to the last hat she had bought. It was a very thorough piece of work, and, indeed, so far as Pearce and Sergeant Thornton were concerned, it answered every criticism.

But Scotland Yard had only come on the scene a good many hours after the discovery in the stables. There remained the conduct of Superintendent Bicknell and other officers of V Division; and while Good was awaiting trial *The Times* came out with a "critical analysis" of the evidence given at Bow Street which was in effect an exposure of the dilatory behaviour of the local police first on the spot. Its importance lay in the fact that its avowed purpose was to impress the Commissioners with the urgent necessity of creating a new detective department.

Why, asked *The Times*, had P.C. Gardner allowed an already accused man to escape? Why had there been no attempt on that Wednesday night to follow the fugitive? Why had Superintendent Bicknell taken nearly two hours to get from Wandsworth to Roehampton, and what had he done when he got there which excused his tardy dispatch of the important route-paper? Why did this message, when sent, contain so few particulars that two of the inspectors on night duty did not think it worth circulating immediately to their men on the beat, an omission for which they had been suspended?

The inspectors in question were those at Marylebone and Vine Street, in both of which divisions there were policemen who knew Good, but who did not learn that he was wanted until late on the Thursday. Three more suspensions were to follow in R Division, for at Woolwich there were also police officers who knew Good, but had not received prompt news of the murder. These punishments, though *The Times* did not know it, were rendered the more necessary because the offenders had very recently been warned. Only a few weeks earlier the Commissioners had issued a stern Police Order[1] on the lack of diligence shown by many of those whose duty it might be to circulate a route-paper.

Used as they were to the perversions of the truth regularly appearing in the *Weekly Dispatch*, the Commissioners may well have been seriously disturbed when the influential *Times*, for so many years a staunch supporter of the new police, raised a sharply critical voice. The "analysis," by implication, rightly exonerated Pearce, who was, in fact, already marked out for early promotion; but few of the divisional superintendents were showing much initiative in the detective side of police work. When such problems arose there were signs of inter-divisional jealousy, especially marked when the Headquarters Division was involved. At this very time, as other newspapers (including, of course, the *Weekly Dispatch*) did not fail to remark, a series of impudent highway robberies in the Highbury and Islington districts was baffling all the resources of N Division. Nor were the Commissioners given more than a few days to digest the strictures in *The Times* before a fresh tragedy shocked all London and led to another outburst of criticism of police methods.

[1] March 5, 1842.

3

Just a month after the horrid discoveries in Mr Shiell's stables, on May the 5th, late in the afternoon, P.C. Moss of A Division was on special patrol duty in uniform on the outskirts of Islington. He noticed that a gentleman was being followed by another man in labourer's clothes.[1] Seeing the policeman, this man ran off into a field. Moss followed, and found him hiding under a hedge, with two old-fashioned horse-pistols by his side. When the policeman threatened to take him into custody the man fired and again took to his heels, turning to fire his second pistol as he ran. Moss was hit in the shoulder, but gamely continued the pursuit until the fugitive, reloading, wounded him again, when he fell. Others had now taken up the chase, among them a local policeman, Timothy Daly; towards Highbury the hunted man ran into a cul-de-sac, but, having once more recharged both his weapons, refused to surrender. A journeyman baker who tried to grapple with him was shot down. Daly, undeterred, rushed in, and a second shot killed him on the spot. The murderer was then seized and tied up.

There were reasonable grounds for the outcry caused by this affray. The man who had killed one constable, and severely injured a second and a member of the public, was even better known to the police than Daniel Good. A bricklayer named Thomas Cooper, he had a long record of convictions, some for crimes of violence. It was thought that he belonged to a gang, on account of whose activities P.C. Moss had been sent from Headquarters to assist the divisional police, and it was asked why single unarmed officers in uniform were allowed to risk, and lose, their lives in such circumstances. One other arrest was, in fact, made locally, but Cooper alone was brought to trial. He was duly sentenced to death.

He was still awaiting trial, and Good had just been hanged, when a third sensation startled the whole country, and added to the Commissioners' immediate perplexities. On the 30th of May occurred the second attempt on the life of the young Queen.

With Prince Albert she was returning to Buckingham Palace along Constitution Hill. A young man named John Francis, who was standing against the Palace wall within a yard or two of P.C. Trounce of A Division, stepped into the road, produced a pistol, and fired at the royal carriage. No one was harmed, and the Queen once more showed the greatest coolness. Francis was seized by Trounce and a

[1] The contemporary accounts of this murder are more than usually unreliable. The version given here is mostly obtained from counsel's speech for the prosecution and witnesses' statements at Cooper's trial at the Old Bailey, as reported in *The Times*.

soldier. From the station he was taken to the Home Office, as was then the custom in such a case, to be examined by the Privy Council. Among those hastily summoned to attend were Rowan and the Chief Magistrate, Mr Hall.

Francis was sentenced to death, but was reprieved on the day, July the 3rd, when another weak-minded youth named Bean levelled a pistol at Her Majesty as she was driving to the Chapel Royal, St James's. The weapon failed to go off. Bean, a hunchback, escaped at the time, and until he was caught, a few days later, humpbacked men were being apprehended all over London.[1]

According to Greville, the Queen was warned by Scotland Yard that an attempt might be made on her on the 30th, the information being based on a conversation said to have been overheard in St James's Park the day before. P.C. Trounce, on the other hand, so far from being on the alert, had been idly watching Francis for half an hour, even noticing that he was trying to avoid observation. Yet he did nothing about it, and the actual attack obviously took him completely by surprise.

It is known that within a fortnight, their deliberations hastened by this series of events, the Commissioners had decided to press for the immediate establishment of a separate Detective Department at Scotland Yard. A "Memorandum relative to the Detective Powers of the Police," containing the outline of a scheme for such a branch, was forwarded to the Home Office on June the 14th. When Peel's Bill for the Better Protection of the Queen's Person, introduced on July the 12th, was finally amended, it did little more than authorize the ordinary courts to deal with offenders like Francis and Bean without recourse to the Privy Council: but it is possible that during the preparation of the Bill discussions about police protection in such cases took place between the Commissioners and Graham, and even with the Prime Minister.

The Commissioners' "Memorandum" of June the 14th has disappeared, but it seems that they asked for the appointment of two inspectors and eight sergeants to the new Detective Branch at rates of pay which would mean modest promotion for the men selected. A reply received on the 16th, when, incidentally, March Phillipps forwarded to Rowan a letter containing a threat to assassinate the Queen,[2]

[1] Bean's pistol was loaded with gunpowder and small pieces of tobacco-pipe. Up to May 1842 some thirty-seven persons had come under cognizance of the police for offences against the Queen since her accession. Most of the charges were for throwing letters into her carriage or trespassing, like "the boy Jones," in Buckingham Palace.

[2] P.R.O., H.O. 65. 14 (Entry Book).

accepted the proposals in principle; the Home Secretary, however, required further enlightenment on a number of points, chiefly dealing with finance. In view of future developments, it is interesting to find Graham wanting to know what regulations would be introduced "to ensure the proper employment of the detective officers when not immediately occupied in the pursuit of offenders."

It is in a rather lengthy letter sent by the Commissioners two days later that the earliest details of their proposals are to be found. The two detective-inspectors were to be paid £200 a year, and the eight detective-sergeants four shillings a day. The annual cost, £984, would be charged on the general funds of the police establishment. In reply to Graham's query about the duties of the men of the new branch when not employed on any particular case, the Commissioners said it was intended that every member of it was to be "employed in gaining information as to the facilities" that might "be afforded from time to time for the commission of particular species of crimes, and by the habits, haunts and persons or parties known or suspected to live by the commission of crime, so as to prepare themselves for tracing and detecting offenders when any case occurred." The Commissioners, it was added, "would require reports to be made to them to ascertain that the time of all was fully occupied."

With this cumbrously worded information the Home Secretary, who was at this time suggesting to the Middlesex magistrates the establishment of a "permanent Metropolitan Court for trials of common larcenies and frauds within the Metropolitan District," with "a paid judge"—the present-day London Sessions—was apparently satisfied; he thought, however, that to begin with six sergeants instead of eight would suffice. On June the 20th permission was formally granted for the experimental establishment of a "Detective Force."

4

During the next few weeks a number of newspapers referred briefly to "the new police arrangements." Apparently no details were allowed to be known, and though the Commissioners, with ample material in the existing force, had no intention of looking outside it, at least one application for enrolment was received from a member of the public who believed himself to possess unique qualifications as a detective. A working nucleus of the new department was already in being in the persons of Inspector Pearce and Sergeant Thornton, and the former as a matter of course became one of the two detective-inspectors. His colleague was a younger inspector from P Division, John Haynes. The pair were in theory on an equality, no provision having been made for a single head of the Detective Office. This rather strange omission was soon remedied, and from the first Pearce was generally regarded as the senior, which he was in age, seniority of rank, and experience of detective work. In any case, he takes precedence in the list of Metropolitan detectives.

As a matter of record, the first detective-sergeants should be named. The original six were Stephen Thornton (E Division), William Gerrett (A), Shaw (R), and Braddick (F), all sergeants, together with two constables promoted to that rank—Goff (L) and Whicher (E). Of Whicher much was to be heard, as one of the most successful and most unlucky of detectives; he is regarded as the original of Sergeant Cuff in Wilkie Collins's novel *The Moonstone*. For some reason Gerrett resigned from the force at the end of the year, his place in the Detective Branch being taken by Sergeant Shackell of G Division. When, in November 1844, Pearce became Superintendent of F, Shackell was promoted to detective-inspector, and his resignation a year or two later brought into the new force from Woolwich Dockyard another officer who was to become famous in fact and fiction, Inspector Charles Frederick Field, the Inspector Bucket of *Bleak House*.

Such, with headquarters in Scotland Yard, was the original personnel of the Detective Office, which was to expand into the present Criminal Investigation Department. It seems to have had no fixed appellation in these early days; the terms office, department, and force were all used in official correspondence, and even 'Detective,' in the sense of the office as well as of the men who worked there. Dickens refers to this usage in his *Household Words* articles, and in *Bleak House* Inspector Bucket is introduced as "Mr Bucket of the Detective." The office itself came into being in the most unobtrusive manner. By the 12th of July the *Morning Post* had heard of it, but it was ignored by *The Times*, and even by the *Weekly Dispatch*, which missed an opportunity, for among the few criticisms of the new force which date from its early months the name "Defectives" was first thought of in another quarter. This neglect by the Press, which it is tempting to think may have been encouraged by the Home Office for reasons of secrecy, was more probably due to the dearth during this period of spectacular crimes—a state of things which always tends to thrust the police into the background of the news.

Obscurity, no doubt welcome to Inspector Pearce and his little force, was not to last. The Detective Office soon came in for its share of the censure and abuse for a long time to come too readily showered upon the police as a whole by certain newspapers and the correspondents whose views they aired. "The strength of the prejudice against the detective force," says Sir John Moylan, "can be gauged from the fact that not until 1864 was there any increase in the establishment of the detective branch, and in 1868, when Sir Richard Mayne died, it was just a small section of the Commissioners' Office, fifteen strong in a force nearly 8000." From the beginning, however, it also had its friends, not the least powerful of whom was Charles Dickens, who in 1850 published in *Household Words* his three articles, "The Modern Science of Thief-taking" and, in two parts, "A Detective Police Party," which is based on a visit paid by almost the entire detective force to the journal's offices in Wellington Street. The officers' names are only slightly disguised, Field, for example, becoming Wield, and Whicher, Witcham, and their appearance is described in some detail. They told stories of their exploits, which Dickens elaborated; he is not always accurate in his details, but the articles are the expression of cordial admiration for a body of hard-working and conscientious men. They are compared very favourably with the Bow Street Runners, "who never lost a public occasion of jobbing and trading in mystery and making the most of themselves." (It was later to be considered a fault in Inspector Field, the most famous of them all, that he played to the gallery.) A sequel to a "party" which no doubt was authorized with an eye to counter-propaganda was that Whicher had his pocket picked on his way home.

Eight years later Dickens thought he had cause to complain of the police. In a letter to his sub-editor, Wills, he asks the latter to protest to Scotland Yard about alleged inquiries made by a policeman into the private lives of Maria and Nelly Ternan. Dickens suspected that the officer's services had been hired by some "swell."[1] At this time, in addition to official awards of money for exceptional good work, officers of the Detective Branch could be hired by private persons, with the consent of the Commissioner, for quite long periods, a practice which was to develop throughout the force, on an "off-duty" basis, until it became mischievous. It will be remembered that Lady Verinder, in *The Moonstone*, hired Sergeant Cuff.[2]

[1] Professor Rolfe, *Nineteenth-century Fiction*.

[2] Mr John Carter's *New Paths in Book Collecting* (Constable, 1934) contains an interesting section on "Detective Fiction." Of the period when Dickens and Wilkie Collins were writing Mr Carter lists the following works in this *genre*. An early and successful effort was a yellow-back, *Recollections of a Detective Police-officer*, by "Waters" (1856), which was followed by a second series (1859). Preface signed "C.W." (Charles Waters). The real author was William Russell. There had been a Runner named Waters, who was not

5

The Detective Office was not to come into the news in connexion with a crime of the more sensational sort until the end of the decade. While it was still feeling its way, however, a murder occurred which is of some importance in police history, though it offered no scope for the type of work for which the new branch had been created.

On the 20th of January, 1843, Mr Edward Drummond, Peel's private secretary, was shot in Whitehall, dying of his wound five days later. The murderer, David McNaughten, had mistaken his victim for Peel himself. McNaughten, who suffered from persecution mania, was tried at the Old Bailey in February, when he was acquitted by the jury on the ground of insanity and ordered to be confined in an asylum. The verdict was felt to be unsatisfactory, and, the matter being raised in the House of Lords, certain questions were referred to the judges, who delivered their opinions, ever since known as the McNaughten Rules, on the 19th of June. In reply to the question, "If a person under an insane delusion as to existing facts commits an offence in consequence thereof, is he thereby excused?" they replied unanimously that the party accused was in law equally liable with a person of sane mind. The form of the verdict to be returned in such a case has since been altered to "Guilty, but insane," and the sentence one of detention during Her (or His) Majesty's pleasure.

Police Orders of this period include a number relating to the detective force. Within a few weeks of its establishment on the 15th of August, 1842, an anomaly was removed when Pearce, though still only an inspector, was officially put in charge. An Order of the 1st of September lays it down that weekly reports of unsolved cases are to be given to the Inspector of Detectives and kept by him as a record of undetected crime. No doubt a good deal of jealousy of the new force was felt by the uniformed branch, but that there were faults on both sides is indicated by an Order of the 24th of March, 1845, three months after Pearce, on promotion to F Division, had been succeeded as Inspector of Detectives by Shackell. The detective force was reminded

---

at Bow Street, but it is very doubtful if he had anything to do with the book. Possibly some of the sketches were based on fact, but in general they were imaginary. Most of them originally appeared in *Chambers's Journal*. Russell also wrote *Experiences of a Real Detective*, by Inspector "F" (1862); *Undiscovered Crimes* (1862); and *The Autobiography of an English Detective* (two vols., 1863). Other early fiction purporting to be fact includes *Revelations of a Private Detective*, by Andrew Forrester, Jnr. (1863), the author taking the name of the famous Forrester brothers, City detectives; *The Detective's Note Book* (1860); and *The Diary of an Ex-detective* (1860), these last two being by "Charles Martel," whose real name was Thomas Delf.

that it must co-operate with the uniformed branch, and must show due respect to senior officers. A memorandum by Mayne of the same date reveals the names of the offenders whose conduct provoked this order. He wrote that he had pointed out to Sergeants Whicher and Smith, in the presence of Inspector Shackell, the great impropriety of any of the detective force showing want of respect to their senior officers with whom they came in contact. The conduct of the two sergeants on this occasion had been "most indiscreet and legally unjustifiable." As it was the first instance "in which any of the Detective Force had improperly come into collision with the officers of a Division," Mayne added that he had limited his action to admonition and caution for the future, but Inspector Shackell was to make known to all the Detective Section that any further offence of this kind would be severely dealt with.

Police Orders of the 11th of November, 1845, include a "Memorandum for Guidance of Police to be specially employed to observe all Burglars and other Felons throughout the Police District and to prevent the commission of any crime by them." This memorandum referred to a development of the detective organization which came into effect six months later, on the 11th of May, 1846. The duties and strength of the little detective force at Scotland Yard remained unchanged, but each superintendent of a division was instructed to select "two intelligent constables" to be employed on the above-mentioned duties—*i.e.*, as detectives—until further notice. These men were to move among the divisions, co-operating and exchanging information. Superintendent Pearce of F Division was for the time being to supervise and direct the whole body, and for the purpose of training its members was to arrange with Inspector Shackell for the loan of sergeants from Scotland Yard when their other duties permitted. Presumably these divisional detectives wore plain clothes, though a month after the Memorandum of the 11th of November Rowan was writing: "I have reiterated to the Superintendents that there shall be no particular men in the Divisions called Plain Clothes Men, and that no man shall disguise himself without particular orders from the Superintendent, and that this should not be done even by them without some very strong case of necessity being made out."

Among the growing stream of Orders affecting the whole force one other should perhaps be mentioned. On the 5th of February, 1846, it was directed that whistles should be substituted for the familiar rattles. The rattles, however, were to return.

The 29th of June, 1846, which was marked by the brutal murder of

P.C. Clarke at Dagenham, a crime which remained unsolved, saw the resignation of the Peel Ministry, in consequence of the Government's defeat four days earlier on the second reading of the Irish Coercion Bill. In Lord John Russell's new administration the Home Secretary was Sir George Grey. The change had barely taken place when a tremendous storm of rain, hail, and thunder broke 7000 panes of glass in the new Houses of Parliament, and 300 at Scotland Yard. Other storms were affecting the police throughout these years, the Chartist demonstrations and riots increasing in gravity until in the revolutionary year 1848 the annual augmentation of the force by about 100 leapt up by special recruitment to 600. A total of 150,000 special constables had been enrolled, and, in preparation for the pitched battle with the Chartists expected on the 10th of April, the Duke of Wellington, in his eightieth year, took command of the military and police in the Metropolis. There was no conflict, but two months later all the superintendents of the Metropolitan Police were at Scotland Yard, receiving instructions for the next day, June the 12th, when another immense demonstration was feared. So great was the alarm that public buildings in London were garrisoned, and the Houses of Parliament were provisioned for a siege. The background of revolution all over Europe made the Chartist agitation appear to Londoners in lurid colours out of all proportion to its real strength and character in the Metropolis; and, the great demonstration proving a dismal fiasco—"there was nothing," said *The Times*, "that could be called an assemblage, except by the merest courtesy"—these elaborate precautions must have seemed a little silly. Even the Detective Office was involved in its specialized capacity, and Inspector Haynes and Sergeant Thornton were sent as far afield as Halifax, to keep an eye on the Chartists drilling in the North.

The first half of the century was running out, and the Detective Branch was eight years old, before it was engaged on its first big case. On the 10th or 11th of August, 1849, the Bermondsey police were notified that a Custom House officer, a gauger named Patrick O'Connor, had been missing from his lodgings since the 9th. He was a man of considerable property for his position in life, and had no known reason to disappear, but the prompt action of the police suggests that suspicious circumstances had been brought to their notice. They went at once to the house of a couple named Manning, who lived in Miniver Place, Bermondsey. Mrs Manning, in particular, was a close friend of O'Connor. At a first rather cursory search of the house no trace of him was found; but immediately after, on the 12th, the Mannings themselves disappeared. By now, it would seem, the Detective Office had been called in, and Inspectors Haynes and Field, with Thornton, Whicher, and others, were on the case. A more thorough search was made of the house in Miniver Place, and O'Connor's body, tied up and covered with quicklime, was found buried in the back kitchen. Mrs Manning, it was learnt, had been at his rooms the day after he vanished, and had taken away railway scrip and money.

Within a few days, as Mrs Smith, she was trying to sell the scrip to a stockbroker in Edinburgh. It had been advertised, and on the 20th she was arrested. Eight days later her husband was found in Jersey. They were a singularly unpleasant pair, and each accused the other, Manning's story being that his wife, having asked O'Connor to dinner and sent him downstairs to wash, gripped him round the throat with one hand and shot him with the other. This may have been the truth, but any vestige of sympathy for Manning must have been dispelled by a remark which deserves a place in an anthology of callous sayings. "He moaned; I never liked him well, and I battered his head with a ripping-chisel." Ripping-chisels, since the Ratcliffe Highway murders, had perhaps become popular weapons.

Tried and convicted at the Old Bailey in October, the pair were hanged in front of Horsemonger Lane Gaol on the 13th of the following month, Mrs Manning wearing black satin and a long lace veil. In a letter to *The Times* Dickens wrote of "the wickedness and levity of the immense crowd collected at the execution." "Cries and howls" at midnight "came from a concourse of boys and girls already assembled in the best places." Such spectacles were a commonplace in the England of the Great Exhibition, and another twenty years were to pass before executions in public were abolished.

At a very early stage of this case Inspector Haynes was promoted to superintendent, and appointed to his old division (P), which included Bermondsey, where the crime had taken place. He thus remained in control of the investigation, working no doubt in close co-operation with his old colleagues of the Detective Office. In a letter to the Home Secretary,[1] recommending for special notice Haynes, Inspector Field, Sergeants Whicher, Thornton, and eight others, with one constable, the Commissioners spoke of their "extraordinary exertions and skill in bringing to justice F. G. Manning and Maria Manning." All were granted awards of money—Haynes and Field £15 each, the sergeants £8, and P.C. Locker £5.

[1] December 14, 1849.

12

"KING" MAYNE

By 1850 the original 3000 men of the Metropolitan Police had grown in twenty-one years to a force of some 5500. In the meantime, in 1840, the police district had been enlarged sixfold, and its population had risen from a million and a half to nearly two millions and a half. There were still seventeen police divisions, a number soon to be increased, one of the new divisions being originally formed for a special and temporary purpose—the Great Exhibition of 1851.

The year 1850 was only a few days old when the partnership which had carried the force through the first two difficult decades of its existence came to an end. Rowan, who had been knighted, retired, to die at his house in Norfolk Street, Park Lane, rather more than two years later. The long continuance of Mayne's Commissionership, and the feelings aroused by the autocratic behaviour attributed to him, have caused his original colleague's admirable services to be almost forgotten. Yet it was Rowan who was most heard of during those first twenty years; he was the senior in age and experience, and the outward and visible tokens of the force's growing efficiency were largely due to him. Due largely to him, too, to his equable temper and kindliness, must have been the almost unexampled success of the risky experiment of placing two men together, with equal and very considerable powers, at the summit of the new organization. Mayne, as events were to show, was a man of decided opinions, and full of self-confidence, and that for so long he allowed himself to be to some extent overshadowed, at least in the public mind, by his fellow Commissioner is perhaps the most striking evidence of Rowan's qualities, and, in especial, of his gift for friendship.

There was a rumour,[1] surprising in view of the attitude of the City to the Metropolitan force, that he was to be succeeded by the Commissioner of the City Police, the rather eccentric Daniel Whittle Harvey, but the new joint head at Scotland Yard was Captain Hay, who had completed ten years as Inspecting or Visiting Superintendent. Hay was thought to have done well during the Chartist alarms, and

[1] *Illustrated London News*, November 17, 1849.

RUFFIANLY POLICEMAN ABOUT TO PERPETRATE A BRUTAL AND DASTARDLY ASSAULT ON THE PEOPLE

Punch on the Hyde Park Riot in 1866.

Reproduced by permission of "Punch"

[*See p.* 146.]

BOW STREET, 1851

Showing the Police Station (with Royal Arms) in its old site on the same side as the Opera House.

BOW STREET, 1879

On its present site, showing horsed Black Maria.

"The Illustrated London News"

he may have seemed the obvious choice for the post. But he was not the man to work well with Mayne, nor, perhaps, was Mayne the man to work well with anyone except Rowan. By denominating Hay Second Commissioner the Home Office intended him to be subordinate to Mayne, but to what precise degree was not defined. Mayne seems to have been annoyed because he was not left sole Commissioner. Other reasons apart, he must have felt that such a combination as that of himself and Rowan was exceptional. Hay was succeeded as Inspecting Superintendent by Captain (afterwards Lieutenant-Colonel) D. W. P. Labalmondière.

As the first year of the new régime drew to a close the Commissioners began to be exercised by police problems arising out of the Great Exhibition. Traffic control must have been relatively simple, but vast crowds, for that time, were expected. The figure of half a million visitors to London is mentioned as a possibility. The failure of revolution abroad had filled the capital with political refugees, and there would be an influx of foreign criminals unknown to the police. Towards the end of 1850 the Home Office was being asked to sanction a large augmentation of the force. The Commissioners, stressing their immense responsibilities, would have liked another 1400 men: they felt compelled to ask for a thousand. This increase was granted, the whole being allocated to various duties in connexion with the Exhibition, as follows:

Interior:	3 inspctrs.	10 sgts.	200 p.c.'s
Entrances and Approaches:	6 "	21 "	300 "
Divisions (Special Duties):	4 "	20 "	430 "
Receiver:	4 "	20 "	100 "
	17 "	71 "	1030 "

Superintendent Pearce was in charge of the temporary division thus formed, and responsible for all arrangements, and at the end of the year Mayne is found thanking him for the excellence of these and informing him that the Royal Commissioners of the Exhibition had granted him a sum of money. The whole proceeding, however, seems to have given offence to Hay, whose relations with Mayne were already deteriorating, and who appears to have thought that his own services in regard to the Exhibition had been ignored; and a little later (11th of February, 1852) Mayne was writing a very stiff letter to his fellow Commissioner, expressing astonishment at his conduct and referring to "the evils of the present system." Further trouble between the pair was soon to follow.

On the 14th of September, 1852, the Duke of Wellington died at Walmer Castle. The police arrangements for his lying-in-state, two months later, broke down so badly that the immense crowd got out of control, and two or three people were crushed to death. Without informing Mayne, still less consulting him, Hay caused a paragraph to be printed in the *Globe* contradicting statements that he was responsible for the ineffective police measures. Mayne, while accepting full responsibility, wrote angrily that such action as Hay had taken "must destroy that good understanding and cordial co-operation between the Commissioners which is absolutely essential in carrying on the police service." Hay apologized, but a year later was offending in rather the same way, sending proposals for a revision of police duties to the Home Office in a letter marked "private," which he refused to show to Mayne. From these proceedings it seems clear that Hay was trying to take advantage of the failure to define his subordinate position. The situation between the Commissioners now became very strained, until, early in 1855, Hay fell ill. He died in August that year, and, the Home Office having taken the lesson to heart, the experiment of having two Commissioners with equal, or almost equal, powers was not repeated. Instead, by a Metropolitan Police Act passed in the following year, the force was placed under a single Commissioner. Two Assistant Commissioners were appointed—Labalmondière, who seems to have acted in this capacity after Hay's death, and Captain W. C. Harris.

2

For thirteen years more Mayne reigned alone. He too had taken the lesson to heart. It was inevitable that a strong-willed man, who in partnership or single-handed controlled for nearly forty years a new and increasingly powerful force, should become very much the autocrat, if on the whole a benevolent one. He seems to have resented the fact that he was not made sole Commissioner immediately after Hay's death, but had to wait several months for his position to be regularized by the Act of 1856. At any rate, after his experience of Hay he was determined to delegate as little as possible. He had two capable assistants—particularly in Labalmondière—but everything must go through his hands. So long as he retained his remarkable energy and grasp this system might work; once his capabilities began to fail it led to trouble and dissatisfaction, and the end of a long life of achievement was cloudy and unhappy.

These thirteen years saw the force developing in some ways, but remaining almost stationary in others. It had begun as a relatively simple organization. "Division of police administration into departments began in 1842 with the formation of the detective branch."[1] Between 1856 and 1869 this decentralizing process continued with the creation of an executive department, others to deal with dangerous structures and police buildings, and, most widespread of all in its effects, the Public Carriage Department. This branch was not entirely new. By the London Hackney Carriage Act of 1843 the Police Commissioners were given authority to allot cab-ranks, and, another Act in 1850 having transferred to them the duties of the Registrars of Metropolitan Public Carriages, a small Public Carriage Branch was formed at Scotland Yard three years later. But by the Public Carriage Act of 1869 the Home Secretary, the licensing authority, delegated all his powers to the Commissioner, who has ever since controlled, down to the smallest detail, a road traffic which has multiplied in volume and changed in character to a degree undreamed of by Mayne and his immediate successors, becoming, in fact, one of the major problems of the Metropolitan Police.

The first predecessor of the present Assistant Commissioner "B" was a Colonel Paschal, who was appointed to the infant branch in 1853, apparently on a temporary basis to organize it and get it under way. His appointment was made permanent in 1857; but though by then he had a staff of 200, he and his work cut so small a figure in police history of the time that little or nothing is known about him. In 1867 Mayne was trying to get rid of him, though he liked him personally. There was great slackness in the department, and Paschal failed to examine the accounts he signed. He was suspended, but five months later, by order of Gathorne-Hardy, the Home Secretary, he was restored to his duties. This incident is of interest only because it was one of the troubles connected with the Carriage Department which were to have an unhappy influence on the closing years of Mayne's career. After the comprehensive Act of 1869 the branch was put in the charge of one of the Assistant Commissioners.

During this period three Metropolitan divisions were added to the original seventeen—W (Clapham), X (Paddington), and Y (Highgate). X was the division temporarily created for the Great Exhibition; it was made permanent in February 1862. It has been seen that in 1841 the force took over the naval dockyards at Deptford and Woolwich from the dockyard police; now, in 1860, under considerable pressure from the Admiralty and the Horse Guards, Mayne reluctantly agreed

[1] Sir John Moylan, *Scotland Yard and the Metropolitan Police* (Putnam, 1929).

to police all the principal naval dockyards in the country, together with the War Office establishments at Portsmouth, Devonport, and Chatham. For this purpose five small dockyard divisions were formed. In some cases their powers were at first extended beyond the limits of the dockyards, and there was occasional trouble with the local police; but this matter was regulated, and the arrangement was to continue for nearly seventy years.

An innovation which aroused indignation in some quarters, and mirth in others, was the replacement of the tall hat by a helmet, similar in essentials to that worn to-day. On the one hand, the old cry of militarism was absurdly raised; on the other, papers like *Punch* and *Fun* found the subject excessively amusing. The introduction of police bands a few years earlier had also been thought highly comical, and constables with guitars were shown serenading cooks. The novelty of a police force having worn off, such jokes and criticisms might seem somewhat *vieux jeu*, but they were to go on for a long time. Something will be said of this later.

More important than helmets and bands was the adoption for police purposes of the new electric telegraph. It was not so new that use could not have been made of it earlier than was the case;[1] expense, perhaps, stood in the way. Only on the 30th of December, 1867, eighteen months after the Atlantic cable was finally completed, was Mayne able to write: "I have a telegraph to every police station."

In 1855 the Emperor of the French and the Empress Eugénie paid a State visit to London. In the absence of any written record, the 19th of April in that year may be suggested as a possible date of an incident of minor historic interest to the police of London, for on that evening the Queen and the Prince Consort escorted the Emperor and Empress to a State performance of Beethoven's opera *Fidelio* at the Covent Garden Theatre. All that is known is that on some similar occasion between the opening of the theatre for Italian opera in 1847 and the death of the Prince Consort in 1861 Queen Victoria took exception to the blue lamp over the door of Bow Street Police Station, immediately opposite what was to become the Royal Opera House. She ordered the lamp to be removed, and removed it was. Bow Street was until very recently the only police station in the Metropolis without a blue lamp, and was rather proud of the fact. It now shares the distinction with Northwood, which was deprived of its lamp in 1947 for mysterious æsthetic reasons connected with the Town and Country Planning Act.

[1] In 1845 a murderer had been apprehended by the use of the telegraph.

3

Taking, as he did, far too much into his own hands, it is not surprising that Mayne, as he grew older, ignored or deferred certain serious problems that now demanded solution. Everything was growing and changing, including, in some respects, the Metropolitan Police itself; but in organization and methods it stood still. To take only two instances, there was the Detective Branch, and there was the question of pay.

Pay, though from time to time it had been increased, was by the 1860's lagging behind the rise of industrial wages, and was even, to quote Sir John Moylan, "below the rates of pay of some other forces." The pension conditions were also rightly considered unsatisfactory. Complaints about the long hours of duty were only another aspect of this question of money. As a result, the early rush of those anxious to join the force had died away, and too few men of the right physique and character were now coming forward. The strength of the force by the end of 1868 was less than double what it had been in 1840, though by the latter year the area of the Metropolitan Police District had been multiplied by six and a half, and now had a population approaching three millions and a half. The situation was put very clearly in a pamphlet[1] published in 1868, possibly with the connivance of some senior police officers.

At the end of 1867, wrote the pseudonymous author, the numbers of the force stood at 7840;

> but inasmuch as this number included about 1200 men who were employed in the Government Dock-yards, at Military Stations, and for other special purposes, and are, moreover, not chargeable on the Metropolitan rates, the number of men under the orders of the Heads of the Metropolitan Police Force for ordinary Metropolitan duty was 6640. During the present year, 1868, a further increase of 1120 men—equivalent to, exactly, one-seventh of the whole—has been authorised by the Secretary of State; but as this augmentation has been made chiefly, if not entirely, for the purpose of allowing every man on the Establishment to obtain one day of rest in the week, the number available, on any one day, for the ordinary duties of the Force, is not greater than it was prior to the date of the Secretary of State's order.

"Custos" goes on to point out that deductions on account of sickness, and clerical, station-house, and other duties, left no more than 6000 men, in round numbers, available for street duty, a proportion of

[1] *The Police Force of the Metropolis in 1868*, by Custos.

1 to about 566 inhabitants of the police district. As the constable's turn of duty, except in times of pressing emergency, was eight hours and a half in the twenty-four, the actual number doing duty at any one moment was little more than 2000. "The dangers of the night being considered to be greater than those of the day," duties were, in fact, so arranged by a system of day reliefs that this total was doubled between the hours of 10 P.M. and 6 A.M.

The augmentation of 1120 referred to was sanctioned on the 6th of February, 1868. Between this date and the 29th of July, when a Police Order apportioned the recruits among the divisions, two new police stations were established (at Enfield and Streatham)—an instance of the way in which development of clerical and station duties alone went hand in hand with any increase in the numbers of the force. Much more serious was the annual wastage. To quote "Custos" again (though these figures cannot be checked):

> The extent to which this evil exists will be understood, when it is stated, that in the course of twelve years, from 1856 to 1867, both inclusive, the annual average of casualties from resignations and other causes, but principally from resignations, in a Force averaging 6800 men, amounted to 1069—figures which accurately represent the number of men who, during the whole of that period, could have been practically but of little use.

The writer points out that many men joined the police because they were out of work through seasonal fluctuations of trade; as soon as this improved, and they could get a better job, they resigned, as a constable could then do by giving a month's notice. One way or another, at any rate, wastage was very largely due to the inadequate pay of the force.

Mayne, of course, was well aware of this grievance, and from time to time is found pressing the Home Office for an increase. Perhaps he did not press hard enough, for nothing was done until 1867, when the then Home Secretary, Spencer Walpole, sanctioned enhanced rates of pay which, as they affected the great mass of the force, were not over-generous. While third- and fourth-class constables got no increase at all, an extra two shillings and one shilling a week to first- and second-class men respectively raised their pay only to 25*s*. and 23*s*. That of second-class sergeants went up by two shillings to £1 8*s*. On the other hand, rises of £50 a year for superintendents, and one of £100 for the chief superintendent (A), brought these officers' salaries to £300 and £425 per annum. Constables, it will be seen, did not greatly benefit, and the sergeants' pay, to quote Mayne's successor, was still "obviously and confessedly too low." Further slight increases were to come into force as a result of the report of the Departmental Committee which deliberated in 1868, Mayne's last year; but they were too slight, and they came too late, to avert trouble.

The Departmental Committee said of the detective force that it was very efficient, but in numbers wholly inadequate. This understatement was an implied criticism of Mayne, who seems never to have appreciated fully the importance of enlarging and in other ways developing this branch. Yet he had had a lesson in events which had done nothing to render more popular the ordinary policeman's lot.

Since the Penal Servitude Act of 1853 transportation of criminals overseas had gradually ceased. It came to an end ten years later. The released convict, thrown again upon the world, generally relapsed into his old ways, and was often the more dangerous because embittered. There were soon thousands of this type in London. One result was the outbreak in the capital in 1862 of a form of violent crime novel in this country—garotting.

Victims who looked well-to-do were half throttled from behind, and perhaps stunned as well. These attacks were soon taking place in daylight, and in the centre of London. A Member of Parliament was felled and robbed in Pall Mall. Concentrations of police in the areas most affected resulting in a number of arrests, the accused were almost always found to be old offenders, some of them with many convictions. Very heavy sentences, up to penal servitude for twenty years and even for life, and methods of publicity adopted by judges and police, eradicated the evil in its wholesale and organized phase, though there was to be a recrudescence of garotting in the Borough thirty years later.

The public, angry and alarmed—for weeks many people were afraid to go out after dark—inevitably blamed the police. The fault lay not with the men, who were too few, but at the top; and even more with the Home Office. The ticket-of-leave system, a product of the Act of 1853, was intended to ensure supervision of convicts released on licence before their sentences expired, but the Home Office issued instructions that the police were on no account to question or interfere with these men, who, of course,

> almost invariably destroyed their licenses (which they were not compelled to keep), and if apprehended for a fresh offence, or on suspicion, stoutly denied that they had previously been convicted: nor was it easy for the authorities to prove the contrary in the absence of any proper system for the registration of convicts.[1]

[1] Melville Lee, *op. cit.*

As for Mayne, it is not surprising if he was disgusted by this ill-directed humanitarianism; but he carried his disgust too far when he washed his hands of the whole affair. It is astonishing to hear him telling the Select Committee on Transportation in 1856 that until a few months before he had never seen a ticket-of-leave, and did not know what was endorsed upon it. "It was no business of mine," he said.

This, as he seemed to realize, was a strange saying. The non-enforcement of the conditions under which these licences were issued was very much the business of the constable on the beat, who could take no action inconveniencing criminals who might be known to him unless he caught them actually committing a crime. Such a state of things did not encourage initiative.

There was indeed a detective force, created to deal with crimes which, on the whole, seldom came the way of the constable on the beat. But at the time of the garotting scare it still numbered less than a dozen. Presently there was a considerable increase in the number of divisional detectives,[1] but the Detective Branch itself, which Mayne kept under his own hand at Scotland Yard, had at the time of his death only crept up to a strength of fifteen men.

4

The general history of the force during this period, and such outside events as directly or indirectly affected it, must—with the exception of certain occurrences—be summarized briefly.

The year 1850, that of Rowan's retirement, saw the death of its founder. Peel was thrown from his horse on Constitution Hill, and died three days later, on July the 2nd.

By this time the agitation in Australia against the transportation of criminals was coming to a head, and the whole question of the treatment of convicts was being widely discussed, in particular conditions in the overcrowded hulks lying in the Thames and at other ports. It is difficult to-day to realize that only a hundred years ago this medieval system was in existence. It was only in 1850 that the first convict prison was opened, the great war prison on Dartmoor, which had been lying derelict, being adapted to receive the inmates of the hulks.

The year 1855, which saw the first pillar-boxes in London, was marked by two notable events in police history: the Sunday Trading

[1] Police Orders, 14.8.62. Police to be specially employed in plain clothes in the divisions for the prevention of robberies, etc.—17 sergts., 176 p.c.'s.

Riots and the arrest of Dr Palmer of Rugeley for the murder of John Parsons Cook. The demonstration in Hyde Park on Sunday, July the 1st, against Lord Robert Grosvenor's Bill to prevent Sunday trading, has been described as "in the nature of a comic relief to the anxieties of the Crimean War."[1] If it was taken too seriously at the time the Home Office order prohibiting a "meeting or assemblage in large numbers" perhaps helped to turn what might have been a noisy but harmless gathering of the "Leave-us-Alone Club" of street traders and the like into an invasion of the Park by thousands of roughs less interested in the pros and cons of Sunday observance than in annoying well-dressed people and baiting the police. The latter, grouped about the Park beforehand, took no action until the mob began to throw missiles at carriages driving by the Serpentine; then there were charges, and truncheons were used. Some seventy persons were arrested. As forty-nine policeman were injured, it is difficult to believe the newspaper reporter who declared that "everybody was as quiet as possible." The affair, however, had been mismanaged, and a Royal Commission appointed to investigate complaints, while finding ample testimony to "the moderation and forbearance" of the great majority of the police, found that "excesses were shown to have been committed by some." As usual, little was said of excesses by the crowd, which was estimated at 40,000. The number of police in the Park, or held in reserve, was 450. Also as usual, scapegoats had to be found, and after the inquiry several constables were dismissed.

In the following year the launching of the London General Omnibus Company was of interest to the new Public Carriage Branch. Only a few antiquarians can have regretted the demolishing, at Jarrow, of the last gibbet in England. Acts passed in 1835 and 1839 had brought into being paid borough and county constabularies; maintenance of such forces by the counties, however, only became compulsory in 1856, by an Act which also created a Home Office Inspector of Constabulary to enforce a uniform standard of efficiency, based on that of the Metropolitan Police, throughout the country. Though the Home Secretary's approval is required for certain appointments, he is not the police authority for the county and borough forces, as he is for the Metropolitan Police; county constabularies are administered by Standing Joint Committees of the County Council and Quarter Sessions, and borough constabularies (since 1835) by Watch Committees.[2]

It is unlikely that the detective force at Scotland Yard heard of an experiment of great forensic importance made in India at this time.

[1] Moylan, *op. cit.*

[2] Troup, *op. cit.*

Several hundred years ago the Chinese, whose soldiers in the nineteenth century still carried umbrellas, employed fingerprints for purposes of personal identification. While Mayne was drafting an order forbidding the use of umbrellas by police on duty in uniform, Sir William Herschel, in Bengal, had started his fingerprint registration of Government pensioners and contractors. In connexion with later developments of this science, as it has become, various claims have been put forward which may be disregarded, because they produced no practical results; not only was Herschel indisputably the originator of modern dactyloscopy, but his personal influence may be traced forward to the present day, for towards the end of the century there followed him in Bengal an Inspector-General of Police named Edward Henry.

Critics of the police always ready to believe that the force was being militarized may have read a sinister interpretation into the order forbidding umbrellas, and in the same year, 1859, they learnt with dismay that constables were being drilled in Regent's Park, at the Foundling Hospital, and, worst of all, at Wellington Barracks, "by experienced sergeants now serving in the police-office." *The United Service Gazette*, on the other hand, thought this "a very proper proceeding. It gives additional security to London, and may ultimately enable the inhabitants to dispense with the presence of guardsmen, who seem not to know how to conduct themselves."[1] By implication this was a high compliment to the general behaviour of the police. In April this year the detective force was earning praise from Holland for the recovery from the hands of thieves in London of a picture by Vanderwerff, valued at £2000, which had been stolen from the Picture Gallery at Amsterdam.

In 1860 occurred the Road murder, which, with the Rugeley poisoning cases and the first train murder, will be considered separately. The last execution for attempted murder took place in the following year, when the practice of handing over murderers' bodies for dissection was also definitely abolished, and the police, having lost their umbrellas (though about to gain helmets), had a part of their summer uniforms, the white duck trousers, taken away from them. Their superannuation fund, being found insolvent, was put on a new footing in 1862, but the revision of pensions and retiring allowances[2] did not give satisfaction, and was to lead to trouble later.

The City Police, having failed to keep order during Princess Beatrice's visit to the City in 1863, survived another threat of

[1] *Daily Telegraph*, 5.3. and 28.5.59.

[2] Police Orders, 23.9.62. For instance, on completion of fifteen years' service 15/50ths of pay (instead of 15/30ths), and increase by 1/50th for each successive year up to thirty.

absorption in the Metropolitan Police.[1] Alterations in the uniform of the latter continued: Wellington boots, never in general use, went in 1864, and in 1866 the swallow-tail coat was replaced by a tunic. In March of the former year died Mr Charles Yardley, a veteran of Waterloo, who as Chief Clerk at Scotland Yard had been Mayne's right-hand man for thirty-four years.

The closing years of Mayne's own career were now to be embittered by a series of events which brought obloquy, often most unfair, on the police force and on himself. The first of these troubles followed a change of Government in June 1866. Lord John Russell's short-lived second administration was ended by a defeat in the committee stage of a Bill for extending the franchise. The Bill satisfied nobody, least of all the radical Reformers; the Reform League held meetings in Trafalgar Square and elsewhere, and the new Conservative Cabinet was barely in office when Spencer Walpole, Home Secretary for the third time, was faced by the threat of a huge political demonstration in Hyde Park. It was decided to prohibit it, and Mayne posted notices all over London to this effect.

The proposed demonstration was a threat in the sense that it fell in a different category from the protest of street traders and the like in 1855. The Reform League organizers were responsible persons, including Members of Parliament, and their action had the blessing of John Bright, and later of John Stuart Mill. They must have known perfectly well what would happen if they persisted in marching with bands and banners to the Park; however orderly the procession itself, it would be accompanied by a huge rabble delighting in the opportunity of making mischief. The expected did happen. The procession was turned back by the police at the Park gates. While, however, it retraced its steps peaceably to Trafalgar Square, the rabble remained. Stones had already been thrown at the police; the Park railings were now pulled down in Park Lane and Bayswater Road, and the mob streamed through. The police present, though numbering some 3000, were insufficient to control what had now become a riot, and Foot and Life Guards were summoned—the first use of the military on such an occasion since the force had been formed. Late in the evening the Park was cleared. Mayne himself, on his horse, was there throughout, giving orders in the thick of the affray, blood running down his face from a wound caused by a stone. Scores of police were injured, some being disabled for life.

[1] Mayne to Delane of *The Times*, 9.6.63: "I had an opportunity, if I had pleased, to commit a *coup d'état* and carry off the Lord Mayor and aldermen."

As in 1855, the police arrangements seem to have been defective. But in prohibiting the meeting, for which he was arraigned as if he were some irresponsible tyrant, Mayne was merely acting, as before, on the authority of the Home Secretary, who had previously defended the ban in the House of Commons. After the event Walpole took a different attitude; receiving a deputation from the Reform League, he was "much affected," and practically apologized for the action he had taken. He might more properly have been affected by the thought of the aged Commissioner, wounded, shaken, and humiliated because he had tried to carry out the duty for which he had been appointed.

It had already been forgotten, as it has so often been forgotten since, that the Metropolitan Police was primarily created to maintain order. What enabled Peel to push his Bill through Parliament was not anxiety about traffic control, or supervision of dangerous structures, or petty robberies, but recent memories of riot after riot, of London mob-ridden and in flames, of daily crimes of violence committed with impunity.[1] If this essential responsibility must always be in the mind of every Commissioner, it was a very present care during the first fifty years of the force's existence, when Londoners repeatedly showed that they had not lost their turbulent habits. This responsibility, however—and the fact being so often overlooked at this time must again be emphasized—is subject to the Commissioner "obtaining the approval of the Home Secretary to all his standing regulations, and to all important matters affecting the public." It is the Home Secretary who is the final "Police Authority."

But above the Home Secretary, again, is the House of Commons. "I am the servant of the House," said Sir William Joynson-Hicks in the debate on the Savidge case in 1928, "and every action I take, every decision I come to in regard to the police, can be brought up and discussed here." Of this ultimate controlling power Sir John Moylan remarks that it has the defects of its virtues: "Like any large assembly, it may be swayed by emotion." In the nature of things, the emotion is often political, and views of police action are likely to be coloured by party prejudice. In July 1866, for example, two quite different aspects of the case preoccupied the Commissioner and the politicians. Three days before the trouble in Hyde Park John Bright was writing to the Council of the Reform League about the right of "millions of intelligent and honest men" to meet in a royal park or anywhere else. This

[1] "The prime necessity a hundred years ago was the introduction of unity, order and efficiency into the confusion and helplessness of the numerous petty police jurisdictions in the Metropolitan area."—MOYLAN, *op. cit.*

was no concern of Mayne's; his duty was to protect ordinary citizens, and public and private property, against the less intelligent and honest, who, as he knew, would come in their thousands armed with sticks and brickbats. The disorders he foresaw have their importance in police history because they were the first on a large scale, since the creation of the force, which had purely political origins. An unfortunate if inevitable precedent was set up, and on similar occasions in the future criticism of the police was in the main to follow party lines.

The legal aspect of the prohibition order was thrashed out in the House of Commons and in the Press. A Royal Parks Bill, introduced by Walpole's successor at the Home Office, Gathorne-Hardy, was withdrawn. The outcry had at least the effect of drawing attention to the lack of proper control in normal times in Hyde Park and Green Park, where people were constantly being molested, and in the following year the police took over from the keepers of these Parks the dubious duty of keeping order.[1] The Park gates, which up to that time had been closed at ten o'clock, have since remained open until midnight.

It was in this year, 1867, that politics of another kind involved Mayne in fresh trouble. There were Fenian disturbances in Chester, where an attack was made on the castle, and in Manchester, where a police sergeant was shot dead while resisting an attempt to rescue two of the conspirators. Some months earlier Inspector Williamson, of the Detective Branch, had been sent by Mayne to Liverpool to investigate Fenian activities; and in March 1867 the latter was writing of "many rumours here of impending outbreaks, but nothing definite." In London another officer of the Detective Branch, Inspector Thompson, arrested two Fenians named Burke and Casey, for which Mayne promoted him to the rank of superintendent. Burke and Casey were committed to Clerkenwell Prison, and in December Mayne received an anonymous letter giving particulars of a plot to rescue them. There were other warnings, which were passed on to the governor of the prison, but no special precautions seem to have been taken by the police. On the 12th of the month a constable in Corporation Row, which was bounded by the prison wall, actually witnessed an attempt to blow down the wall; the fuse was damp, and the parcel of gunpowder failed to explode. The constable was so little interested that he allowed the conspirators to return and remove the package. The next day they tried again, with a cask of gunpowder on a barrow, and were more successful. It was a quarter to four in the afternoon, the hour when prisoners were usually exercised on the other side of the

[1] The first police station in Hyde Park was established in the barracks of the Magazine.

wall; the explosion blew down a length of this, and tore away the fronts of the houses and shops in Corporation Row; four people were killed, and forty injured, among these being many children playing in the street. The outrage was as futile as it was wicked, for Burke and Casey, with the other prisoners, were being exercised in an inner yard. Police, though apparently only one or two, were patrolling the wall, and three of the criminals, one of them a woman, were captured. A fourth, Michael Barrett, who fired the powder, was afterwards caught in Glasgow. His execution on the 26th of May, 1868, was the last public hanging in England.

The Clerkenwell explosion caused something like a panic. Fifty thousand special constables were enrolled, and Parliament authorized an increase in the Metropolitan Police. The natural fear of further outrages to come would have been aggravated had the public known of a tithe of the anonymous letters and other warnings that reached Scotland Yard during the weeks about Christmas and the New Year. There were plots to blow up the Crystal Palace and the ironworks at Erith, to cut the Atlantic cable, to put the street water-plugs out of action by filling them with strong cement, to place bombs in the water-mains themselves. Two men had gone to the Isle of Wight to damage Osborne, where one of the gardeners should be watched. An illiterate letter threatened the Queen. Sinister inquiries were being made about the magazines, and a memorandum from the Horse Guards informed the Commissioner that the Commander-in-Chief (the Duke of Cambridge) was seriously perturbed by rumours of attempts to seize the arms at the Tower and at Woolwich Arsenal. Numerous vague reports came in of suspicious gatherings and hidden gunpowder and weapons; a clergyman's daughter of sixteen, who had been at the British Museum, overheard talk in a coffee-shop in Museum Street. "I know a jolly Fenian," the proprietor had said, "who supplies money to buy powder." Much treasonable matter was bandied about in public houses, and "A Publican's Daughter" learnt "that a quantity of Gunpowder and Greek Fire are on board a Barge now lying in the river; and that Incendiarism, Explosions and Assassinations are in contemplation." While dreadful happenings were prophesied for Christmas Day, a nervous public, happily unaware of all this, was suffering from practical jokers who set off home-made fireworks in gardens and backyards.

Every rumour and anonymous letter had to be followed up. The Museum Street coffee-shop turned out to be above suspicion; there was no gunpowder or Greek fire on any barge in the Thames. Th

Commander-in-Chief was reassured, and a special eye was kept on water-plugs as well as on magazines. A curious episode of the time was the hunt for a man calling himself "Michael Justice," thought to be perhaps the same as "M.J.W.," who offered information if an advertisement, accepting his conditions, was published in the *Morning Star*. Mayne actually ordered such an advertisement to be inserted, but cancelled a repetition when "M.J.W.," like Oliver Twist, asked for more. There are tantalizing glimpses of another mysterious affair in a report, dated January 14, 1868, from Superintendent Durkin of Bow Street. An anonymous letter caused the superintendent to send officers to a house in Peckham, where the man who had fired the gunpowder barrel at Clerkenwell was alleged to be lodging. A lodger had left the house some weeks before; his description did not tally with what little was known of the wanted Fenian, but the landlady had her own reasons for wishing him found. Giving the name of R. J. Prytherch, and calling himself a secretary at an address in Buckingham Street, off the Strand, he had offered to be responsible for the first quarter's rent of the Peckham house in return for a room there. He had left without paying anything. At Buckingham Street it was found that chambers had been sublet early in 1867 to Prytherch, who on his first visit gave the name of James. He was then accompanied by a clergyman, a Mr Sharp. Afterwards "James" himself became the Rev. S. Brereton, and appeared to be conducting the affairs of "The Clergy Assurance Aid Society." According to a printed prospectus, enclosed with the superintendent's report, this body was "under episcopal sanction," and had a treasurer, trustees, and three banks; the Rev. S. Brereton was the Organizing Secretary, and was to be found at the Buckingham Street office. He was not found there, however, by the police; having paid no rent for six months, in October he disappeared, and his goods had been seized. Nothing more seems to have been heard of him. He was probably a common swindler, for neither the Rev. S. Brereton nor the Clergy Aid Assurance Society can be traced.

It was known that there had been repeated warnings before the Clerkenwell outrage, and there was much criticism of the laxity, from the Commissioner's Office downward, which had more or less ignored them. Mayne admitted that he had been gravely at fault, and tendered his resignation. Walpole did the right thing in refusing to accept it; "We told Mayne," the Under-Secretary is reported to have said, "that he had made a damned fool of himself, but that we weren't going to throw him over after his long public service."

Mayne was now seventy-one, and had been Commissioner for six years beyond the maximum retiring age in the Civil Service. Overworked and disillusioned, and haunted, as a man with his strong sense of responsibility must have been, by the thought of deaths and injuries which foresight might and should have prevented, for the remaining months of his life he was again to be the victim of constant attacks in the newspapers, most of them unmerited and some disgraceful. His energies, however, were still vigorous, and his eye, where petty detail was concerned, all-seeing; and at this very time he was beset by fresh anxieties which he had brewed for himself by his inquisition into the affairs of the Public Carriage Department.

His dissatisfaction with Colonel Paschal has been mentioned. The trouble came to a head in December 1866, when three inspectors of the department were dismissed, and the veterinary surgeon, Cherry, was suspended. In Police Orders Mayne accused the inspectors of making out accounts for payments founded on misrepresentations, and of charging for expenses not incurred, or, if incurred, unauthorized.[1] Later, the Commissioner allowed some of the items to which he had objected, but the inspectors were not reinstated. One of them, Jackson, brought an action for libel against Mayne, and throughout the rest of that year and the next, until his death, the latter was harassed by the long-drawn-out course of the proceedings. The action was heard in the Court of Common Pleas in the first days of December 1868; the judge held that the publication of the charges in Police Orders was a libel, but the jury could not agree upon a verdict. In this unsatisfactory state the case remained; for by the end of the month Mayne was dead.

There had been more demands for his resignation; he had just lost a beloved daughter; and there can be no doubt that the worry and humiliation of the libel action itself put the last unendurable strain upon his declining health. It was a sad ending to a remarkable public career. Since Mayne died there have been a dozen Commissioners of the Metropolitan Police, whose years of service in that post, put together, amount to little more than double his own. With Rowan he raised the force which Peel had founded from a not too popular experiment to an essential institution. Later criticisms directed against it, though in general ill-informed and often malicious, tacitly recognized this fact, and were an unconscious tribute to the man who, above all others, was responsible for the achievement.

[1] Police Orders, 8.12.66. For Cherry's case: Police Orders, 13.3.67.

5

Leading London newspapers in the middle of the last century gave even more prominence to police matters than those of to-day; but, their readers being a relatively small and well-informed class, the emphasis was not on the sensational side of police work, but on discussion and criticism of the administration of the force, its relations with the public, and kindred topics. It was still a new force, and considered fair game for attack; the Press of those days, on the other hand, had not yet rid itself of old habits of intolerance, violence of language, and, in general, of a pontifical attitude which it was always ready to discern and rebuke in Home Secretaries and Commissioners. Numberless leading and other articles on the police are, almost without exception, carping and one-sided. The comic papers, *Punch*, *Judy*, and *Fun*, as a rule took the same tone.

No one reading the Press reports of the inquiry by a Royal Commission into the Hyde Park riots of 1855 would expect the Commission's finding to be that the great majority of the police behaved on that occasion with "moderation and forbearance." The *Illustrated Times*, while admitting that so little interest was taken in the inquiry that only twenty or thirty members of the public troubled to attend on the opening day, filled several columns with the testimony of persons who professed to have witnessed or experienced police brutality, and in a leading article summed up the day's proceedings as follows: "Witness after witness has come forward; violence after violence has been reported; the most shameful brutality has been narrated with the most harrowing details."[1] Rebutting evidence on behalf of the police then began to be heard, and of this the journal remarked artlessly in its next issue that as it was "of a negative character, we only make a few brief selections." Mayne himself having pointed out on the first day that in prohibiting the meeting in Hyde Park he was acting under instructions from the Home Secretary, and that the notice he drafted was approved by the Under-Secretary, so small was the attention paid to his words that the leading article referred to goes on to say: "We never yet quite understood how Mayne acquired the power of forbidding assemblages by his own act, or why he assumed the airs of a dictator."

Next to Mayne the villain of the piece was Inspector Hughes, who was variously described as white with rage, distorted with rage, and behaving like a madman. One witness said picturesquely that the

[1] *Illustrated Times*, July 28, 1855.

inspector was "on a pale horse—pale did he look and diabolical was his countenance." The Commission's Report, issued in November, censured Hughes, who in the meantime had become a superintendent, for want of judgment and forbearance, and no doubt some of his men lost their tempers. Innocent passers-by, as usually happens, became involved, and there were complaints of the treatment at Vine Street of persons taken into custody. It was a rough age, however, when a mob of 30,000 or 40,000 people, including "vagabonds and scoundrels of the lowest description,"[1] who had come on purpose to foment trouble, was not to be dispersed by adjurations. Men were seen to fill their pockets with stones, and it was only after volleys of these had struck the police that the latter began to retaliate in earnest.

Eleven years later the results of the Reform League's ill-advised challenge to the ban on its proposed meeting in Hyde Park were handled by the Press with rather more restraint; but while prominence was given to cases of injury among the vast crowd—"St George's Hospital," it was remarked, "was very favourably placed for the occasion"—again little or nothing was said of the casualties, some very serious, suffered by the police. A scandalous accusation against the latter was contained in the last verse of a parody in *Fun* of Macaulay's "Ivry":

> Hurrah! the force are moving! Hark to the mingled din
> Of fife, and steed, and tramp, and drum, and voices thick with gin!
> The fiery Chief is pricking fast across the dusty plain,
> With all the hireling chivalry of Harris and R. Mayne.

By this time the comic papers were seizing every opportunity to ridicule the police. *Punch*, always the least malicious, had the courage and good sense to stand up for the force after the Reform riots, a cartoon of August 11, 1866, showing a constable, wounded in the face, his helmet knocked off, confronting alone a mob of roughs brandishing sticks and throwing brickbats; the description reads: "Ruffianly policeman about to perpetrate a brutal and dastardly assault on the people." In general, however, when the police were not represented, to a tedious degree, as figures of fun, they were pilloried as a force for the errors and misdemeanours committed by a few.

A ridiculous outcry was raised in 1868 over what was called Mayne's "barbarous dog edict." There had been cases of hydrophobia from

[1] *Illustrated Times*, November 10, 1855. This journal's columnist, "The Lounger," took his own line, which did not always agree with the editorial view. "These Hyde Park riots," he writes under this date, "are getting beyond bearing, and it is high time that Government should interfere in a marked and stringent manner."

dog-bites, and the Commissioner issued a muzzling order. At once the newspapers were filled with angry letters from "Snarleyow," "Cynophile," "Humanitas," "The Dog of Gray's Inn," "A Retriever in the Suburbs," and the like. *Fun* and *Judy* revelled in the opportunity, and satirical verses and articles were poured out weekly. With the rather heavy humour of the time, *Fun* announced that police armed with cutlasses[1] and revolvers were to round up all mosquitoes found going about Woolwich, Deptford, and Plumstead Marshes without muzzles. All stray flies were to be captured and taken to the nearest police station. Ridicule and sentimentality killed the order; not many years later a similar one was enforced without any of this clamour, and with beneficial effects.

Mayne, at this time, was also under fire for ordering the confiscation of children's hoops. These were of iron, and were a nuisance, and even a danger in some circumstances. *Judy*, dedicating "A Pleasant Ditty" to him on this subject, went out of its way to slander the whole force:

> The hoop-stealers of London,
> Who call themselves police,
> But leave the classes criminal
> Most carefully in peace.
>
> The hoop-stealers of London,
> Who never, never shrink
> From taking bribes to see or not,
> And ne'er refuse a drink.

Fun had made the same charge a little earlier, after two constables had been prosecuted for perjury, in verses addressed to "An Unprincipled Policeman":

> I charge him with the crime of being tight,
> And hint that he will have to pay a fine,
> Unless he chooses to set matters right,
> By half-a-sovereign as a counter-sign!
> Often he yields, nor dreams of showing fight,
> For perjury is also in my line!

The last lines of this doggerel embody a staple joke about the police, who were supposed to have a particular fascination for cooks, as Guardsmen for nursemaids, until cooks and nursemaids alike ceased to be common objects of the social scene:

> Oh, culinary fair, whose eyes are bright,
> Say, will you have me for your Valentine?

[1] Cutlass drill had been introduced in 1866, when *Fun* heard "that considerable consternation and distress were caused in fashionable circles (of certain areas) by the intelligence that Sir Richard Mayne had ordered the police to learn the cut-lass exercise."

If not actually accused of brutality and corruption, the police were almost always pictured in the Press as inefficient and stupid. *Fun*, which never tired of gibing at the force, began in 1861 a series called "Figures of Fun" with an essay on the policeman: "His face shines not with intelligence, but soap. He is often wanted, but seldom found at the right time." Among "Popular Delusions concerning the Police," which appeared in the same periodical three years later, are the following: "That the police are our legal guardians; the name having been only applied in a bitterly sarcastic sense." "That a policeman ever has conscientious scruples against taking an oath on any subject whatever." "That the police are in any way useful to prevent the commission of crime." The more responsible journals gave their readers the same impression; to take instances only from Mayne's last year, 1868, the *Daily News* was writing (October 28): "Of late years the old confidence in the police has diminished. Whether as detectives or protectives, the public mistrusts them." On November the 4th this paper speaks of the public recognizing the truth of the harlequinade, in which the police are always running after little boys, but are never there when the clown is stealing,[1] and mentions a suburban district whose inhabitants had formed a sort of vigilance committee "to supplement the protection which they pay for but do not get from Sir Richard Mayne's subordinates." This last grievance was raised again at the end of the month in the *Penny Illustrated Paper*, an article headed "Help! Police!" beginning: "The latest achievements of Sir Richard Mayne and the activity and intelligence of Scotland-yard are so surprising that we shall soon see district after district joining with St Pancras, Marylebone and Lambeth in measures for self-protection." Two days later the *Daily Telegraph* was animadverting on the "delicate forbearance" shown by the police towards criminals:

> They give a glance down some Short's-Gardens or Seven Dials lane; they see lounging about two men let out last week after "three years for burglary": another lurking about who had garotted a gentleman in the Strand: a third five times convicted of picking pockets; four or five boys looking up to these, serious with admiration and taking in ideas of crime almost at every breath. The police see all this, and pass by on the other side. They then parade up and down some quiet, respectable street, and while they are engaged in this senseless sentinel-work, the loungers plan a burglary, easily effected when the policeman has just passed one point on his beat, and will not be back for half an hour.

[1] Tradition in the theatre has caused this caricature of the early police to be perpetuated long after the feelings which made it popular have been forgotten.

Obviously there was some truth in this flood of fault-finding, flouts, and jeers. The standard of character and intelligence in the police force was indeed much lower then than it is to-day. Insufficient care was taken to recruit the best type of man for the job. The police themselves, however, were representative of the populace of the time—a populace that still retained the turbulent individualism of a past age. In a recent review of a book on contemporary social life in England the critic speaks of "the respect for the rule of law (or the rules of the game) which we regard as an essential part of our make-up." But feelings of this kind were rare in the 1860's. No particular respect was felt for the law, and there were no rules of the game. It was not only criminals who were suspicious of the police; the flavour of militarism still hung about them, and sober persons talked of *gendarmerie* and swallowed the wildest tales of "savagery and butchery."[1] At the other end of the scale the most childish grievances were aired in the Press, and the people who lived in the "quiet, respectable streets" which the police were said to parade when they should have been hunting malefactors were the first to complain angrily that when they went for a walk there was not a policeman in sight. The public, in short, did not give the force the support and co-operation to which it was entitled, and without which it could not be expected to show overmuch zeal or efficiency.

With regard to combating crime, one weakness, which cried out for correction, appears to have been overlooked by everybody, including the Commissioner. This was the negligible size of the Detective Branch. A uniformed constable on a beat, to which he was tied, held few terrors for "loungers," even if they were habitual criminals known to him, when all they had to do was to keep out of his way. The value of the plain-clothes detective with freedom of action should by now have been recognized. It was not; a number of detectives were indeed scattered among the divisions, but little is heard of them, and all serious investigation of crime seems to have fallen upon the fifteen men attached to A Division at Scotland Yard.

A very powerful element in the Press campaign against the police was the hostility felt towards the Commissioner himself. Mayne had reigned too long for his own good, and perhaps for the good of the force. This, however, does not excuse the disgraceful tone of the attacks upon him, which reached a crescendo in the last troubled year of his life. That he ignored them was in itself a grievance; he was rebuked for not listening to the Press. A major charge against him, and a particularly absurd one, was that he wished to model the force upon

[1] *Daily Telegraph*, July 27, 1866. Narrative of "W.B."

Continental patterns. *Fun*, after asserting that the streets of London at night were "as much under the tyranny of the Mayne force as the streets of Paris are under the despotism of the French police," accused the Commissioner a year or two later of admiring the Austrian police system and visiting Vienna "in order to take a hint as to the organization of the English constabulary," being "ambitious to make his 'Blues' *the* great power in the Metropolis."[1] The humorous periodicals were not always satirical, and attacks of this kind were intended to be taken as seriously as the following from one of the newspapers:

> Sir Richard Mayne has again exhibited that capricious temper which has done so much to lower the efficiency and popularity of the force under his command and to set them upon duties that are altogether repugnant to themselves and to the public at large. That the Chief Commissioner is quite above control seems to be inferred from the fact that he never condescends either to defence or explanation. Magistrates, members of both Houses of Parliament, and, for aught we know, the chiefs of the Home Office themselves, seem to be paralysed by his dumb authority. He treats all their questions with utter contempt, declines to discuss the question with anybody concerned, seems able to obtain all sorts of enactments for securing to himself all sorts of functions, and goes on like an irresistible fate in a blue uniform, amenable to nobody, and probably not even acquainted with popular opinion.[2]

This tirade was occasioned by the Fenian outrage at Clerkenwell, but just censure of police laxity was not strengthened by distortions of the Commissioner's character and intentions. (The newspaper made the common mistake of calling him the "Chief Commissioner.") Some months later the *Daily Telegraph* was raising this spectre of autocracy in a leading article on the muzzling order: "'I, the Commissioner'—notice how naturally our Prefect of the Thames falls into the old Castilian style of 'Yo, el Rey'—'do hereby require'—it is a pity he does not say command. . . ."

"The Satrap of Scotland Yard," *Fun* called him in April of this year, in a "Fun-Done Letter" which ends: "the sooner he retires, or is *retiré*, as his French admirers would say, the better." "Sir Richard," said the *Daily Telegraph* in August, "has served for many years—so long, indeed, that a generous and enlightened public would gladly release him from any further exertions." "How much longer," asked *Judy* in November, "is suffering London to put up with the aged imbecility of Sir Richard Mayne?"

[1] *Fun*, August 4, 1866.
[2] *Penny Illustrated Paper*, January 4, 1868.

A month later Mayne was dead. The chorus of vituperation was stilled. Among the usual formal obituaries, *Judy*, to do her justice, openly acknowledged past offences in some rather poor verse, of which one stanza ran:

> Which of us who roughly cavill'd,
> Did not wish the words unsaid—
> Did not feel a quick repentance,
> When we heard that he was dead?

Where the police were concerned, however, the Press as a whole did not allow repentance, if felt, to stay its hand. While for years Mayne had been condemned by every periodical in London, complaint and ridicule of the force he had done so much to mould drowned the few faint voices heard from time to time in its praise; and if this handful of admirers hoped that with a fresh start, under a fresh Commissioner, the flood of abuse would be in any way abated, they were mistaken. Within a year the *Graphic* was writing in the old strain: "The police of London are inefficient and insolent. . . ."

13

ROAD, RAIL, AND RUGELEY

THE Metropolitan Police was not directly concerned in the case of Dr Palmer of Rugeley, but a tinge of reflected glory was cast upon the force by newspaper enterprise. The case was among the first to be reported in what may be called the modern manner, one journal devoting to it a special supplement as large as its normal issue. The English law of libel having developed through a long series of judicial decisions, a hundred years ago reporting in general was outspoken to a degree that must arouse strong feelings of envy in the breasts of editors to-day; and it seems likely that the freedom of comment and speculation allowed in the middle of the last century has done much to hand down the name of Palmer the Poisoner, as a household word, to generations who could not say for whose murder he was hanged. Even a classical chestnut of the period reappears now and then as a new story, and, for future reference, may perhaps be told again. The inhabitants of Rugeley, tired of the wrong sort of notoriety, petitioned the Prime Minister for permission to change the name of their town.[1] The P.M., Lord Palmerston, was most obliging: let them call it Palmerstown—after himself, of course.

The *Illustrated News* published its special Rugeley Number, or supplement, on the 2nd of February, 1856, more than three months before Palmer's trial began. Its opening article said of the accused, but in theory still innocent, doctor: "Unhappily, his medical studies appear, by the well-thumbed pages of a work upon poisons, to have been chiefly directed to the properties of prussic acid, strychnia, and deadly narcotics; while the best-filled bottle in his surgery is said to have been one of tartarised antimony. So fond, indeed, was he of fatal drugs that he once owned a horse named Strychnine." Of Palmer's mother-in-law it was related: "She is reported to have said that if she went to reside under the same roof with him, she would not live a fortnight. These forebodings proved to be true, for she subsequently went to live with her daughter, and four days afterwards she was a

[1] The people of Hilldrop Crescent made a similar plea as a result of the publicity given to the Crippen case; Filleted Place was one of the suggestions offered.

corpse." Of Mr Bladen, to whom Palmer was alleged to owe £400, the *Illustrated News* thought it probable "that the hope of recovering this sum induced the unfortunate man to become the guest of his debtor. However this may be, he had no chance of taking it out in board and lodging. In less than a week he fell desperately sick." Mr Bladen died, and the article goes on: "Poor Mrs Palmer was greatly agitated when she heard of Mr Bladen's death, and exclaimed, 'My poor mother died when she was on a visit here last year—and now this man. What will people say?' What will people say, indeed? Beyond these deaths, there were also other grounds for suspicion. Of five children, the offspring of their marriage, four died in infancy. . . . Ere, too, a few short months had gone by, it was destined to be the poor mother's turn."

When this article appeared Palmer was in Stafford Gaol, having been arrested on a coroner's warrant, charged with the murders of his wife, his brother Walter, and John Parsons Cook. He was tried on the last charge only. He was never formally accused of the murder of his mother-in-law, or of Bladen, or of any one of his children; but the *Illustrated News*, not content with three homicides, threw in a few more for good measure. Local talk, even less inhibited, credited him with a dozen, just as in another little town, many years later, a number of sudden deaths were attributed to the arsenic of Major Armstrong; and it was on the ground of local prejudice that what is known as "Palmer's Act" was passed, by which it was made possible to remove the venue of the trial from the Staffordshire Assizes to the Central Criminal Court. But the *Illustrated News* may have helped to make legal history.

Its special supplement, which was lavishly illustrated, had a section on "Inspector Field at Rugeley." The ordinary issue of the paper of the same date published a Memoir of that officer. He was incorrectly described, possibly with his own connivance; he had, in fact, retired from the Metropolitan Police in 1852 after a very successful career, first as a sergeant in E Division, then, as inspector, in L and at Deptford and Woolwich Dockyards, and finally as chief of the Detective Branch, where he succeeded Inspector Shackell. In this capacity he investigated a number of crimes which made news, from murders and jewel robberies to Chartist sedition. As the *Illustrated Times* put it, "Fortune, fickle creature, smiled on Field, and ever since has continued to pour down upon him her bounteous gifts"; and these may indeed have been financially more bounteous after his retirement than before, since he then set up as a private-inquiry agent, and, being well known, was employed on confidential work of all kinds. It was at the instance of an insurance company that Field went down to Rugeley in November 1855 to play his part in one of the most famous criminal cases of the century.

It was a minor part, as events turned out. When Palmer was arrested in December on the capital charge, Field was still investigating the doctor's financial activities, particularly the curious affair of "G. Bate, Esq.," who, according to Palmer, wished to insure his life for £25,000, but who was found by Field hoeing turnips. Mr Bate, who may have had a lucky escape, made the briefest of appearances at the trial, the defence's objection to his evidence being sustained; and though the prosecution made use of Field's information, they did not call him as a witness.

Field's use, after his retirement, of his old rank of inspector, and some of his proceedings as a private-inquiry agent, got him into trouble with the Commissioner's office. Police Orders for the 7th of January, 1862, include the following:

> Restoration of Pension: Mr Field, late Inspector in the Metropolitan Police, the payment of whose superannuation allowance has been stopped (Police Orders, 17th August, 1861), on account of his conduct in connexion with a Private Inquiry Office, has given assurance to the Secretary of State that no cause for the future shall be given for disapprobation, and that he will take steps at once to remove any impression that may exist that he acts in any connexion with the Government.

Field had a reputation for boasting and playing to the gallery, and even after this warning he seems to have failed to regulate his conduct as he had promised, for his case was raised again in 1865. But by then he had severed his connexion with the private-inquiry business, and the Home Secretary, Sir George Grey, wrote to the Commissioner that in these circumstances he did not take away Field's pension, "on the understanding that he is not again in any way connected with that office."

2

Early in July 1860 Mr Stancomb, a magistrate on the Bench at Trowbridge, in Wiltshire, had an interview with the Home Secretary. As a result, Detective-Inspector Jonathan Whicher, of the Detective Branch at Scotland Yard, was sent to the village of Road, five miles from Trowbridge, and just over the county boundary in Somerset. The inspector was to assist the Wiltshire Constabulary in their inquiry into the murder of Francis Saville Kent, a child less than four years old, whose body had been found on the 29th of June, wrapped in a blanket, in the servants' privy in the garden of Road-Hill House,[1] in that county.

The family at Road-Hill House, a considerable mansion situated a short distance from the village, but in Wiltshire, consisted of Mr Samuel Saville Kent, an assistant inspector of factories, his second wife, seven children—three of them by his second marriage—and several servants. Mr Kent appears to have been a trying and tactless sort of man who lived in a style above his means. He was unpopular with the villagers of Road, and with the managements of the local cloth factories he supervised. At home he was what has come to be regarded as the typical Victorian father, very much the head of the family, and a selfish if on the whole well-meaning tyrant. In addition to the four surviving children of his first marriage, six others had died, five of them in infancy. Before their mother herself had died, worn out, she had shown signs of insanity, which is said to have been inherited. Her successor was a governess-companion who had been called in nine years before to look after the children and the house. Mr Kent married her in August 1853.

The murdered boy, Francis, was the second child of this second marriage. He and his younger sister, aged two, slept with the nurse, Elizabeth Gough. The latter woke at five o'clock on the morning of the 29th of June and saw that the boy's cot was empty, but she supposed that his mother had come in unheard and taken him to her own room. At seven o'clock it was discovered that Francis was not in the house, and an hour or two later his body was found in the privy. His throat had been cut, and he had been stabbed in the chest.

The conduct of the investigation by the local police, under Superintendent Foley of Trowbridge, was perhaps no worse than might be expected. County constabularies had been in being only twenty years, and had no officers trained in the detection of the more serious types of crime. Foley had no natural qualifications for the task; he seems to have been a stupid sort of man, and is thought to be the original of Superintendent Seegrave in *The Moonstone*, as Whicher was undoubtedly Collins's model for Sergeant Cuff. It appears to have been realized from the first that the murderer was almost certainly a member of the large household at Road-Hill House, numbering, with servants, a dozen; Foley's suspicions fastened on the nurse, Elizabeth Gough, while the people of Road and the neighbourhood were convinced that

[1] The Ordnance Survey now spells the name Rode. It will be simpler to use the contemporary spelling here.

the unpopular Mr Kent had committed the most unnatural of crimes. So little is heard of his two eldest daughters, both approaching thirty, and of their full-brother William, aged fifteen, that they seem scarcely to have been in the running as suspects, and the same is true of the cook and housemaid and the two outdoor servants, a coachman and boy. But the case of the remaining surviving child of the first marriage, the sixteen-year-old Constance Kent, was felt even then to be rather different.

An excellent local paper, the *Somerset and Wilts Journal*, thus summed up the situation at Road-Hill House before the crime:

> Of the family we are only justified in saying that it is alleged that some time since there was, as so often happens with a stepmother, some uncomfortable feeling generated, and that three years ago, conceiving themselves to be unkindly treated, the two children, Constance and William, then eleven and ten years of age respectively, started off, both attired in boy's clothes and with the girl's hair cut short, intending, as they afterwards said, to go to sea. They were recognized, however, at an hotel in Bath, and after two days' absence were returned to their parents. A somewhat unusual number of servants have been discharged from this establishment, a fact which some have thought affords a probable clue to the murder.[1]

It may have been these discharged servants whom Whicher was seeking when, later, he extended his inquiries to Bristol, Frome, and other places. But the root of the matter lay in the "uncomfortable feeling" in the household to which the newspaper refers—the not uncommon jealousy felt by children of a first marriage towards their stepmother and her children; and Whicher's suspicions seem to have centred from the start on Constance Kent. Psychology, as a science—if it is one—was then little studied by detectives, but the inspector was an experienced officer, who must have learnt much about human behaviour; and an idea which shocked people quite ready to believe that a father had murdered his three-year-old son may have appeared far less improbable to him. Several days' researches into the history of the Kent family, as locally known, prejudiced and garbled as such gossip might be, must have thrown a good deal of light on the character of Constance Kent. It was a strong character; the girl was old for her years, passionate and determined, and in the escapade with her brother William (when both were rather older than the newspaper report stated) it was she who was the leading spirit. After this episode

[1] Quoted in *The Case of Constance Kent* (Bles, 1928), by John Rhode, a very full and careful account of the case

she was removed from a boarding-school in London to one within two miles of her home, but still as a boarder, an arrangement which caused comment. There were other indications that her position in a somewhat difficult household, to which her older sisters seem to have reconciled themselves, was not a happy one, though the unhappiness may have been largely the product of her own feelings and imagination. At home she is said to have concealed her growing jealousy of the little boy Francis, a clever, healthy child, and his mother's favourite, but she may have been less discreet elsewhere, and Whicher perhaps picked up a hint or two in village gossip. One curious story, with which there is no evidence to connect Constance beyond the fact that she had just returned home for the holidays at the time of the incident, was that when Francis was about two the nurse woke up one morning to find his bedclothes stripped off him and his bed-socks removed. One of the socks was later discovered hidden in Mrs Kent's room. "A favourite terror of mid-Victorian days," to quote Mr John Rhode, "was that of 'catching one's death of cold,'" and in the case of a child of two the danger was very real. Whoever the culprit on this occasion, even if no serious harm was intended, the mischievous trick showed how easily some one could enter and leave the nursery while the nurse was asleep.

Whicher knew these things, and he knew that the first Mrs Kent had shown symptoms of a deranged mind long before Constance was born. Both Constance and William Kent, the last of that stock and nearly of an age, had been delicate and abnormal children. Other factors, however, would be needed to persuade a jury of Constance's guilt. Almost from the first a significant circumstance was known to the local police, but they were not impressed by it: one of the girl's nightgowns was missing. The murder was discovered on a Saturday morning, and on the Monday morning the housemaid put the nightgown with other dirty linen in one of the baskets sent weekly to a washerwoman in the village. She noticed no unusual stains or marks on it. Nevertheless it disappeared, almost certainly before the baskets left the house. Constance, by sending the maid on an errand, had an opportunity to abstract it. The importance of the incident was at once realized by Whicher, who goes at length into it in his official report. His explanation of it was given by a rather more practised pen in the *Somerset and Wilts Journal*:

> Constance Kent had three nightgowns on the night of the murder—A and B in her drawers (not one in the wash, as has been said), and nightgown C in wear. Supposing that it was wished on Friday night to destroy

nightgown C, nightgown B could be taken into wear and worn until next day, and could then be inspected by Mr Foley and Mr Parsons, the police surgeon, and would present the appearance of being "very clean, not having even the starch out of it." Nightgown A would still be in the drawer. Then on Monday let B be put out to be washed, and A put on the bed to wear. Then let B be brought back from the washing basket to the bed, and A be put back in the drawer. Nightgown C would then appear to be missing at the wash. . . . This, be it remembered, is only theory, first propounded by Inspector Whicher, and now adopted somewhat reluctantly perhaps by the local police.

A more disgraceful episode was the suppression of evidence by Superintendent Foley and his men, presumably to cover up their own carelessness. During the search of Road-Hill House after the discovery of the crime "a bloodstained woman's shift" was found in a boiler-hole in the back kitchen. The superintendent ordered it to be put back there, and, like the nightgown, it disappeared. "Not one word," said Whicher afterwards, "was said to me or to the magistrates, or indeed to anyone, about the finding of this dress or shift. . . . It would not have come out had it not been for a Sergeant Watts of the Somersetshire Constabulary letting it out in some way." Whicher clearly thought that the "shift" was the missing nightgown, and though play has been made with the fact that these are different garments, it seems as likely that a man would mistake one for the other, or would use the same term loosely for both. It is improbable that a shift as well as a nightgown should have been mislaid that night.

Whicher, it will be seen, had his difficulties; and the inefficiency of his colleagues of the local constabulary was not the half of them. Scotland Yard had been called in too late, as has been known to happen since, and the fact that it had been called in at all was deeply resented by Foley and his men—an occurrence also not unknown in similar cases in later days. Whicher met with obstruction from those he had come to help, and he had none of the authority which now attaches to a senior officer of the C.I.D. In every other respect the affair had been mishandled before he appeared on the scene. At the inquest, which was over in five hours, the foreman of the jury was the Rector of Road, a friend of the Kent family, whose feelings, as he said frankly, he wished to spare, and it was only because of the insistence of the other jurymen that Constance and William Kent were called as witnesses. The verdict was one of wilful murder against some person or persons unknown. Within a week a number of local magistrates, not unnaturally dissatisfied with the conduct of the case, took the strange step of holding an examination of their own in the Temperance Hall at Road, summoning witnesses who could not have been compelled to attend and who were not under oath. Among these was poor Elizabeth Gough, who all this time had been under a sort of open arrest. These irregular proceedings at least resulted in her being released, though her troubles were by no means over. With greater propriety, the magistrates had already sent their delegate, Mr Stancomb, to the Home Secretary; and with the arrival of Whicher in time to attend the fourth session at the Temperance Hall, the examination, which had been held behind closed doors, but with few other precautions of secrecy, came to a timely end.

This was on July the 16th; and four days later Whicher obtained a warrant and arrested Constance Kent. This was quick work, and his action may have been impulsive in the sense that he was angered by the incompetence and actual obstruction that met him at every turn. There was still much to be done, and in his telegram to the Commissioner reporting the arrest the inspector asked for assistance; could Sergeant Williamson or Sergeant Tanner be sent down to him? He was joined by Frederick Williamson, later to become the best known of all the members of the Detective Branch and the first Chief Constable of its successor, the Criminal Investigation Department.[1]

At this date Whicher's case was based mainly on the evidence of the missing nightgown, but he said afterwards that he counted on Constance Kent breaking down under the shock of arrest. There he was mistaken; she was not the sort to break down; and once he had discovered this, Whicher must have feared that his throw had failed. Before the magistrates whom he already knew only too well, the prisoner was charged, on the 27th, with the murder of her stepbrother, and at the end of the day was released, her father being bound in £200 to produce her when called upon.

It was not an acquittal; and it can only be conjectured how the case would have gone had the police been properly represented at the proceedings. In the days before Scotland Yard employed a firm of solicitors to handle such business it relied upon a legal adviser, who on this occasion seems to have done nothing, or not to have been called upon to advise. Whicher, scarcely an educated man, as his reports show, had to conduct the police case in the Temperance Hall; the defence, on

[1] Whicher's telegram, on a form of the Electric and International Telegraph Company, is addressed to the "Chief" Commissioner, though Mayne was then reigning alone. The inspector's reports on the case, and his and Williamson's claims for expenses, are also sent direct to Mayne, an instance of the Commissioner's personal handling of affairs in these early days of the force and of the Detective Branch.

the other hand, briefed a barrister from Bristol, who set the tone of what followed by a savage attack on the interloper from London—"a man eager in pursuit of the murderer, and anxious for the reward which has been offered."[1] In the result, the discharge of the accused is generally held to have ruined the inspector, because Mayne allowed himself to be influenced by popular clamour, and made his prejudice so clear that Whicher, disheartened and disgusted, soon resigned from the force. Whicher himself, however, in a letter to the Press written long after his retirement, attributed this to ill-health.

During what must have been an unhappy period he no doubt followed with cynical amusement the further proceedings in Wiltshire and Somerset, where every one, relieved of his embarrassing presence, began to do everything all over again. More irresponsible magistrates held more irregular inquiries. A Bath solicitor, vaguely authorized by the Home Office, held one on his own account. A consequent application by the Attorney-General for a writ *ad melius inquirendum* sanctioning a fresh inquest was refused by the Court of Queen's Bench. "Many of the most influential citizens of Bath," who were in no way concerned in the affair, were among those who begged the Home Secretary to appoint a special commission to inquire into it. The body of Francis Kent was exhumed, apparently in the hope that the missing nightdress would be found buried with him. A man with the singularly appropriate name of Gagg gave himself up for the murder, but it turned out that he was confusing Road with Roade, in Northamptonshire; and he had not been long disposed of when Superintendent Foley, free again like the rest to follow his own bent, had the satisfaction of securing the arrest of Elizabeth Gough. She was committed to Devizes Gaol and brought before her old friends the Trowbridge Bench on October the 1st, accused of killing the child of whom she had been in charge. The proceedings came to the same unsatisfactory end as those against Constance Kent; though the chairman held that there was a case of grave suspicion against the much-tried nurse, she was released, bound in two sureties to appear again if called upon. The extraordinary nature of this decision will appear from the fact that four of the magistrates had arrived at a similar one in the case of Constance only two months before. If Mr Kent could have been brought before them, as he very nearly was, there might have been three people simultaneously at large under bond on "grave suspicion" of the same murder. None

[1] £100, by the local magistrates. After Constance Kent's confession they seem to have suffered a change of heart, for they wrote to the Commissioner asking that the reward should be divided between Whicher and Williamson, but the offer was declined.

of these justices appears to have noticed his own inconsistency. Nor, apparently, did anyone else.

Long before this the Kent family had left Road, where life amid these antics and inquisitions had become intolerable. Mr Kent was still the favourite suspect with many people; others were again beginning to wonder about his daughter. Constance had been sent to a convent in France, returning to England in 1863 to stay as a visitor at a religious retreat in Brighton. It was in the following year, on the 19th of March, that Whicher resigned from the Metropolitan Police, in which he had served with distinction for twenty-five years, his name often appearing in Police Orders among those of officers granted rewards for good work. Another twelve months went by, and then, in April 1864, it was announced that Constance Kent had confessed to the murder of her stepbrother.

Thus, it would seem, was Whicher vindicated. Whatever the reason for his retirement, he was now a middle-aged man, and it does not appear that any attempt was made, then or earlier, to recover his services for the Detective Branch. He was not too old or infirm, however, to undertake private-inquiry work, and it will be seen that he helped to investigate the past of the Tichborne Claimant.

Convicted on her own confession, Constance Kent was sentenced to death, the sentence being at once commuted to penal servitude for life. She was released in 1885, a woman of forty-one. Of her later life little or nothing that can be called authentic has been disclosed; but interest in her case has never died. As recently as 1954 the latest of many imaginative versions of the events at Road-Hill House, nearly a hundred years ago, appeared in the book-shops.[1] It attempts to show that Samuel Kent was the killer of his son, a theory held by many at the time. However ingeniously developed, this remains a theory, since it is based on an assumption unsupported by any evidence other than gossip of the day, and on problems presented by the daughter's confession itself, some details of which do not tally with medical and other ascertained facts. Such discrepancies could be accounted for; and even less convincing is the argument put forward to explain the confession —that Constance Kent, aware of her father's guilt, was moved by strong religious feeling to save his life, or at least to clear his name. Four years after the murder Mr Kent was no longer in any danger, and falsehood merely revived waning interest in the tragedy; and it seems scarcely conceivable that so fearful a lie could be prompted by religious motives.

[1] Yseult Bridges, *Saint with Red Hands?* (Jarrolds, 1954).

Fortunately there has survived the destruction of Metropolitan Police records during the removal of headquarters in 1890, and also subsequent losses, a considerable bundle of documents on the murder at Road. There are, of course, the usual letters from busybodies, in those days as a rule educated persons who should have known better. Only one out of more than twenty such letters preserved is anonymous, and it is the only one in an uneducated hand. Two clergymen, one from as far away as Lancashire, thought fit to instruct the Commissioner on his conduct of the case. A colonel suggested that chloroform had been used. Of another writer Whicher commented, "He appears to be insane." In general these accusations fastened either on Samuel Kent, on William Nutt, a servant about the house, or on some unknown nocturnal visitor—the guilty person in almost every case being the clandestine lover of the nurse, Elizabeth Gough. Not only Superintendent Foley considered poor Elizabeth fair game, though there is no evidence that her character was anything but exemplary. Whicher himself wrote that the charges of improper conduct levelled against her (and by implication against her employer) by the local police were "incorrect." Yet so far did gossip and persecution go that long after Elizabeth Gough had returned to her parents at Isleworth the Wiltshire magistrates were writing twice to Scotland Yard, pointing out that she was still under recognizances and asking for inquiries to be made into allegations that she was leading a dissolute life. The Brentford police reported that she was leading a most respectable one, and earning her living as a seamstress.

The busybodies' letters being passed to Whicher, he endorsed them invariably as "of no assistance to the inquiry." Rather out of the general run, however, was a private communication to the Commissioner from an acquaintance at Blandford who also knew the Kent family well. Medical evidence had shown that the murdered boy was probably unconscious, if not nearly dead, before the knife was used. Mayne's correspondent, writing in August 1860, suggested that Mrs Kent, trying to quieten the child, had suffocated him by accident—an early instance of this theory of causation, put forward again in the latest reconstruction of the crime.

But it is another letter, never seen by Whicher, that contains matter of genuine interest. After the boy's funeral four friends of the family were driving back together to Road-Hill House. They were Dr Mallam, the child's godfather, two other medical men, and a solicitor. Having met in this way, they found that they were at one in the opinion that Constance Kent, whom all of them knew well, was guilty of the murder; and as soon as they reached their destination they took Mr Kent aside and gave him their views. It must have been a painful occasion for all, and the four gentlemen, feeling that they had done what they considered their duty, seem henceforward to have held their peace. Not until May 1865, a year after Constance Kent had confessed, did Dr Mallam write to the Commissioner to relate these events. He added that Samuel Kent and his second wife had always slighted the children of the first marriage. The doctor may have been moved to act because by this date the suggestion that the daughter had sacrificed herself for her father's sake was already being aired; at any rate, he requested that a police officer should be sent to interview him. If this was done, which is improbable, there is no record of the interview.

By themselves these dead leaves might scarcely seem worth disinterring; but they have some importance as a background to Inspector Whicher's own report and memoranda, with which, so long ago, they were filed. Much of the report deals with the missing nightgown, but the notes show that Whicher had not overlooked the possible significance of the earlier episode, when the little boy's bedclothes were turned back and his socks removed. Whicher pointed out that on the night of the murder both nurse and child might have been sleeping more heavily than usual; Elizabeth Gough had cleaned out the nursery that afternoon, and would be tired, while the boy had missed his daily rest; he could therefore have been carried from the room without waking, and without the nurse being roused. The inspector then went on to note, without comment, the very curious incident of *The Times*.

When Constance Kent was thirteen there occurred a *cause célèbre* which aroused public interest as intense and long-lived as her own case was to do. In July 1857 Madeleine Smith, a young woman of good family, was put on her trial at Glasgow for the murder by poison of her lover, Émile l'Angelier. The jury brought in a verdict of "not proven." It would seem that Mr and Mrs Kent thought it inadvisable that Constance should read about the trial, and copies of *The Times* containing reports of it were hidden in a writing bureau. There, apparently, they were forgotten, at any rate by the father and stepmother. Exactly three years later, in July 1860, when Whicher made a thorough search of the girl's bedroom, which the local police had omitted to do, he found these issues of *The Times* under her mattress.

Such pointers, and others in his report and in the notes made for his own reference, still leave the matter very much where it was. On the one hand there are puzzling circumstances, which after so long an interval of time are likely to remain mysterious; on the other stands the opinion of an experienced, intelligent, and unbiased police officer, and a confession of guilt. As against guesswork, this sort of testimony will usually be accepted in the ordinary affairs of life.

3

The first known murder in an English train took place on another July day in 1864. It was the 9th, a Saturday, and a Mr Briggs, one of the chief clerks in the Lombard Street banking house of Robarts, dined that night with his niece and her husband in Peckham. He lived at Victoria Park, Hackney, and after dinner his host saw him board an omnibus which would take him to Fenchurch Street Station, on the North London Railway. At the station he was seen by the ticket inspector, who knew him well, since he travelled on this line daily. A healthy man of seventy, Mr Briggs was carrying a stick and a small black bag. With his gold watch and Albert and gold-rimmed spectacles, he no doubt looked the responsible man of business that he was.

Leaving his niece's house at 8.30, he had ample time to catch the train which left Fenchurch Street for Chalk Farm, Camden Town, at 9.50. It reached Victoria Park, or Hackney Wick, at 10.5, and Hackney some six minutes later. Here two bank clerks got into an empty first-class compartment; it may fairly be described as a strange coincidence that they were also employed by Robarts'. As they sat down one of them touched the seat, and found blood on his hand. He was able to call the guard before the train moved on; more blood was then found on the cushions, the window, and the offside door handle. There were a hat, a bloodstained stick, and a small black bag in the compartment. The carriage was locked and taken on to Chalk Farm.

Here the guard found news waiting for him. At 10.20 the driver of a train of empty coaches travelling from Hackney Wick to Fenchurch Street saw a body lying on the six-foot way between Hackney Wick and Bow. It was Mr Briggs; his skull was fractured, and he had other head-wounds. He was still alive, but he died during the next day without regaining consciousness. His gold watch and chain and spectacles were missing, but a gold ring had been left on his finger, and in his pockets, with other articles by which he was identified, were four pounds ten shillings and a silver snuff-box.

The police of K Division, under Inspector Kenessey, having taken charge, a constable was sent to the victim's house with the hat, stick, and bag. Mr Briggs's son recognized the stick and bag, but the hat, a black beaver stamped with the name of J. H. Walker, of 49 Crawford

Street, Marylebone, was not his father's. Kenessey handed it over next day to Detective-Inspector Tanner, of the Detective Branch, who had been sent from Scotland Yard to assume control of the inquiry. Tanner, whose name has already been mentioned, had only recently been confirmed in his rank after serving for a year as temporary inspector. His advancement leaving a vacancy among the sergeants in the Detective Branch, it had been filled by promoting a constable, transferred from C Division, whose name was to acquire unhappy notoriety thirteen years later—Nathaniel Druscovitch.[1]

The murderer of Mr Briggs having lost his head and his hat, for it was a safe presumption that the black beaver was his, Inspector Tanner had a straightforward case once he had identified the wearer.[2] It took him a week to do so; the Marylebone hatter was no help, and the actual purchaser did not read the newspapers; and this short lapse of time enabled the criminal to set up a precedent, which was not to be repeated until Crippen and Ethel le Neve fled to Canada in 1910. Publicity, which included the offer of substantial rewards by the Government, the firm of Robarts, and the railway company, soon, however, produced other results. On the Monday, the 11th, a young man speaking good English with a German accent came to the shop of a jeweller named Death and exchanged a gold watch and chain, valued at £2 10*s*. for a chain and ring of the same value. A description of the missing watch and chain having been circulated among jewellers and pawnbrokers, Death discovered that he had them; and before long a pawnbroker came forward with the chain and ring given in exchange. Inspector Tanner now knew the sort of man he had to look for, but nothing more about him, for the name and address given to the pawnbroker were fictitious. And by the end of the week, had the inspector known it, his quarry was out of the country.

It was on the next Monday, the 18th of July, that affairs began to march in earnest with the appearance of a cabman named Matthews. His story was that his elder daughter had at one time been engaged to a German, Franz Müller, a tailor by profession. The engagement was broken off, but Müller continued on friendly terms with the Matthews family. Recently the father had seen his other and much younger daughter playing with a small cardboard box, given her by Müller, on which was the name of Death. What was more, Matthews had once bought for Müller a black beaver hat at the shop of J. H. Walker in

[1] Police Orders, October 31, 1863.

[2] Some eighty years later another murderer ruined his chances of escape by forgetting his hat. Because of its amusing sequel the case will be referred to in its turn.

Marylebone. Asked why he had not come forward with this valuable information before, Matthews said that he did not read the papers and did not discuss current topics with his friends. He had only heard of the murder eight days after it took place, when the jeweller's name struck a chord in his memory. Thanks to this attitude of detachment, his information had come very nearly too late.

The Detective Branch, however, in the person of Inspector Tanner, who has been described as the most brilliant officer then at Scotland Yard, showed that with the limited resources it possessed eighty years ago it could strike as quickly and efficiently as the immense machine which has grown out of it. Within twenty-four hours, armed with much information about Müller and a warrant for his arrest, the inspector was on his way to Liverpool to sail in the steamship *City of Manchester* for New York. With him and Detective-Sergeant Clarke were the jeweller Death and the cabman Matthews, who were getting a free trip across the Atlantic.

Müller was also heading for New York, but in a sailing-ship, the *Victoria*. Like Inspector Dew forty-six years later, who reached the St Lawrence in front of Crippen, Tanner, in the faster ship, overtook the fugitive somewhere in mid-ocean. He was at New York on the 5th of August; and it was the 25th before the *Victoria* arrived. The jeweller and the cabman must have spent an interesting three weeks, for the Civil War was drawing to its end, and no doubt while they were there the city was *en fête* for Farragut's victory in Mobile Bay. Mr Matthews, perhaps, found something to talk about at last.

Müller was arrested on board ship and brought back to England in the s.s. *Etna* under the extradition treaty concluded with the United States in 1842, the oldest of such treaties still in force. Declaring his innocence of the murder, he stood his trial at the Old Bailey at the end of October. A native of Saxe-Weimar, aged twenty-five, he was out of work at the time of his attack on Mr Briggs, and this appears to have been a sudden desperate act by which he hoped to procure enough money to pay his passage across the Atlantic. This he did, but he could not afford even to buy a new hat, but wore the one he had taken in his agitation from the railway carriage, cutting it down to alter its appearance. The evidence against him was conclusive; he was sentenced to death, and hanged in front of Newgate on the 14th of November. At the last moment he confessed.

In matters of murder the Press had now got its hand in. It is amusing to find the *Illustrated Times*, which during the Palmer case started a new line in sensational journalism, now adopting a self-righteous tone.

"Whatever may be said of the detectives in relation to the murder of Mr Briggs," it wrote, "it must be admitted that the penny-a-liners have excelled themselves." That the detectives had done extremely well was generally recognized, and among rewards granted by the Home Secretary were £20 to Inspector Tanner and £10 each to Inspector Kenessey and Sergeant Clarke.[1] Tanner received a gift of £5 5*s*. from the son of the murdered man.

The murder had a curious international repercussion. Prussia had gone to war with Denmark, and early in 1864 had overrun the Schleswig-Holstein Duchies. The Prince of Wales having recently married Princess Alexandra of Denmark, English sympathies were wholly with the Danes, and though the latter were left to their fate, there was much public censure of the action taken by Prussia. This criticism was strongly resented throughout Germany, and, the Müller case occurring when excitement in that country was at its height, the normal processes of law were taken to be an instance of British malevolence. It was natural that the German Legal Protection Society in London should undertake Müller's defence, but in his own country other societies and the Press raised an ill-informed outcry. It was even asserted that what in fact was a most fairly conducted trial had been influenced by the pro-Danish British aristocracy, behind whom was the Princess of Wales. Like sensational journalism, the inability of the Germans to understand other people is no new thing. In fairness it should perhaps be added that the British chose the occasion to display a national characteristic far from endearing to foreigners. There were too many smug comments and leading articles in the newspapers on the superiority of British judicial methods, as exemplified at this trial, over those obtaining in less enlightened countries abroad.

[1] Police Orders, February 8, 1865.

BOOK THREE

The Modern Police

14

A NEW COMMISSIONER

A POLICE force which has been in existence for just on forty years can no longer be described as new. It is for other reasons, however, that the appointment of Sir Edmund Henderson as Commissioner in February 1869 marks a fresh point of departure in the history of the Metropolitan Police. Sir Richard Mayne's very long tenure of office at Scotland Yard was to be followed by the second longest Commissionership, and a total of fifty-seven years from the enlistment of the first "Peeler" carries the story definitely forward into modern times. Mayne, born before the Battle of the Nile, could remember Wellington at the height of his powers and Napoleon I in the decline of his, and he himself was a product of those days; Henderson's ideas were moulded when reform of every sort was in the air, and when great social and material changes were transforming the country. Perhaps the most important of all the factors which make 1869 a turning-point in police annals in this country was that Mayne's own position was unique. The newspapers might deride him, and clamour for his resignation; he might even, in his old age, offer to retire; but for thirty-nine years he was, in fact, almost irremovable. It is doubtful if any Home Secretary during this period would have been strong enough to demand his resignation. The future was to hold a different story. No Commissioner since Mayne has acquired an authority approaching his, and within twenty-one years of his death his three immediate successors had, one after the other, felt compelled to resign.

There is no evidence that after the sequel to the Clerkenwell explosion, at the end of 1867, Mayne himself repeated his offer of resignation, or thought seriously of doing so, but during the last year of his life certain hostile newspapers affected to believe that his retirement was imminent, and were busy disposing of his office. In January 1868 the *Penny Illustrated Paper* perceived "at last a faint chance that the administration of the Metropolitan Police will be confided to a distinct Government department, and not to one apparently irresponsible Commissioner." The idea had been broached from time to time, but seems never to have been seriously considered; it was thought to be too Continental. At the same time there was a horrid suspicion abroad that the next Commissioner, when the time came to appoint one, would be a soldier, and the Home Secretary was warned that this would not do. Opinion in general was in favour of another lawyer, but some unlikely candidates were proposed, among them the author of *Tom Brown's Schooldays*. Mayne fell ill, and in two leading articles, one published immediately before his death, and the other immediately after, the *Daily Telegraph* instructed the Home Secretary in his duties, summed up the special attributes required in the new Commissioner, and added: "We feel certain that no retired soldier in this country combines these essential qualifications." There was an interregnum of two months, during which Labalmondière was acting Commissioner, and this was regarded as ominous. The *Penny Illustrated* feared that his appointment would become permanent. The public, like Eric, was now roused—at least, churchwardens and others, meeting in the Vestry Hall of St James's, Piccadilly, considered "the propriety of memorializing the Secretary of State on the appointment of a Chief Commissioner of Police," and a similar gathering of delegates of vestries and district boards at the Court House, Marylebone Lane, resolved to ask for an interview with the Minister. All this was in January 1869; a little later the worst was known. A new Home Secretary—H. A. Bruce, afterwards Lord Aberdare—ignored the commands of editors and the more respectful arguments of vestries, and on the 2nd of February the *Daily Telegraph* was asking plaintively, "Who is Colonel Henderson?"

Henderson, in fact, had many of the qualifications which the *Telegraph* had been demanding, in particular "some practical insight into the characteristics of our criminal classes." Few men knew more about these classes than he did. For thirteen years he had been head of the convict establishment in Australia, and for another six Director and Surveyor-General of Prisons at the Home Office. He was, of course, a regular soldier, his corps being the Royal Engineers, the old Sappers and Miners, but as Commissioner, observes Sir John Moylan, "he was very little of a military chief." He seems to have possessed much tact and common sense, for he got on well with a succession of

Home Secretaries, all determined now that the Commissioner should not be another Mayne, and not the least forceful of them, Sir William Harcourt, said of his rule that "things went very smoothly both inside and outside Scotland Yard." He showed the same qualities from the start in his handling of the police themselves, as is illustrated by a trivial matter better remembered than many of his more important reforms: by an order issued when he had been in office less than two months all members of the force were permitted to wear beards and moustaches.[1] Apparently this was a felt want, and *Judy* sang the gratitude of Constable XYZ:

> Three cheers for our new commander!
> HENDERSON'S the man for me;
> For he likes his bold perlicemen
> Ever beautiful to be.

There were other desiderata, more essential than beards. Many of them had been recommended by the Departmental Committee of the Home Office set up (as mentioned in a previous chapter) after the Clerkenwell outrage. Some of these proposals were now carried into effect. The force was to be increased, and the Detective Branch also, and opportunity was to be taken to modify the existing organization. The Committee had pointed out that a system designed for 3000 men (roughly the total in 1830) was not well adapted for 8000, and still less so for a larger number. There was, for instance, too high a proportion of superior officers to sergeants and constables. It was thought that every division should have quarters for married men, as was already the case in Paddington, and that there should be canteens; the latter were a success, but in days when there was no housing shortage married quarters were not popular, and the scheme was eventually abandoned. The same fate nearly befell an ambitious plan which grouped the divisions into four large districts, each Assistant Commissioner having charge of a pair,[2] and each district being under a District Superintendent. It seems to have been the idea of the Committee that this arrangement would in course of time render the Assistant Commissioners redundant; but things fell out otherwise. Three of the new District Superintendents were drawn from outside, and for this reason, among others, the experiment was at first not altogether a success. The Divisional Superintendents resented the authority of the newcomers, whose duties were ill-defined, and who soon found themselves with

[1] Police Orders, March 30, 1869.
[2] Police Orders, May 7, 1869.

very little to do,[1] and two of these appointments presently lapsed. They were revived after Henderson's resignation, when the title of Chief Constable replaced that of District Superintendent. To-day, in charge of Commanders, with Deputy Commanders under them, the four districts are an essential part of the Metropolitan Police organization.

Henderson took immediate steps to augment the ridiculously small Detective Branch, as the Departmental Committee had recommended. He found fifteen men under Chief Inspector Williamson, who as a sergeant had been with Whicher on the Road case, and who took Constance Kent into custody after her confession five years later. Williamson was promoted to superintendent, and other promotions and transfers brought the number of detective officers above the rank of constable to twenty-seven, and the total personnel of the branch to nearly 200. It was further increased to some 260 in Henderson's time. Among those now advanced were three officers whose names were soon to become only too well known—Inspector Clarke, to chief inspector, Sergeant Druscovitch, to inspector, and Second-class Sergeant Meiklejohn, to first-class sergeant.[2]

Much was done by Henderson to make the life of the constable on the beat less unattractive. As the strength of the force increased, the beats themselves were shortened, and fixed points were established at which a policeman could be found when wanted. Police stations were rebuilt or reconditioned, and recreation-rooms provided where the men could smoke and play billiards when waiting to go on duty. When off duty they were allowed to wear plain clothes. Schoolmaster sergeants were appointed in the divisions to meet the need for a higher standard of literacy. The Metropolitan and City Police Orphanage[3] dated from Henderson's day. The growth of the force went on steadily throughout his seventeen years at Scotland Yard, the annual increase averaging 300; and when he resigned in 1886 the total had risen from about 8500 to 13,804.

As the force increased, so did the responsibilities of the man on the

[1] Moylan, *op.cit.*, and Sir Basil Thomson, *The Story of Scotland Yard* (Grayson, 1935). The first District Superintendents, with their headquarters, were: District 1, Lieutenant-Colonel R. L. O. Pearson (King's Cross); District 2, A. C. Howard (Albany Street); District 3, H. Baynes (Rochester Row); District 4, R. Walker (Brixton). Walker, the only one of them taken from the force, had been Chief Superintendent, A.

[2] Police Orders, May 15, 1869. The pay of a superintendent in the Detective Branch was £300, with 15*s*. a day travelling expenses. Chief inspectors got £250 and 15*s*. for daily expenses, inspectors £200 and 13*s*., and first- and second-class sergeants £150 and £110 respectively, with a 10*s*. expense allowance. There was a general allowance of £10 per annum for clothes.

[3] Now replaced by the Metropolitan and City Police Orphan Fund.

beat, who was now expected, as Police Orders show, to apply his mind to an infinite variety of affairs, ranging from the serious to the trivial, according to new regulations, or amendments to old ones, which appeared almost daily. Henderson was barely in office when the attention of Divisional Superintendents was called to existing orders on the game of Tip-cat, and the police were instructed to do all in their power to prevent the dangerous pastime (April 27, 1869). There was more about Tip-cat early in 1870, and the dangers of other youthful pastimes in the streets must have been constantly in an alert officer's mind; thus it was pointed out (November 1871) that Mayne's much-abused order on the "Trundling of Hoops" was still in force, and presently reports were called for from divisions on the prevalence of catapults (May 22, 1875). The untidy habits of Londoners were a constant worry, and references to General Orders, "Orange Peel," Paragraph 1, "which is to be strictly complied with" (November 27, 1874), were to go on for years, though in time the invention of safety-matches relieved the police of the tedium of recovering all "Vesuvians or Lucifers lying on the pavements" (July 30, 1873). The manners of the police themselves were not overlooked, and slang terms were forbidden on duty; the words "taken into custody," for instance, should be used instead of such phrases as "running them in" (November 25, 1869). Outside influences were at work in the cause of uplift, and on April 30, 1870, the force was informed that the United Kingdom Band of Hope Union had presented to the police libraries copies of its prize stories *Frank Oldfield* and *Tim's Troubles*.

An Order of the 14th of December, 1871, requiring returns to be made by divisions of "all places known as Greenyards," is a reminder that eighty years ago, and for some time after, London resembled a great congeries of market towns. A prominent feature of the Metropolitan scene appears to have been the numbers of stray animals—horses, cattle, pigs, and sheep—wandering in the streets. Police had to intermit the collection of orange-peel and Vesuvians, and the counting of catapults, to round up these creatures, which were herded in pounds called greenyards, usually established in such places as livery stables and the yards of public houses. Stray dogs were more common than they are now, for 4500 were collected in three months in 1874, or fifty a day.

Rearrangements in the organization of the force included the amalgamation, in 1869, of E (Holborn) and F (Covent Garden) Divisions as E (Holborn) Division. As soon as the Detective Branch at Scotland Yard was sufficiently augmented a number of its trained men were attached to divisions to supplement the old divisional detectives, hitherto considered none too efficient, and the immediate success of this move is perhaps indicated by the remarks of Mr Serjeant Cox, Deputy Assistant Judge at the London Sessions, when commending two detectives of D: "No institution within my memory has done so much towards the prevention, as well as the punishment of crime."[1] In Henderson's first year the Register of Habitual Criminals was begun at Scotland Yard; designed on too comprehensive a scale to be practical, it was nevertheless a step towards the Criminal Record Office of to-day. The most important of all developments in this direction was the transformation of the Detective Branch itself, in 1878, into the Criminal Investigation Department, of which more will be said later.

By the Public Carriage Act of 1869 the licensing of all public vehicles plying for hire completed the work of earlier Acts by vesting all licensing functions in the Commissioner of Police. Licensing fees were reduced, and standards of fitness set up, no fewer than 1500 vehicles being taken off the streets within twelve months. Paschal retired, and was not replaced, the Commissioner and one of the Assistant Commissioners dividing the work. London then had 5872 cabs and 900 stage carriages or omnibuses, the successors of the "Shillibeers" of 1829; seventeen years later there were 7020 hansoms, 3997 Clarences (four-wheelers, the later "growlers"), and 2531 omnibuses. Natural growth was much helped by Henderson's interest in this department, and in the welfare of the cabmen, omnibus-drivers, and others under its wing. He set about at once increasing the number of hackney-carriage stands, enabling more vehicles to be on the streets, and he introduced the cabman's shelter. The one in Piccadilly known to the West End as the "Junior Turf Club" goes back almost to his day. He was so popular with the cab-driving fraternity, a class by itself, with its own customs (among them that of getting very drunk and "driving furiously," which got it the name of Jehus), that after his resignation the cab-owners and -drivers of London presented him with a silver model of a hansom cab.

2

It might be thought that newspaper editors, once they had got over the shock of having their commands ignored, would at last begin to see some good in a force which was growing in efficiency and popu-

[1] Police Orders, June 9, 1871.

larity,[1] and in a Commissioner who was the reverse of an authoritarian. But bad habits die hard, and for some years the old parrot-cries of Mayne's day persisted, as though set permanently in type to be brought out every few weeks. December 1869, when the *Graphic* found the police of London still "inefficient and insolent," was perhaps a little early for a change of heart; but in 1870 the *Daily News* was running a series of articles on police incompetence, and the *Daily Telegraph* discovered that the existing system had "collapsed," because "the upper staff, with one notable exception, has proved an utter failure. . . . We want more brains at headquarters, not more men in the streets." "Never," said the same journal a month later, "did the Metropolitan Police stand so low in the eyes of the public," and a fortnight after that another leading article spoke of "the incompetency and vexatious military proclivities of the Chief [*sic*] Commissioner."[2] In 1871 the *Telegraph* had almost as many leaders on this fruitful topic as there were months in the year, and printed scores of bilious letters from "Vigilans" and others, besides, of course, giving prominence to every case in which the conduct of the police was questionable, or even questioned.

This stage in the long campaign of vilification of the force had one amusing feature—the editorial *volte-face* in the case of the late Commissioner. Mayne was now discovered to have had virtues completely overlooked when he was alive. "He knew—no one better," said the *Telegraph*, "what really were the duties of the superintendent, of the inspector, of the sergeant, of the constable. . . . He lived close to his business, and by day and night he was unwearied in the discharge of his important functions." Now, alas, things were changed: "the tradition of hard work is fading at Scotland Yard." Mayne, it was reported, had dreamed of a Ministry of Police, "with himself, of course, as 'Minister,'" and readers who remembered what had been said only a year or two before about "the Prefect of the Thames," whom the public "would gladly release from any further exertions," might have been wondering if their eyes now deceived them when they read that "a worthier man could scarcely have been found," had they not already blinked at the startling pronouncement that "those were the palmy days of the Metropolitan Police."[3]

[1] By 1871 the number of candidates on the waiting-list had risen to 689.—Commissioner's Report, 1871.

[2] *Daily Telegraph*, May 17, June 10, June 27, 1870. "The one notable exception" to the general rot at Scotland Yard was evidently well liked by the editor, for he was referred to anonymously again.

[3] *Daily Telegraph*, May 17, 1870; August 15, 1871.

Things changed again—or, at least, opinions did, though it is not easy to see why. By the end of 1873 the new Commissioner, so far from being incompetent, was "a man of high character and ability." Two years later there was "fair cause to pronounce that Colonel Henderson had every reason to look with pride on the force under his command, and that the public at large are equally warranted in feeling a high degree of satisfaction with the general state, organization, and discipline of the municipal army so laboriously and energetically directed from headquarters in Scotland Yard"—where, so recently, the tradition of hard work had been "fading." Better police stations, and provision in them for amusements, of which it was said at the time that the community had "scarcely benefited by these innovations," were now, only a few years later, matters for pride.[1] There is no need to stress this eating of words—in which almost the whole Press took part, as it had taken part in the original misjudgment—but one more amusing instance should be noted. In the early months of 1874 there was renewed alarm about the spread of hydrophobia in London. "Colonel Henderson," said the *Daily Telegraph* of the 1st of May, "cannot too soon follow the example of his lamented predecessor, and enforce the most stringent precautions." The Colonel having done so, "with commendable promptitude," it was remarked that an Act of Parliament of 1871, giving the police the fullest authority in such an emergency, might have gone a little further, so that "an ownerless dog would be, as it ought to be, promptly destroyed." As things were, "a policeman's duty should include the arrest of every dog he finds loose in the streets unaccompanied by its master." Did it, for a moment, flash across the editor's memory that only six years earlier the Colonel's lamented predecessor had been accused of "rather unscientific and irrational energy on the subject of 'mad dogs,'" and that his Dog Laws, it was feared, would "do more mischief than they prevent"? The spirit of Mayne, remembering how he had been abused and ridiculed by every paper in the country for issuing instructions now so heartily approved, may have smiled a little. In time it was to appear that he had been wiser than "the best veterinarians," who still held the opinion that muzzling was "a precaution of little value."[2]

The change in the general attitude of the London Press towards the police was permanent; there were, indeed, to be many relapses, but they were of a relatively mild nature, and not long sustained. It was time, for perpetual carping and abuse had a serious aspect which does

[1] *Daily Telegraph*, November 12, 1873; August 19, 1875.
[2] *Daily Telegraph*, May 1, 7, 8, 1874.

not seem to have been recognized then or since. The effect upon the force as a whole must have been most mischievous. Every policeman reads some newspaper sometimes; his friends read others, and the humorous papers, in particular *Fun*, *Punch*, *Judy*, and the new *Vanity Fair*, were widely quoted, and had their counterparts in the music-halls. The man on the beat, doing his best, as he generally was, knew that he could scarcely open a paper when he went off duty without finding himself pilloried in it as a nincompoop, a figure of fun, or a downright brute. If he made a mistake it was reported at length, and probably made the subject of a leading article; if he did a good piece of work that was not news in those days. Letters headed "Police Brutality" were a commonplace; when the police themselves were assaulted they read that "people are getting tired of hearing about" such cases.[1] Yet in Henderson's first four years as Commissioner attacks on policemen increased from 2858 in 1869 to 3692 in 1872, which meant, it was pointed out, that every man on duty in the streets might expect to be so attacked once every two years.[2] What he might also have expected, some appreciation of the risks he ran, was a very long time coming.

3

When Mayne was still Commissioner, on Christmas Eve, 1866, Arthur Orton, alias Thomas Castro, arrived with his wife and family at Ford's Hotel in Manchester Square. For the next seven years the Tichborne Case dominated the English scene. It culminated in two trials of incredible length, of which Lord Maugham remarks: "The civil case heard before the Chief Justice of the Common Pleas lasted for no less than one hundred and two days before the jury intimated that they did not desire to hear any further evidence; and the criminal trial went on for one hundred and eighty-eight days before the jury found the claimant guilty." An imposture which, as the same learned writer says, hypnotized half the world, and which must rank with the frauds of Mme Humbert among the classics of human gullibility, cost the successful defendants, the unfortunate Tichborne family, upward of £91,000.[3]

The case was merely a part of the background to police history until the end of the civil trial in March 1872, when officers of the Detective Branch arrested Orton and took him to Newgate; but an old member

[1] *Daily Telegraph*, September 3, 1875. [2] Commissioner's Report for 1872.
[3] Lord Maugham, *The Tichborne Case* (Hodder and Stoughton, 1936).

of the Branch had for some time been working in that background for the solicitors for the family. When the gross creature who claimed to be Sir Roger Tichborne came to Ford's Hotel six years before, having just landed at the Victoria Docks after a voyage from New York, he had no sooner had dinner than he set off on a mysterious journey in a four-wheeled cab. The next day, Christmas Day, he was away again on unspecified business of his own. It was ex-Detective-Inspector Whicher, now, like Field and others, taking on confidential inquiries, who found out that both these journeys had ended at Wapping, a place of which Roger Tichborne could scarcely have heard, but the home of the Orton family. There Whicher ran to earth Charles Orton, to whom his brother Arthur had promised money if the imposture was successfully carried through. Because from an early date he maintained that the Claimant was a fraud the ex-inspector was much abused.

Two years after Arthur Orton was sentenced to a total of fourteen years' penal servitude, another legend was started when Police-Constable Cock was shot dead at Whalley Range, Manchester, in August 1876. Two brothers named Habron were tried for the murder; one was acquitted, and the sentence of death passed on William Habron was commuted to one of penal servitude for life, it being thought that an accomplice had actually fired the shot. The day after the trial ended Arthur Dyson was shot dead at Ecclesall, a suburb of Sheffield. The murderer was seen and recognized, but the local police appear to have been satisfied with inquiries in the neighbourhood which failed to find him. Another two years went by before a man caught in the act of burglary at Blackheath was identified as Charles Peace, the killer of Dyson. In resisting arrest he shot and wounded P.C. Robinson, of R Division. While two Pentonville warders were taking Peace in handcuffs to Sheffield he threw himself out of the railway carriage window, but was knocked senseless by the fall. An habitual criminal, who made his livelihood by burglary, Peace, under the name of Thomson, had been living at Peckham, and the numerous stolen articles found in his house seem to have suggested many of the stories soon current of his remarkable abilities. The newspapers elaborated them; for months even a sober journal like the *Daily Telegraph* was full of "The Convict Peace" and his sham artificial hand and folding ladder and musical gifts. A stream of fiction about him, dressed up as fact and coloured by a false romanticism, has been appearing ever since. A little, wizened, dark-skinned man, who had shown early ability as an actor—he certainly deceived his neighbours at Peckham for several years—he was, in fact, a cold-blooded and cowardly criminal of the worst type.

Before he went to the gallows in February 1879 he confessed to the murder of Constable Cock, three years earlier, at Whalley Range. At first this confession was scarcely believed, but a comparison of the bullets which killed Cock and Dyson and wounded P.C. Robinson showed that they had been fired from the same weapon—an early use of the science of ballistics. William Habron was, of course, released and compensated. His case appears to be a striking illustration of how misleading circumstantial evidence may be, for this had convinced not only a judge and jury, but also the Home Secretary, who studied it closely, of Habron's guilt.

Peace, of whom the *Telegraph* said that he was, "like most other musical amateurs, an amiable and obliging person," gave the police a list of receivers of stolen property all over England, and something seems to have been done to investigate this traffic in London. The police of B Division made a good haul at the premises of a marine-store dealer in Pimlico, where they found "gold coins, travelling bags, bank notes, blue serge, watches, chains, tablecloths, brooches, lockets, studs, silver plate, pieces of alpaca, cutlery, artificial teeth, slippers, shawls, lead and brass, and articles of almost every description."[1] But though it was said that the receivers in the country known to the police numbered over a thousand, a majority of these, disguised as pawnbrokers, marine-store dealers, jewellers, assayers of gold and silver and the like, carried on their trade with impunity; and Peace's revelation revived interest in a proposal which had been in the air for some time—that a Director of Public Prosecutions should be appointed, to aid and stimulate the police, and ease the work of the Treasury Solicitor's office. In 1884 the proposal was carried into effect; but the functions of the first Directors were very limited, and after a time the office lapsed. It was to be re-created, with much wider powers, in 1908.

Two other capital cases of this period of unusual interest were the murder of Mrs Thomas at Richmond in 1879, and the shooting of P.C. Cole at Dalston on the 1st of December, 1882. Kate Webster, who hacked her elderly mistress to death with a cleaver, was a ferocious tigress of the type of Mrs Manning and Mrs Pearcey. She anticipated some of the methods of Patrick Mahon, boiling her victim's trunk in a copper (she said the grease would come in useful), and carrying the head about in a black bag until she could dispose of it. The Criminal

[1] *Daily Telegraph*, April 12, 1880.

Investigation Department, as it was by then, was called in on this case. The murder of Constable Cole was committed on its own ground, and the subsequent investigation, in the hands of Detective-Inspector Glass, is an early classic of its kind. Cole's murderer, like Peace, was an armed burglar, and, like Franz Müller, he left his hat behind. He also left a couple of chisels, scratched on one of which, though only legible under a magnifying-glass, was what appeared to be the word "rock." After patient inquiries among tool-makers and cabinet-makers in Dalston and the neighbourhood the chisel was traced to a carpenter named Orrock. He had a police record, and was by this time serving a sentence for another burglary. It has been suggested that he allowed himself to be caught, thinking prison the safest hiding-place. He had underrated the pertinacity of Inspector Glass, and, perhaps, the general improvement in the methods of the reformed Detective Branch. The police must have pursued him with special zeal, for not only was robbery under arms on the increase, but little more than a month before Cole was murdered a burglar had shot and wounded P.C. Ellingham, of S Division, in Hampstead.

With the conviction of a murderer, his case normally passes out of the hands of the police; but as macabre curiosities the fate of three murderers in Henderson's last years, though only one of the crimes was committed in London, may be referred to here. In 1885 John Lee was sentenced to death for killing Miss Emma Keyse at Babbacombe, in Devon. Three attempts were made to hang him, but each time the drop failed to act. Lee was reprieved, and after serving twenty-two years of his life sentence capitalized his experience as "The Man they could not Hang." The hangman was Berry, who was unfortunate, to say the least, in his technique, for in the same year Robert Goodale had his head torn from his body while being executed, while in 1886 Berry was concerned in another horrible business in Wales, when in hanging David Roberts he underestimated the drop required; the wretched victim struggled, and had to be dispatched by other means.[1] Hanging was still carried out by rather empirical methods; in course of time a simple formula was worked out for estimating the drop, but it was not until the late 1930's that the question was approached scientifically, on humanitarian grounds, by Sir Bernard Spilsbury and Mr Bentley Purchase, the London coroner.

In 1876 a man named Fish, who committed a murder in Blackburn, was caught by the aid of bloodhounds—the first case of the kind in this country. The Home Office sent the relevant documents to Scotland

[1] Alan Brock, *A Casebook of Crime* (Rockliff, 1948).

Yard, where the idea was received with some scepticism. It was revived at the time of the "Jack the Ripper" murders, twelve years later, when bloodhounds were used.

An oddity in 1880 was the attempt to stop the execution of Charles Shurety by means of a forged reprieve. Among miscellaneous domestic events in Henderson's time was a second replacement of the rattle by the whistle for day patrols; the first use (in the same year, 1885) of steam launches by the Thames Division; and the purchase, also in 1885, of a site on the Embankment, opposite Westminster Hall, for a new headquarters building later to be called New Scotland Yard.

15

THE COMING OF THE C.I.D.

THREE outstanding events in Henderson's seventeen years' Commissionership were the police "strike" in 1872, the startling disclosures five years later of corruption at Scotland Yard itself, in the trusted and privileged Detective Branch, and the rioting in the West End of London in 1886, which brought about the Commissioner's resignation. The first and last of these occurrences were, in themselves, far less serious than they were made to appear at the time.

The Departmental Committee of 1868 had failed, as other similar bodies have failed, to face squarely a recurrent cause of complaint among the police—the inadequate pay of the lower ranks. This question has a positive and a relative aspect. When compared with the wages that can be earned in industry the pay of a policeman, like that of a soldier, must always seem inadequate. On the other hand, the policeman and the soldier are not affected by bad times, and can look forward to retiring on a pension at an age when they can find other work. Relatively, however, they are periodically affected, because the cost of living is always going up, while their pay is controlled by the amount of money which can be wrung from the Treasury. During the trouble in 1872 Henderson pointed out to the advocates of increased pay that he simply had not got the funds. That these were afterwards found was a complete justification of the men's demands. Where the latter went wrong was in the methods adopted to air their complaints, but it is at least difficult to say how else this could have been done effectively at that time. A secondary motive behind the strike—the word, adopted from industry, does not altogether meet such a case—was the question of the formation of some sort of police trade union, which no Government could allow. This question was to be raised again, and was eventually solved by a compromise—the creation of the Police Federation. At the same time a system of allowances to meet rises in the cost of living was introduced.

All this was a long way ahead when in the autumn of 1872 a number of constables, and a few sergeants, almost all from D, E, and T

Divisions, refused to report for duty. There were meetings and small demonstrations—Constable Goodchild, of E, hired an omnibus drawn by four greys, in which he drove about from station to station, haranguing—and a rather pushing Member of Parliament named Eykyn, who considered himself an authority on police matters, took the chair at some of the gatherings, and wrote letters to the papers. A demonstration in Hyde Park was a fiasco, but roughs from the East End enjoyed a field day there. It was considered rather serious that a centre of disaffection was historic Bow Street, the oldest of police stations, and still regarded (apart from the nature of its accommodation) as a model. Here the firmness of Labalmondière quelled the trouble at the start, and Henderson dealt as promptly with the situation as a whole. Altogether 180 men were suspended. It was then announced that the question of increased pay would be submitted immediately to the Home Secretary. The agitation collapsed; Goodchild and a few more were dismissed, and the other culprits were reinstated. The increases which came into force in November ranged from fifty pounds a year for superintendents to a shilling or two a day for constables, now formed into three classes instead of four. There were modifications of hours of duty, by which the eight hours on the beat was divided into reliefs of four hours. The Commissioner further undertook to raise the question of pensions, the inadequacy of which was another grievance; but it was to be a long time before this matter reached a satisfactory settlement, and it was to be a source of trouble in the future.

Henderson reduced the strike to its right proportions when he wrote:

> Of this occurrence, which was much commented on at the time, it is sufficient to say that it was repented of almost as soon as committed, has been amply atoned for, and has left nothing behind it but a regret that by the unjustifiable conduct of a few men, a stain should have been left on the honourable annals of the force.[1]

The strike, nevertheless, had its after-effects. The growth among the public of a more favourable opinion of the police was checked. The Home Secretary, now Robert Lowe, of *ex luce lucellum* fame, spoke of a "dead set" against the force. There was an outcry over the arrest in Gray's Inn of Mr Belt, an eccentric barrister whose behaviour led a constable to think him drunk, and the Chief Magistrate at Bow Street, Sir Thomas Henry, held an inquiry into the case. When a similar charge was brought against officers of the Life Guards, after a fracas

[1] Commissioner's Report for 1872.

outside a notorious dancing saloon in the Haymarket, an addition to the rather numerous actions for perjury against the police was averted only by the intervention of the Duke of Cambridge, the Commander-in-Chief. The Detective Branch came in for much adverse criticism because several brutal murders in the London area in 1872 and 1873 remained unsolved. "The Inspector Buckets, of 'Bleak House,' the detective heroes of Mr Wilkie Collins's novels, have created an utterly false impression as to the capabilities of our police force," said the *Daily Telegraph*. The bodies of two murdered women having been recovered from the Regent's Canal within six months, the *Telegraph* did indeed point out that when such victims remained unidentified the detective force was "all but powerless." Reference in a lighter vein to certain disappearances about this time which had also baffled the police reads oddly to-day; among those missing was a Mr Bauer, of whom the *Telegraph* said: "It may be that the Skoptchi, or some other terrible secret sect of which nobody but the author of 'Free Russia' knows anything, have spirited Mr Bauer off from his friends and his betrothed."[1]

The Detective Branch, like Mr Midshipman Easy, was also accused of too much zeal; in one or two of these cases of murder it was over-hasty in making an arrest. It was thought to have erred in the other direction when Warren, Bidwell, and Macdonell, the leaders of a gang of American swindlers dealing in forged securities, were given time to escape across the Atlantic. It has never been suggested that there was any collusion in this affair, but to one at least of the detective officers specializing in financial trickery the case of Warren, Bidwell, Macdonell and Co. should have brought sobering thoughts. For by March 1873 Sergeant Meiklejohn, one of Inspector Druscovitch's "merry men," had been for some months in the toils of another gang of rogues, working on very similar lines. During the next few years the gang was to enlist Druscovitch himself, and other officers of long and creditable service were to be involved in a net of corruption and deceit happily unique in the history of the Metropolitan Police.

In 1877 Superintendent Williamson, of the Detective Branch, had immediately under him four chief inspectors, his right-hand men. Chief Inspector Clarke was sixty, Chief Inspector Palmer forty-three, Chief Inspector Druscovitch only thirty-seven; the rise of the last-named, a very able man who spoke several languages, had been rapid.

[1] *Daily Telegraph*, June 29, 1872. If history repeats itself it is perhaps because nations do not change. Nearly eighty years after the disappearance of Mr Bauer the papers were to be full of missing "diplomats" and others, generally presumed to have been "spirited off" to Russia.

The fourth chief inspector plays no part in the lamentable story. So far as Scotland Yard was concerned, the villain of the piece was none of the other three, but Meiklejohn, by now an inspector. As far back as 1872 Meiklejohn had begun taking bribes from William Kurr, who made his money as Warren, Bidwell, and Macdonell made theirs, by creating bogus firms, though Kurr's were concerned with betting on horse-races, not with so-called securities. Soon after this Kurr became associated with a mind far more brilliant than his own. Harry Benson was the son of a respectable Jewish merchant; he was partly educated in Paris, and before he was twenty-four he had carried out a series of swindles, some of which, though small in scale, bore the stamp of genius. This phase of his life came to an end in 1872; as the Count de Montagu, Mayor of Chateaudun, terribly damaged in the Franco-Prussian War, he got £1000 out of the Lord Mayor of London, but he was arrested within a few days. At Newgate he tried to take his life by setting his bed on fire, and as a result was for some years afterwards a cripple, confined to a wheeled chair. His sentence of twelve months' imprisonment was spent in the prison hospital. Released in July 1873, he took the name of J. H. Yonge, and, having got in touch with Kurr, an even younger man—he was then only twenty-three—he became the brains of a partnership which in the next four years defrauded of a good many thousand pounds that section of the public which is always hoping to make money easily and quickly on the turf.

The *modus operandi* was the establishment of firms with fancy names in London, Edinburgh, and Glasgow, and the advertisement of their infallible betting systems by circular and in sporting journals printed for the purpose. Benson, who soon moved to a large house at Shanklin, in the Isle of Wight, wrote the circulars and articles. A staff of lesser knaves was recruited, and with the help of Inspector Meiklejohn, who gave warning whenever some transaction roused suspicion at Scotland Yard, the gang was able to carry on with impunity and profit for several years. A feature of its method was the employment of dupes as 'agents.' Benson being able to write fluently in French, the field of operations was eventually extended to France by means of a publication called *Sport*, which was numbered and priced as though a genuine periodical. Its carefully selected readers were told how the wicked bookmakers had boycotted the editor and proprietor, a "Mr Montgomery," because of his successes on the turf, and were invited to help him to defeat the boycott and circumvent the rules of the Jockey Club by placing bets for him in their own names. Those who consented received Mr Montgomery's cheques, drawn on an imaginary bank, and dealt with them as requested. The sight of all this money in transit often had the desired effect; the agent risked a bet of his own. He was allowed to win until he staked a considerable sum, after which he heard no more of his bet or of Mr Montgomery.

While Kurr and his *aides* worked from various offices in London, Benson was living in great style at Shanklin, where it was soon known that the cultured Mr Yonge was a French nobleman of the Murat family, and a friend of the Empress of Austria, to whom he actually wrote, "in the name of the inhabitants of Shanklin," when that ill-fated lady was on a visit to England.[1] It will appear that Benson was a man of imagination and ideas, and one of these—for which, unhappily, there was some justification—was that most policemen had their price. Meiklejohn was extremely useful, but how much more useful one or two of his seniors in the Detective Branch would be. It was generally agreed that Superintendent Williamson could not be bought; it might, however, be worth tempting Chief Inspector Clarke, the next senior officer, and Druscovitch would be an even more valuable prize. A specialist in the type of fraud the gang was engaged in, Druscovitch had once or twice been uncomfortably near tracking some of them down, only a warning from Meiklejohn averting disaster. The latter learnt that Druscovitch was in a financial difficulty; he had backed a bill for his brother, and now had to find the money. Meiklejohn, who was now buying house property with his bribes, and could have found the necessary sixty pounds, professed to be unable to help. But there was his friend Bill Kurr: no doubt he would do something.

Detective officers, as part of their duty, mix with very queer people. In this way Meiklejohn had first met Kurr, and it is most improbable that Druscovitch did not know a good deal about the latter. But for sixty pounds, which benefited him not at all, he put himself in Kurr's debt; and repayment, as he must have suspected, would not be demanded in money. It is a very sad story, for Druscovitch was an able and kindly man, who might have gone far. Williamson thought very highly of him, and at the Old Bailey gave a long list of rewards and commendations, including one from the Emperor of Russia, earned by Druscovitch in the course of his rapid rise to chief inspector. Anyone who has been tried as he was tried must have some understanding of his case. For Meiklejohn, the traitor, there can be nothing but contempt.

Blackmail of another sort was employed to entangle Chief Inspector Clarke. His case became urgent when he ran down two members of

[1] George Dilnot, *The Trial of the Detectives* (Bles, 1928), from which many details of the story are taken.

the gang, Murray and Walters, in 1875, and at the same time obtained a warrant for Kurr. He had written Walters a letter which could be thought compromising; Benson obtained it, and Clarke did himself no good by having several interviews with the descendant of Marshal Murat in the fine house at Shanklin and at the Langham Hotel. His accounts of these meetings differed from Benson's, and it was not proved that he accepted bribes. He maintained that he reported all that went on to Williamson, who at the trial did his best for his old colleague. A jury took the view that the senior chief inspector, on the verge of retiring, had merely been foolish. It had no doubts about Chief Inspector Palmer, whose involvement in the case remains, however, somewhat obscure.

A good deal of anxiety is entailed in such frauds as those engineered by Benson and Kurr, but both were young men, and seem to have played the game with gusto. Benson may have found in it release from pain and infirmity. Kurr had no nerves, and any amount of audacity. New schemes were continually in hand; old offices were always being hastily closed, and fresh ones opened; sham companies and false names would have filled a page of the directory. Shielded by Meiklejohn, and later by Druscovitch, Kurr and others for long ignored warrants out against them under their aliases. Kurr himself was always travelling about England and Scotland, to France and the United States, sometimes with Benson, as the latter's disability became less crippling. There were many secret meetings with Meiklejohn and Druscovitch at railway stations and hotels, and presently as far afield as Derby and the Bridge of Allan, in Stirlingshire. In July 1876 Kurr and Benson, the latter once more the Count de Montagu, were in Paris. It was soon after their return, and a convivial evening with Meiklejohn at the Cannon Street Hotel, that Mr Montgomery was invented. The connivance of Druscovitch was necessary, for he handled Continental matters at Scotland Yard, and he was led to believe, or tried to convince himself, that the circulation of *Sport*, and Mr Montgomery's use of agents abroad, were harmless evasions of the Betting Act.

The new scheme had not long been under way when a really big fish was landed. The Comtesse de Goncourt, a very wealthy woman, became one of Mr Montgomery's go-betweens. Entranced by the sums the proprietor of *Sport* appeared to be winning, the Comtesse put £1000 of her own on a horse. Told it had won, she staked more, until by September of this year, 1876, she had parted with £10,000, for which she held cheques on the "Royal Bank of England," Mr Montgomery explaining that by English law these could not be presented until a later date. With the £10,000 in their hands, Benson and Kurr should have been content; but success had gone to Benson's head. The Comtesse was now urged to invest no less than £30,000 with one "Thomas Ellerton," that *rara avis* (in Mr Montgomery's words), an honest bookmaker. The foolish woman was quite willing, but to raise so large a sum she had to consult her lawyer. What the lawyer said can be imagined. He put the matter in the hands of a London solicitor. Greek now joined Greek, for Mr Abrahams, like Benson, was a Jew. He went at once to Scotland Yard.

A swindle on so large a scale roused the powers there to energetic action. Poor Druscovitch, still unsuspected, was sent by Williamson to interview Abrahams. The distracted chief inspector then sought out Kurr, to whom he said, "I must arrest somebody." "Arrest me, if you like," said Kurr, still confident that he could bluff his way out. Druscovitch did not dare to go so far—perhaps because Kurr knew too much about him. But the game was up; minor members of the gang were brought in one by one. Benson went to Holland, and Druscovitch, with several other officers, was sent to fetch him back. Kurr stood his ground at the public house he owned in Islington, and there he was arrested by Detective-Sergeant Littlechild, whom Williamson had warned to keep the business secret, even from his fellow-officers.

These must have been terrible days for Clarke, Palmer, and Meiklejohn at Scotland Yard, and even worse for Druscovitch at Rotterdam, for he had to wait there for some weeks while extradition proceedings were completed. All four had had to play their parts in hunting down men whose arrest they dreaded; and they must have known by now that their own actions were closely watched. Williamson, as has appeared, had begun to suspect the truth, and some time before Kurr's arrest on New Year's Eve the Treasury Solicitor had started an inquiry into the police handling of the case. It is said that other officers of the Detective Branch were under suspicion. It was a bad time for Williamson, too, and for Henderson; they did not know whom they could trust. *Fun* thus summed up the position:

> SUPERINTENDENT WILLIAMSON. I have to report another very serious jewel robbery, sir. About £5000.
>
> COLONEL HENDERSON. Now, then. How many of you fellows are in this?

Benson, Kurr and his brother Frederick, and two others stood their trial at the Old Bailey for fraud and forgery in April 1877. Benson was sentenced to fifteen years' penal servitude; the two Kurrs (though little is heard of Frederick in the earlier stages of the case) and a man named Bale to ten years each. In the meantime the Treasury Solicitor's office had been accumulating evidence against Druscovitch and Meiklejohn; and now happened what all the detectives involved had been dreading—Benson and Kurr, in the hope of getting some remission of their sentences, betrayed their confederates, or all except Chief Inspector Clarke, who at this time does not seem to have been suspected. His turn came, however, in the course of the police-court proceedings against the other three, which dragged on at Bow Street for months, and in September he joined his fellow-officers in the dock, where there was also a solicitor named Froggatt, who had acted for Benson and Kurr. As poor Clarke, who seemed bewildered by his position, took his stand beside Palmer, the latter shook him by the hand and burst into tears. On the 24th of September the five accused were committed for trial on a charge of conspiring to obstruct justice, Clarke and Froggatt being allowed bail.

The famous trial of the detectives, with whom was Froggatt, began at the Old Bailey exactly a month later. It lasted twenty days, six of which were taken up with the evidence of Kurr and Benson, brought from prison in convict dress. The conspiracy charge was a Common Law offence, though by a fairly recent statute this was punishable by imprisonment with hard labour. The prosecution of public servants in the peculiar position of police officers had not been foreseen; had it been, the judge observed in his summing up, it was probable that "the Legislature at some period or another would have created the offence into a particular and statutory crime, and would have annexed to its commission a punishment far beyond that which the prisoners under any circumstances can receive." For this reason, when Palmer, Druscovitch, Meiklejohn, and Froggatt had been found guilty, Baron Pollock, who described their crime as one of peculiar enormity, disregarded the jury's plea for special consideration in the cases of Palmer and Druscovitch. Sentences of two years' hard labour seemed indeed light when compared with those passed upon Benson and the Kurrs. Clarke, who owed much to his counsel and namesake, Edward Clarke, was acquitted.

Druscovitch, the least guilty, did not long survive his release. Of the others concerned, Benson and Kurr, even younger than the unfortunate chief inspector, were irreclaimable; Benson, released at the end of ten years, continued his career of swindling, and, having deluded Mme Patti, on one of her visits to New York, into accepting him as her agent, he collected several thousand pounds in Mexico for a concert she was to give there. He was once more arrested, in New York. Learning that extradition to Mexico had been granted, he threw himself to his death from an upper storey of the Tombs Prison.

2

More than two months before the trial of the detectives began it had been decided to appoint a Home Office Departmental Commission "to inquire into the state, discipline and organization of the Detective Force of the Metropolitan Police." The order of reference from the Home Secretary is dated August 13, 1877; and the four members of the Commission held their first meeting on the 16th of November, four days before the trial ended. Some of the newspaper forecasts of their conclusions, which were not published until early in the following year, may have been inspired; thus as early as the 22nd of November the *Daily Telegraph* was taking it for granted that the head of the remodelled Detective Branch would be an Assistant Commissioner, "who should, under any circumstances, be an astute and experienced lawyer."

The astute, if not then very experienced, lawyer was to hand. Mr Howard Vincent, a young barrister, had made a special study of the subject—"hurriedly," says Sir John Moylan,[1] and all accounts (including his own) agree that Vincent saw his chance and took it. He went to Paris and studied the centralized French detective system. His report, which he is said to have redrafted eighteen times, impressed the Commission, which adopted some of his recommendations. In particular, the head of the new department was not to be a policeman, but a lawyer ranking as an Assistant Commissioner. Vincent applied for the post, and obtained it.

The Criminal Investigation Department was created in March 1878. Its members were to receive higher pay, rank for rank, than the rest of the force, and enjoyed a rather superior status, and at first they were far from popular with the uniformed men. The new organization was thought to be too French; even Vincent's title of Director of Criminal Investigations was, as Moylan points out, a translation of the French Directeur des Recherches Criminelles. "There was undoubtedly," says the same authority, "an idea at first of making the C.I.D. an entirely separate organisation, as in Paris, and the Director was given almost *carte blanche* to carry out any change he thought fit."[2] This idea,

[1] *Op. cit.* [2] *Op. cit.*

however, was abandoned, and it was later laid down that detectives attached to divisions, though responsible to senior officers at Scotland Yard, not only must co-operate closely with Divisional Superintendents, but must send in their reports through these officers, whose control of investigations in their own areas was thus preserved. Later each division was given a Divisional Detective-Inspector who was responsible, under his superintendent, for detective work in the division.

One of the Commission's recommendations was modified in a way which restricted Vincent's powers. Though his only superior in the force was the Commissioner, he himself was made Director, not Assistant Commissioner, a distinction which meant that he was really responsible to the Home Secretary. He had no statutory authority over his department. This unhappy arrangement was not persisted in; Vincent's successor, Monro, was made an Assistant Commissioner, with the powers of that office.

Vincent found a detective force of about 250 men. A month after his appointment he reorganized the department as follows. The Central Office at Scotland Yard was to have one Chief Superintendent, three chief inspectors, three first-class and seventeen second-class inspectors, with an office staff of six sergeants and constables. To the divisions (including the Thames Division) were allotted fifteen detective-inspectors and 159 sergeants, the men under them being divided into sixty divisional patrols and twenty special patrols.[1] This was on paper; three months later the authorized strength of the department was still only 260; but in six years Vincent augmented this to 800.

He was a man of enterprise and organizing ability, and he carried out many other reforms at Scotland Yard and in the divisions. He was fortunate in having as his right-hand man the experienced Superintendent Williamson, who became Chief Superintendent within a month of Vincent's appointment. The pair were faced with great difficulties at the start, for the machinations of Benson and Kurr had not only seriously depleted the senior ranks of the department, but had left hanging over it an unhappy aura of suspicion. No one knew how far corruption had gone. The proceedings of the Departmental Commission contain some interesting information about the senior detective officers left at Scotland Yard, and about some of those in the divisions. The latter normally supplied the personnel of the Detective Branch, but at an early stage it became the practice to recruit a few men from outside the force. The Branch had to deal with foreign criminals, and

[1] Police Orders, April 6, 1878.

there were cases, such as the recent turf frauds, which took detectives abroad, and these outsiders seem usually to have been linguists. Several were of foreign extraction; Lavite was a Frenchman, and another was named Marchand. Apart from poor Druscovitch, who came from F Division and who was part Russian or Polish, the foreigners were not always a credit to the force. Marchand was dismissed for bad conduct, and Williamson said of Lavite, who was recruited for a special job, that he was of no use afterwards. Other reasons for the introduction of civilians into the Branch were the need of a good standard of education and the belief that detectives who had been in the uniform branch were known to criminals by their "manner and carriage." The well-educated man was represented by Detective-Inspector Greenham, who had been a draughtsman with an engineering firm, and who spoke French.

Detectives from the uniformed branch were jealous of the outsiders, another of whom, Sergeant Andrews, who spoke Russian and had been a valet, thought that a detective should serve at least two years in uniform, and then three years as a divisional detective, before coming to Scotland Yard. There was general agreement on this point, and the recruitment of outsiders was in time done away with. Most of the police officers examined also favoured a greater degree of decentralization of the Detective Branch than the Commission was to recommend; but two officers of great experience took the opposite view, Detective-Inspector Shore wishing to see all divisional detectives transferred to Scotland Yard. In effect, though detectives were henceforth gathered together in one body, quite distinct from the uniformed police, decentralization has in a sense won the day.

There had been disturbing evidence before the Commission of leakage of information from Scotland Yard. Greenham said that the detective force was under a system of espionage by criminals, and described how he had been startled to hear one of his most secret reports quoted accurately by a French swindler whom he apprehended. A Divisional Superintendent thought that too many people at Scotland Yard saw confidential correspondence, which was never locked up—a fact that had come out during the trial of the detectives. Williamson admitted that there was insufficient secrecy in his office; he had no messengers of his own, and papers went through too many hands, including those of clerks, who saw secret reports.

The Departmental Commission had gathered valuable evidence concerning the state of things in the Detective Branch,[1] and had made

[1] And concerning the force as a whole, for the Commissioners roamed rather far beyond their terms of reference. One of their proposals for the general good deserves remembrance. "Some gentleman placed in the position of Secretary, through whom all papers

sensible recommendations, many of which were based on Howard Vincent's own. The new Director was therefore in a strong position—with the one drawback that he had no statutory or disciplinary powers. "That this arrangement did not break down within a twelvemonth," says a later head of the Criminal Investigation Department, Sir Robert Anderson, "is a notable testimony to the personality of my friend Howard Vincent." Otherwise Vincent's *carte blanche* enabled him to reorganize and reform freely. Besides raising the detectives' pay, he improved the standard of training and education of recruits to the C.I.D. He simplified the criminal record system, and in general cut through much red tape. He compiled a Police Code and manual of criminal law which every policeman could understand—continually revised, it was in use until recent times—and he brought the *Police Gazette* from its old home at Bow Street to Scotland Yard, remodelled it, and gave it illustrations. Some of his methods were thought to be undignified—his revival of the Fieldings' use of the Press, for example; and so energetic and unconventional a man was bound to have his failures. One was an attempt to keep alive the system of using "outsiders" by selecting civilians with special qualifications of breeding and intelligence. These men were much more unpopular, and less useful, than their predecessors had been, and with their departure[1] the experiment came to an end. Vincent also got into hot water because of his use of the *agent provocateur*—a means of combating crime thought peculiarly un-British, though under other names it will always be employed by every police force. A chemist named Titley was known to be selling drugs to procure abortion; to obtain evidence against him a policeman's wife pretended to need his aid. "Similar action by the police in another case ten years earlier had passed without challenge," says Sir John Moylan, who adds: "Such actions cannot, without an abuse of language, be called incitements to crime." But there was a great outcry over the wretched Titley, and Harcourt, the Home Secretary, had to repudiate Vincent's action. An indictment was brought against the police officers concerned, but it was quashed.

Long before Vincent retired, in 1884, the incident was forgotten. He was that rare specimen in official life, a man who wanted change,

should pass from the various departments of the office at headquarters to the acting Commissioner, would be of considerable value to the Commissioner and the Assistant Commissioners in the management of what may be called the office staff." Half a century later, when that "office staff" had grown from a dozen or two to some hundreds, this idea was carried into effect by the appointment of a Secretary of the Commissioner's Office, who is a civil servant with the status of Assistant Commissioner.

[1] It is said at the instance of Mr Winston Churchill, when Home Secretary. See *Scotland Yard*, by George Dilnot.

and he left Scotland Yard in order to start a new career. He will be best remembered, however, as the founder of the modern Criminal Investigation Department.

3

The new Department was very new indeed when Charles Peace was arrested for burglary, and he soon passed out of the ken of the Metropolitan Police, his crimes in the north of England taking precedence of the attempt to kill P.C. Robinson. The C.I.D., however, was soon investigating several notorious capital cases in the London area, among them being the second known murder in an English train, that of Frederic Isaac Gold when travelling to his home at Brighton on the 27th of June, 1881. The murderer, Percy Lefroy or Mapleton, was detained before the body of his victim was found in Balcombe tunnel, since he left the train at Preston Park covered with blood, telling a most improbable story, and with a gold watch in his shoe. He escaped for a time by a simple ruse—the only sign of intelligence he showed—but was arrested three weeks later in Stepney. His behaviour was on the whole so foolish that the case has few points of interest, but it made a sensation at the time. The same may be said of one that followed in December of that year, for though the name of 'Dr' Lamson holds a prominent place in the roll of medical or quasi-medical murderers, the 'doctor' (like Pritchard, Neill Cream, and Crippen, a medico of dubious qualifications) carried criminal eccentricity to the verge of madness. Described as "a high-toned Christian gentleman of unsound mind," he poisoned his paralytic young brother-in-law with enough aconitine to kill a large household, in circumstances which at once directed suspicion upon himself.

A Metropolitan Police Act in 1884 creating two additional Assistant Commissioners, one for Civil Business, the other to be in charge of the Criminal Investigation Department, Howard Vincent's successor, James Monro, assumed control of the department with the new status. Monro had been Inspector-General of Police in Bengal, a province several times associated with the Metropolitan Police. A new series of Fenian outrages in London had begun in 1883, the work of Irish-American conspirators since known as the Dynamiters; on March the 15th of that year, after an explosion at *The Times* office, there was a second and more violent one outside the Local Government Office in Whitehall. Attempts of a similar kind continued through 1884 and into the following year. A wall of Scotland Yard itself was blown down, a bomb went off near the Nelson Column in Trafalgar Square, and another Constable Cole distinguished himself by prompt action which saved Westminster Hall.[1] One of Howard Vincent's last acts, carried into effect by Monro, had been the formation of the Special Irish Branch of the C.I.D., to deal with the dynamiters. Under Monro himself, the work of the new branch was directed by Chief Inspector Littlechild, who arrested Kurr. His chief assistant was Detective-Inspector Sweeny, who had a fortunate escape when his office was wrecked by the explosion in May 1884; most of the original officers of the branch were Irish. The dynamiters having been stamped out, with the help of the inevitable informers, the Special Branch remained, dropping the word 'Irish' and becoming a very important part of the machinery of the C.I.D.

These events, it should be noted, put a heavy strain on the resources of the Metropolitan Police as a whole—a strain more onerous than that caused in the later 1880's by the repeated unemployed demonstrations and rioting to be described. In the latter case the police were called out in large numbers from time to time, but during and for months after the dynamite outrages a considerable proportion of the force was on permanent duty guarding public buildings. Besides such places as Buckingham Palace (where there were sixty-three uniformed and plain-clothes police), the Houses of Parliament, the Government offices, the Law Courts, and the Thames bridges, in January 1885, similar protection was demanded by the Home Secretary, Harcourt, for St Paul's, the National Gallery, and the museums. Out of a total strength of just over 13,000, 1100 were already immobilized on these duties, and in a memorandum of the 10th of February Henderson said that the new requirements would absorb another 200 men. Among the resources called upon was the Royal Irish Constabulary, of whom fifty were brought over. "To avoid friction," it was laid down that they were to be kept separate as much as possible from the Metropolitan Police.

Of the three Commissioners who were to see the C.I.D. through its formative years, the period from 1878 to 1890, Henderson and Monro did much to influence these—though Monro's important work in this sphere was naturally accomplished when as Assistant Commissioner he was head of the new department. In his brief Commissionership he had little time to devote to a side of police work in which, a

[1] An admirer of P.C. Cole, Mr C. Gray Robertson, presented to each divisional library two copies of R. L. Stevenson's *The Dynamiter*, which is dedicated to Cole. (Police Orders, 30.10.1885.)

trained policeman himself, he was specially interested.[1] Warren, who immediately succeeded Henderson, had the reputation of being uninterested in criminal investigation, and in his annual reports he did not refer to it.

In these early days the C.I.D. had little or no technical equipment. Modern science, other than medicine—and the Smethurst and Staunton cases were a poor advertisement for pathology—began to be applied only experimentally to criminal investigation in 1894, with the introduction of Bertillonage. Galton's system of fingerprint identification was tentatively adopted in the following year. It was Henry, from 1901 onward, who improved and encouraged this and other innovations in detective methods; but in some respects Scotland Yard was to lag behind Continental, and even provincial, police forces for a long time to come. A scientific laboratory, for example, was not to be established until 1934.

The C.I.D. has, however, always been fortunate in its departmental heads. During this formative period Howard Vincent, Monro, and Anderson laid the foundations of what is now an institution of international fame. Anderson's appointment as Assistant Commissioner in 1888 coincided with the passing of an era. Adolphus Williamson, who had joined the force in 1852, and who had become the first Superintendent of the old Detective Branch, was still Chief Constable of the renamed organization. He retired in the summer of 1889, and died in December of that year.

[1] It may have been in 1885, when Monro was A.C. "C," that the Black Museum was started in a small back room on the second floor of the Convict Supervision Department in Great Scotland Yard. The first curator was Sergeant Bradshaw. (*Chambers's Journal*, April 25, 1885.) By some accounts the Museum is older.

16

THE COMMISSIONERS AND THE HOME OFFICE

DURING these years the constables on their beats, the station sergeants, the inspectors, and the Divisional Superintendents were as usual kept busy with tasks that were seldom spectacular, and often tedious. Besides the daily round, their activities in 1878, the year when the C.I.D. was created, ranged from supervising the erection of Cleopatra's Needle on the Victoria Embankment to helping to save life after an appalling disaster on the river itself, the sinking of the pleasure steamer *Princess Alice* with a loss of 700 lives. One hundred and fifty police from the Thames Division and Woolwich Dockyard took part in the work of rescue, and a Police Fund raised £179 for the afflicted families and survivors. The people's sports entailed duties that at least offered some entertainment; the growing popularity of the bicycle took members of the force to a meet at Hampton Court that year, and to many similar occasions later on; and in November 1880—a little late in the rowing season—272 foot police and seventeen mounted had a good view of the Hop-bitters World's Regatta from Hammersmith Bridge and the towing-paths to Mortlake.

The lighter side was conspicuously absent from the tedious business of escorting processions of unemployed and social reformers through the streets, another common pastime of the period; in 1886, the last of a few relatively quiet years, six demonstrations at Clerkenwell, Hyde Park, and Trafalgar Square required the presence of bodies of police ranging from 300 to 2400 in number. The serious troubles in 1887, when eventually Trafalgar Square was closed, led to the issue by Sir Charles Warren, then Commissioner, of a definition of a disorderly meeting which clarified the policeman's powers and responsibilities, hitherto vague, on such occasions. "Should a procession, crowd, mob or band, perambulating the streets, break into a run, or make rushes, or terrorize the inhabitants by hooting or yelling in any thoroughfare, the Commissioner deems it a disorderly meeting, and directs that it shall be dispersed, and the principals arrested."

A little before this time a new truncheon, to be carried in the pocket instead of in a case, had been issued to the force, and constables may have the more appreciated their greater freedom to use it because their old truncheons had been turned against them. Nine hundred and fifty of these weapons, having been condemned, were so imperfectly split by the War Office Artificer that they were sold in the East End, bound with wire or cobbler's waxed string, and employed to bash their late owners.

This period also saw the final disappearance of the rattle. It had come back for a time, but in 1885 the whistle again took its place, except for night patrols; and in 1886 all rattles were withdrawn. Police Orders for the former year show that the Londoner's passion for oranges was as uncontrollable as ever, and combined with his careless habits was producing "lamentable effects." Throwers of peel were henceforward to be cautioned; if they persisted in casting it about their names and addresses were to be taken, and reports made.

An event which affected the Metropolitan Police in many ways was the creation in 1888 of the London County Council, though happily its claim to control the force came to nothing. "It seems improbable," Maitland had written in 1885, "that the new corporation will be endowed with the powers of the Commissioner; he has become very necessary to us." In 1889, when the L.C.C. began to exercise its functions, it took over the charge of all the royal parks except Hyde Park, where the police station had been moved to a pleasant site on the slope above the Magazine. The year 1888 also saw the important Local Government Act, of interest to the Metropolitan Police because it "gave the County Councils which it established some share in the administration of the police by substituting for the justices joint committees of county councillors and justices."[1]

A problem which, at the time of writing, when the force is much below establishment, has become so pressing that it is being considered by special committees and working parties, was no problem at all in the 1880's. To-day more than a thousand policemen (in addition to as many civilians) are employed permanently at Scotland Yard and in the divisions on indoor office work. In 1886, when the strength of the force was almost what it is now, and when there were no typewriters or other modern aids to speed and efficiency, the clerical staff at Scotland Yard totalled 66, including 12 civilian clerks in the Receiver's Office. The 54 policemen were distributed as follows: Executive Branch, 26; Public Carriage Branch, 13; Lost Property Office, 6; C.I.D., 7; Convict Office, 2. It was still the age of simplicity

[1] J. M. Hart, *The British Police* (Allen and Unwin, 1951).

—and cheapness. The annual cost of the Metropolitan Police was little more than £500,000.

This was, indeed, too cheap. The men had many just causes of complaint. Henderson did much for the accommodation, but far more remained to be done. There was insufficient supervision of contractors by the Receiver's Office, and some of the clothing was shoddy; in 1890 the Commissioner (Monro) was complaining about the "wretched trousers." Above all, pay and pensions were a constant grievance.

2

In March 1886 began what may be described in the language of cricket as a collapse of the Commissioners. First Rowan and Mayne, and then Henderson, between them carried the score to fifty-seven years; during the next four, three wickets fell—those of Henderson himself, Warren, and Monro. Bradford and Henry then stopped the rot, staying in for thirteen and fifteen years respectively.

It is possible that Ireland, which has upset or ruined so many careers, had a good deal to do with the abrupt and undeserved termination of Henderson's. On February 1, 1886, Gladstone began to form his short-lived third administration, which was to last only seven months. The new Home Secretary was Hugh Childers, who had been Secretary for War in the previous Liberal Cabinet. The Prime Minister and most of his colleagues were wholly absorbed by the Irish question, which was the reason for their taking office, and which within two months was to split their ranks; and from the first some of them must have doubted whether in any case they would hold office long. In these unstable conditions the Home Secretary, who had little to do with Irish Bills, enjoyed an unusually free hand.

Childers was new to the work, and he had been at his desk only a matter of hours when he heard on February the 8th, apparently by chance, that a mob of roughs was roving about the West End of London, smashing windows and looting shops. There had been rival meetings in Trafalgar Square that day of the unemployed and the Social Democratic Federation, and a considerable force of police was at hand, though only some sixty were in the Square itself. There was the usual attendance of rowdies and criminals, and District Superintendent Walker had his pocket picked. When the meetings were over a crowd said to number at least three thousand headed for Hyde Park, wreaking destruction and pillaging on the way. From the Park they turned back and did more damage in Oxford Street and Mayfair. In those days the small body of mounted police, which would soon have dispersed the rioters, was used to patrol semi-rural suburban districts, and through the misreading of an order the reserves, hastily summoned, marched to the Mall instead of to Pall Mall. The main body of the mob was eventually broken up in Oxford Street by sixteen men from Marylebone Lane Police Station, led by Inspector Cuthbert. But in the meantime a great deal of harm had been done, the streets looked like battlefields, and shopkeepers and householders were in a state of mingled rage and panic.

Most unfortunately, some of them received a warning that more trouble was expected in two days' time, on Wednesday the 10th. They were advised to barricade their premises. It was said then, and has been repeated since, that these instructions were Henderson's; but it appears that he had nothing to do with them, and they probably came from some over-anxious senior officers. In the event, the Wednesday passed in perfect quiet, in spite of a dense fog. This did not placate the indignant sufferers from Monday's disturbances, of which the newspapers also made the most, and the infection spread to the very new Home Secretary, who had barely had time to master a single paper in his in-tray. With unbecoming haste Childers announced that he had appointed a committee to inquire into the conduct of the police, and that he would preside over it himself.

This was a very improper proceeding, rendered worse by the Minister's lack of experience of his office. As chairman of the committee Childers drew up a report which he handed to himself as Home Secretary,[1] and it is only too plain that he was determined from the first to find a scapegoat, and that the scapegoat was to be Henderson. It had to be somebody important, to save the face of the harassed Government, and Childers may have been under pressure, but this does not excuse him.

Henderson did not wait for the committee's deliberations. He knew that he was to be "thrown over by the Government," and, "conscious of a successful administration of seventeen years, at once resigned."[2] It was a sad and indeed disgraceful business, of which even the Treasury was a little ashamed, for it approved without hesitation a proposal to grant the late Commissioner the highest rate of pension allowed.

[1] " 'I'll be Judge,
I'll be Jury,'
said cunning
old Fury."

[2] *Dictionary of National Biography.*

All in all, Henderson had been a great success in a post which he accepted with reluctance. He added many enduring features to the solid foundation built by Rowan and Mayne, and during his seventeen years the force began to acquire the characteristics for which the British Police are admired to-day, though it was some time before the permanent improvement in men and methods became generally realized. As late as 1880 it could be written:

> The present Chief Commissioner of the Metropolitan Police, Sir Edmund Henderson, being a man of high principle, and acknowledged prudence in the control of the immense machine over which he presides, we have had for some years past comparatively few of those outrages which a Government police is so constantly liable to commit, owing to the extensive and unconstitutional powers placed in their hands. But under a less prudent or conscientious chief the scene will change.[1]

These fears were groundless. Whatever criticisms were directed against the police in the future, the force as Henderson left it had never been less like the oppressive *gendarmerie* which the writer envisaged.

It has been alleged that towards the end Henderson was out of touch with the lower ranks. His apparent lack of interest in the District Superintendents, who were intended to be a link between the divisions and Scotland Yard, but two of whom he dropped, is cited as an illustration of his absorption in other matters, and even of his preference for centralization. By all with whom he came in contact, however, he was liked as well as respected, and the manner of his dismissal—for that was what it came to—was resented by a force which under him had acquired a strong *esprit de corps*. Two years afterwards Sir Robert Anderson, just appointed Assistant Commissioner, met the veteran Williamson, by then Chief Constable, C.I.D., and within a year of his retirement, whose memories went back to the very early days of the Metropolitan Police. "You are coming to a funny place," said Williamson. "You'll be blamed if you do your duty, and you'll be blamed if you don't." It may have been apparent to the Chief Constable that the fate of Henderson created a precedent; a few more weeks, in fact, and a second Commissioner was forced to resign.

3

The case of Sir Charles Warren, it is true, was very different from that of his predecessor. Warren had little of Henderson's tact and forbearance; he was combative and opinionated, and rather enjoyed

[1] *Government by Police.* Anonymous. (London, Dyer Brothers, 1880.)

baiting the Home Secretary. Before long he played straight into the latter's hands.

If this continued use of the analogy of cricket suggests a contest between the Home Office and Scotland Yard, for some four years there was, in fact, almost continual friction between the two. That the Commissioners concerned were men so various as Henderson, Warren, and Monro also suggests that the fault was not all on one side. Nor was it; Childers was a bad choice for Home Secretary, and though his Conservative successor, Henry Matthews, afterwards Lord Llandaff, was described by Lord Chief Justice Coleridge as the best Home Secretary he had known, it was also said of him that he was "a departmental success but a parliamentary failure," which implies that where he failed was in handling men. During the greater part of his Home Secretaryship his relations with Scotland Yard were far from happy. The attitude of his Permanent Under-Secretary, Godfrey Lushington, did not improve them.

Warren, like Henderson, was a regular soldier, and an engineer. He had had administrative experience in Bechuanaland and elsewhere, and at the time of his appointment to Scotland Yard was Governor of the Red Sea Littoral. The selection of another soldier by a Liberal Home Secretary caused surprise, but Childers seems to have thought that what the police needed was a little discipline. Warren himself understood that he had been "specially chosen at a critical time for the reorganization and administration" of the force. He was given little time to carry out administrative reforms. Repeated disturbances in London, the Cass case, differences with the Home Office, with the Receiver, and with one of the Assistant Commissioners, Monro, to say nothing of the Jack the Ripper murders in the Whitechapel area and a short-lived agitation among elements of the police force itself, together kept him fairly fully occupied during the two years and nine months he was at Scotland Yard. His only lasting work of reorganization was the appointment of four Chief Constables, with three Assistant Chief Constables, to take over the moribund District Superintendencies.

The trouble in the force was fomented, and possibly engineered, by outsiders for political purposes. In the spring of 1887 every Divisional Superintendent was sending to Scotland Yard copies of a handbill which was being distributed by civilians among the lower ranks. One was thrust into the hand of a constable on duty outside the Commissioner's office. Headed "Police Grievances," the bill called on taxpayers to assemble in their thousands on May the 8th at the Reformer's

Tree in Hyde Park. On that date a crowd, presumably of taxpayers, was addressed by a Mr Dyke, who claimed to speak for the police, on the subject of pensions, punishments, and other matters of interest to the force, some of them genuine grievances. The eyes of impartial onlookers may have been opened when Dyke was followed by H. M. Hyndman; and while a speech by P.C. Murphy was giving a gloss of authenticity to the proceedings John Burns arrived with a following from a Socialist meeting at Marble Arch. Some senior officers were present with the police detailed to maintain order, but not needed, for most of the taxpayers appear to have been merely curious, and soon bored, and a Divisional Inspector of A stated that the gathering numbered about a thousand. His Chief Superintendent added a caustic note: "I entirely disagree with my inspectors as to their estimate of numbers; they always appear to go in for thousands." The Superintendent and others (not inspectors) thought that there were scarcely more than three hundred persons at the meeting.

A week later there was an echo in the House of Commons in the form of questions about constables' hours of duty and the promotion, said to be too rapid, of officers employed in clerical duties at Scotland Yard. There were real causes for dissatisfaction in the force, that before long were to have results more serious than a dull meeting in Hyde Park; but as to this it was strongly felt in the Commissioner's office, and minuted accordingly on the report quoted, that a few discontented men had been exploited by persons who had no genuine concern for their well-being.

Demonstrations by unemployed and various Socialist bodies were renewed on a large scale in the late autumn of that year, 1887. For days thousands camped in Trafalgar Square, where well-meaning but injudicious people kept them supplied with food. "These assemblages," to quote Melville Lee,

> led by demagogues, encouraged by foolish agitators, and reinforced with the scum of London, became so frequent and intolerable that Sir Charles Warren had to make a bold move in the interests of order, by altogether forbidding the use of Trafalgar Square as a place of public meeting. His action was endorsed by the Home Secretary, but only in such a half-hearted fashion that the forces of disorder, confident that they were masters of the situation, determined to fight it out.[1]

In fact, there had been more than a month of the weakest shilly-shallying with the forces of disorder, though Warren warned Matthews almost daily of what would happen if the police were not given fuller

[1] *Op. cit.*

powers. What in the circumstances amounted to a forcible occupation of Trafalgar Square started in the beginning of October; three weeks later, on the 25th, the Commissioner was pointing out that while he had to employ 2000 men to shepherd processions through the streets of the West End, the City Police had dispersed similar gatherings; "there is one law for the City, and one for the Metropolis." On the 31st came another warning: "It is in the highest degree impolitic to allow a hostile mob to perambulate the streets day after day, even under police supervision. . . . They will soon get out of hand." "It appears," Warren wrote on the 2nd of November, "that the Commissioner of Police and the Secretary of State take a totally different view of the state of affairs." Two days later he was complaining with justice of a speech by Gladstone, whose preoccupation with the Irish question, exacerbated whenever he was out of office, had already led him into mischievously irresponsible utterances; it was thought that the dynamiters had been encouraged by his pronouncement that the wrongs of Ireland would never be redressed without the use of force. Now the statesman who had been three times Prime Minister declared that "persons when interrogated by the police should answer 'Walker.'"

Matthews continued to equivocate. Memorials from tradesmen, from the Mayor of Westminster, from the Metropolitan Board of Works, failed to rouse him from his indifference or timidity. Then, as Warren had prophesied, the mob did "get out of hand," and the Home Secretary, in a flurry, granted the Commissioner some of the powers which, had they been enforceable earlier, would have nipped the trouble in the bud. On certain days only, meetings in Trafalgar Square were forbidden. The challenge was taken up, and on November the 13th, a Sunday, there was a regular battle in the environs of the Square, which had been cordoned off by the police. Seven thousand special constables, and the Guards, were held in reserve. More rioting occurred on the 17th, when several policemen were injured, and on the 23rd a couple of thousand roughs were brawling in Westminster Abbey. It was another week before these disgraceful scenes, which were abetted by certain newspapers and politicians, came to an end.

Matthews, at last thoroughly alarmed, had by then forbidden all meetings in Trafalgar Square, and all processions within a certain radius of it. This edict remained in force for more than a year. In October 1888, when there was a threat of further disturbances, the Lord Mayor decided to cancel what Warren called his annual "circus"; instead he would drive along the Strand with a few carriages. Warren must have enjoyed pointing out to the Home Secretary that under the latter's order of the previous year this constituted a procession, and would be unlawful.

In the meantime both the Home Secretary and the police had been in very hot water over the Cass case. This was one of those unfortunate affairs that are almost bound to occur from time to time, and its repercussions in 1887 appear a little disproportionate to the cause. They illustrate the intense interest still felt in police matters. On Jubilee night Miss Cass was taken into custody in Regent Street by P.C. Endacott and charged with soliciting. Witnesses came forward to say that she was a respectable young woman, and at the magistrate's court she was dismissed, but with a reprimand. Feeling for and against her was so violent that a heated debate followed in the House of Commons, and the Government was defeated by five votes, a result largely due to Matthews' inept handling of the case. The First Lord of the Treasury, W. H. Smith, then announced that an inquiry would be held by the Commissioner of Police and a London magistrate. Before it began Warren saw Miss Cass and her lawyer at Scotland Yard, and the police made some investigations of their own. Miss Cass, who had been only a few years in London, came from Stockton-on-Tees, and Superintendent Ball, of the Stockton police, collected information about her conduct there which did not amount to very much.

The witnesses summoned to the inquiry were not under oath, and the proceedings were valueless. No one was blamed except P.C. Endacott, though it was thought that more tact might have been shown by all concerned—in other words, by the magistrate, Mr Newton, who had reprimanded Miss Cass. The Lord Chancellor, upon whom Miss Cass made a favourable impression, interviewed Mr Newton, who, as the *Law Journal* pointed out, had been entitled in the circumstances to accept Endacott's uncorroborated evidence. Endacott was the inevitable scapegoat; he was suspended from duty, charged with perjury, and tried at the Old Bailey. Mr Justice Stephen told the jury that in his opinion the charge was not sustainable, and Endacott was acquitted. He was at once reinstated.

4

Upon this storm in a tea-cup there followed just a year later the horrifying series of murders attributed to the unknown Jack the Ripper. There were eight of these crimes in nine months; but at the most five of them, and perhaps only four, were the work of the maniac whose frightful methods have given his nickname to the English language. All the eight took place in a narrow strip of the East End of London about a mile long; on the west it enters the City, and it stretches eastward into Stepney, but the series is generally known as the Whitechapel murders, Aldgate and the Whitechapel Road bisecting the strip longitudinally. Until the bombing raids of the last War the scene had changed little; Mitre Square, just within the City, was much as it was when the body of Catherine Eddowes was found there, and at the opposite end of the strip Durward Street, where Mary Nichols was killed, just across the Whitechapel Road from the London Hospital, had scarcely altered from the days when it was called Buck's Row. Hanbury Street and Dorset Street, in Spitalfields, though the Market had swallowed up Miller's Court, were still almost as they had been known to poor Annie Chapman and Mary Kelly.[1] Though beside squalid tenements are busy factories, warehouses, and prosperous businesses owned mostly by foreigners and Jews, who form a considerable element in the local population, as a whole the dreary district has long been one of the most poverty-stricken in London.

The four cases of murder just mentioned occurred between the 31st of August and the 9th of November, 1888. The dreadful technique of disembowelling, and other details, stamped them as the work of the same hand. Less than an hour before Catherine Eddowes died, in the early hours of the 30th of September, Elizabeth Stride, a Swede, had been killed in a yard off Berners Street, which runs into Commercial Road half a mile from Mitre Square. Her throat was cut, but she suffered no other injuries, and it is doubtful if her murder is one of the series. There were no doubts at the time, of course, and two earlier murders of women in the same ill-omened neighbourhood, on April the 4th and August the 7th, were credited to the silent and invisible killer now known throughout the country as Jack the Ripper—a name taken from a letter, written in red ink, which was sent to the Central News Agency.[2] An eighth murder, early in 1889, was added to the list by popular belief;[3] and similar crimes in which prostitutes in poor neighbourhoods were the victims—especially those of Neill Cream—long kept the legend alive.

During the months of panic in the autumn and winter of 1888 the C.I.D. and the City Police were working day and night in the East End. A great number of arrests were made. An outbreak of anti-

[1] William Stewart, *Jack the Ripper* (Quality Press, 1939).

[2] Sir Robert Anderson, in *My Official Life*, says it was "the creation of an enterprising London journalist."

[3] As were some mutilated female remains found in 1888 hidden on the site of New Scotland Yard.

Jewish feeling in Whitechapel added to the difficulties of the police; after the murder of Catherine Eddowes, a portion of whose apron was found in Goulston Street, near Mitre Square, some one wrote in chalk in an archway there, "The Jews are the men that will not be blamed for nothing." Warren went himself to Goulston Street, and ordered the words to be wiped off. There seemed to be strong grounds for suspecting an unbalanced Polish Jew named Pizer, a tailor known as "Leather Apron," but the case against him collapsed. The assumed medical knowledge of the murderer then turned the thoughts of the police to medical students and doctors,[1] and in a letter to the Home Office in November Warren refers to inquiries being made about a demented student living in St John's Wood. The Home Office was continually writing to complain that no progress seemed to be made; an article in *The Times* prompted a demand for bloodhounds, and though Anderson, the new head of the C.I.D., had little faith in these animals, two were hired from a Mr Brough of Scarborough, at a cost of £100. Then the Home Secretary wanted a general clearance of brothels in the East End, to which Warren replied that the eviction of owners of brothels was no remedy—the women would merely be driven on to the streets, while "in driving the brothel-keepers away from certain neighbourhoods much would be done to demoralize London generally. It is impossible to stop the supply where the demand exists." The Commissioner gave some figures relating to this traffic; at least sixty-three brothels were known to W Division, and there were probably more. There were about 1200 prostitutes in the district, "mostly of very low character." Common lodging-houses, also a bad feature, numbered 233, accommodating 8500 persons.

The audacity of the murderer in committing his fearful crimes at an hour when people were still about the streets, suggested the trial of boots for policemen with "indiarubber, waterproof, or silent soles," so that their distinctive tread should not give warning of their approach; but these soles were found unsuitable for a constable's varied duties in all weathers. Warren put less faith in indiarubber, bloodhounds, and a campaign against brothel-keepers than in substantial rewards for information; anonymous letters were pouring in, and money might induce some one with knowledge to come forward. He referred to cases in which the Home Office had refused to allow such offers, but, he said, "I look upon this series of murders as unique in the history of our country, and of a totally different character to those mentioned

[1] A friend of the writer's possesses one of two surgical knives said to have been left by the Ripper beside his victims.

above." The Home Office remained adamant; Sir William Harcourt had said, "I have a profound distrust of rewards," and the words of the only strong Home Secretary of recent times were law. Warren was much annoyed because his request was refused point-blank, without further consultation. Among those who advocated rewards was a Member of Parliament, Samuel Montagu, who wished to offer £100 in the name of his fellow-Jews.

The Home Office was perhaps rather shocked by some of the Commissioner's ideas. On the 4th of October Warren wrote: "I am quite prepared to take the responsibility of adopting the most drastic or arbitrary measures that the Secretary of State can name which would further the securing of the murderer, however illegal they may be, provided Her Majesty's Government will support me." He thought this contingency doubtful, and he was right. The Secretary of State had no constructive ideas of his own to offer, but continued to complain, and a fortnight later Warren was writing: "The Police and C.I.D. have *not* exhausted all means, etc. They have barely begun."

Nevertheless, all means were in time exhausted, and dozens of detectives, working on an average fourteen hours a day, found themselves at the end of the year no nearer discovering the identity of Jack the Ripper than they had been in August. His identity is unknown to this hour, though definite claims to the contrary have been made, and numberless theories propounded. Sir Robert Anderson, who succeeded Monro as Assistant Commissioner, C.I.D., just after the second Whitechapel murder, says that the murderer was a low-class Polish Jew. According to Sir Basil Thomson, "in the belief of the police he was a man who committed suicide in the Thames at the end of 1888," and who "had probably been at some time a medical student." A third head of the C.I.D., Sir Melville Macnaghten, appears to identify the Ripper with the leader of a plot to assassinate Mr Balfour at the Irish Office. Where experts disagree, there is a fine opening for fancy; others have held that the Ripper was a sailor, a mad West End doctor, and even a midwife.[1] This last theory is a fascinating one, but will not bear close examination. The only points on which there is very general agreement are that the murderer lived close to the scene of his crimes, and that since these ceased as unaccountably as they had begun, either

[1] W. Stewart, *op. cit.* Sir Melville Macnaghten, in *Days of my Years*, quotes the following anonymous verse received at Scotland Yard:

"I'm not a butcher, I'm not a Yid,
Nor yet a foreign Skipper,
But I'm your own light-hearted friend,
Yours truly, Jack the Ripper."

THE ATTEMPT TO BLOW UP GOVERNMENT OFFICES
IN CHARLES STREET, WESTMINSTER

Showing "A" Division's Police Station in King Street.

"*The Illustrated London News*"

[*See p.* 194.]

THE BLACK MUSEUM AT SCOTLAND YARD IN ITS EARLY DAYS

he was dead by the end of the year, or a few months' dreadful madness had suddenly spent itself. The notion of a dual personality, nowadays tediously exploited in novels and films, but new in the 1880's, which did not know the word schizophrenia, was popularized by Stevenson's *Dr Jekyll and Mr Hyde*, published in 1886, and two plays based on the story were running together in the autumn and winter of Jack the Ripper's year.

5

It was a bad year in every way at Scotland Yard. Not only was the Commissioner constantly at odds with the Home Office, but he was in disagreement with the Receiver, Sir Richard Pennefather, and he quarrelled outright with his Assistant Commissioner, Monro. Oddly enough, his grounds of complaint against Monro were very similar to those held against himself by the Home Secretary. Personalities apart—and the three men represented three antagonistic types—the question at issue in both cases was who was responsible to whom, and to what extent.

Warren's chief bone of contention with the Home Office was the Home Secretary's meddling with the internal affairs of the police, or, what came to the same thing, the Minister's refusal to allow the Commissioner the free hand in this respect which he claimed under the Statute appointing him. On the 7th of April, 1887, Warren was complaining in strong terms of Home Office interference, retarding of reforms, and offensive letters. This letter he withdrew, but he continued the attack. On the 8th of March, 1888, he wrote that after two years in office he was still not given enough discretion, and his scheme for administration had been ignored. There should be an inquiry into the relations between the Home Office and the police. Matthews and the Permanent Under-Secretary, particularly the latter, had, in fact, done little to better these relations; and when, the very next day, the *Pall Mall Gazette* printed a letter from Lushington to Bradlaugh, the independent and combative Member for Northampton, in which the latter was told that if he had any charge against a member of the police force he was to lay it before the Director of Public Prosecutions, Warren was justifiably angry.

So things went on, Warren taking his stand on the Statute, Matthews and Lushington being irritatingly departmental, and referring to reports and memoranda which the Commissioner said he had never seen. His trouble with the Receiver is referred to in a letter of the 28th of April, 1888, when he wrote that he was never informed that the

Home Office and the Receiver's Office could intervene between the Secretary of State and the Commissioner. At this time the *Pall Mall Gazette* was campaigning against the police, the attacks, in Warren's opinion, being inspired by some one connected with the force, probably in the Receiver's Office. Wontner's, the firm of solicitors now acting for the police,[1] had been inquiring into the conduct of three members of the Receiver's staff who were not only bankrupt, but were thought to be taking bribes from contractors, and there were now grounds for suspecting that these persons were the newspaper's informants.

To this unpleasantness was added the complication of Monro. It has been seen that Monro succeeded Howard Vincent as head of the C.I.D., with the statutory rank of Assistant Commissioner, in 1884. The C.I.D., says Sir John Moylan, "had from its inception been almost an independent department."[2] Though this state of things had worked under Henderson, and suited Monro, it was not likely to suit such a man as Warren; and its dangerous possibilities are obvious. To make affairs more difficult, Monro had been acting, and was still acting, in a rather mysterious capacity as secret agent for the Home Office, though this was originally only a temporary appointment, and though, as Warren pointed out, the work of the C.I.D. should absorb all the Assistant Commissioner's time. Monro seems to have felt that this additional link with the Home Office strengthened his claim, as head of the C.I.D., to be independent of the Commissioner and responsible only to the Home Secretary. It can be seen now that it was an impossible situation, in which Warren, in particular, was deserving of sympathy. It is usually held that his want of tact made the situation worse, but at least he did not make too much of Monro's attitude, thinking the latter's assertion of independence "an ephemeral matter"; and Monro himself, though possessed of admirable qualities, was not an easy man to work with, as the Home Office was soon to discover.

Matthews and Lushington, unfortunately, seem to have enjoyed playing off one against the other, and must take most of the blame for what followed. In May 1888 Warren was grumbling because Monro was writing direct to the Home Office about the appointment of an Assistant Chief Constable, and refusing to let Warren himself see the correspondence. Next month the Home Office was writing direct to Monro, and ignoring the Commissioner. This could not go on; Warren put his foot down, and in August Monro resigned.

[1] They were appointed in 1887, replacing a short-lived legal adviser. [2] *Op. cit.*

Four months later Warren himself had gone. In November his attention was drawn to a Home Office circular of the 27th of May, 1879, which claimed powers over the internal administration of the police. "Had I been informed that such a circular was to be in force," he wrote back, "I should not have accepted the post of Commissioner. The Commissioner's duties, and those of the Metropolitan Police, are governed by statute. The Secretary of State has no powers under this to issue orders to the force." Declining to accept the implications of the circular (which he did not see until next day), he offered his resignation. The matter appeared to be smoothed over; but Warren had already made a false step. It was a surprising one for a soldier to make—unless, of course, the indiscretion was calculated. *Murray's Magazine* for that month contained an article by him in which he set out his views of the Commissioner's powers and duties, and criticized the attitude of the Home Secretary and the Government as a whole towards the police. It is often said that Warren claimed to be as independent of the Home Office as Monro had claimed to be of him; but this is to twist his arguments, which merely recapitulated those he had advanced again and again in his official letters. A Commissioner of Police, in his view, is in the position of a colonel of a regiment, who for general purposes is under higher authority, but who controls the internal administration and discipline of his unit. The Home Office of those days thought differently. The appearance of the article, of course, precipitated a first-class row; and on December the 1st Warren resigned. He had offered to do so more than once before: this time, perhaps, he was determined to force the issue, and in a way that made it clear to the public.

6

What the public thought can be seen from the humorous papers. In August *Punch* had "A Nursery Rhyme for the Times" which began:

> "Who chased Cock Warren?"
> "I," said the Home Sparrow,
> "With my views cramped and narrow,
> I chased Cock Warren."

Four days after Warren's resignation *Fun* came out with the following:

> *A "Two-M." Rule*
>
> Mr Monro, C.B., hath Sir
> Charles's late post
> (Thanks to Matthews, the
> muddling and prosy).

He is no doubt a good man,
but he won't need to boast;
For while Matthews rules o'er
The Home Office "roast,"
His path will not be too
Monro-sy.

Monro, in fact, had been brought back from retirement to replace the man with whom he had quarrelled. It was not perhaps a very happy augury. Monro was an able man, popular with the force, and universally respected, and his differences with Warren, in Sir Robert Anderson's opinion, if not actually fomented by Lushington and others at the Home Office, would never have been allowed to come to a head under a different *régime* there. But Monro was just as determined and opinionated as Warren, and he was something of an idealist. After he in turn felt compelled to resign he devoted the rest of his life to the work of a medical mission in Bengal. In thinking that such a man would work well with the Home Office, where there were then few or no ideals, Matthews had made another mistake.

Monro was Commissioner for little more than eighteen months. He was barely in office when more demonstrations by the unemployed and so-called unemployed were tolerantly and successfully handled by the police. An attempt to hold a meeting at the Wellington Statue at Hyde Park Corner raised one of those curious points which surely no police force but the British would allow to complicate and impede necessary action. There was a serious discussion between Monro and the Home Office about the precise status of the "island" on which the statue stands. Was it a portion of Green Park, as it once had been, and therefore still subject to park regulations, or should it be considered "part and parcel of a thoroughfare," which, in fact, it now was? It is not clear whether this problem was solved, but common sense dictated that a tumultuous meeting at one of the busiest road-junctions in London would be highly inconvenient, and it was forbidden.

The great Dock Strike followed in the autumn of 1889, and again, under Monro's guidance, police measures were excellent, and as unobtrusive as possible. Monro complained that Matthews had been flippant about it in the House, though expecting the police to provide him with all sorts of information about the dockers—how they were paid, how they lived, to what trade unions they belonged, and whether the public sympathized with them. There was a good deal of intimidation, and many complaints from the dock authorities of "besetting," or picketing; but Monro refused to allow the police to interfere unless their aid was invoked for adequate reasons. Some 700 extra men were drafted into H and K Divisions, and one sergeant and six constables went afloat for a week on the s.s. *Arawa*, at the expense of the Shaw, Savill, and Albion Line.[1]

It was in these early days of Monro's short Commissionership that the Local Government Act of 1888 brought into being the London County Council, which entered on its duties on the 21st of March, 1889. From the start a very powerful body, it was within limits a necessary one; but it was altogether too grasping when it aspired to control the Metropolitan and City Police forces. Such control would be disastrous, for the control of the L.C.C. itself has become a matter of party politics. Whether or no the Government of the day foresaw the full extent of this danger, the proposal received no encouragement, and it is to be hoped that it will never seriously be considered.

This was the age of Parnellism, and in the autumn of 1888 *The Times* had published, under the heading of "Parnellism and Crime," the letters attributed to the Irish Nationalist leader, some of which were afterwards shown to be forged. While the Special Commission inquiring into these charges was sitting—it held its last meeting in November 1889—there were first rumours and then threats of renewed Fenian outrages. In February of that year the Metropolitan Police was providing protection at Lord Salisbury's house in Arlington Street and at the Foreign Office; and in June Monro sent to the Home Secretary what he described as a direct incitement to the murder of Mr Arthur Balfour, Lord Clanricarde, and Captain Featherstone. Early in 1890 there was some alarm over alleged threats to blow up St Paul's.

Monro took a rather gloomy view of the resources of the police in face of these various heavy calls upon the force. Its numbers were steadily rising, and by the end of 1889 had reached 14,725; but the Commissioner wanted more. The matter was being discussed by a Parliamentary Committee on the vote for supplies, and on the 2nd of December that year he was urging upon Matthews the need for the acceleration of the committee's report. Unless no other course was possible, he was not prepared to consent to a temporary increase of the force.

[1] Purists who maintain correctly that there is no such post as that of "Chief Commissioner" of the Metropolitan Police may be interested to learn that Monro seems to have so described himself in his correspondence with the Chairman of the London and St Catherine's Dock Company.—Report of an Extraordinary General Meeting of the Company. It has been noted that Inspector Whicher, at the time of the Road Murder of 1860, addressed his reports to the "Chief Commissioner."

He had as little patience as Warren with the Home Secretary's timid handling of the perpetual labour troubles, which added to the work of the police. Not only were large numbers absorbed by meetings and processions of unemployed and others, but smaller detachments had now to be kept permanently on guard at such places as Trafalgar Square, where, during July 1889, an inspector, three sergeants, and thirty constables were on duty, doing nothing most of the time, though needed elsewhere. The public suffered, too: "Socialists and Friendly Societies do not care one jot for the public convenience." However, "the Secretary of State's instructions would be carried out," though "causing serious inconvenience and interruption of traffic." As late as the 11th of June, 1890, ten days before his resignation, Monro was returning to the charge, and posing a series of awkward questions to the Home Secretary.

A year earlier, in a letter to the Chairman of the Dock Board, he had said almost apologetically that "he must to some extent take his tone from the Home Office." This can scarcely have been the spirit Matthews expected to find in the new Commissioner after the lesson administered to the two previous ones. Plainly Monro had soon discovered, as they had done, cause for complaint of what Warren called the obstacles thrown in their way by the officials across the street in Whitehall. It seems very probable that this alone would before long have provoked a third resignation. Before this could happen, however, Monro's persistence over another grievance, not his own, brought about the crisis.

From the beginning he had taken up very strongly the old sore point of police pensions. Dissatisfaction with the inadequacy of these was growing throughout the force. The men knew that the Commissioner sympathized with their grievances, which also had the support of the Press. On the 29th of April, 1890, Monro forwarded a strong protest about the existing pension scheme, which was most unsatisfactory, and "in no way a fulfilment of the Secretary of State's promise in 1881." He agreed with the men's demand that after twenty-five years' service they should receive pensions amounting to two-thirds of their pay, without medical certificate or reference to age. A month later two petitions for increase of pay and improved superannuation rates were pinned up on the notice-boards at police stations in A and Y Divisions—forewarning of the worse trouble that was to break out in July. On the 5th of June Monro submitted another memorandum on the pension question. The next news, surprising everybody, was that he had resigned.

One of his reasons was resentment at a proposal that a vacant Assistant Commissionership should be filled by Matthews' own Private Secretary, Mr Ruggles-Brise. It seems doubtful whether this was ever more than a suggestion, and the post was filled by Monro's nominee, Charles Howard; and the main cause of a hasty and "somewhat quixotic departure from Scotland Yard"[1] was a sudden loss of patience with what he thought was a continual disregard of the men's claims, and of his support of them. He knew that a Police Pensions Bill was about to be introduced in Parliament, but he had convinced himself that it would not meet those claims. It would seem that the Home Office was quite as much to blame in not acquainting the Commissioner beforehand with the details of the Bill, which should have satisfied him.

7

Monro's resignation, accepted with alacrity by the Home Secretary, but deeply regretted by the force, coincided with one event of considerable importance in the domestic history of the Metropolitan Police, and was to be followed, in the same year, by another development affecting both police and public, the ultimate consequences of which still lie in the future.

Monro himself stayed long enough to give the name of New Scotland Yard to Norman Shaw's tall building on the site by Westminster Bridge. It was completed in the summer of 1890. More will be said of it in the next chapter.

During these troubled years the Public Carriage Department was probably the one least affected by the prevailing discontents. It went unobtrusively on its way, coping competently with hansoms and Clarences and knife-board omnibuses and the new trams (the introduction of tickets next year was to cause a strike of drivers), siting new cab-ranks and erecting shelters, hopefully trying to check furious driving, and buying from Messrs Tilling 500 enamelled plates, bearing the words "Keep to the Left," which were affixed to street refuges. Regardless of their doom, the little victims played. An enormous revolution was at hand. In 1890 the first motor-car was seen on the road.

[1] Moylan, *op. cit.*

17

NEW SCOTLAND YARD

THERE is a book to be written about the Commissioners of the Metropolitan Police—if the material can be found. They constitute as a whole a remarkable body of men, who too often, however, seem to have been as self-effacing and shy of publicity as they were capable and versatile. In the case of Monro's successor, for example, the *Dictionary of National Biography* can offer little more in the way of sources of information than the memoirs of a Field-Marshal and the somewhat arid pages of Volume XVI of Crisp's *Visitation of England and Wales*. Yet Sir Edward Bradford was a distinguished figure long before he came to stamp his personality upon Scotland Yard.

Like so many eminent public servants, Edward Ridley Colborne Bradford came of a clerical family, and, like other Commissioners before and after him, he had made his reputation in India. Born in 1836, he left England as an East India Company's cadet, served in two Madras cavalry regiments and then, in the Persian War, with the 14th Light Dragoons. He was soon seeing service again in the Sepoy Mutiny. As adjutant and then second in command of Mayne's Horse, an irregular unit, he took part in the long pursuit of Tantia Topee after the collapse of the revolt. In 1866 he was married to a great-niece of Jane Austen. An excellent and enterprising officer, fearless but "singularly modest," according to his friend Sir Evelyn Wood, he showed at this time the gift for handling men which was to make him one of the most successful Commissioners.

In 1863 Bradford had an arm so badly mauled by a tigress that it was necessary to amputate the limb without chloroform. As soon as the stump was healed he was hunting and shooting again, and even spearing lions, holding his reins in his teeth. Recognition of his varied abilities led to his appointment, in 1874, as General Superintendent of Thuggee and Dacoity, his first experience of police work of a kind. Other purely political offices followed, and in 1887, as Sir Edward Bradford, K.C.S.I., he was called home to the India Office to become Secretary of the political and secret departments. Two years later, fortunately for the Metropolitan Police, he refused an offer of the High Commissionership at the Cape.

Described by Sir Richard Temple as "the very best Anglo-Indian type," Bradford was probably already in Matthews' mind as a successor to the difficult Monro when the unexpected but welcome news of the latter's resignation reached the Home Office. This was on June the 12th, 1890, and the resignation took effect on the 21st. Until that date the public was kept in suspense, and in the interim, which saw the introduction, on the 17th, of the text of the Pensions Bill, the Press suggested other names. 'Suspense' is not too strong a word, for the newspapers were also full of reports of spreading dissatisfaction among the police, to whom Monro's sudden decision seemed a proof that their grievances were once more to be disregarded, or at best met in a half-hearted manner. On the 16th, to quote the *Daily Graphic*, "The agitation among the Metropolitan Police developed a practical phase . . . when numerous meetings of bona fide constables were held in various parts of the Metropolis to consider their position in view of the issue of Mr Matthews' superannuation scheme." The text of this being now available, the same paper, in "Topics of the Day," found the measure "fair almost to the point of generosity," adding, "It is difficult to understand what Mr Monro found to object to in it." A further comment voiced suspicions then very generally held: "The Bill thickens the mystery of Mr Monro's retirement, but is it, in its present form, exactly the same document as that which induced the ex-Commissioner to abandon his post?"

Many of the police themselves were in no mood to discover the virtues of the Bill. After an adjourned conference of superintendents held at Scotland Yard on the 18th, though proceedings were of "a strictly private nature," it leaked out that the scheme had been condemned "in toto" by the men. Monro presided at this meeting as Commissioner. He was referred to as Acting Commissioner on the following day, when events were moving to a crisis. There were more meetings of the men, attended by much excitement, particularly in Y Division, which included Paddington and Kensington, and where there was talk of sending a deputation to Monro.

A memorandum of the complaints and resolutions having been sent to Members of Parliament, on Friday, the 20th, Matthews was under fire. The name of the new Commissioner was now known. Monro, in the Distinguished Strangers' Gallery, heard the Home Secretary attacked by the inevitable Cunningham Graham and then by Harcourt, who, it was said, "sat down with the feeling that he had so pulverised

Mr Matthews as to leave him no alternative but immediate resignation." If Harcourt ever thought this he did not know Matthews as he should have done. The Minister remained "jaunty," and now, as it was to turn out, with some reason; he could well afford to ignore the usual ill-informed carpings at the new appointment, for, whether or no he fully realized it at the time, he had found a Commissioner who combined the best qualities of his three predecessors—the sympathy of Monro, the firmness of Warren, and the tact of Henderson.

2

Bradford took up office knowing that his capabilities were immediately to be put to the test, and that firmness in handling a dangerous situation must take precedence of other measures. It was no accident that again a soldier had been called in; a quixotic temperament at odds with the views of the Home Office had also, in eighteen months, had an unfortunate influence on the police force itself. "The line taken by Mr Monro, and the discontent of the police over pay and pensions, called for a disciplinarian rather than a crime expert,"[1] and though Bradford's gift with men and his administrative experience were no less urgently needed, it was as a disciplinarian that he was first called upon to act.

While, at midday on Monday, June the 23rd, he was being introduced by Monro to the senior officers at Scotland Yard, elsewhere malcontents among the junior ranks had themselves abandoned talk for action. In the Borough a sergeant and a constable were suspended for disobeying an order; what was more ominous, they had to be reinstated when the men parading that evening refused to go on duty until this was done. Delegates from various divisions came to Bow Street, where they were refused admission, and by 4.30 P.M., according to a news agency, four hundred constables in plain clothes were demonstrating before the station, encouraged by their comrades inside. An official statement issued later denied that there had been a demonstration, but the new Commissioner, having been at his desk only a few hours, had already circulated a private order to superintendents forbidding any such meetings.

As a result of this step, for a fortnight there was an uneasy lull. It was said that at Bow Street, on the 25th, a number of constables were reported for shouting and cheering, it being thought that they were defying the ban on organized meetings. There was another sort of

[1] Moylan, *op. cit.*

meeting that day, of Conservative Metropolitan Members of Parliament, at which it was agreed that the Pensions Bill should be pushed through the second reading as it stood, to be then referred to a Select Committee with special instructions.

The second reading was moved on the 28th. In the meantime, among the police, petitions were being handed about for signatures, and contributions, averaging *6d.* were collected for a fund for Monro, who must have disapproved heartily of the idea. Bradford, watching events and feeling his way, addressed a minute, on July the 1st, to the superintendent of the troublesome Y Division, promising his careful consideration of the men's complaints. "Everybody," said the *Daily Graphic* on the 7th, "will be glad to notice how the police difficulty is diminishing"; but on the same page the Press Association was quoted as announcing that the agitation had assumed an alarming phase—"as in 1872, Bow Street is the centre of the agitation." During the evening parade on the 5th, at the order "Fall out for traffic," no one moved until the inspector in charge had promised to forward the men's demands. Among these, the cry for a police union had again been raised by extremists.

July 5th was a Saturday. Bradford, like Monro before him, refused to meet a committee of delegates, and he now decided that things had gone far enough. He was satisfied that insubordination was confined to a minority in one or two divisions, and that he had ample reserves of loyal police, and having called for particulars of the men who had refused duty at Bow Street, he attended there in person on the Sunday. The active malcontents were paraded before him, one by one, and were told that they had disgraced their uniforms and were dismissed. It did not take long to dispose of thirty-nine in this way; "I was out of the room again," one of them said, "before I properly understood what had happened."

This summary justice broke the little rebellion. That there was an outbreak of serious trouble the next day was due less to the men who had been dismissed than to allies whom the most discontented constable must, in his sober moments, have treated with contempt, as his natural enemies. The thirty-nine blustered indeed, and, in a telegram to the Home Secretary, threatened that if they were not reinstated there would be a general strike of the police. It was said that their well-wishers at Bow Street "resolved to notify the public to safeguard their houses, as a strike of the police is now inevitable." More frothy nonsense of this kind was heard at a meeting of the dismissed constables at a public house in Long Acre, as when one of them said he would knock down the first man who dared to go on duty from Bow Street; and pot-valour was fanned by the encouragement of a growing mob from the worst quarters of the district, and by political agitators equally delighted by so novel an opportunity of making mischief. Handbills were ready, announcing that "Now is the time for the social revolution," and summoning "the People" to Trafalgar Square that Monday evening. Bow Street, however, offered more entertainment, and by eight o'clock, though it was raining, the neighbourhood of the police station was the scene of wild disorder. "Rule, Britannia" was sung, rather incongruously. Howard, the new Assistant Commissioner, Monro's nominee, had arrived at the station, and mounted police were summoned. They were too few to break up the crowd, now thoroughly out of hand. Bags of flour were thrown about, and a basin was hurled from an upper window of the station. Howard went into the street, and was hustled, but when some of the dismissed men, "who evidently had been drinking," refused to move from the station steps, the Assistant Commissioner, to their surprise, invited them in.

By this time Howard had called for troops, an action afterwards criticized, and attributed to undue alarm or inexperience. But though the crowd probably numbered far less than the current estimate of 5000, disorder had to be quelled before it could spread. Mounted men, on well-trained horses, can disperse a mob more effectively, and at a smaller cost in injuries, than several times their number of men on foot; but there were not enough mounted police available. When a troop or two of Life Guards arrived the combined force of horsemen speedily cleared the narrow streets. Rain also damped enthusiasm for social revolution, and by midnight the situation was normal.

Memories of mob rule, and the talk of agitators, kept public alarm alive for some days. The Press did not help when it circulated absurd rumours, as that discontent had spread to the Grenadier Guards. There were a few minor disturbances, but they were the work of rowdies. Bradford, in the meantime, was further enforcing discipline in the police by some suspensions, followed by dismissals, in Y Division, and by the transference of a small number of constables from their own divisions to others. He fully understood that many more, who had remained loyal, were in a dissatisfied mood, though often they scarcely knew why. "Most of the force," said the late head of the C.I.D., Howard Vincent, now a Member of Parliament, and President of the Police Pensioners Association, "don't know what the alleged grievances are." The next step was to clear away doubts and misconceptions. Vincent himself, with the authority of his past and present connexion with the police, emphasized in a newspaper article the merits of the Pensions Bill, and the Government's determination to see it passed, substantially unchanged, before Parliament rose. Bradford, having put before the Home Secretary recommendations of his own, took in hand remedial measures within the force. There were other grievances besides pay and pensions to be considered, and the Commissioner began by visiting police stations, where he met all ranks and listened to complaints.

In Parliament, in spite of factious opposition and pages of amendments, and attempts to refer it to the procrastinating procedure of a Select Committee, the Bill was forced through both Houses in a few weeks. As it affected the policeman on the beat, its chief features were these: on joining constables received 24*s*. a week, as before, but with a yearly rise of a shilling a week up to 32*s*.; classes of constables were abolished; a maximum pension of two-thirds of a man's pay was due after twenty-six years' service, and one slightly less than the maximum after twenty-five years, the normal retiring period. There was no age qualification. Senior ranks benefited in a lesser degree. Sub-inspectors went, and were replaced by station sergeants. Some dissatisfaction was expected in the C.I.D., which remained outside these adjustments, but its members, with their special allowances and comparative freedom of action, were still better off than their colleagues of the uniformed branch, and they did no more than grumble.

Bradford, in his annual report, reduced this affair, of which so much was made by the Press, to its proper proportions. An early incident had shown it even more clearly in its true light. H. M. Hyndman's Social Democratic Federation, always ready to foment trouble, had lent the malcontents a room at No. 337 Strand, and a meeting was called there for the evening of the 12th of June. Of nine persons present at the start, two were policemen; three others came in, and went out again. Acting-Superintendent Wells, of E Division, in reporting this fiasco, commented drily that the Social Democratic Federation had chosen the wrong day. It was that of the division's annual excursion, "and it is extremely unlikely that such a day would be selected by the police."

3

If the appointment of Henderson as Commissioner in 1869 marked the end of an era, that of Bradford, twenty-one years later, was scarcely less significant in the annals of the Metropolitan Police. Not only was a period of uncertainty and friction ended, but 1890 has a claim to distinction of its own. The force was then sixty-one years old, and it seems happily appropriate that what is now a half-way stage should have been signalized by the move of the machinery of administration from the scene of its birth to new and more suitable quarters.

From its early home at No. 4 Whitehall Place the Metropolitan Police Office had spread untidily in and about the area from which it took its popular name. Sixty years after the formation of the force its headquarters was still "a dingy collection of mean buildings." Of what these were like inside, *The Times* wrote in May 1890: "Innumerable books are piled up on staircases, so that they are almost impassable, piles of clothing, saddles and horse furniture, blankets and all manner of things are heaped up in little garrets in a state of what outside Scotland Yard would be called hopeless confusion." Amid such conditions the Commissioner's Office and the staffs of the several departments had to find room and quiet in which to work, and from early days there must have been talk of finding better accommodation; but no definite step to this end seems to have been taken until the 1870's, when the opportunity to acquire a most desirable site for an entirely new police headquarters first presented itself.

Riverside Westminster was undergoing great changes. In 1860 a beginning was made on the Victoria Embankment, and from Chelsea to Blackfriars a strip of land, or, rather, mud, was being reclaimed. Behind it scores of old alleys and wharves were swept away. When the stretch of the Embankment from Westminster Bridge to Blackfriars was opened for traffic in 1868, much final tidying remained to be done; in particular, reclamation and clearance had left a rectangular empty space close to Westminster Bridge itself. This piece of land was bounded to east and west by the river and Parliament Street, on the north by Richmond Terrace and Mews, and on the south by certain structures on the north side of Bridge Street—the new Westminster Bridge Station of the Underground Railway, the building of the Civil Service Commission, and the houses on the west side of Cannon Row, those on the east side having been pulled down to make room for the Commission's grounds. At the top of Cannon Row, where it entered the empty space, Derby Street, now Derby Gate, came in from Parliament Street, which was only half the width that it is to-day. Opposite Downing Street the wide thoroughfare of Whitehall then split into two branches, the easterly one being Parliament Street and the westerly King Street. On the far side of King Street stood the chief police station of A Division, later to be moved to the head of Cannon Row.

The roadway of the new Embankment was necessarily laid on solid foundations, but of this rectangular plot inside it, where there had been a timber-yard and a narrow street of gabled wooden warehouses ending in a wharf, about half was reclaimed land, and unfit for building until the soil had settled. The whole area was accordingly left derelict for some years; but since to do nothing about it was to have an ugly patch of mud and weeds in the heart of the capital and the Empire, it appears to have been laid out, as a temporary measure, as a public "pleasure garden." The Ordnance Survey of 1870 shows a semi-circular shrubbery on the Embankment side.

So things remained until 1875. A Mr J. H. Mapleson, sometimes called Colonel Mapleson, then formed a company to purchase the site from the Metropolitan Board of Works and erect on it a Grand National Opera House. Backed by prima donnas (whom Mapleson was accused of stealing from Covent Garden), the scheme was not merely grand but grandiose; the building was to be a third as big again as its rival in Bow Street, with an auditorium measuring 100 feet by 102 feet, and a stage having a clear depth of 80 feet.[1] In September 1875 Mme Titiens laid the first brick of the foundations; and on December the 16th a number of police, who must soon have been reflecting on the queer twists of fortune, were on duty at a more august ceremony, the laying of the foundation-stone by the Duke of Edinburgh. The Brigade of Guards found the guard of honour, music was played by the bands of the Coldstream and the H.A.C., and the Mayor and Sheriff of Westminster, peers, junior Ministers, and Members of Parliament were among those present. Nothing is said about prima donnas.

Seldom can so much pomp and circumstance have been followed by so swift a disillusionment. A sum of £40,000 had already been spent, and if the prophets of woe had not then been heard they were soon audible. Within another six months the manager of the Royal Opera House in Covent Garden, who was perhaps not altogether disinterested, was predicting that little in the way of returns would come to the subscribers to the new enterprise. From then onward ominous reports appeared periodically in the newspapers. Though the vast structure was going up, it was by fits and starts; the *Building News* of September the 16th, expressing surprise because "all visible signs of work had ceased," referred to "temporary fiscal difficulties." In October the architect, Francis H. Fowler, exhibited his design at the Royal Academy; with its conical roof above the foyer and grand staircase,

[1] Interesting facts about this extraordinary building will be found in *Jimmy Glover—his Book* (Methuen, 1911), pp. 195–200.

and its female figures carrying musical instruments, it was plainly inspired by the new Opera House in Paris. Like the design of the building which was to arise on its foundations, it met with a mixed reception. "Piled up tea-chests," was one description, but the *Building News* thought it "not wanting in antithesis and variety," the "thoroughly French treatment" having "sportive and allégresse qualities." This otherwise favourable pronouncement ended upon a too familiar note: "the work has not been going on so fast as could be wished, owing to temporary difficulty in obtaining the amount necessary for the monthly advance to the builder." The building had then reached the level of the Grand Tier, and there were hopes that by the next spring it would be "in a fair state for the opera season."

They were vain hopes. The Grand National Opera House was never completed. So short was its young life, and so short are memories, that how much of it was completed is difficult to ascertain. In August 1877, in a letter to *The Times*, Mapleson said that £10,000 was still wanted for the roof. In reply to a critic, who alleged that the original estimate of a quarter of a million had already been considerably exceeded, he explained that, the site being little better than a swamp, an extra £30,000 had literally been sunk in concrete foundations. (These were not to be altogether wasted, being to-day mingled with the cellarage of New Scotland Yard.) Before this there had been questions in the House about the work, "now long stopped for want of funds," and Lord Ernest Bruce asked for information "as to when it might be thought proper to remove the present remarkable building on the Embankment exactly opposite the windows of Her Majesty's Office of Works." There were rumours that the Opera House was to be converted into a hotel. In February 1878 it was stated officially that no rent had been paid for the site since Michaelmas of the previous year. References to the still-missing roof imply that externally, at least, the pretentious edifice was all but finished.[1]

Whether or no there was any truth in the rumour about a hotel, by 1878 many persons must have been considering the future of the great shell, or of its site. Among them was Henderson, the Commissioner at the time. The site, only a few hundred yards from Great Scotland Yard, was in every way suitable for a new police headquarters. A file dated the 16th of April, 1878, is minuted: "Correspondence relative to a proposal to convert the New Opera House on the Victoria Embankment as a Police Office and a Chief Station for A Division." The minute, however, is endorsed, "To be Registered"; and registered,

[1] And see Glover, *op. cit.*

COLONEL SIR EDMUND HENDERSON

Victoria and Albert Museum. Crown copyright

[*See pp.* 169 *et seq.*]

JAMES MONRO

Victoria and Albert Museum. Crown copyright

[*See pp.* 195–196 *and* 212–215.]

SIR CHARLES WARREN

Victoria and Albert Museum. Crown copyright

[*See pp.* 201–211.]

SIR EDWARD HENRY

[*See pp.* 249 *et seq.*]

1829 1956

A CONSTABLE

1920 1956

THE WOMEN POLICE

or filed away, it was, in November. The Home Office, presumably, did not see its way to find the purchase price.

Early in the next year Henderson tried again. The opportunity might be lost; a French company was in treaty for the site, with a view (or so it said) to building offices and flats. In April the Receiver wrote that he was "not in a position at present to open any negotiations." "At present," however, sounded a little more hopeful. The French company withdrawing, the huge derelict eyesore remained, rusting and crumbling behind unsightly hoardings, a spur to the Commissioner's aspirations and a standing reproach, as Lord Ernest Bruce had pointed out, to higher authority.

In December 1880 Henderson was referring once more to "an opportunity which will probably never recur," and the Metropolitan Police Surveyor, Butler, in a memorandum to the Receiver, said that he had been offered the building privately for £25,000. He could convert and adapt it to the needs of a police headquarters; a particularly useful feature was the tunnel designed to bring opera addicts direct to the auditorium from the platform of Westminster Bridge Station. By this means, in time of emergency, 2000 men could be fetched by rail from all over London and concentrated unseen at the nerve-centre of operations. This tunnel still exists, and is occasionally used; but happily London has been spared a New Scotland Yard built for opera. No police force could have lived this down.

Though the authors of *London Past and Present*,[1] writing of Whitehall at this period, say that "at the Westminster Bridge end were for many years the unfinished walls of the ill-fated Grand Opera House," these years were few. The offer to Butler showed how the wind was blowing; soon after, with ground rent owing and stockholders clamouring, Mapleson was compelled to accept a firm offer for his white elephant. It is said that the price was £29,000, and that the structure itself was resold, as building material, for £500, its demolition costing the new owners another £3000.[2] The site, once more available, must have been much sought after, but now at last the Receiver, Sir Richard Pennefather, was in a position to negotiate for it, through the Home Secretary, Childers, with the Board of Works. No doubt he had priority, but it was a case of Greek joining Greek, and the sum ultimately paid was £186,000. Childers and his Permanent Under-Secretary, still Godfrey Lushington, at least deserve credit for appreciating the opportunity.

[1] Wheatley and Cunningham, p. 367.
[2] Glover, *op. cit.*

It was apparently Henderson and the Receiver who now asked Butler to design the new police headquarters. No one can have known better than Mr Butler what was wanted in the way of office accommodation. The Government, however, rightly decided that so important a position, in the shadow of Big Ben, demanded something worthy of it externally, as well as suitable within. Butler's plan was put aside, and Norman Shaw, as one of the leading architects of the day, was commissioned to design the building for which, among all his works, he is most famous. It was a happy choice, and must appear especially so when the result is compared with "the sportive and allégresse qualities" favoured by his luckless predecessor Fowler, and apparently thought not inappropriate by Butler himself.

Shaw was to have his troubles with departmental foibles. When he sent in plans he could not get them back. Upwards of 140 offices, to say nothing of store-rooms and the like, were required, and these were not enough to satisfy the departments, each wanting more rooms than it could have. The C.I.D. alone demanded forty. There were criticisms of turret staircases, of the lay-out of the Lost Property Office, of what were called "service rooms." "What is a service room?" asked Monro, among others. The forceful Warren had succeeded Henderson as Commissioner, and proved very hard to please, expressing his objections in his usual energetic manner. He approved of Butler's design, and did not see why an outside architect should have been called in. "I have to observe," he wrote to the Receiver, "that the internal arrangements are not nearly so convenient and commodious as those proposed by Mr Butler. . . . As for its [the building's] external appearance, from what I have heard no doubt it will be hideously ugly."

Warren at least put his finger on the great weakness of the design. It was not the fault of the architect, who worked to specifications; the whole project, however, had been so long in fruition that when the building began to go up it was already too small. In 1887 the Commissioner wrote prophetically: "Possibly before we get inside the building we shall have outgrown it. In my opinion we should have a building suitable for the Police Force for at least 30 to 40 years to come." By 1890, with the administrative needs of the force still expanding, it was only too clear that the great structure was not big enough.

Shaw's design, an experiment in the philosophy of architecture, was intended to convey an idea of the purpose of the building. It was, in effect, an immense tower with an interior courtyard, a parallelogram having the proportions of a Norman keep, 130 feet high, its longest side being 168 feet and its shortest 128. Sir Reginald Blomfield, in his *Richard Norman Shaw*, calls it "a magnificent building . . . the finest in London since Somerset House." Many modern architects no doubt disagree violently, but such things are largely matters of current taste; oddly enough, Fowler's tea-chests, though without his "sportive" ladies, have become fashionable. New Scotland Yard received a mixed reception in 1890; it "has already," said the *Daily Graphic* of June the 12th, "given rise to severe criticisms." Some of these were as ill-informed as they were violent. Shaw was abused for using granite wrought by the convicts at Portland, though this material was imposed on him for reasons of economy. The building was attacked in the House of Commons; of one particularly acrimonious speech Shaw wrote to a more appreciative M.P., "I do not suppose that anything would make it bearable to Mr Cavendish Bentinck's taste." Harcourt was as bad, chiefly, it is said, because he believed the architect to be a police official, presumably Butler, whom he particularly disliked, though surely a politician of Cabinet rank should in those days have heard of Norman Shaw? Harcourt's architectural taste may be judged by his earlier suggestion that for a building which would have to bear close comparison with Westminster Abbey and the Houses of Parliament an Engineer officer should be borrowed from the War Office.[1]

Sober opinion, as expressed in *The Times* and the *Daily Telegraph*, the *Builder* and the *Building News*, on the whole approved. The elevation was considered original and impressive, and that judgment will stand. Internally, though *The Times* thought that "for all practical purposes New Scotland Yard is an unqualified success," the design had the practical defects of most public and many private buildings of that age. A good deal was sacrificed to show, and above the second floor, to which few important visitors penetrate, and where the main staircase ends, the great quadrangle becomes rather a rabbit-warren.

The total cost, with the price of the site and the expense of lighting and furnishing, rose to above £300,000, of which £95,000 went on what can be seen of the tall structure above ground. Only £11,000 had to be spent on the foundations, an estimated saving of £40,000 being effected by embodying those of the Opera House, tunnel and all. The site was then still so waterlogged that these old foundations are sunk to a depth of 22 feet 9 inches below pavement-level.

Though Monro named New Scotland Yard, he did not remain to

[1] Harcourt may have had in mind the work of Captain Fowke and Major-General Scott on the Albert Hall.

move into it. Among Bradford's early tasks was the supervision of the change-over. As police work never ceases, this must have entailed a considerable feat of organization, details of which have not survived destruction of documents at the time. Departments were moving down Whitehall into Parliament Street during November and December 1890; the Commissioner and his staff occupied their new offices on December the 15th. With the brickwork still sweating, there were complaints of damp, and the Receiver sanctioned extra fires.

Warren's forebodings being realized, departments found they had not enough room, and those first in appear to have staked claims to the quarters of later comers. Readjustment took some time. Thus the Public Carriage Department and the Lost Property Office were left out in the cold, or at any rate in Whitehall Place and Great Scotland Yard, for eighteen months. The architect was soon being consulted about the erection of an additional building on the remainder of the site, to the south of New Scotland Yard. Shaw was reluctant to have anything to do with a plan which destroyed his conception of a single isolated tower. Though the details of this are followed in the annexe begun in 1895, and completed within a few years, under his general supervision, Sir Reginald Blomfield thinks that much of the design of what became Scotland House, with its abrupt ending in a flat gable to the south, "was the result of the well-meant efforts of an architect to the Police." Mr Butler had been given his chance at last.

It will be convenient to deal here with this addition, and later ones. There being a public right-of-way between New Scotland Yard and Scotland House, they are joined by a bridge. The Receiver's Office moved across to Scotland House, leaving room in the older building for the Public Carriage Department and the Lost Property Office, which occupied the quarters Shaw had designed for it on the Embankment. Still there was a demand for more accommodation; with the police printing office in the basement of Scotland House, the Receiver had to move sideways into rooms above the adjoining Cannon Row Police Station. In 1927 the Lost Property Office, the Public Carriage Department, the Receiver's Store, and the Police Garage were to cross the river to another new building in Lambeth Road. In the meantime the personnel and activities of the C.I.D., especially on the technical and scientific side, were also developing to an extent never foreseen by Howard Vincent or Monro; and now that department has a whole block of offices and laboratories to itself. Like Scotland House to the south, the North Building (as the new block is usually called), the fourth and latest of the series, a box-like structure in the modern style, is linked by a bridge with New Scotland Yard, which has become the Commissioner's Office.

Still other adjuncts to the Metropolitan Police Headquarters, such as Peel House and the Hendon Police College, are not administrative. They will be mentioned in their turn. As to the headquarters itself, no right-minded person, when he talks of Scotland Yard, is thinking of the Lost Property Office, and it may be doubted whether even the average Londoner yet recognizes the North Building. It is the original New Scotland Yard and Scotland House that symbolize the Metropolitan Police, with its 16,000 officers and one hundred and seventy-five stations; and the two buildings together form one of the dozen landmarks in the capital—there are scarcely more—known by hearsay, if not by sight, to almost everybody everywhere.[1]

[1] The three buildings at Westminster are here given the names by which they are generally known, and by which, probably, they will continue to be known. Officially, the whole group is called New Scotland Yard. Such individual mouthfuls as New Scotland Yard (Central), New Scotland Yard (South), and New Scotland Yard (North) may be left to the purists.

18

THE 1890's

WITH the passing of the Police Act of 1890, "a pension charter," as Sir John Moylan describes it, "for all forces in England and Wales," the Metropolitan Police entered into a period of domestic calm after storm. Apart from the beneficial effects of the Act, something may be attributed to Home Secretaries of a different stamp from Childers and Matthews (the latter was to depart unlamented, at any rate at Scotland Yard, with the fall of Lord Salisbury's administration in August 1892), but still more to the new Commissioner. Bradford, who contrived to work well with Matthews during their two years' official association, was active from the start, even while disciplinary measures were still in hand, in acquainting himself with the conditions under which his 15,000 men had to work and live. His visits to police stations, and consideration of grievances and minor complaints, were interrupted in August, a fall from his horse in Hyde Park disabling him for a short time, during which Howard, though the newest Assistant Commissioner, as head of the Executive Branch functioned under Royal Warrant as Acting Commissioner. As soon as Bradford resumed his duties he continued his tour of the whole Metropolitan Police District, until he had visited every station. The results of this thorough inquisition, and of a lively personal interest in the men's welfare, were reforms in all directions, carried out during his tenure of office; towards economy of work, by the provision of more stations, and of signal-boxes and fixed points; towards recreation and physical fitness, by the encouragement of sport; and towards raising the standard of the force by insistence upon a more careful selection of recruits.

In the very new New Scotland Yard, where the Receiver noted a regrettable habit of knocking nails in the walls, the functions of the different departments were still far from clearly defined. Monro had found that when he became head of the C.I.D. he was also expected to supervise the police attached to dockyards and military stations. He passed this work to his fellow Assistant Commissioners, and when one of these, Anderson, succeeded him in the department, dockyards and military stations became in practice the business of the senior A.C., Bruce. In December 1890 Bradford was writing to the Home Secretary to have this temporary arrangement put on a regular footing. A minor complaint of the Assistant Commissioners, of long standing, had already been adjusted; allowances, unchanged since 1857, "to cover hire of gig, feeding horses and tolls when visiting Police Stations and Section Houses in the exterior Police District," were at last increased. (Tolls in the London area had been abolished only a few years before.) By the end of the year the first motor-cars were on the roads; but since they were classed as locomotives, limited to a speed of four miles an hour in towns, and, even when provided with "a lamp, bell or horn as a warning instrument," compelled to be preceded by a man carrying a red flag, Assistant Commissioners, however mechanically minded, were for some time to come to find gigs a much speedier means of conveyance. The traffic problem in London was still in so elementary a stage that only in the following year were tickets introduced on omnibuses and trams, an interference with the privileges of drivers and conductors which at once caused a strike.

In March 1891 the rearguard was able to march out from Whitehall Place and Great Scotland Yard. The Public Carriage Department gained possession of at least some of the rooms in the new building allotted to it, and at the same time the Lost Property Office evicted intruders from the small low range of buildings which, after some argument about the plan, Shaw had designed on the Embankment side for the convenience of absent-minded persons, whose forgetfulness was extraordinary. Another aspect of accommodation was raising its ugly head, for among the results of growth and progress which the specifications of public buildings of this era failed to take into account was the enormous annual increase of documentary matter. The tradition still lingers at Scotland Yard of a receptacle called the Commissioner's Cupboard, but even in Mayne's day cupboards soon ceased to meet requirements, and papers were piled on stairs; and a few bonfires during the removal made insignificant inroads into the accumulating reports and returns, written on stiff foolscap that after long folding acquired the properties of a steel spring, which were now a matter of almost daily routine. To take only a handful of those demanded from Divisional Superintendents in 1892, there were returns for each of the twenty-two areas of empty houses, new houses built, and doors and windows left open; of police points and hackney-carriage standings; of the number of public houses and greenyards (which were increasing); of summonses applied for by private individuals, of street accidents, persons taken to hospital, and dead bodies found. That senior officers should be fully occupied in this period of domestic calm their attention was further drawn to such things as the Contagious Diseases (Animals) Act of 1878, and the Pleuro-pneumonia Orders of 1890 and 1891, to the Kent Animals Order, London (Cowsheds), of 1887, the Swine Fever Order of 1890, and the allied Rabies (City and Metropolitan Police Districts) Order and the Muzzling of Dogs Order of 1889. It is perhaps worth remembering that sixty years ago police paper-work had assumed dimensions that would have made Peel's head spin, and that there were no typewriters. (The first machine seems to have been introduced by Henry in 1901.) Nor was there any proper provision in New Scotland Yard—or, for that matter, in the Home Office or any other public building—for the storage of documents speedy reference to which might become necessary at any moment. In the course of time thousands of box-files were to find their way to the Registry immediately below the water-tanks under the roof.

2

In marked contrast with preceding years, the Commissioner's relations with the Home Office now became so harmonious that almost the only correspondence of interest between the two departments in 1891 concerned the visit of a police band to Constantinople and arrangements for Bradford to meet the Turkish Ambassador, the question whether Mr X—— was a fit and proper person to be Consul in Bulgaria, the duties of police employed at the Post Office, and an optional clause in the new Police Act affecting the Commissioner and the three Assistant Commissioners. Bradford wrote in April that Anderson and Howard accepted the provisions of the Act, "but Mr Bruce and myself have elected to refuse them."

Towards the end of the year, however, a graver topic was causing some anxiety on both sides of Whitehall. If the C.I.D. had ceased to be responsible for dockyards the Special Branch, once the Special Irish Branch, was still keeping a watch at certain home and even foreign ports. So far as London was concerned, Fenianism was scotched, if not dead; but the anarchists, whose methods it had borrowed, having been too active on the Continent, a number of them, mostly Italians, had taken refuge in England. No watch at the ports could keep out more than one or two old friends. Psychologists may explain, if they can, why these fanatics should feel a grudge against the only country in the world where, so long as they behaved themselves, they could live in peace. On rational grounds it was extremely stupid to antagonize their tolerant hosts. Unlike the Fenians, fortunately, anarchists seem as a rule to be thoroughly inept, and those who tried to frighten the citizens of London in the early 1890's were no exception. The Fenians, trusting no Englishman, worked in secret, but the simple Italians and their few British confederates not only associated themselves with the genuine unemployed and the windbags of the Social Democratic Federation, but advertised their intentions in public prints. Some of them probably had not got their hearts in the job, others were informers, and altogether it is not surprising that every one of their plots came to nothing.

Early in 1892, "on information received," the Staffordshire police raided a house in Walsall where bombs were being made. Six men were arrested, two in London by the Special Branch, and at the Stafford Assizes four of them were given long sentences of penal servitude. In March, before the trial, Bradford was sending to Matthews, still Home Secretary, copies of periodicals called *Commonweal* and *The Walsall Anarchist*, in which articles by D. J. Nicoll, "a well-known London anarchist," contained threats against Matthews himself, Mr Justice Hawkins, and Inspector Melville of the Special Branch. Nicoll, probably a Scot, was later charged with incitement to murder and sentenced to a term of hard labour. At the same time the Commissioner was forwarding information about a Sheffield anarchist with the Irish name of Creagh, an advocate of dynamite who claimed the degree of L.R.C.S. and who was thought to have supplied one of the Walsall gang with chloroform found in his possession. Men of this type, with some education, might have been far more dangerous than illiterate Italians, but their education betrayed them; they all had to talk or write.

The police and the Government were less worried about the anarchists themselves at this stage than about the trouble they were fomenting among the unemployed and unemployable. In November 1892 there was talk of a midnight march through London; this was at once forbidden, a precedent having been set after a similar parade, with torches, in 1886, had resulted in something like a riot and much damage. The Social Democratic Federation, having been quiescent for some years, was active again, and planning demonstrations, and the new Home Secretary, H. H. Asquith, was asked to authorize a temporary augmentation of the Metropolitan Police by a hundred men. There were weekday meetings of the unemployed at Tower Hill and elsewhere, and the need to keep a small reserve of police near Trafalgar

Square on Saturdays and Sundays was depriving the officers concerned of their fortnightly day's leave.

This instance of the recurrent problem, in a force none too big, of finding men to watch meetings and shepherd processions in which there was usually an element of mischief-mongers, coincided with an amusing example of revolutionary logic and impudence. The patience and good feeling of the police, and the tenderness of higher authorities towards any demonstration which by a stretch of fancy could be called political, encouraged anarchists to hope that a few bombs were neither here nor there. On the day when the Commissioner applied for his extra hundred men he received from a Mr H. R. Samuels a request "on behalf of the Allied Anarchist Groups of London," who wished to meet in Trafalgar Square—possibly with bombs in their pockets, but, unless they started to throw these about, protected by the police. At this date the Walsall bomb-makers had been in prison only a few months, most of their accomplices were, in fact, in hiding, and the Special Branch, busily hunting for other bomb factories, had an eye on two Italians, Polti and Farana, who before long were arranging to blow up the Stock Exchange at its most crowded hour. Even in England, in these circumstances, it was felt that the right of free speech should stop short of advocacy of dynamite; but, the English being a little mad, Mr Samuels's request was forwarded through the usual channels to the highest quarters, and its eventual refusal was couched in the following respectful terms:

> SIR,
>
> I am directed by the Commissioner of Police of the Metropolis to acquaint you that having submitted your application to the Secretary of State, he is unable to give the necessary permission.

During the rest of the year, and throughout 1893, so far as the public was aware, the anarchists had ceased from troubling. The Special Branch knew better. Polti and Farana, among others, were still under observation. Early in 1894 they were being shadowed day and night, a Mr Thomas Smith, manager of Cohen's, a firm of iron-founders, having given information that he had received an order for the manufacture of bomb-cases. When Polti, a youth of eighteen, left the factory carrying a brown-paper parcel he was followed to an omnibus by Inspector Sweeny, who had helped to run down the Fenians and had narrowly escaped death or injury at the time of the dynamite outrage at Scotland Yard ten years before. As Polti left the omnibus Sweeny arrested him. Farana, a much older man, was taken a few days later in his bed. At the Old Bailey, in May, Farana was sentenced to twenty years' penal servitude; he had pleaded guilty to a charge of conspiring to cause an explosion in the Stock Exchange, and his only regrets were for his failure. Polti received a sentence of ten years. For arresting Farana. Inspector Quinn was granted a reward of fifty pounds, and another fifty pounds went to Mr Smith.

As at the time of the Fenian outrages, much extra trouble was caused to the police by practical jokers and reports of suspicious objects which, after anxious handling and immersion in buckets of water, proved to be innocuous. To Italians and others who had to be watched were added a number of Spanish anarchists from South America. After a quiet year the public was becoming alarmed; explosions and murders all over Europe culminated in the assassination of the President of France by an anarchist named Henry, and a people used to stones and brickbats as political arguments, but shocked by the revelations at recent trials, was further startled by an extraordinary affair in Greenwich Park. The overworked police deserved a little luck, and, though they seem to have overlooked a young French tailor called Bourdin, his own ineptness removed him before he could do any harm. It seems too grotesque for belief that anyone could regard a standard meridian, or even the Astronomer Royal, as a symbol of tyranny; but Bourdin set out with a home-made bomb to blow up Greenwich Observatory. He was near the building when the bomb exploded in his hand, tearing off his arm, and he died before he could receive medical attention. The peculiar imbecility of this attempt so fascinated at least one novelist, Joseph Conrad, that he abandoned his usual *genre* to make the episode the basis of *The Secret Agent.*

At the end of the year a bomb in Mayfair damaged property, but injured no one; and then these senseless outrages virtually ceased. An explosion in an Underground train in April 1897, though attributed to anarchists, remains unexplained. It caused one death, and a number of persons were wounded. Until well into the next century the Special Branch continued to watch the dwindling band of dynamiters, but the creed survived only among talkers; the men of action who later called themselves anarchists, the foreign ruffians of Tottenham Marshes, the Houndsditch murders, and Sidney Street, were common bandits.

3

The high rate of increase in the numbers of the Metropolitan Police which marked the ten years from 1880 to 1889 was due to special circumstances, and was not maintained during the next decade. The force, however, continued to grow. In 1890 its strength rose above 15,000, and by the close of 1899 the total on establishment was 15,763. This was more than the actual number of men then available, some being returned as 'off-pay' on rejoining the Army at the outbreak of the war in South Africa.

The need for further augmentation was already foreshadowed. By the Locomotives (on Highways) Act of 1896 the motor-car was freed from its most crippling restriction; the speed limit in towns was raised from four miles an hour to fourteen, and as even a running footman could not have maintained this speed the man with the red flag necessarily disappeared. By 1898 the work of the Public Carriage Office had so expanded that twenty-one members of the staff were distributed among divisions. The first electric cabs were on the road, and during 1899, when the dying era was still represented by 5000 horse-drawn omnibuses and trams, there was a short-lived experiment with electric buses. Another novelty was the taximeter, originally introduced on horse-drawn cabs.

At the end of 1894 members of the C.I.D., in particular, were probably reading with interest the report of the first of two Home Office Committees, appointed during this decade, whose proceedings will be considered in the next chapter. They were to revolutionize the work of the department, which was also to be influenced by Bordet's discovery of reliable blood tests in 1893, and, more profoundly, by Marconi's experiments in wireless telegraphy six years later. The Special Branch, with its eye on Italian and Spanish anarchists, had for a time to find men to watch an Armenian revolutionary group. A story that several hundred Armenians had arrived from the United States in the White Star liner *Britannic* proved to be unfounded. Genuine refugees from Asia Minor, where the Turks were harrying their country, were on the whole harmless, and in the following year the police were instructed to inform them that they could hold meetings. As many were said to be destitute, a house was found for them in West Hampstead, and those who have read Stephen Leacock's tale of the poor Armenians in Canada may wonder how they prospered in North-west London.

The Special Branch was also concerned in 1893 in a minor international incident. Detective-Sergeant Ratcliffe having gone to Paris on official business, the French judicial police were dissatisfied with his credentials, put him under arrest, and, it was said, handled him rather roughly. Profuse apologies which accompanied his release were considered to close the matter.

In general, these 1890's, after a bad start, became so uneventful in Metropolitan Police domestic annals that Chief Superintendent A. W. Rowlerson, creator of the Museum at Bow Street and the compiler of a book of "Interesting Incidents" drawn from the force's history, can find nothing more noteworthy during this period than the opening of a new police station in Gray's Inn Road and the adjustment of E Division's boundary. The world at large was less peaceable; the ten years saw the Dreyfus Case, the Jameson Raid, wars between Japan and China, Turkey and Greece, and Spain and the United States; the British Army was fighting in Ashanti, and presently in South Africa. President Carnot and the Empress of Austria were assassinated. At home tempers ran high over the rejection by the Lords of another Home Rule Bill, and Gladstone, at eighty-five, left office for the last time. In London the police were very busy indeed, for the great age of ceremonial occasions had reached its climax. Among these were the marriage of the Duke of York, in 1893, to Princess Mary of Teck, and the first visit to England, two years earlier, of the young German Emperor and his Empress. It was to be some time before Wilhelm II came to be known disrespectfully as Kaiser Bill, but within five years of this visit his telegram to Kruger after the failure of the Jameson Raid provoked almost the last outburst of British national pride—or jingoism, if taste prefers the word. A new Conservative Government took action, and the Flying Squadron of fast cruisers was commissioned for sea.

The Emperor had been forgiven by the year of Queen Victoria's Diamond Jubilee, the culmination of a long series of pageants at which the Metropolitan Police had assisted. There were few or none of the fears of anarchist or Fenian outrages which had been a serious worry in 1887, but there were foreign revolutionaries and criminals to be kept under routine supervision, and the arrival of potentates, the receptions, the dinners, and the daily crowds (drawing a swarm of pickpockets) threw an increasing strain upon the resources of the police, until on the day of the Queen's drive through London to St Paul's 9000 men were on duty in connexion with the procession alone.

Two years later the police were concerned in other martial occasions, in the same atmosphere of confidence and high spirits—soon, however, to be dashed. In September 1899 troops were marching through London, police reservists among them, on their way to embark for the Cape.

One other event of the 1890's held the seeds of much tribulation to come. No one had divined this when the century closed, least of all

Inspector Froest, of the C.I.D., who in December 1895 had been instructed to look into what appeared to be a trivial and commonplace case of fraud. It was suspected that the accused was the culprit responsible for a series of recent complaints of similar offences, and the Chief Inspector was to settle this question, one way or the other. He accomplished his task only too well; nearly ten years later he was still to be embroiled in the case of Adolf Beck, and what in 1895 had not even been recognized as a cloud on the horizon was bringing a storm about the ears of the police, the prison authorities, and the Home Office itself.

4

Among investigations of graver crimes, the C.I.D. was concerned during the 1890's in the three notorious cases of Mrs Pearcey, Neill Cream, and the Muswell Hill murder. The case of Mrs Pearcey presented no difficulties, and it is of interest in police history only because it belongs to a type rare in these islands—the ferocious killing, from jealousy, of one woman by another. The criminal career of Neill Cream, and the Muswell Hill murder, on the other hand, are instructive examples of detective work in its least impressive form, and at its best.

The mangled body of Mrs Pearcey's victim, Phœbe Hogg, was found in the early hours of an October morning in 1890, in a new road on the boundary of Hampstead and St John's Wood; and with the Whitechapel murders a very recent memory, the horrible features of the crime started rumours that Jack the Ripper was at work again. Two years later the poisonings in the neighbourhood of Waterloo Station raised a similar theory, the known victims of Thomas Neill, commonly called Neill Cream, belonging to the same class as the Ripper's. At Cream's execution, according to Billington, the hangman, the former cried out, "I am Jack——," but the sentence and his life were cut short by the pulling of the bolt. He had an inordinate share of the vanity of criminals, and dates and other factors dispose of any such claim, if he made it.

Born in Scotland and taken to Canada as a boy, Cream obtained some sort of medical diploma in the United States, as Crippen was to do a little later. He was suspected of causing the deaths of two women before being sentenced to life imprisonment for poisoning his mistress's husband with strychnine. This sentence was reduced to one of seventeen years, which again was soon shortened to two—an inexplicable remission. Thus casually let loose, this born poisoner, at the age of forty-one, returned to the British Isles, which he reached on the 1st of October,

1891. Within less than three weeks he had accomplished the next instalment of his crimes.

On the 12th of the month Ellen Donworth died, and on the 19th Matilda Clover. The cause of both deaths was strychnine poisoning, but in the case of Matilda Clover a doctor who apparently did not even see the corpse certified that death was due to delirium tremens and syncope. The truth was discovered only many months later, when the body was exhumed. There were other women who at this time came to know the bald-headed doctor, with his respectable top-hat, his squint, and his spectacles, but they were lucky, or suspected his white pills, and escaped with their lives.

In January 1892 Cream went to Canada for three months. Back in London again, on the 9th of April, he wasted even less time than before. On the 13th two more women, Alice Marsh and Emma Shrivell, were taken dying from a house in Stamford Street, off Waterloo Bridge Road, both victims of strychnine poisoning.

What distinguishes Cream's predecessor in multiple murder, Jack the Ripper, from almost all criminal lunatics of this type is that he never advertised. Apparently without any of the vanity of Cream, he remains a dreadful shadow with a nickname. In Cream, on the other hand, exhibitionism ran wild; by foolish talks and hints and pseudonymous letters, most of which found their way to Scotland Yard, he fairly thrust himself upon the notice of the police. Finally he even claimed their protection. Before this, however, within a fortnight of the deaths of Alice Marsh and Emma Shrivell, one of his letters, coming into the hands of Detective-Sergeant M'Intyre, recalled something to that officer's mind. Signed "W. H. Murray," the letter contained threats to a doctor and his son in connexion with these fatalities. Sergeant M'Intyre knew of another letter similarly signed; it had been sent to the coroner who conducted the inquest on the bodies of the two women. Moreover, the threatening letter to the doctor reminded M'Intyre of an earlier series which, over different signatures, had accused two well-known men of being concerned in the deaths of Ellen Donworth and Matilda Clover in the previous October. And Ellen Donworth, like the latest victims, had certainly died of strychnine poisoning.

When these earlier letters were taken from their file a feature which at the time had been overlooked, or disregarded, increased the sergeant's interest. One of them opened with the statement that Matilda Clover, supposed to have died of syncope following delirium tremens, had also been poisoned with strychnine. The police are accustomed to accusations of this kind, which usually turn out to be baseless; but was it not possible, with all this strychnine poisoning of women of the same class, living in the same district, that the writer of the letter was telling the truth? If he was, he was almost certainly the murderer of Matilda Clover, if not of the other three, for who else could know how she died?

Sergeant M'Intyre went to his superiors, and it was decided to exhume the bodies of Matilda Clover and Ellen Donworth. In the remains of the latter, as was expected, strychnine was found; it was also present in the second body. With four cases of poisoning by this means now on their hands, linked together by the letters and other circumstances, the police turned their attention in earnest to Dr Neill Cream. He was still doing his best to ensure that they did not forget him; and on the 3rd of June he was arrested on a provisional charge of attempting to extort money by false pretences. The capital charge followed, the victim selected for the occasion being the woman whose body might have rested undisturbed in its grave if the accused had not gone out of his way to draw attention to the true cause of her death.

Cream was hanged, no one protesting. His actions in incriminating himself seem so clear a proof of insanity that to-day they might have saved him from the gallows. They would no doubt have led to his arrest on a similar charge had the letter about Matilda Clover remained forgotten in its file at Scotland Yard. But his two later victims might not have died as they did if more thought had been given to the letter at the time of its receipt six months earlier. Normally it is a matter of routine to follow up all such accusations, however improbable, and had this course been pursued in the case of Matilda Clover the doctor who gave the death certificate would have been examined and exposed, and suspicion must at once have been directed to the letter-writer himself.

There were no mistakes in the investigation of a case of murder at Muswell Hill in February 1896. This was still a semi-rural district on the fringe of North London. The Alexandra Palace, designed to be the Crystal Palace's rival north of the Thames, rose above steep hills and extensive patches of woodland, which still remain, embedded now in suburban streets. The police division concerned was Y, one of the huge divisions on the perimeter of the Metropolitan Area. The largest piece of woodland in the region was Coldfall Wood, which stretched north and south for a mile; and backing on to it was a rather isolated house, Muswell Lodge, which had been built for a Mr Smith to his own design. The rockery at the end of his garden was in the shade of the trees of Coldfall Wood. In 1896 Smith was aged seventy-nine, and a widower; his only help about the place was a gardener named Webber. A man of some means, Smith was supposed by his neighbours to be richer than he was, and there were stories of considerable sums of money kept in the house. The situation of the house, with the thick wood behind, and the fact that the old man was alone there at night, caused him to take the precaution of fixing a spring gun in the rockery, which Webber set every evening when he finished his work in the garden.

On the 12th of February the gardener set the gun at sunset, and left Muswell Lodge at 5.30, his employer being then in the house. As was usual, however, Webber returned later, at about 11.30, to stoke the boiler of the greenhouse; Muswell Lodge was then in darkness. By seven o'clock in the morning he was back again, knocking at the front door to be let in. Getting no answer, he went round to the kitchen door, which was also locked. Flower-pots which he had left on the kitchen window-sill had been moved, and there were marks of a tool on the window-frame; and still getting no reply to his knocking Webber in some alarm went to examine the spring gun. Its mechanism had been disconnected, and a gate leading from the garden to Coldfall Wood was unlocked, which it should not have been. He returned to the kitchen window, peered in, saw something white on the floor, and ran to the nearest house, the home of a Major Challen, for help. Between them the pair forced the kitchen door. Old Mr Smith lay dead on the floor in his nightgown, his legs bound at the ankles and knees, a duster round his neck, a towel forced into his mouth, and a rag tied over that. There were severe injuries to his head.

The police of Y Division found some very interesting evidence, both in the house and in the garden, of the events of the night. On the kitchen table was a drill-brace, and on the floor two pocket-knives, the blades open, which were the murdered man's property. A small bull's-eye lantern, found in the sink, seemed less likely to belong to him. The bedroom upstairs had been ransacked, and the safe there opened with its key. At the end of the garden near the wood were two clear sets of footprints in the mould of a bed, one made by large boots, the other set by a small, pointed pair. There was also picked up in the garden a tin tobacco-box, with tobacco in it. It was not Webber's, and his employer did not smoke.

At Scotland Yard two inspectors of the C.I.D., Marshall and Nutkins, were put in charge of the case. Inquiries showed that among dangerous criminals likely to commit burglary with violence, and at that date at large, were two men named Albert Milsom and Henry Fowler. Both had many convictions, including a sentence apiece of five years' penal servitude, both were on ticket-of-leave, and Fowler was liable to arrest for failing to report. Milsom lived with his wife and mother and a young brother-in-law, Fowler in cheap lodging-houses, and neither could be found at his home or in his usual haunts. Shortly before the murder at Muswell Hill two men resembling this pair had made inquiries about Coldfall Wood of a Miss Kate Good. She was to see them again, three days after the crime, at Paddington Station.[1]

The most important witness interviewed by the two inspectors was Milsom's brother-in-law, a boy of sixteen. The bull's-eye lantern was his. He identified it, in particular, by the wick (now in the Black Museum at Scotland Yard), which he had made from the material of a child's dress. Since the night of the murder the lantern had been missing from the place where he usually kept it. He also identified the tin tobacco-box as Milsom's.

Both the latter and Fowler had been seen in London the day after the murder. They were wearing new suits, carrying revolvers, and talking of going to Australia. Miss Good's recognition at Paddington Station of the men who had questioned her at Muswell Hill suggested, however, that the Great Western Railway might be a pointer to their whereabouts; and before long they were run to ground at Bath, in the troupe of a travelling circus, Fowler, a very powerful brute, doing a turn as Ajax, the strong man of the company. He was arrested only after a struggle. He was in every sense the strong man of the pair, whose association resembled that of Browne and Kennedy, the murderers of Police-Constable Gutteridge in 1927; Milsom, like Kennedy, was the weaker vessel, and he tried to save his neck by incriminating his confederate. At the trial, Mr Justice Hawkins having summed up and left the court, Fowler suddenly brushed aside the warders in the dock, caught Milsom by the hair, and threw him to the floor. Half a dozen warders proved incapable of mastering the infuriated man. Milsom was got away to the cells, but the struggle went on; with warders hanging to him, the ex-'Ajax' thrashed about the dock, smashing the glass screen, while women in the gallery screamed and barristers stood on tables to see better. Fowler was subdued and taken below only when half a dozen large officers of the City Police came to the warders' aid. Never, before or since, has the Old Bailey witnessed such a scene.

The two men were convicted, it may be said largely on the evidence

[1] Alan Brock, *op. cit.*

of the lamp-wick; and such was the fear of what the powerful Fowler might do when he saw his treacherous confederate again, for the last time, on the scaffold, that another murderer named Seaman, who was also to be executed that day, was placed between them, which led Seaman to remark that it was the first time he had ever been a bloody peacemaker. There is said to have been a final incident in which the macabre and the comic were mingled; the assistant executioner was standing on the trap when it was lowered prematurely, causing him to disappear.[1]

5

From its early days the Detective Branch was occasionally called upon to deal with a class of crime it was then little fitted to investigate; and in course of time officers were recruited with the education and gifts required to counter large-scale financial trickery—with disastrous results to one of the ablest among them, Chief-Inspector Druscovitch, and to some of his colleagues. It has been mentioned that Druscovitch's "Fraud Squad"—the name was not then used—came under fire for its conduct of the inquiry in 1872 into the forgery of securities by the American Bidwells and others, though the leading members of this gang were later trapped, convicted, and given sentences of penal servitude for life. The heyday of financial fraud, however, lay in the future; when it may be said to have begun, in the 1890's, the resources of what had become the Criminal Investigation Department were far in advance of those at the service of Superintendent Williamson twenty years earlier.

The Metropolitan Police itself was only seven years old when an Act was passed to regulate building societies. In 1868 was founded the Liberator Permanent Building and Investment Society, which some twenty years afterwards came under the control of Jabez Spencer Balfour, to whom regulations were things to be circumvented. Combined with the Land Allotment Company and several more, it became the leading company of the Balfour Group. Said to have a capital of £7,000,000, and backed by the London and General Bank, another of Balfour's creations, this body issued glowing prospectuses and attracted investors and depositors in tens of thousands. In 1892 the showy edifice collapsed. The bank closed its doors; and official liquidators, assisted by officers of the C.I.D., began the enormous task of unravelling falsified accounts and balance-sheets, paper payments by one company to

[1] F. W. Ashley, *My Sixty Years in the Law* (Lane, 1936).

another out of fictitious profits, the vanishing of cash into the pockets of directors, and trickery in general on an unprecedented scale. More than £5,000,000 had disappeared.

So, with a good deal of it, had Jabez Balfour. One of the best riverside skylines in London, close to Great Scotland Yard, is a surviving monument to his misdirected ingenuity; and from his palatial quarters in Whitehall Court he got away across Europe to Genoa, and so to Buenos Aires. "On no condition," as the song ran, "is extradition allowed in Callao," and it was the same in Argentina, and it took more than two years, and some high-handed proceedings by Detective-Inspector Froest, to get the embezzler back to England. Three of his confederates had already received heavy sentences; others stood in the dock with him at his two trials in April and November 1895. The sentences passed on Balfour himself totalled fourteen years.

The careers of some of the greatest financial swindlers this country has known overlapped during this era. While the hunt was up for Balfour, Ernest Terah Hooley and Whitaker Wright were deluding investors in the same grand style, and Horatio Bottomley, a beginner, was heading for his first libel action. The *modus operandi* was always the same, being based on the quite extraordinary credulity of persons who think they are acute business-men. The swindler's apparatus consists of expensive quarters in the West End of London, a large country house, and very little else except his brains. The large house—in this case Papworth Hall, in Cambridgeshire—so impressed an impoverished young man not long down from the University that he gave himself body and soul to Ernest Terah Hooley, putting his name to bills of exchange for thousands; while, at the other end of the scale, one of the acute business-men, equally impressed by Papworth Hall and the splendours of the Albemarle Hotel, in Piccadilly, not only bought 75,000 shares, at 10*s*. a share, in a company which never paid a dividend, but cheerfully parted with another £10,000 for shares in a worthless mine in Canada. When men of substance of this type, out for easy money, lead the way, the small investor, thinking of his old age, may be forgiven for following.

Investigation of one of these elaborate systems of fraud is very largely the task of civil lawyers and accountants. By the end of last century the C.I.D. had a small but accomplished section, specializing in company finance, which has now become a sub-department, C.6; but when the police are called in to assist in unravelling the affairs of a Balfour or a Hooley a very great part of their work is the usual routine drudgery of interviewing, questioning, and taking statements.

No private organization can do this on the scale required. In the case of Hooley scores of statements were obtained from his own confederates, his men of straw appointed to directorships, his wealthy dupes, and the unfortunate smaller fry who had only a few pounds to spare, if they could spare those. From these documents the big swindler's technique emerges, and that of Hooley is of more interest than some because he was perhaps the ablest and the most slippery of them all. At this turn of the century, moreover, he had to keep in the background. He was a bankrupt, though this did not abate his style of living at Papworth Hall and in Piccadilly, since he had salted away some of his ill-gotten gains in his wife's name.

One of the façades behind which he worked at this time was a group of companies controlled by his friend and confederate, H. J. Lawson. It was no doubt the latter, an engineer, who saw the possibilities, from his and Hooley's point of view, of electric traction. The Electric Tramways Construction and Maintenance Company had been founded in 1886; Lawson obtained sole control of it when it was in a moribund state, for the purpose, according to his prospectus, of acquiring bills and concessions for tramways all over the country. He appointed as managing director a man whose rent and rates he paid, in addition to a monthly salary, and who admitted, when interviewed by the police, that he "knew nothing about company work." The secretary was one of Hooley's creatures. From the E.T.C. and M. Company sprang more than a dozen others, such as the Blackpool Tramways (South), the British Electric Street Tramways, and the Great Horseless Carriage Company. Most of these concerns existed only on paper, or at most had a scantily furnished office. Also affiliated to the parent body, rather oddly, was the Moore and Burgess Company.

When, early in the new century, proceedings were instituted against Hooley and Lawson, one of the fraud specialists at Scotland Yard went through the minutes of the board meetings of the E.T.C. and M. Company, and selected items that seemed to him of interest. They are interesting even to the uninstructed in high finance. Thus, at one time in 1901 the company had to be helped by Mrs Hooley, who lent it £3000; yet a little later that year a cheque for £5305 was made out to Lawson, and another for £2138 to Hooley. At a board meeting on the 30th of July, 1902, when the company's balance at the bank stood at £129, two cheques, each for £700, were made out to Lawson, perhaps on the strength of a letter from the philanthropic Mrs Hooley guaranteeing her shares in the City and Surrey Electric Railway. So it went on, the bank balance fluctuating violently, but money being always available for the two manipulators at the top, and even for the managing director who knew nothing about company business. Very shortly before Hooley was arrested six acceptances for large sums were made out in his favour; the bank balance, when next noted three weeks later, was down to £10 11*s.* 4*d.* The police and the accountants could no doubt explain how all this was done. It does not appear that any one of the affiliated companies, in theory operating from Yorkshire to the Home Counties, whose ghostly assets were juggled in this way, ever put a single tram on the roads anywhere.

The City Police take as keen an interest in financial wizards, who often operate from the City itself, as does the Metropolitan force; but though by now the two were working happily together, there was not the very close co-operation in such cases that exists to-day. Towards the end of the 1890's both were keeping a close eye on the affairs of Hooley and Lawson. While the latter's concerns had their offices and boards of directors, who might or might not meet, scattered about the country, Hooley (for reasons not unconnected with his bankruptcy) was handling personal transactions in the shares of the Coruna Company and the Canadian Corundum Mine in the cosy and informal atmosphere of the Albemarle Hotel; and his victims, associates and underlings, who met him there, had become the special care of the Metropolitan C.I.D. One of the underlings was an ex-inspector of police, but when, in the summer of 1899, his old colleagues would have enjoyed a talk with him it was found that he had left the country, it was thought by ship from Liverpool.

If the more wary rats were now deserting the ship, it was a long time sinking. Hooley and Lawson, themselves always optimists, were continually trying new casts to redress the adverse balance of the old; among other ventures there were some complicated dealings in the affairs of the Maria Farina Eau de Cologne agency in London; and it was in this connexion, on a charge of attempting to defraud the manager of the Windsor Castle Public House at Victoria, that the two were taken into custody in May 1904. Lawson was convicted of issuing false statements; the more ingenious Hooley was acquitted, and continued for years to elude the grasp of the C.I.D. At long last, in 1912, he was brought to book for defrauding a very young man who in eighteen months was induced to part with £21,500 out of an inheritance of £27,500, besides incurring obligations totalling £16,000 more. Hooley wept in the dock as he enumerated the country mansions he had been forced to sell, and the judge took so broad-minded a view of the case that, in his own words, he decided to punish the accused only in respect of a specific item of £2000. The officers of the "Fraud Squad," having devoted some fifteen years' hard labour to unravelling Hooley's transactions, may have felt that a sentence of twelve months in the Second Division was an anticlimax.[1]

[1] *The Times*, February 10, 1912.

19

FINGERPRINTS AND THE BECK CASE

AMONG early Police Orders for the year 1900 those of February the 1st dealt, besides other matters, with newsvendors crying false news. The partial successes near Ladysmith with which the Boer War opened being followed by defeats that seemed inexplicable, and rather shameful, the light-hearted rush for news in the week of Talana Hill and Elandslaagte had become a tendency to hope for the best while expecting the worst; and some newsvendors, perhaps with excellent intentions, turned every skirmish into a victorious battle. Those who were called to order may have felt ill-used, for it was editors who had begun the game with large headlines describing tactical offensives undertaken to cover a retreat as "Victory upon Victory."

The police had to handle large crowds that year when the C.I.V. marched through London to embark for the Cape, and still larger ones when the volunteers returned with Lord Roberts in October.[1] The hysterical mobs parading Central London on Mafeking Night, May the 18th, and throughout the next day, were beyond handling. Excitement had to be allowed to spend itself, and though in retrospect it was wildly disproportionate and rather absurd, another aspect of a happier age passed with it. It was a glorified Bank Holiday, even for pickpockets; and policemen wedged in these throngs who were to be on duty eighteen year's later, on Armistice Night, and who lived to see another May day—VE Day, 1945—must have reflected on the progressive decline in London manners.

During this year the force was granted a Rent Aid Allowance, and allowances to married reservists recalled to the colours were adjusted, by a reduction from 12*s*. a week to 9*s*. 10*d*., to meet increased separation grants sanctioned by the War Office. Since the previous November a Relief Fund had been in existence for immediate help to the wives and families of policemen called up.

[1] At the outbreak of war Sir Howard Vincent, late of the C.I.D. and then Colonel of the Queen's Westminster Volunteers, had proposed the formation of picked volunteer units for South Africa. Senior regular officers were contemptuous of the idea. It was officially adopted after the series of defeats in December 1899.

In 1901, when the population of London had grown to 6,554,449, the strength of the Metropolitan Police was approaching 16,000. That of the Police Reserve, having been revised, stood at 1372 of all ranks. The war in South Africa was still dragging on, and permission was refused, as against regulations, for police officers to distribute medals and tickets at a Monster Patriotic Fête held at the Crystal Palace in aid of the Soldiers' and Sailors' Families Association. It was a symptom of the changed attitude towards the force that its members were now in frequent demand for purposes which, only ten or fifteen years earlier, a policeman would have been thought to contaminate; regulations had to be invoked again somewhat later, there being a precedent against the appointment of constables as Sergeant Buglers of Church Lads' Brigades. When the Dame President of the Cheltenham Habitation of the Primrose League wished to know if police officers could become members, the Commissioner was able to point out that he had no authority in Gloucestershire.

The overshadowing events of 1901 were the death and funeral of Queen Victoria. Another of great importance to the force was the appointment of a new head of the Criminal Investigation Department. In May Sir Robert Anderson retired, and Edward Henry, from India, took his place as Assistant Commissioner.

Henry was not long to remain in charge of the C.I.D. He had been brought from India to introduce his system of fingerprinting; but he was also under consideration, on the strength of his experience and reputation, as a potential successor to Bradford. In May 1903 the latter in turn retired, at the age of sixty-seven, after a Commissionership of thirteen years, the more valuable because domestically it was so uneventful. Bradford's firm but placid rule had steadied and raised the morale of a force which, when he took up his post, was in an unhappy mood. Towards the end, however, Bradford appears to have been overburdened by his responsibilities, and in his last year his worries were aggravated by his own vacillating attitude towards the problem of the London unemployed, whose numbers were temporarily increased when the reduction of the Army to a peace footing after the close of the South African War suddenly threw thousands of men on the labour market. There were constant processions of unemployed marching about the streets with collecting-boxes, disorganizing traffic and straining the resources of the police. Advantage was, of course, taken of this licence to beg by the more aggressive of the genuine out-of-works, and by the usual element of idlers and others to whom it offered an easy way of making a little money. The processions became a form of intimidation, feared as well as resented by the public, which remembered the riots of the 1880's. It appears that memory of these scenes unduly influenced Bradford himself; determined that they should not be repeated, he shrank from the remedy immediately and successfully applied by Henry, with Home Office authority—the regulation of street collections. Those who had taken part in the demonstrations merely because these were lucrative naturally lost interest in long tramps which brought them nothing.

The year 1902 had also seen demonstrations of another sort. The Boer War having long ceased to be what the public regarded as one, the June rejoicings over peace had a rather artificial air; but it was a different matter when in August King Edward VII was crowned, after a postponement of the ceremony because of his very serious illness. There had been a succession of new Home Secretaries, Sir Matthew White Ridley replacing Asquith in 1895, and being himself replaced by C. T. Ritchie when a Conservative administration was returned to power in 1900; and in the autumn of 1902 Ritchie in turn was succeeded by Aretas Akers-Douglas. At Scotland Yard, in the same month, Sir Charles Howard resigned his Assistant Commissionership, having served the Metropolitan Police in that office, and previously as Chief Constable, for thirty-three years. A precedent was created when Major E. F. Wodehouse, who for two years had been Assistant Commissioner of the City Police, was invited to fill the vacant post.

From time to time Bradford had been reminded of the case of Adolf Beck. When Beck was committed to prison in March 1896, as the result of Inspector Froest's inquiries, it was as John Smith. As far back as 1877 a German or Austrian Jew calling himself by that name had been convicted of defrauding women. Beck was positively identified as Smith by the retired police officer who had arrested the latter nearly twenty years before. Mr Gurrin, the handwriting expert, was equally positive that Beck's handwriting was that of Smith. Beck, a Norwegian and an engineer, something of a rolling stone and possibly an adventurer, in vain protested that in 1877 he had been in Peru; he was sentenced to seven years' penal servitude, and in Portland Prison was given the registration D.W.523, which indicated that he was John Smith and that he had been convicted before.

He immediately began through his solicitor, Mr Dutton, a long and fruitless series of petitions and protests. Mr Dutton, with other well-wishers of the prisoner, was convinced that Beck was neither the John Smith of 1877 nor guilty of the offence for which he had now been sentenced. In 1898, learning that Smith bore physical marks which might decide the question, Mr Dutton applied to the Commissioner for leave to inspect Smith's record. Commissioners, like all busy public men, have to rely on what appear to be minor matters on the knowledge and advice of subordinates; but when, most regrettably, the solicitor's application was refused by Sir Robert Anderson, then head of the C.I.D., the ultimate responsibility was Bradford's. The Home Office supported this decision; but only two months later, persistent efforts having induced that Department to request the Governor of Portland Prison to compare the official descriptions of the two convicts, the Governor reported that Augustus Wilhelm Meyer, or John Smith, was a Jew, and circumcized, and that neither distinction applied to Beck. What followed is the most incredible, and perhaps most discreditable, feature of this lamentable case. The Home Office instructed the prison authorities to give Beck a new number, and did nothing more. It did not inform the police, or even its own official known as the Public Prosecutor. (The present Department of Public Prosecutions, under a Director, was not created until 1908.) What was worse, Beck was made to serve the rest of the heavy sentence passed upon him when he was supposed to be an old offender. The Report of the Commission of Inquiry into the Beck case does not comment as severely as it should have done upon this aggravation of the Norwegian's unmerited sufferings; and of the mishandling of the case in general by the Home Office at this stage it merely commits itself to the understatement, "We regret to have to say that its action was defective."

Beck was released on licence in July 1901. He was still protesting and petitioning when Bradford retired, leaving the storm to burst upon his successor.

2

It is a striking coincidence that while the most notorious miscarriage of justice due to confusion of identity that has occurred in recent times was dragging its long course through the courts, the Press, and the prisons, an infallible method of preventing such errors was being introduced at Scotland Yard. It came too late to help Adolf Beck; but his case was to prove the final exposure, as it was the most damning, of the methods of criminal identification employed in these islands up to the turn of the last century.

The fallibility of visual recognition had been a problem to police forces throughout the world. Among the more notable instances of its pitfalls, France had Lesurques and Dubosc, England the Tichborne Case, the United States the Hoag-Parker mystery, in which each of two wives, supported by seven other trustworthy witnesses, positively identified the accused as her husband. Much was hoped of photography, but the camera proved as unreliable as the human eye. Faith in it brought about in England, within a few years, a wrongful conviction and the imprisonment, as a first offender, of a violent habitual criminal whose lenient treatment in gaol gave him the opportunity to murder a warder. By this date other countries had gone ahead; Bertillon, in France, attacking the problem scientifically, evolved his anthropometric system of criminal registration, in which photography played only a part, and this was adopted by the French police about 1880, and presently elsewhere. The system had its limitations, as was to be abundantly shown in another case in America, that of the two Wests, in 1903; but it was the first great step forward, so far as official police work was concerned, out of the welter of visual identification, photography, and the rest, on to firm ground. Yet by the time of its adoption it was already out of date. Every one, Bertillon included, ignored the earlier experiments of an Indian Civil Servant who had, in fact, disposed of every difficulty completely and for ever.

Sir William Herschel was only one of many who must have known that fingerprints, usually in the form of thumb impressions, had for some thousands of years been used in China and other Eastern countries not merely as sign manuals in diplomacy and trade, but to identify illiterates and even for police purposes. There was a slight stirring of interest in dactyloscopy in Europe in the seventeenth and eighteenth centuries, but from the scientific and physiological, not from the utilitarian, point of view. In 1823 a Breslau physiologist, J. E. Purkinje, suggested a system of classifying the ridge patterns which cause the characteristic and individual markings of fingertips; but his thesis, written in Latin, attracted so little attention that sixty years later only three copies could be found. That memory lingered of the individuality of these patterns, and of the uses to which this feature might be put, is suggested by the instance of Thomas Bewick's well-known wood engraving of his thumb, and by one or two earlier examples, such as the document on which, in 1691, certain citizens of Londonderry impressed their thumb-prints beside their signatures.

Herschel, beginning with the imprint of a road contractor's palm in 1858, developed a system of fingerprinting to counter corruption and impersonation in Bengal, where the mass of the people were illiterate. He foresaw that this preventive measure had enormous possibilities in the field of criminal registration and detection, but little came of his efforts to interest the authorities concerned. His work, however, came to the notice of Francis Galton, already interested in Bertillonage in connexion with his own study of heredity and genetics. Galton's *Fingerprints* was published in 1892, and his *Fingerprint Directories* of 1895 outline the first system of digital classification, or "lexicon," as he called it, to appear in print.

Whether independently, or because news from Bengal had crossed the Pacific, while Herschel's countrymen, both in India and at home, continued to ignore him, interest in fingerprinting was stirring in the two Americas. A simple system was employed in 1882 by the leader of the United States Geological Survey in New Mexico, to prevent frauds on the commissariat; and during that decade a novelist and a police official were thinking on the same lines. A chapter in Mark Twain's *Life on the Mississippi*, published in 1883, contains the first detective story dealing with fingerprint evidence, and both the autobiographical element in the book and the writer's acquaintance with the technique of the subject suggest that this was a fairly common matter of talk. He returned to it some ten years later with *Pudd'nhead Wilson*, the first detective novel on the same theme. In official quarters nobody paid any attention to a writer of fiction, and a humorist at that, except possibly a Dalmatian named Juan Vucetich, who in 1888 had emigrated to Argentina and joined the police force at La Plata. From a French scientific periodical Vucetich learnt of Galton's fingerprint system, and on it based a system of his own. This was adopted in Argentina in the 1890's, at first in combination with Bertillonage, but eventually, when further modified, as the basic method of criminal registration throughout the Republic.

In England, in the meantime, Galton's interest in dactyloscopy, his references to Herschel's work in India, and the apparent success of the Bertillon system in France, at last combined to draw attention to the chaotic state of police and prison records in this country, largely due to the lack of any efficient and uniform method of registering habitual offenders. The most shocking exposure of the existing system was yet to come; but in 1893 the still new Home Secretary, H. H. Asquith, appointed a committee "to inquire into the best means available for identifying habitual criminals." The chairman of the committee was Mr C. E. Troup, of the Home Office, the other members being Major Arthur Griffiths, Inspector of Prisons, and the Chief Constable of the C.I.D., Melville Macnaghten. Two of the witnesses called, Galton and Dr J. G. Garson, were questioned about fingerprints. The committee's report, published in October 1894, recommended the adoption of the Bertillon system, and suggested that a subsidiary experiment might be made with Galton's classification by fingerprints. Bertillonage was accordingly introduced at Scotland Yard for a provisional period of six years, Garson, who had worked with Galton for a short time, being appointed adviser to the Home Office, where he established what he called a "metric office," and to the C.I.D. Tentative use was made of fingerprinting by that department, but not much faith seems to have been placed in it, except by a small band of enthusiasts. Galton's system, in fact, was too complicated for police work, for which an essential is simplicity, because this means both a saving of time and easy comprehension by men with no scientific training.

In the meantime Edward Henry, of the Indian Civil Service, had been appointed Inspector-General of Police in Bengal. He took up Herschel's fingerprint system where the latter had left it, pruned and developed it into a readily workable method, and applied it to normal police purposes along two distinct lines—the tracing of the criminal antecedents of convicts and the maintenance of their records, and the identification of criminals who leave accidental or "casual" fingerprints on the scenes of their crimes. In 1894 he commented in a report on the shortcomings of Bertillonage; and in 1897 his own fingerprint system was adopted by the Indian Government, which, three years later, ordered the printing of his *Classification and Uses of Fingerprints.* This short work, as an official text-book, was to go into many editions. In 1899 the Home Office appointed a second committee, under the chairmanship of Lord Belper, to investigate the still very unsatisfactory methods of criminal identification, and, Henry being in England on leave, he was called as a witness. Another witness was Dr Garson, still adviser to the Home Office and the C.I.D. on anthropometrics and, to some uncertain degree, on fingerprints; he had, at any rate, devised a fingerprint system of his own, which he submitted to the committee. Dactyloscopy, in fact, was the chief subject of that body's deliberations; not only had Henry's system proved highly successful in India, but that of Vucetich had been adopted by other states of South America and by some countries in Europe. Bertillon was soon to incorporate it in his anthropometric system. No one perhaps foresaw that Bertillon would next discard Vucetich for Henry, still less that Bertillonage itself, to all intents and purposes, would be driven from the field by fingerprinting; but, to look a little ahead, the Belper Committee was so impressed by Henry's evidence that it reported unanimously in favour of the adoption of his system as the primary method of criminal identification in England and Wales. The next step was obvious; Henry himself must introduce the system at Scotland Yard.

His appointment as Assistant Commissioner in charge of the Criminal Investigation Department was dated the 8th of July, five weeks before Adolf Beck was released from Portland Prison on licence.

3

Among the events of Henry's first seven months as Commissioner which directly concerned the police was a Motor-car Act increasing the speed limit of this still-novel vehicle to twenty miles an hour, and compelling drivers of cars to be licensed. Licences issued included those to the drivers of the first petrol-driven cabs. The last steam trains were running on the Underground Railway, electricity being the new motive-power used. There were still 7500 hansoms on the London streets, and 4000 horsed four-wheelers. The police were busy that year at the scenes of two disasters at opposite ends of the London area—an explosion in Woolwich Arsenal, causing the deaths of sixteen men, and a shocking fire at Colney Hatch Lunatic Asylum in which fifty-one women perished.

In the autumn of this year, as afterwards became known, Augustus Wilhelm Meyer, or John Smith, *alias* also, at an earlier period, the Earl of Wilton and Lord Willoughby de Winton, was in London again. He was now calling himself William Thomas, or, alternatively, "a member of the House of Lords." Also in London was Adolf Beck, after March no longer a convict on licence, but a free though much embittered man. It may have been resentment against the police that led to an impulsive action for which he was fined five pounds for obstructing a constable in Oxford Street. Walking in Hyde Park in November, Beck met Inspector Froest. Though at this date Froest can have had no comprehension of the fearful tangle of injustice which had sprung from his routine inquiry into the frauds of 1895, he may have had occasional doubts about the case; he certainly seems to have felt some sympathy for Beck, who, for his part, cherished so little personal animus against the Chief Inspector that he now asked him for advice and help. Froest recommended a petition to the Home Secretary (as if this resource had not been tried many times already), and promised to use his influence to forward it. Another petition, however, was a luxury Beck could not afford; he was very poor, and his solicitor (not Mr Dutton) wanted twenty pounds for drawing up a new appeal. Discouraged again, the unfortunate man returned to his lodging-house in Percy Street, off Tottenham Court Road, to brood over his wrongs. These were far from over—so far, indeed, that in police history they were to dominate the next year.

Otherwise 1904 would have recorded only peace and progress at Scotland Yard. The Fingerprint Branch being now well established, the new Commissioner made his next move towards improving the efficiency of the force by introducing more up-to-date and comprehensive methods of instruction for recruits. The plans for Scotland House were now virtually complete, though building was not to be begun until the following year. The Public Carriage Department was dealing with a further development of the traffic problem, the replacement of horse-drawn omnibuses by motor-buses on a large scale; and the Government, realizing that conditions in the streets of every big city were being revolutionized, appointed a Royal Commission to examine the question. But if Henry had hoped for a quiet twelve months of such uncontroversial tasks and interests he was soon disillusioned. The legacy of trouble left by Bradford was to bedevil the Commissioner's Office for most of the year; for by the middle of April Adolf Beck was in the news again.

In the previous August, John Smith being then back in town, a new series of petty frauds on women had begun, similar in every respect to those for which Beck had been imprisoned. The women, with one exception, were of the same class, and the *modus operandi* of 1895 (and of 1877) was faithfully repeated. The first case reported, in March 1904, at once turned the attention of the police to Beck, who was traced from the Percy Street lodgings to a room he had now taken in the neighbourhood, in Store Street, where later Crippen was to have an office. On the 15th of April he was arrested in the street and charged with defrauding Paulina Scott of a watch, a ring, and one pound in money. Other victims then came forward, and on the 30th Beck was charged with three more offences. A fifth charge followed on the 12th of May. All five women confidently identified Beck, who was committed to take his trial at the Central Criminal Court.

Before this took place Beck wrote from prison to Chief Inspector Froest, protesting his innocence. The letter, dated June the 6th, was endorsed by Superintendent Hare of the Central Office: "This is a wicked persistent old thief and most dangerous." Having been tried and convicted a second time, Beck wrote to Froest again, on July the 7th; after referring to "these terrible and monstrous false accusations," he goes on, underlining the words, "*I am not John Smith nor am I the man who has robbed this woman.*" These letters, on grey prison paper, affect the imagination more movingly than all the books and pamphlets and reports on the case, conjuring up a picture of this tragically bewildered man groping in a fog of injustice that seems to have an active malevolence of its own.

An application by Beck's counsel for the postponement of the trial to the next sessions having been granted, the order to this effect was then rescinded. The malevolent influence was still at work. The prisoner accordingly appeared before Mr Justice Grantham at the Old Bailey on the 27th of June, and was found guilty. The Criminal Evidence Act of 1898 enabled him to go into the witness-box. Fifty years' experience of the working of this privilege seems to show that while, as often as not, it is very damaging in the case of guilty persons, it may be of great value to the innocent; and it is possible that something in Beck's demeanour strengthened the misgivings which the judge admitted that he felt. These misgivings, at any rate, caused him to defer passing sentence until he had made further inquiries. At long last Beck's luck was turning, for during the interim the whole sham edifice of the case against him collapsed resoundingly.

How this came about can be told in the words of the police memorandum later drawn up for the information of the Committee of Inquiry.

"During Beck's imprisonment, from 15th April till 7th July [1904]," says the memorandum,

> no similar complaints were made to the police, but on the latter date the man William Thomas was given into custody for an offence similar to that for which Beck had been tried. In consequence of a communication from Inspector Kane, some 28 hours after Thomas's arrest, Inspector Ward, at 8.30 P.M., the 8th, saw the former, who showed him a letter received by Beulah Turner,[1] presumably sent by Thomas, and which was precisely in the same handwriting as that produced in evidence against Beck. The officers, after conferring, came to the conclusion that there was a possibility of a mistake having been made by the witnesses. Inspector Ward returned to Paddington [Police] Station and reported the facts to his immediate superior, Superintendent Ferrett, who accompanied him the following morning to New Scotland Yard, and laid the facts before the superior police authorities.
>
> In consequence of this, the inspector was directed to attend Brixton Prison to see the man Thomas. This he did on the same day. Bearing in mind the remarks made by Beck when in the dock at the Central Criminal Court—which were to the effect that he had been wrongfully convicted in 1896, and that a previous conviction against him as one John Smith, a

[1] One of two sisters whose complaints resulted in Smith's arrest as Thomas.

circumcised Jew, had been wrongfully proved, he [Beck] being a Christian and not circumcised—the prison authorities were requested to carefully examine Thomas with a view to determining whether this was the case or not. The examination was made, and it was reported by the prison authorities that Thomas was circumcised.[1]

Through the rather clumsy wording of the memorandum the long disconnected parts of the puzzle are seen falling into their places like elements in a problem by Euclid. "William Thomas" was John Smith, convicted in 1877. But according to the Home Office and the prison authorities, Adolf Beck was John Smith. He was therefore also William Thomas; which was absurd.[2]

4

Every department of justice concerned in this case contributed its share to the monument of perversity, obstruction, and downright wrong. Before and during Beck's first trial in 1896 it was taken for granted by the prosecution that he was the John Smith of 1877. Four of the fourteen counts in the indictment against him referred to a previous conviction in that name in that year. The assumption was alluded to in court, as was the essential denial by the defence, which further contended that Smith, and not Beck, had committed the new series of offences with which the latter was being charged. Nevertheless, by what can only be described as a piece of legal chicanery, the four counts charging a previous conviction were not proceeded with, and the defence was thus deprived of the opportunity of proving that Beck was in South America in 1877, and so could not be Smith. Such evidence, though strictly speaking irrelevant to the remaining ten counts, by bringing into the open the question of mistaken identity must have raised doubts about the validity of these charges. Mr Horace Avory, counsel for the Crown, whose denial of this opportunity to the defence was supported by the judge, characteristically maintained to the end of his life, when he had become a judge himself, that his action was correct in law.[3] Equity, however, which is defined as the use of principles of justice to supplement law, was disregarded, and in a wholesale

[1] "The Case of Adolf Beck. Statement of the Action of Police, with complete Copies of all Papers and Reports."

[2] This represents the police point of view on the date in question, the 9th of July, 1904. The Home Office and the prison authorities had, of course, known and concealed the truth for six years.

[3] Mr Eric Watson, who edited *The Trial of Adolf Beck* for the "Notable British Trials" series, remarks that all the witnesses before the Committee of Inquiry who had been instrumental in obtaining Beck's convictions expressed their deep sympathy with the wronged man, "with one notable exception." The exception appears to have been Avory.

manner, since the very heavy sentence, for the type of crime involved, passed by Sir Forrest Fulton, the Common Sergeant, seems to show that he was influenced throughout by the assumption he professed to ignore—that Beck was an old offender. All pretence that the procedure adopted was in the prisoner's interest was indeed soon abandoned; after conviction Beck was at once given the prison number of the man whose name and offences had been excluded from public reference, and whose identification with Beck had never been proved.

The "defective" action, or inaction, of the Home Office, from the very start, has been touched upon. This department, in those days, appears to have cultivated a detachment from the normal affairs of life equalled only by the proverbial innocence of judges; thus Mr C. E. Troup, in 1904 Assistant Under-Secretary (he has already been mentioned in connexion with Bertillonage and fingerprints), told the Committee of Inquiry that he knew nothing of Beck's second arrest until after the latter's conviction. Yet between the arrest and the trial the newspapers were full of the case, and all London was talking about it. Back in 1898, Mr Troup's predecessor, Mr Charles Murdoch, meeting Inspector Froest six months after the Home Office knew that Beck and Smith were different persons, did not think of mentioning a matter of vital importance to the police, who for another six years were allowed to go on supposing that the two were one. When the Home Office did bestir itself the results were disastrous, largely because—it is astonishing to relate—these very involved criminal proceedings were handled by officials who had no legal training. Such was Mr F. J. Sims, whose apathy or ignorance wrought enormous harm. It was Mr Sims, a layman, who prepared the briefs for prosecuting counsel at both trials, and who, though "specially careful" during police-court proceedings to avoid reference to past convictions, in each brief described Beck as a previously convicted man. It was Mr Sims who denied that Inspector Waldock reported to him, after Beck's second arrest, that the prisoner's physical marks did not correspond with those of Smith, a denial which the Committee of Inquiry was unable to accept. In short, to quote Mr Eric Watson, the lawyer who has edited the fullest account of the case, Mr Sims's conduct of it "proved to be in the last degree lamentable." The ultimate responsibility, however, as with the police, rested with a higher authority.

The working of routine, upon which the Home Office relied a good deal in its defence, was the only argument put forward by the prison authorities. Such and such a thing was not customary. In 1879, when John Smith was a prisoner at Portland, he applied to change his religion, and it was then learnt that he was a circumcized Jew. This absolutely distinctive mark was not entered on his prison form because, said Major Clayton, Secretary to the Prison Commissioners, it was not customary to enter such marks. In May 1898, when Smith had long been at large, the omission was rectified, at the same time that the Home Office was informed that Beck had no such mark, and therefore could not be Smith. No similar notification was sent to the police, because it was not the custom to do this. To red tape was added sheer carelessness; when, two months later, in July, one of Beck's numerous petitions reached the Home Office, the endorsement by the Governor of Portland stated that the appellant had previously been convicted as Smith.[1] (It does not appear that the Home Office, with fresh information to the contrary, from the same source, in its hands, troubled to point out the error.) Moreover, at some period—perhaps during the highly important weeks between Beck's first arrest and trial—the photograph with Smith's descriptive form was mislaid.

There remains the question—to what extent were the police responsible for this miscarriage of justice? No blame attaches to the officers who arrested Beck on either occasion; he was twice identified in the street by the victims of Smith. Next, perhaps, to Mr Sims, the evil genius in the case was an obscure busybody named Russell Davis, who on the 18th of December, 1895, two days after Beck's first arrest, called at Scotland Yard with a story that Beck was really Smith. "This," says the confidential memorandum already quoted, "was the first intimation the police had as to any connection between John Smith and Beck." All stories of this kind have to be checked, and the next step, in these days before fingerprints, was to find some one who had known Smith. Two officers concerned in his arrest in 1877 were fetched from retirement. In spite of the lapse of time—nearly eighteen years—both confidently identified Beck. The ages of the innocent and the guilty are of interest in this connexion: Beck was born in 1841, Smith apparently in 1850. Most unfortunately, though one of the retired policemen gave evidence at the police court, owing to the line taken by the prosecution at the ensuing trial neither could then be called; had either been, such an advocate as C. F. Gill, who defended Beck, would no doubt have made short work of a feat of memory which unhesitatingly recognized, in the lineaments of a man of fifty-three, those of another who when last seen was only twenty-seven.[2]

[1] *The Trial of Adolf Beck* ("Notable British Trials"), Introduction and Appendix V.

[2] In *The Trial of Adolf Beck* Mr Watson says of one of these witnesses: "Eliss Spurrell, who had been so confident as to his [Beck's] identity with Smith, whom he had never seen between 1877 and 1896, failed to recognise in 1901 the man he had sworn to five

He had, in fact, been seen much more recently, and by policemen too. He had actually been in their hands for a fortnight, only eight months before Beck's arrest. On the 8th of April, 1894, in the name of Augustus Wilhelm Meyer (which may have been his real one, though he claimed to have been christened William Augustus Wyatt), Smith was charged with obtaining £300 on a worthless letter of credit. Since his release in 1881 he had been practising as a doctor in Australia; he had grown stout and had shaved his beard, and his hair and moustache had gone grey. To quote the memorandum again: "All the means then at the disposal of the police were made to establish his identity, but unsuccessfully. . . . After being remanded for a fortnight, he was discharged for want of evidence, and was lost sight of by the police." How Mr Meyer must have laughed eight months later, and from time to time during the next ten years, when Adolf Beck made one of his periodical headlines in the Press. His own brief appearance in the curtain-raiser of April 1894 is certainly not the least remarkable feature of this remarkable case.

If, in the following December, the police were altogether too credulous of recollections of long ago, they were gravely to blame for failing to secure existing official evidence which would have settled the question at once. At Portland Prison was Smith's descriptive form, to which was attached his photograph, taken on his release in 1881. Apart from differentiating physical marks, such as small scars and moles, and the fact that while Beck's eyes were blue, Smith's were brown, the photograph shows very clearly the latter's right ear. No expert in Bertillonage (in December 1895, still something of a novelty at Scotland Yard) need have been called to pronounce that the formation of the ear was totally unlike that of Beck's; anyone can see this at a glance. It does not appear that the police even asked the prison authorities for Smith's photograph at this time. If they did it may have been then that it was mislaid; but in such a case the Portland officials should have been made to ransack their files until it was found. This was the vital record which subordinates at the Home Office, and Anderson, head of the C.I.D. at Scotland Yard, refused Mr Dutton permission to inspect.

The third factor in the case which influenced the police in their too facile acceptance of appearances was the evidence of Mr Gurrin, the handwriting expert. They were perhaps entitled to think that what was

---

years before." At Smith's trial, as Thomas, in 1904, he gave his age as sixty-five, but no reliance can be placed on this assertion. The older he then made himself out to be, the more hope he might have of a light sentence.

good enough for judge and counsel was good enough for them. Mr Gurrin, in fact, proved as unreliable as the witnesses to identity. Several of these, who had sworn that Beck was the man who defrauded them, as confidently later identified Thomas, or Smith; and Mr Gurrin had eventually to admit that he had been equally at sea. It appears that Mr Justice Grantham's misgivings at the trial in 1904 were in part caused by the nature of the handwriting evidence.

There were police officers who were exceptions to the general rule, and who from an early date had their misgivings too. Inspector Waldock, of A Division, who was in charge of the first inquiry until superseded by Inspector Froest, had known Beck and liked him. In the course of the second inquiry, in 1904, when the police were still ignorant of the absolute proof existing that Beck was not Smith, Waldock, to satisfy his own doubts, examined Beck's physical marks, concluded that he could not be Smith, and reported accordingly to Mr Sims. Inspector John Kane, of D Division, was in court during both of Beck's trials; he was of the opinion all along that two men were being confused, and that Beck was innocent; and it was his initiative, after "Thomas's" arrest, that led to the discovery of the truth.

It was apparently Kane who was instrumental in drawing attention, during the last days of Beck's purgatory in July 1904, to the evidence of Mrs Chapman, a lady of position and cousin of a Cabinet Minister. For some months before Beck's arrest in 1896 he had been considered as good as betrothed to Mrs Chapman's sister, a state of affairs scarcely compatible, as the superintendent of D Division remarked in his report on this episode, with Beck's "prowling about the streets picking up unfortunate women and robbing them of small articles." It was a great pity, the superintendent thought, that the sister could not be discovered at the time of the arrest. She was abroad, and for reasons which can only be conjectured no serious attempt seems to have been made to find her.

After Beck's conviction Mrs Chapman persuaded herself that he had probably stolen three bangles and some money from her house, but, said the superintendent, "she has not an atom of evidence to support this suggestion." The adage about giving a dog an ill name is only too well exemplified in the file on Adolf Beck; after each arrest signed and anonymous letters came to the police containing allegations, subsequently disproved. He had been imprisoned in Norway and in South America; he was "an adventurer of the worst type." Two years after it was all over an anonymous writer took the trouble to write, "Keep your eye on Adolf Beck."

Beck was then already drifting to his end. He soon spent, or misspent, the £5000 granted him with his rather derisory free pardon. He died in hospital, almost penniless, in 1909. It is regrettable that apologists for the police and other authorities have harped on these last years, and on Beck's supposed faults of character. What has his character to do with the case? As for his mode of life after his vindication, he came out of prison for the last time a man of sixty-three, prematurely broken by ten years of mental and moral degradation for which he was in no way whatever responsible. If £5000 went to his head it is not surprising. It may even be thought that the legal machinery which had ruined him should bear some of the blame.

Eighteen months before Beck died, Thomas, or Smith, or whatever name he should be known by, was released from prison on licence, having earned a remission of his sentence of five years' penal servitude. (Only five, it may be noted, whereas Beck got seven.) To the annoyance of the police, the Jewish Prisoners Discharge Aid Society, apparently (though strangely) ignorant of tickets-of-leave, rescued him from a Rowton House and paid his fare to Vienna. Nothing more is known about him; but he had made judicial history.

During the prolonged course of this extraordinary case minor mystifications were introduced by news of another Adolf Beck, a German, who, like his unhappy namesake, had been in Peru, and by the appearance in custody, at the very end, of a second Jew, a signal fitter, calling himself John Smith. There were even two Sims in the field; one representing the powers of darkness, the other Mr G. R. Sims, the journalist, who led the Press agitation for a full disclosure of the facts.

5

The great importance of the Beck case in the history of the Metropolitan Police lies in the time of its occurrence. The force to-day has to undertake a great number of duties and responsibilities unknown fifty years ago, when its strength was approximately what it is now; in those times, accordingly, it was associated in the public mind almost exclusively with the preservation of order and the enforcement of law. After a long period of mistrust it had become a source of pride. The Beck case seemed to have put the clock back. It was by no means the first of its kind: in 1878, for instance, when John Smith had been a year in prison, Edmund Galley was "pardoned" after serving forty-three years of a sentence of transportation for life for a crime, committed in Devonshire, of which he was wholly innocent; but the circumstances of Beck's convictions made a more profound impression than those attending any other miscarriage of justice of recent times. The public could scarcely be expected to weigh the facts, and apportion the blame. It knew little about the Home Office or the Prison Commissioners; but it knew the police, and its faith in a force it had come to like and trust was badly shaken.

The Committee of Inquiry exonerated the police, and if this was somewhat generous the force came better out of the affair than the Home Office. But the case had exposed in a startling manner the weakness of a system upon which the Criminal Investigation Department had hitherto relied. Existing methods of criminal identification and registration (with one new exception) were shown to be thoroughly untrustworthy, and a common resource of everyday police work, the evidence of visual recognition, was proved as fallible as the rest. On this point the Master of the Rolls, Sir Richard Henn Collins, who presided at the Inquiry, made the following observation: "Evidence as to identity based on personal impressions, however *bona fide*, is perhaps of all classes of evidence the least to be relied upon, and therefore, unless supported by other facts, an unsafe basis for the verdict of a jury." But for a scientific development, already though only recently in practical use, which transformed the whole process of criminal identification, these words might well have been posted up in every police station in the country. The Beck case is again important because its final stages coincided with this innovation, thanks to which such a tragedy of errors should never happen again.

In the confidential police memorandum on the case it is remarked of the change in the appearance of John Smith between 1877 and 1894, when he was again arrested but discharged, that "his non-identification by the officer in the case is not to be wondered at. . . . The means upon which we now rely, the fingerprint system, which would certainly have established his identity, had not then [in 1894] been introduced." The system was introduced in 1901, and, an essential feature of it being the fingerprinting of all persons under arrest, both Beck and Thomas (or Smith) must have had their prints taken when they were charged in 1904, in April and July respectively. There is no record of a comparison of their prints; Beck was released on other grounds, and his own prints would then be destroyed, in accordance with custom in the case of an arrested person's discharge or acquittal. But had he been in appearance as indistinguishable from Smith as Will West was from William West in the classic American case—indeed, had he and Smith been twin brothers—fingerprints would have differentiated the pair.

The public was scarcely aware, in 1904, of the value of fingerprint evidence. Its infallibility was certainly not generally recognized, even on the Bench. It was only two years since the first conviction in England, on such evidence, had been obtained in a case of felony. Few people heard of the trial of Scheffer, in Paris, in the same year, 1902, in which Bertillon, who had incorporated Henry's system in his own anthropometric method, proved the identity of the murderer by his fingerprints. In 1905, however, ten months after the disturbing revelations of the Beck case, the Stratton brothers were charged with murder at the Central Criminal Court, and the very important part played by fingerprint evidence in their conviction, broadcast by the publicity attending a sensational capital trial, did something to restore confidence in an aspect of police work affecting guilty and innocent alike. It began to be realized that at last an insurance against the human element had been discovered.

In the early hours of the 27th of March, 1905, an elderly couple named Farrow were murdered at 34 High Street, Deptford. The crime was marked by great brutality. Farrow, who managed an oil-and-colour business on the premises, was killed when he came downstairs to confront the intruders—for there was evidence that there were at least two. Mrs Farrow was callously dispatched to silence her, or merely because the murderers wished to search the bedroom where she lay. Their motive was robbery, and a small cash-box, broken open, was found under the bed.

Suspicion fell on two young brothers named Stratton, who had bad records, and who after the murder disappeared from their usual haunts. They had been seen coming out of the shop, in broad daylight, but when, within a week, they were arrested, they were at first confident and truculent. Perhaps they thought of Adolf Beck, or remembered the words of the Master of the Rolls; and, in fact, the evidence of the eyewitness, a schoolboy, would not in itself have been enough to bring the crime home to them. Their attitude changed, however, when their fingerprints were taken. Criminals were naturally more alive than the general public to the potentialities of the new science, and one or other of the pair might have been careless; as, indeed, was the case.

On the tray of the Farrows' cash-box the police had found a clear thumb-print. While the search for the Strattons was in progress this print was compared with those of everybody who had access to the house, including the murdered couple and a young detective-sergeant who admitted handling the box. All these persons being eliminated, it was hoped that the thumb-mark had been left by one of the murderers.

It proved to be the impression of the right thumb of Alfred Stratton, the elder of the brothers.

Faced with this evidence, before their trial came on each of the pair accused the other of the murders. At the Old Bailey, in May, the Fingerprint Branch was represented by Inspector Stockley Collins (as he now was) and Inspector Steadman, who gave the jury figures showing the growth of the Fingerprint Collection at Scotland Yard. A juryman had his thumb-print taken in court. A very curious feature of the trial was the appearance of Dr J. G. Garson, recently employed by the Home Office and at Scotland Yard, as a witness for the defence, and his dismissal by Mr Justice Channel as "an absolutely untrustworthy" one. The judge, in his summing up, displayed the conservative instincts of the Bench when he expressed his belief that the jury would not like to act on fingerprint evidence alone. Whatever evidence most impressed the jury, the inevitable result was a verdict of guilty against both prisoners, who were duly hanged. Judicial caution was not shared by the public, to whom this advertisement of a safeguard against human error came just when it was needed.

20

MME D'ANGELY AND INSPECTOR SYME

MRS PANKHURST'S Women's Social and Political Union was two years old when, in 1905, its more violent members began the campaign of forcible annoyance to all and sundry which was to involve the police throughout the country, but especially in the Metropolitan District, in the most unpleasant and humiliating duties they have ever had to perform. The Genius of the Language once more proving too strong for the purists, the word 'suffragette,' described by H. W. Fowler as "a more regrettable formation than others such as *leaderette* and *flannelette*," came into common use, where, as a handy means of distinguishing militant suffragists from others, it has remained.

In January of the following year a General Election established the new Liberal administration with a majority which, including Irish Nationalists and 53 Labour Members, was by far the largest since the reformed House of Commons assembled in 1832. "It contained an exceptional proportion not only of men who were new to Parliamentary life . . . but also of zealots, more anxious for the triumph of some special 'cause' than for Liberalism in the abstract."[1] Once party feeling had come to influence the attitude of M.P.'s towards the affairs of the police, and particularly of the Metropolitan force, the natural tendency in any controversy was for Conservatives to sympathize with the motives of those responsible for keeping order, and for Liberals and their allies to question these; and senior officials at Scotland Yard must have viewed with some dismay the collection of busybodies, ideologues, and plain cranks which formed so considerable a part of an enormous majority likely in any case to be fussy and captious. Such forebodings were soon to be realized.

About midnight on the 1st of May a woman calling herself Eva D'Angely was arrested in Regent Street for "riotous and indecent behaviour," in other words, for soliciting. She was a Frenchwoman, who spoke very little English, and at the police-court proceedings next morning an interpreter was necessary. A man giving the same name, who swore he was her husband, said that on the previous evening

[1] Sir J. A. R. Marriott, *Modern England* (Methuen, 1934).

his wife had been waiting for him, as she had often done before; Sub-divisional Inspector MacKay stated that the D'Angelys, who had been in England only a few months, were so far as he knew a respectable couple; and the magistrate, Mr Denman, who dealt with such charges daily, dismissed the case.

There was at once a great uproar in a section of the Press and in Parliament, recalling the Cass case. The more irresponsible supporters of the new Government made the wildest accusations against the police, going far beyond the question at issue. The Home Secretary was now Herbert Gladstone, who made so small an impression on his times that Sir John Marriott, in the work just quoted, does not include his name in a fairly comprehensive list of Cabinet appointments, or in the index of the book. While paying lip-service to the conduct of the police, Gladstone and the Prime Minister, Campbell-Bannerman, bowed to a storm as ill-informed as it was intemperate; and yet another Royal Commission was set up to inquire into the methods and discipline of the force.

This body did not issue its report for two years, by which time Mme D'Angely had long been forgotten. If similar adjudicators have sometimes been over-tender with officialdom, as in the case of the Beck inquiry, a tribunal appointed by a Liberal Government to investigate a whole series of charges of bribery and corruption brought against a police force was not likely to gloss over shortcomings. Not one of a serious nature was discovered; the force as a whole was completely exonerated. In a leading article on the report, *The Times* of July 1, 1908, referred to the Commissioners' "minute scrutiny of several much disputed cases,"[1] and summed up the findings as showing that "the Metropolitan Police are entitled to the confidence of all classes of the community."

With special reference to the more outrageous accusations *The Times* went on: "Many of us have encountered the sort of people who like to think they have great knowledge of the world, and who, out of the fullness of that knowledge, are given to asserting that the police blackmail unfortunate women or take bribes from them." That charge had been found by the Commissioners to have no foundation. No evidence had been produced to support it; there was, on the contrary, plenty on the other side—the police were more given to helping unfortunates than to hounding them. Actual arrests in such cases made only a small proportion of the warnings given. "We have no hesitation in saying," *The Times* repeated in this connexion, "that the Metropolitan

[1] Nineteen were investigated.

Police as a whole discharge their duties with honesty, discretion and efficiency."

No better example can be given than the D'Angely case itself, *fons et origo* of so many reckless and, indeed, wicked allegations, of the stuff out of which these are too often woven. A very brief further investigation had caused Inspector MacKay to revise his opinion of that "respectable pair," M. and Mme D'Angely. The man was first heard of in London two months after the woman's arrival, when he went under another name. He belonged, apparently, to a well-known type who make a business of lending a reputable air to prostitutes by claiming to be married to them. There seems to be as little doubt about the profession of the injured Mme D'Angely herself. As soon as the couple realized the inconvenient stir they had made they went to Paris, leaving the rent of their London lodgings unpaid and abandoning trunks which proved to be empty. All the blandishments of the French and British police failed to entice them back to England to give evidence of the ill-treatment that had roused the Press and the Commons to frenzy. It need hardly be added that after these and other disclosures the "sort of people" to whom *The Times* had alluded, who in Parliament and out of it had clamoured for an official apology to Mme D'Angely, do not appear to have tendered one themselves to the force they had maligned.

If the Press and Parliamentary, not to say political, reactions to what Mr Rufus Isaacs, a member of the Commission and the future Lord Reading, described as "a very ordinary case," give it a significance altogether out of proportion to its intrinsic interest, there are other lessons to be drawn from it. A Royal Commission was once more shown to be the wrong sort of machinery to decide an issue requiring prompt solution. The majority of newspaper readers were not going to reserve judgment on the police for two years, or to weigh the evidence given at upward of sixty sittings, if they even read half of it; they formed impressions at the beginning, and some of those impressions stuck. Mme D'Angely's discharge by the police-court magistrate was unfortunate. These magistrates are very busy men, and according to where they sit become accustomed to dealing summarily with certain types of cases brought before them. The charge against Mme D'Angely was commonplace to the last degree at Marlborough Street. Since she had been in London only a few months, her past history was unknown to the police, though for some time they had been speculating about her reasons for loitering in Regent Street. The existence of the "husband" for whom she was waiting was also unknown to them. Thus he was able to impose both on them and on the magistrate. Policemen being ordinary human beings, whether an accused is known or unknown to them, in the derogatory sense, may sometimes unconsciously influence their judgment; it is possible that a too ready reliance on untrustworthy evidence in the case of Adolf Beck was partly due to knowledge of dubious actions in the past. In the very great majority of instances, however, the record of an habitual offender is in every way helpful to the police and to justice. It may, for example, though it cannot be cited in court, justify an application for a remand; and such a course would certainly have been taken by Inspector MacKay had he suspected that the couple calling themselves D'Angely, and husband and wife, were nothing of the sort. Necessarily superficial inquiries would then have been carried further, with the probable result that the police force would have been spared a vicious campaign of calumny, the country a considerable waste of money, and Press and Parliament an exhibition of ignorance and folly.

2

Towards the end of 1906, possibly in a slightly chastened mood, the Commons was legitimately and usefully busy with police affairs, and a new Superannuation Bill which became law in December rectified certain deficiencies in the Pensions Act of 1890. The most important clause was that dealing with the not uncommon case of the constable who through illness or some other cause was compelled to retire after a few years' service, and who later rejoined the force and remained in it until he was of pensionable age. Hitherto the earlier period in the ranks had not counted as part of the "approved service" on which the man's pension would be based. With certain stipulations, "approved service" was now extended in such cases to include both periods of service. A similar ruling covered re-enlistment in some other police force, if the other police authority agreed, and if previous service in the Metropolitan Police totalled three completed years. If a constable was called up to the R.N.R. or the Army Reserve his naval or military service was also to count as "approved" in the pensionable sense.

The following year saw a sort of architectural blooming in the police world. Scotland House was ready for use, and the Receiver moved in; another of Henry's reforms took practical shape with the opening of Peel House, in Regency Street, Westminster, as the first Police Training School; and, in the City, an event of interest to every police force in the country was the completion of the uninspired pile of the Central Criminal Court on the site of Dance's grim masterpiece, Newgate Prison and Sessions House, fronting on Old Bailey, from which the new building takes its popular and more manageable name. Like this reincarnation, the entirely novel Training School fulfilled a very long-felt want. Hitherto the police recruit, posted to duty after a few weeks' drill, and armed only with his Instruction Book, had to learn his job by the empirical method; he now underwent a preliminary educational test, and, having passed this, a residential course of instruction at Peel House which included not only police duty but general education, physical training, self-defence, and first aid. Writing of a somewhat later date, Sir John Moylan comments on the great reduction of wastage in personnel brought about by this system of selection and training: "In the old days about 40 per cent. of the recruits left or had to be removed in their first year after joining; now [1928] only 5 per cent. drop out during the probationary year."[1]

Press and public, so gullibly wrought upon by the sufferings of Mme D'Angely, more or less took in their stride the conviction during this year of a constable for perjury, and of two others for being drunk and disorderly, incidents that perhaps would not have occurred had the offenders undergone the testing process now introduced. The Commissioner, as part of his campaign for efficiency, was enforcing discipline in general, and certain laxities, so long established that they had become customs, were from time to time dealt with in Police Orders. Those of the 30th of July, 1907, endeavoured to regularize and abate one of the many unofficial duties which the police were expected to perform—that of "callers-up," for which they received "call money" from grateful sleepers. "Though the police should, when they can, render this or any other service in their power to the inhabitants," said the Order, "this particular service is one which can very rarely be rendered, and when rendered, should be gratuitous; the police cannot undertake to be at a given place at a fixed hour every day." Manufacturers of alarm-clocks must have welcomed this injunction.

A year which began with the murder of William Whiteley, of the great shop which undertook to supply man's wants from the cradle to the grave, found the C.I.D. co-operating with the Dublin Metropolitan Police in the investigation into what, so far as the public has been allowed to know, remains one of the major mysteries of the time—the theft of the Irish Regalia at Dublin Castle. In its less spectacular way the Public Carriage Department, always busy with the cumulative problems of more and faster traffic, accomplished two minor reforms; taxi-

[1] Moylan, *op. cit.*

meters were made compulsory for motor-cabs, and 'privilege' cabs at railway stations, an old grievance with non-privileged drivers, were abolished. The man on the beat continued to have trouble with Suffragettes, though it was in the next year, 1908, that these women's misdirected ingenuity began to assume the dimensions of a national nuisance, damage to public property and assaults on Cabinet Ministers eventually throwing much extra work upon the Special Branch, preoccupied as it was at this time with the activities of Russian criminals and the plots of Indian students which culminated in the murder of Sir Curzon Wylie.

Of considerable indirect interest to the force was another Act passed that year which took effect in the following March. The Port of London had for centuries been controlled by the City, but with the rise of the great trading companies and the growth of the docks a host of lesser authorities, self-administered and each with its private police, became more or less independent of the City's jurisdiction. Competition, jealousy, and inefficiency were ruining London's shipping trade, and, the City Fathers being eventually brought to realize that control of these sprawling and conflicting dock companies and boards, whose territories stretched far outside the limits of the City's own waterfront, was altogether beyond the Corporation's powers, the Act of 1908 created a single over-riding directorate, the Port of London Authority. This body was given its own police, which absorbed the various, and very variously efficient, police establishments of the dock companies. Its authority extends from Teddington to the Nore, and since from Teddington to Dartford the preservation of law and order on the waterway itself is the responsibility of the Thames Division of the Metropolitan Police, it was suggested at the time, and has been advocated since, that this division should also be absorbed by the P.L.A. The proposal received no support at Scotland Yard; sentiment apart, the P.L.A. Police, like the miscellaneous bodies it superseded, is a private force, on the lines of the railway police, with strictly limited functions and powers, while, moreover, long experience had shown that the work of the River Police and of the other divisions ashore is essentially interdependent. The Thames Division, accordingly, has remained unaffected by the administrative revolution in the dock area, except so far as greatly increased police efficiency in that area has made for better co-operation between the two forces, public and private, concerned in the change. A governing factor in the general relations between the P.L.A. police and the Metropolitan force is the division of powers; the former, again like the railway police, can hold a suspect in custody only until he can be handed over to the regular civil arm for the normal processes of justice.

Police Orders of 1909 include an increasing number of references to burdensome duties in connexion with the Women's Freedom League, and on the 1st of July a letter from the Home Secretary was published conveying the Prime Minister's appreciation of the conduct of the police "under great provocation" during Suffragette disturbances on the 29th of June. Two days before the end of the year an Order gave details of reorganization at New Scotland Yard itself, where the departure of the Receiver and his staff provided a suitable opportunity, as well as physical space, for a reshuffling of the duties of police departments. A fourth Assistant Commissioner was appointed, and the machinery of administration assumed the form which, with minor modifications, exists to-day. The work of the four Assistant Commissioners, each in charge of a department, was divided as follows: A.C. 'A,' internal administration and discipline; A.C. 'B,' civil, financial, and legal business, traffic and the Lost Property Office, and matters relating to pay; A.C. 'C,' serious crime, the Special Branch, naturalization and the Convict Supervision Office; A.C. 'D,' complaints by the public, disorderly houses, street collections, pedlars, betting and gaming, fires, and similar matters. 'D' Department later became 'L,' taking over legal and other business from 'B,' which is now solely concerned with traffic.[1]

During Bradford's thirteen years as Commissioner the numbers of the force had increased by little more than a thousand men; there was a far more rapid augmentation under Henry, in whose first six years of office the total rose from 16,517 to 18,657, the figures for 1909. In this year a small recruiting commission toured the country, helping to add another 800 in the next twelve months. For some years more the annual increase was to continue.

3

The years 1909 and 1910 are notable in the annals of the force for a domestic episode repercussions of which were to be felt for many years after; and for the introduction by the new alien criminal element of methods of warfare—they were nothing less—as shocking as they

[1] A further division of labour was made possible by the raising of the Secretariat to the status of a department in 1929; it relieved 'B' of responsibility for the Lost Property Office and other business. The Secretary has the status of an Assistant Commissioner. There are now, for practical purposes, six departments at Scotland Yard, in addition to the new Research and Planning Branch. Deputy Assistant Commissioners were introduced in 1919.

then seemed unnatural in the English scene. They have become a commonplace since.

Like the affairs of Mme D'Angely, and to some extent for the same reasons, the case of Inspector Syme caused a stir quite unwarranted by its relative unimportance. On a night in August 1909 two men were brought to Gerald Road Police Station, in the Pimlico area of B Division, charged with causing a disturbance outside a house in Warwick Street (now Warwick Way). Inspector John Syme, then the senior officer on duty at Gerald Road, thought the charge unjustified and dismissed the accused. The two constables concerned in the arrest later came before Chief Inspector Shervington, at the time Acting Divisional Superintendent, who felt that a reprimand would meet the case. Syme, however, now took the constables' part, and talked about seeing fair play. Shervington, in a report to Major Wodehouse, Assistant Commissioner 'A,' alleged that Syme was "obviously too familiar with the constables," and asked for his transfer to another station. Syme was accordingly transferred to North Fulham, "in the interests of the service," it being made clear that no question of punishment was involved.

The interests of the service plainly called for this decision, for at the root of the trivial affair were personal antipathies. Syme, as events were to prove, was a stiff-necked, contentious type, unpopular with his immediate superiors, who, on the other hand, were lacking in tact and, in at least one case, too ready to discover symptoms of insubordination in the inspector's attitude. This, indeed, was to come; with such a man, cherishing a strong sense of grievance, it was inevitable. Before the end of August Syme was appealing to the Commissioner, the tone of his appeal, in the opinion of Divisional Superintendent Isaac, being insubordinate. Syme referred to his "unjust and oppressive punishment," and on the ground that his travelling expenses from North Fulham were paid out of the Police Fund construed his transfer as a provisional measure which gave him the right to appeal. He was informed that the decision was final, but two months later, in October, in what he called a report, he was disputing the Superintendent's course of action and making serious accusations against senior officers at Gerald Road.

Wodehouse, who had interviewed Syme in August, minuted this document adversely, and called for an inquiry into the allegations it contained. This was conducted by Superintendent Isaac, who reported that though Syme had been "practically canvassing the Division" for support, none of his statements was corroborated. The inspector's conduct amounted to grave insubordination, and authority was requested to suspend him from duty. Wodehouse endorsed this application, "Approved. Place the Inspector on M.R. [Morning Report] for making allegations against superior officers which he is unable to substantiate." Syme appeared before Isaac the next day, the 9th of November, as a defaulter, and, having again appealed to the Commissioner, was relieved from duty until his case had been heard by a Disciplinary Board.

The Board, consisting of the Assistant Commissioner, a Chief Constable, and a superintendent (from another division), held its first meeting on the 11th. Syme refused to reply to questions while under suspension, and asked for an investigation by a special commission, "contrary to the rules of the service." The Commissioner himself now took a hand, and, interviewing his difficult subordinate on the 22nd, persuaded the latter to accept the authority of the Board, which resumed its inquiry, and on the 17th of December issued an interim report. This weighed the pros and cons very fairly: Syme's behaviour had been improper, but he was justified in appealing against his transfer because this was recommended on the wrong grounds. Syme, however, was also in the wrong in his reasons for appealing. He was correct in stating that the strict discipline enforced in B Division had caused some dissatisfaction, but this dissatisfaction was unreasonable, and was exaggerated by Syme, who was moved more by personal feeling than by a sense of duty. The reasons given for his final suspension, on the other hand, were misleading.

There were other witnesses to be called, but the Commissioner agreed with the Board that enough evidence had been heard; and on the 20th of December the Board made its final report. The inspector's conduct was contumacious and insubordinate, and he had pursued his vendetta under the pretext of an appeal; but in view of his length of service and previous good character the punishment his behaviour warranted should be mitigated. He would be reinstated with pay and service, but reduced to the rank of station sergeant, severely reprimanded and cautioned, and transferred to another division.

Syme, however, now the victim of an *idée fixe*, would have none of this. Refusing to accept a reduction in rank, in the first week of 1910 he addressed an appeal to the Home Secretary, Gladstone, who declined to interfere. The inevitable followed before the end of the month; once more the ex-inspector was suspended, and once more, on the 29th of January, he appeared before a Disciplinary Board, which dismissed him from the force.

No Board could have acted otherwise, but there were sincere people who felt that Syme had been hardly done by. How else the dilemma could have been solved they probably did not stop to think. Others, less sincere, in Press and Parliament, took up the cudgels on Syme's behalf. Becoming something of a public figure, he showed himself to possess all the arts of the born agitator, and with the example of the Suffragettes before him adopted some of their methods. During the rest of 1910 (and, as will be seen, for long after) his activities, and still more those of his less scrupulous supporters, were a constant cause of annoyance to the Commissioner's office, which found a routine disciplinary measure noisily exploited as an instance of gross injustice. There must have been some tension at the Home Office, too, for in the course of the year there was a new Home Secretary. At no stage of Sir Winston Churchill's career has he stood in danger of being overlooked by historians or anybody else; and it would have been surprising if a man so unconventional and many-sided, who liked to have a finger in every pie—these were the months, incidentally, of the Battle of Sidney Street—had held himself aloof from a public controversy involving a branch of the department newly under his control. The fact that at this time Mr Churchill was a Liberal in politics probably had nothing to do with his attitude, but no doubt it made the form his interference took, from the point of view of the harassed Commissioner, appear the more ill-considered. What happened was that a journalist named Kempster, already and rightly in very bad odour at Scotland Yard, and now one of Syme's most intemperate champions, so mischievously distorted the facts of the ex-inspector's dismissal that the Commissioner, somewhat innocently, took the unusual step of offering him facilities for discovering for himself where the truth lay. Kempster declined the proposal, and, instead, contrived to obtain an interview with the new Home Secretary. Whatever passed at this meeting, it was used for more publicity on Syme's behalf, and for the purpose, in Henry's words, of "exulting over" the Commissioner, for Mr Churchill went so far as to offer Syme reinstatement as station sergeant, an offer which was refused. In a very outspoken letter to Sir Edward Troup, Permanent Under-Secretary to the Home Office, Henry complained of the Minister's going over his head to reopen a case now eighteen months old. "Never before, I venture to say, has a Commissioner of Police been placed in such an impossible position."

The affair was smoothed over; but the nuisance caused by Syme himself was only beginning. Long after most of his genuine partisans had lost interest in him, through the War and the post-war years, the unhappy man, whose *idée fixe* had developed into mania, was to be periodically in the news. He organized meetings and harangued passers-by in Downing Street and anywhere else where one or two would listen, and his one-time comrades in the force had the distasteful task of arresting him as a disturber of the peace. For more than a decade he was repeatedly in and out of prison, where almost as often he went on hunger-strike. Himself an insignificant figure, he still had a following among mischief-makers to whom he was of use, and since there must always be a small minority of these in any large police force, when Syme revived the idea of a Police Union he was laying up trouble for the future.

It is for such reasons alone that his case merits the space given to it here, and it will be convenient to carry the story to its instructive conclusion. Fifteen years after the original incident at Gerald Road Police Station the first Labour Government took office. This was in January 1924, and all those who were discontented, including ex-Inspector Syme, exerted what would now be called a pressure campaign upon Ministers for the relief of numerous and varied grievances. The Home Secretary was J. R. Clynes, who had a stronger sense of responsibility than some who had gone before him, and he cannot have felt much sympathy with a clamour about so old a song as the dismissal of a police officer fourteen years before. Impelled to pay some heed to it, however, for political reasons, he avoided the mistakes of some of his predecessors in office; instead of the long-drawn and often ineffectual proceedings of Royal Commissions and Home Office Committees, examination of the dusty files of the Syme case was delegated to a small but strong Special Commission appointed by the Lord Chancellor. Not at all the partisan sort of body no doubt hoped for by Syme and his friends, its members were Mr Justice Talbot, Judge J. J. Parfitt, K.C., and Mr Rayner Goddard, K.C., then Recorder of Poole and now Lord Chief Justice. Beginning its work in March 1924, the Commission presented its Report on the 8th of July. It is a document in strong contrast to others of its kind. Censure was distributed freely; Chief Inspector Shervington's first report on Syme was "quite unreasonable," and later action by Divisional Superintendent Isaac "exceedingly unsatisfactory." The handling of the case by the Assistant Commissioner was "not unexceptionable." On the other hand, though the final report by the first Disciplinary Board was "not an impressive production," it was substantially just, and the inquiry itself was full and careful. Summing up, the Commission found the decision to dismiss Syme inevitable, "whether right or wrong. No officer could be kept in the force after appealing to Parliament"—a pronouncement which the agitators, in or out of Parliament, must have found particularly unpalatable. The award by the second Disciplinary Board, like that of the earlier one, was therefore "rightly made."

Syme's monomania, aggravated by disappointment, for a time caused him to be certified as insane, and he was sent to a mental home. When he recovered, and was discharged, he found himself forgotten by the public; but he may have been instrumental in the creation of his ideal, the so-called Police Union, during the First World War. He was an active member, but with his unbalanced views he must have been a somewhat embarrassing comrade, even to extremists, and when the opportunity for which he had striven so long at length arrived, with the mutinies of 1918 and the following year, he made no mark at all.

21

TOTTENHAM AND SIDNEY STREET

THE activities of foreign anarchists in England in the early 1890's led to Parliamentary action, an Alien Immigration Bill being introduced in 1894, only to be dropped after the second reading. The more undesirable class of immigrant at that time came chiefly from Western Europe; when, however, within the next decade or so, events in Russia brought to London and other cities several thousands of political refugees, predominently Jews, from that country, mingled with the minority of convinced revolutionaries was a criminal element of a type hitherto unknown in these islands. It was not until 1909 and after that the public was to realize, what it has learnt only too well since, that robbery under arms is not peculiar to the United States; but the Special Branch had few illusions about some of the latest arrivals in the East End, and, the Home Office also taking a serious view, a committee was formed in June 1902 to study this new aspect of an old problem, while a little later a Royal Commission was appointed to inquire into the whole question of the growing alien population. This Commission's report, issued in August 1903, stated that in the twenty years from 1881 to 1901 the number of foreigners in the United Kingdom had more than doubled, having risen from 135,000 to 286,000. Of more immediate interest to the police, and in particular to the Special Branch, was the report of the Home Office committee, published a few months earlier. From this it appeared that out of 30,000 Russian, Polish, and Roumanian immigrants in the country, nearly 8000 had landed in the twelve months before June 1902. Most of them were in London.

The Home Office was less concerned with the criminal element in this invasion than with its effect on the labour market, but both aspects of the case had to be considered by the department. The competition of these Russian and Polish Jews, says Sir Edward Troup, "lowered the wages in some of the unorganised trades to starvation, and their habits had a demoralising effect on the crowded areas in which they settled."[1] As to this last, the London police, both Metropolitan and

[1]Troup, *op. cit.*

City, had abundant information. The Alien Immigration Bill of 1894 having been dropped, there was no legislation to meet the case later than Grenville's Act of 1793 and some amending Acts of which the last was seventy years old. In 1905, accordingly, a new Aliens Bill was introduced, and, in face of the strong opposition which such measures always encounter, eventually became law. In force until the outbreak of war in 1914 necessitated much sterner measures, it gave the Home Secretary power to make Expulsion or Deportation Orders, either upon information supplied directly by the Commissioner of Police, or upon recommendation by a magistrate. Though this Act did something to check mass immigration into the country, it left many loopholes by which individuals could enter, and statutory appeal boards too often overrode the better-informed views of Aliens Officers and the police. The powers of the police themselves in such matters were still regulated by the Prevention of Crimes Act of 1871, and the influx of foreign criminals and plotters having shown the necessity of strengthening these powers, a second Prevention of Crimes Act, amending the first, was introduced and became law in 1908.

Within a few months a startled public was to learn what sort of persons misplaced tolerance and leniency had permitted to find asylum in Great Britain. In January 1909 an affray in North-east London ushered in the new warfare against law and order imported from Russia.

2

At 10.30 in the morning of Saturday, the 23rd of the month, a clerk employed by a firm of rubber manufacturers in High Street, Tottenham, returned in a car from the bank with the week's wages, a matter of eighty pounds. He was attacked at the gates by two men who had been loitering near the premises. Producing automatic pistols, they seized the bag of money, fired at the clerk, but missed him, and then turned their weapons on the driver of the car, Joseph Wilson, who had jumped out and grappled with one of them. Wilson's overcoat was riddled with bullets. A gas stoker named Joseph Smith ran up, and, struggling with the other criminal, caused him to drop the bag. The pair then took to their heels, firing as they ran, and slightly injuring Smith.

The audacity of the outrage was enhanced by the fact that Tottenham Police Station was opposite the rubber factory. Constables Newman and Tyler, hearing the shots, ran out bareheaded. The former took up the pursuit with Wilson in his car, Tyler following on foot. Two other officers jumped out of the station window, and were followed by more. All these policemen were unarmed. The criminals had turned into Mitchley Road, where the car was overtaking them, when, having reloaded, they opened fire again, putting the car out of action and wounding Newman in the face. He and Wilson continued the pursuit on foot, closely followed by Tyler, behind whom again were more police officers and a number of other persons. From time to time the fugitives turned to fire, and this intermittent fusillade mortally injured Ralph Joscelyne, a boy of ten. As the chase swarmed on to Tottenham Marshes, near the Dust Destructor, Constable Tyler was killed by a bullet in the head.

Some of the police in the rear were now catching up, having commandeered bicycles, traps, and a motor-bus. One and all showed complete disregard of the new portent of automatic weapons, at that time scarcely known in England. In the meantime, at Tottenham Police Station, Superintendent Jenkins and Sub-divisional Inspector Large, capably handling such a crisis as they had never dreamt of, were collecting reinforcements and organizing a cordon round the area. What weapons were available were handed out.

The leading pursuers had also managed to acquire one or two, Inspector Gould borrowing a shot-gun and a revolver, and Constable Nicod a revolver which proved to be defective. The bandits, having crossed the Great Eastern Railway by a footbridge, and the river Lea and a canal by another, stood at bay for a few minutes on Mill Stream Bridge, firing recklessly among the crowd. Nicod, with his useless weapon, rushed ahead and was shot in the calf and thigh, as was a boy named Burgess, in the ankle. Along a footpath past Banbury Reservoir to Higham Hill and Salisbury Hall Farm the chase continued, marked by more casualties, mostly slight, though William Roker, a labourer, was shot in both legs. Constable Ziething, who had been fetched from his bed and had come up in a van, had a bullet through his lapel. A gipsy encampment near Folly Lane was sprinkled with bullets.

The footpath came out on the Chingford Road, and here the fugitives boarded a south-bound tram, turning the driver off, shooting a passenger, a man of sixty-three, in the neck, and compelling the conductor to drive, one of the pair standing by him while the other, from the rear platform, continued to fire back along the road. A terrified woman and child in the tram were unhurt, and the only casualty caused by the rather wild fusillade from the jolting platform was a horse. Both bandits had their pockets full of ammunition, while among the nearer of their pursuers only one police officer was armed. There were now some mounted police on the scene, and others were following in every sort of vehicle.

Near the Victory public house another tram was standing on a loop line. Its driver resourcefully reversed it on to the main line, blocking this, whereupon the two criminals abandoned their own for a milk-cart standing outside a shop. As the milkman, George Conyard, ran out he was shot in the arm and chest. In Forest Road, Walthamstow, the cart was overtaken by a van, which in turn was seized. Diverted north again by the sight of police at Hagger Bridge, the pair drove to Wadham Road, into an area not then built over, where waste land stretched to a tongue of Epping Forest. Headed off from its thickets, they took to the fields. Both were now exhausted by their extraordinary efforts, and one of them, failing to climb a fence by the little river Ching, shot himself in the head as the chase overtook him.

His companion found refuge in a small house, Oak Hill Cottage, in which at the time were Mrs Rolstone and her two young children. The man fled upstairs and locked himself in a bedroom, and, the van of the pursuit being close behind, Constable Dewhurst, who had been off duty when he heard gunshots and shouting, helped the woman and her infants to escape. There were now two armed policemen on the spot, Constables Cater and Dixon, who had revolvers. The noise of the running battle, which in its zigzag course had covered between four and five miles, had roused every one within hearing, and duck-shooters on the marshes, one of them the Prince of Wales's coachman, here joined in, firing at the cottage. Some one was using an airgun.

Constable Eagles, who had also been off duty, turned up at this stage and courageously mounted a ladder to look through the bedroom window. Cater and Dixon had entered the cottage; Eagles joined them, and the three climbed the narrow stairs. Revolver bullets riddled the bedroom door, but the lock held until Eagles, taking Cater's weapon, burst the door open with his shoulder. As he fired round it the hunted man within shot himself in the head, dying instantly.

He was Jacob Meyer, usually known as "Jacob." The other desperado, who lingered a few days in hospital, was Paul Hefeld, an ex-employee of the rubber firm. Both were Russians. The admirable conduct of every policeman concerned in this remarkable affair was suitably recognized, Eagles, Dixon, and Cater being awarded the King's Police Medal, the force's highest award for bravery; with two others they were immediately promoted to the rank of sergeant, the usual examination being waived, while nine more were specially mentioned and rewarded for their part in the pursuit. Nor were the civilians forgotten, though some of the claims made by them verged on the ludicrous, ranging from compensation for nervous breakdown to 12*s.* 6*d.* for a new pair of trousers and 3*s.* 9*d.* for a damaged bicycle. The blood of poor Constable Tyler had ruined a carpet, and another claimant had merely been frightened. Daisy May, who lived next door to Oak Hill Cottage, had cause to complain of shock, and J. Longden and J. Armstrong did not wish to be recompensed for their services, but expressed the modest hope that the Commissioner would recognize these in writing.

3

The cold-blooded preparations for this outrage, the store of ammunition Meyer and Hefeld carried for their automatics, and the trail of dead and injured in the wake of their flight were a clear warning of the new criminal methods let loose upon the country by the laxity of the immigration laws and the mistaken tenderness of those who did not even enforce them. But though the Special Branch and the City Police knew that the East End of London now harboured many foreigners of a similar desperate type, calling themselves political refugees and mingling revolutionary activities with crime, the Tottenham affray appeared at the time to be an isolated incident. "*On a diablement peur de la corde dans ce pays-çi,*" Caroline of Brunswick had observed to the Duke of Wellington in the days before Peel's police; and for this reason, among others, the British-born criminal remained shy of carrying firearms until two wars accustomed him to their use. That there was a considerable influx of aliens prepared to employ such weapons indiscriminately, and to take and lose life with equal callousness, was not yet realized by the police as a whole, still less by the public.

Before many months were out the lesson was driven home. On December the 16th, 1910, after business hours, sounds of knocking were heard at the back of a lock-up jeweller's shop in Houndsditch, just within the City limits. The jeweller having gone home, a neighbour reported the suspicious noises to a constable in Bishopsgate. Behind the shop was a *cul-de-sac* called Exchange Buildings, and, the shop itself being locked, and the knocking appearing to come from the rear, the constable went round to a house in the *cul-de-sac*, No. 11, which backed on to the jeweller's. Not liking the furtive air of a man who came to the door, the policeman summoned assistance, and about 11 P.M. three sergeants and two constables of the City Police descended upon No. 11. Sergeant Bentley entered the house, and while he was examining a room on the ground floor a number of men rushed from the back and down the stairs, opening fire with automatics as they came. Bentley fell dying. The other four officers, Sergeants Tucker and Bryant and Constables Woodhams and Choate, all of whom were, of course, unarmed, were shot down in the dark little street as they tried to grapple with their assailants. The latter got away, for the time being, though hampered by the condition of one of their number, also shot in the confusion. Of the five policemen left lying in the house and the *cul-de-sac*, only two survived, and they were maimed for life. The dreadful nature of the new criminal methods, and of the weapons employed, was instanced by the case of Constable Choate, who died with twelve bullets in his body.

The gang concerned in the attempted robbery which led to this massacre, unprecedented in the history of the British police, numbered at least fourteen, three being women. All called themselves anarchists, and all were Russians or Letts. They were associated with an Italian anarchist, Malatesta, who supplied a cylinder of acetylene-gas found at 11 Exchange Buildings. Probably half a dozen, including a woman, Nina Vassileva, were in the house, of which a man known as Joe Levi had been tenant for a fortnight. The gang also used No. 9, next door. Holes had been knocked through the rear wall of the jeweller's premises, and through the wall of his shop, in which stood his safe.[1]

Four days after the crime the City Police offered a reward of £500 for information which would lead to the arrest of Peter Piatkow, or Schtern, alias "Peter the Painter," "Joe Levi," and a woman then unnamed, but apparently Vassileva. The gang lived in the Whitechapel area, outside the City boundary, its headquarters being an anarchist club in Jubilee Street; and the Metropolitan Police accordingly now came into the picture, co-operating with the City Police in the hunt for the murderers and their accomplices. The division concerned was 'H,' and the operational centre Leman Street Police Station, where the campaign, for such it was, scores of officers being engaged in it, was organized by an outstanding figure in the force, Divisional Detective-Inspector Frederick Wensley, who was to become Chief Constable.

The population of the district was largely Jewish or foreign, including thousands who spoke little or no English. Appearances went for nothing; amid much grinding poverty, shabbiness might conceal considerable means. The average Londoner outside this region knew scarcely anything about the way its polyglot inhabitants lived, though the trial of Steinie Morrison for the murder of Leon Beron, whose body

[1] J. P. Eddy, K.C., *The Mystery of "Peter the Painter"* (Stevens, 1946); Sir William Nott-Bower, *Fifty-two Years a Policeman* (E. Arnold, 1926).

was found on Clapham Common two days before the Battle of Sidney Street, was to throw a curious light on conditions as alien to the normal English mode as those in Pekin or Baghdad. The police of H Division were better informed; and while the hackneyed story of Sidney Street need not be retold in detail, its preliminaries deserve mention as an illustration of the peculiar difficulties attending police investigations in such a neighbourhood.

On the day after the Houndsditch murders the wounded desperado, George Gardstein, was found dead in a house in Grove Street, between Commercial Road and the docks. Under his pillow was a loaded automatic and much ammunition. A Russian woman in the house was taken into custody, and during the next few days one or two more arrests were made; but most of the principal members of the gang were still at large at the end of the year. Inspector Wensley has described how this period of frustration came to an end with a telephone-call on January the 2nd, 1911. He was summoned by Superintendent Ottaway, of the City Police, to Old Jewry Police Station.

Several senior officers of the City force were there. An informant had brought news that two of the wanted men, Fritz Svaars and Joseph Marx, or Vogel, were at 100 Sidney Street, in Whitechapel, in the Metropolitan Police area; they were expected to move about 8.30 that evening to another hiding-place in Nelson Street, a turning off Sidney Street. After dark, vans brought a large number of police, in plain clothes and armed with revolvers, to form a cordon round the Sidney Street house. The two men, however, did not come out, and the informer now having another story, that they were not leaving until the following night, the vans were withdrawn and Wensley returned to Leman Street. Just before midnight Ottaway called him again; the Superintendent did not like the look of things, the informer was not to be trusted, and, rather than let the wanted men get away, action should be taken at once. Wensley was in full agreement, and with all his detective staff he returned to the neighbourhood of Sidney Street. Within a very short time a hundred uniformed police were gathered in Sidney Square, where Ottaway and two other of the City's superintendents had arrived. Though there was still no certainty that the criminals were in the Sidney Street house, it was decided at a conference to proceed with the search in earnest.

It was now 2.30 A.M., January the 3rd, and there was much to be done first. No. 100 must be effectually surrounded, and all other persons living there must be got out, and as quietly as possible. It was not even known who did live there; in this squalid neighbourhood people packed together like herrings in a tin, and there was constant moving. Wensley and the three superintendents, with a Jewish interpreter named Wagner, went to the next-door house, No. 102, where they learnt that an elderly couple named Fleishman had the ground floor of No. 100. The front room on this floor was shuttered; Wagner tapped at the shutters, woke the Fleishmans, and, speaking to them in Yiddish, induced them to come out and take refuge next door, though there was some difficulty over this, as Mrs Fleishman, who it now appeared understood English, was on bad terms with her neighbour. She told the police that the upper rooms of No. 100 were occupied by a Mr and Mrs Clements, Mr and Mrs Shineman and four children, and a Mrs Gershon, who had the two second-floor front rooms. It was in these rooms that the wanted men were said to be hiding. Mrs Fleishman said that as a respectable woman she would not tolerate such a thing; but it seems likely that she knew more than she cared to admit, for when invited to find out for herself she declared that she would not do it for £5000, nor would she let her husband go. She was eventually persuaded to re-enter the house and call up to Mrs Gershon. The latter, when roused and brought down, at first denied having men in her spare room, but under considerable and slightly irregular pressure from Wensley she finally confessed that a cousin of her husband and another man were there, and refused to go. She was taken to Leman Street Police Station. There was still no sound or sight of her lodgers, nor even while the other tenants of No. 100 were brought out into the street, though old Mr Clements objected and had to be carried out by Wagner.

All this had to be done in the darkness of a January night, in a poorly lit street full of police, and as nearly in silence as could be managed. Talking was done in whispers. Though most of the ejected persons were excitable and voluble Jews, apparently the two men in the second-floor front room were not roused at this time; it was later that something woke and alarmed them, perhaps the unnatural silence of the house. This being now empty but for them, Wensley and an inspector of the City Police entered the hall, dimly lit by a gas-jet, and turned off the gas-meter. When they came out it was 4.45 P.M., and no one entered No. 100 again until all was over.

In the meantime it was being cordoned off by armed police. They were in the houses next door, in a house at the back, and in the yard of No. 100 itself. Opposite, in 109 Sidney Street, lived a chemist named Cohen. He could not be roused until a constable got into the adjoining yard with a false key and woke him up. Police with revolvers went to his front windows. Mr Cohen, said Wensley, was very helpful.

An uneasy and prolonged lull followed. After what had happened at Tottenham and Houndsditch the senior officers hesitated to risk casualties among their men by ordering entry of the house in force. Misgivings of another kind, moreover, now assailed the superintendents of the City Police. Though, according to Mr Eddy,[1] Mrs Gershon's lodgers had taken away her skirt and boots to prevent her leaving, their true identity was still in doubt. When Wensley suggested putting men in her own bedroom, to seize the pair instantly if they came out, he was argued down not only because of the risk to life, but because, as one officer said, "If it turns out they aren't the right men we shall be a laughing stock." Sooner or later the couple must rouse themselves. If they were indeed two of the wanted Russians, which seems to have been Wensley's own belief throughout, some opportunity to take them at a disadvantage might then arise.

Heavy rain had now come on, soon turning to sleet. The police in the street sheltered in doorways. The quarry remained invisible and unheard. So more than two hours went by in increasing damp and discomfort; and even when at 7.20, acting on unauthorized instructions from some one whose patience had run out, Sergeant Weston knocked at the door of No. 100, there was no reaction from within. It was time, however, that something was done. As Wensley pointed out, it would not do to have bullets flying when people were about in the street. From the yard of Mr Cohen's house the inspector collected gravel and stones, and these were flung at the windows of Mrs Gershon's rooms. It was 7.30 in the morning. Wensley had gone back for more stones when he heard six rapid shots.

The men in the house were Svaars and Marx, after all. They were awake and on the alert, for the shots came from the ground-floor windows. After so long a wait the next few minutes must have seemed rather too full of incident. Sergeant Leeson, of the Metropolitan Police, came running into the chemist's yard saying, "I am shot"; among others with him, Inspector Allan had a bullet-hole in his cap. A fusillade sounded from the street, and a part of Mr Cohen's yard being visible from No. 100, bullets came whistling over it. Police were returning the fire from their windows. Medical help was needed for Leeson, and Wensley putting his head out of the chemist's front door, and realizing that the street was impassable, a boy named Louis Levy was sent over an outhouse at the back to find a doctor, who

[1] *Op. cit.*

arrived by the same route. The yard backed on to that of Mann and Crossman's brewery; Wensley climbed the wall and sent a brewery employee for an ambulance, which with some difficulty was brought through the brewery to the other side of the wall. A stretcher was passed over, but as Leeson was placed on this more bullets flew about the yard, and he rolled to the ground for safety. Eventually he was lifted over the wall. Though dangerously hit in the chest, he recovered. On all this the rain was beating down, and, battle conditions being now more or less stabilized, Wensley, who was soaked to the skin, went off to Leman Street to change. It was not yet eight o'clock. Fifteen minutes later, returning as he had gone by way of the brewery yard, Wensley found bullets flying and glass splintering as before. The brick frontage of No. 109 was pocked and chipped all over. The front door was full of holes. Early workers were now abroad, but not in Sidney Street.

So began a battle the later developments of which are well known. About this time Superintendents Mulvaney and Stark, of the City Police, as the senior officers then on the spot, telephoned to Scotland Yard to ask for troops. They were presently joined by their Commissioner, Sir William Nott-Bower; soon after nine, however, Major Wodehouse, Assistant Commissioner 'A,' arrived, and took command, the battlefield being Metropolitan. An hour later two squads of the Scots Guards, some twenty men, marched up from the Tower. Some of the soldiers posted themselves in doorways, some on the roof of the brewery, others lay in the street on display-boards from a newsagent's. Such a show of force to overcome two men might seem excessive, but preservation of life was the object. The Russians' reckless use of ammunition showed that they had a great store of it, and though there were now several hundred police in and about Sidney Street, relatively few could play an active part, and these, to take deliberate aim with their revolvers, must expose themselves at short range to the more deadly automatics. The Guardsmen, having rifles, though firing diagonally up the street, could do so from a safer range, giving time to every shot at the windows of the besieged house. Less necessary was the section of a Horse Artillery battery summoned by some alarmist in authority from St John's Wood Barracks. The guns were not used. An occurrence much appreciated by the police was the arrival in Sidney Street of the Home Secretary, Mr Churchill, with whom came Melville Macnaghten, the head of the C.I.D., and Superintendent Quinn of the Special Branch. For this Mr Churchill was absurdly criticized; he was, after all, the supreme police authority—though he made no attempt to interfere—and his characteristic action gratified the tired, drenched men who were there, which his critics were not.

For several more hours the besieged held out, and this extraordinary conflict continued. To those in command outside time was no object, but casualties must be kept down. From first to last there were six, of whom only Sergeant Leeson was dangerously injured. It was after one o'clock when the end was seen to be in sight; No. 100 was on fire. The Fire Brigade arrived with its usual promptness and disregard of everything but the job in hand, and protested when it was not allowed to approach the burning house. This was soon blazing from top to bottom; and at last the fusillade from its windows ceased. There was no final sortie, though this was expected. When at length two charred bodies were brought out from the ruins it was found that Joseph Marx had been shot through the head. Medical examination of what was left of Fritz Svaars suggested that he had died of suffocation; and it seems probable that his last desperate act was to set fire to the house. A final unhappy feature of the affray was that though the firemen were not allowed to get themselves shot, five were injured, one seriously, when a part of the gutted building collapsed.

In the sequel, eight of the surviving members of the gang were run to earth. What the police knew about them, however, was one thing; to prove this in a court of law was another. Essential witnesses, for various reasons, would give no assistance; some were in sympathy with the criminals, some were terrorized, few could understand English, and almost all were natural liars. This Oriental atmosphere of obstruction, together with rigid judicial principles, brought about the discharge of four of the accused at the police-court proceedings, and three more were acquitted after trial at the Old Bailey. Even the conviction of Nina Vassileva for conspiracy was quashed by the Court of Criminal Appeal. The later deportation of the *ex-officio* member, Malatesta, for a different offence, can have brought small comfort to police officers who had seen their comrades shot down.

Three of the original fourteen were never found, and were thought to have escaped abroad. Among these was the man whose name is probably the only one remembered to-day. Because the City Police obtained photographs of Peter Piatkow, known as "Peter the Painter," which after the Houndsditch murders were displayed on bills outside every police station, public fancy, encouraged by the Press, attributed to him a prominence in the gang that seems to be unmerited. The nickname—Piatkow painted scenery for anarchist dramas staged at the club in Jubilee Street—no doubt helped. The leader of the gang was Gardstein, and others in the hierarchy probably ranked above Peter the Painter. Sir Melville Macnaghten's theory, that he had nothing to do with the Houndsditch and Sidney Street affairs, and was not even in England at the time, is to all right-thinking persons untenable; and around his sobriquet legends have gathered almost as thickly as about the shade of King Arthur. Since Sidney Street days the elusive Peter has been seen all over the world. Sir William Nott-Bower held that he had escaped to France. Mr Eddy, whose study of the mystery is most up-to-date, says that there is no evidence of this, and that official Russian correspondence shows that Piatkow fled to Russia (where Jacob, one of the acquitted, is said to have become a member of the Cheka), and was last heard of in Germany. Pinkerton's, the famous American detective agency, believed him to have gone to the United States; and other informants there saw him in a carriage, and also dressed as a woman and wearing a wig. The British Consul at Naples heard of him in Italy—perhaps on a visit to his old friend Malatesta. Australians have claimed that he died in that continent. On the other hand, the late Charles Edmund Pearson, whose knowledge of crime was extensive and peculiar, was told that Piatkow never got out of England, but was buried under a hearthstone at 100 Sidney Street.

Canada was not to be left out of it—Peter had died there too; and it was to Canada, as it happened, that ex-Detective-Sergeant Leeson, gravely wounded in the Battle of Sidney Street and invalided out of the force, retired in later life; and there, in 1934, he met a man who claimed to be Peter Piatkow's brother, and heard an odd story which he passed on to old colleagues at Scotland Yard. It does not throw any further light on Peter and his wanderings, but, for what it is worth, it makes a topical postscript to the events of the winter of 1910–11. Three years earlier, in 1907, as Leeson himself no doubt knew, among the Russian immigrants in Whitechapel upon whom the police of 'H' Division kept an eye was a young man who afterwards was to become very well known indeed. He did not stay in England long; but back in Russia, according to Piatkow's brother, if such he was, the young man continued to influence his compatriots' extra-revolutionary activities in England. Speaking of Gardstein's gang and the Houndsditch shootings, "the crime itself," said Leeson's informant, "was organised by Stalin, now head of the Soviet Government."

22

THE WAR YEARS

THE year 1911, which opened so stormily for the police of London, was to be a very troubled year industrially, and strike duty in the provinces made heavy calls on the Metropolitan force. The new year found 400 of all ranks already on loan to the Glamorganshire authorities. These men came under the orders of General Macready, in command of troops sent to the mining valleys. Many of them were to know him in different circumstances seven years later. It was a useful experience for the General, who learnt to appreciate, and warmly commended, the good temper and impartiality with which these London policemen faced hostility and rough treatment. He said of their conduct that "for tactful, firm, good-tempered handling of an angry mob so as to prevent, if possible, resort to force, the Metropolitan Police Officer stands out far beyond his country comrades," and later he was to remember, when for a short time these same men fell from grace, how sturdily they had helped him in the past.

The Glamorganshire detachment returned to London in February 1911; but by the summer more than a thousand were away on the same thankless duty—500 at Hull, 250 at Salford, and 330 in all in South Wales again. In two years the force had been increased by as many, a special recruitment to meet the demands on the strength entailed by the granting, in 1909, of a weekly rest day instead of the one day off every fortnight which had been the rule until then. Another 1600 were needed to make the weekly day a practical possibility, and this shortage, together with so much strike duty out of London, reduced the fifty-two days to which every man was now entitled to an average of thirty-eight. This was also the year of coronation of King George V, and while unpleasant constabulary duty took so many of the force to the northern counties and the Principality, the latter was visited briefly by another thousand for a happier reason, the Investiture of the Prince of Wales. A twelvemonth which saw such exceptional calls on the Metropolitan Police, who are expected to help everybody, saw also the usual incidence of meetings and processions in the Metropolis itself, the most foolish, perhaps, being a demonstration by the Men's

League for opposing Female Suffrage (only a women's league for this purpose would have had any significance), and two days' junketings in Trafalgar Square by the Social Democratic Federation, which took upon itself to protest against the action of the Russian Government in suppressing popular liberties in Finland, a country which few of those present could have found on the map. From time to time it is worth recalling, what it would be tedious to mention too often, the many annual occasions of this kind which waste the energies and strain the resources of London's police forces.

There was another and more prolonged series of strikes in 1912, among them a railway strike. They were mainly, however, in the London area. Thousands of watermen and lightermen were out from the end of May until the beginning of August; more unusual was a six-weeks strike of tailors, men and women, many of whom in the East End, as a result of the competition of foreign immigrants, worked for starvation wages. Police pensioners were recalled, and thanks to this temporary augmentation of the force, and another 400 recruits, the average of weekly rest days, notwithstanding strike duties, rose to forty-six. Towards the end of this year, on November the 27th, the force was shocked by the attempted assassination of the Commissioner; a young man who had been refused a cab-driver's licence fired a revolver at Henry, inflicting a wound from which the latter suffered to the end of his life. At his intercession the life sentence passed on his attacker was reduced to one of fifteen years.

In 1913 a further large increase in strength, to 22,048, enabled the rest-day ideal to be attained. Every man had his fifty-two days off—just in time to appreciate the luxury before the outbreak of war caused it to be suspended altogether. What was known as the Police Reserve was discontinued this year. It had consisted of certain men, who wore an 'R' on their collars, earmarked for special functions and emergencies and drawing extra pay. Their work was now to be carried out by that proportion of the force, about one-tenth, normally absent on weekly leave, this being deferred for the occasion. In June 1913 Sir Melville Macnaghten retired after ten years as Assistant Commissioner (C). He was succeeded by Sir Basil Thomson; and in December the Commissioner was endeavouring in vain to extract another £100 a year from the Home Office to pay the salary of a superintendent of the C.I.D., this rank having been allowed to lapse for parsimonious reasons. A specialized force of nearly a thousand men was under a chief inspector. In the same month Police Orders issued a warning that was to be recalled five years later. A Standing Order prohibited members of the force from joining any such outside body as the Police Union, a newly formed organization whose name embodied an old demand. Much was to be heard of it in the future.

A welcome and useful innovation of these pre-war years was the authorization, in proper circumstances, of the use of bicycles on duty. By 1914 nearly 3000 men in suburban and semi-rural districts patrolled and performed other work on cycles. Though the Golden Age of modern vehicular traffic was drawing to a close, progress had not yet outstripped facilities; the annual issue of licences for public carriages in the Metropolitan Area was still under 20,000, and if the great majority were mechanically propelled the nerves of the populace were protected by police action, some 10,000 buses, vans, and cabs being reported every year as unduly noisy.

2

Not for one moment after the outbreak of war did the phrase 'business as usual' apply to the police anywhere in the country. To the other disciplined forces, the Navy and Army, war was a projection of their training; the police had to begin at once to undertake new duties and responsibilities. More than five pages of Metropolitan Police Orders came to be filled with regulations covered by the Defence of the Realm Act. The conscientious policeman must make some attempt to memorize these, because, while carrying out a routine visitation of hotels to see that friendly or neutral aliens were properly registered, not only had he to be on the watch for balloons, kites, and pigeons, and for mysterious signals by day or night, but he was expected to know what military authority was competent to permit the ringing and chiming of bells and the striking of clocks during certain hours of darkness, and a continually growing host of other novel enactments likely to be infringed at any moment. There was, it was true, less crime against property; it was a reflection on the too tolerant granting of a right of asylum that this factor was largely due to the internment of thousands of aliens neither neutral nor friendly. The Traffic Branch, again, benefited by the virtual halving of the issue of licences. But on the whole there was an immense increase of duties, and at the same time a serious reduction of manpower. Just over a thousand reservists were called up to the Forces in August, and before the end of the year another 300 had gone, some of whom joined the Army voluntarily. The Dockyard Divisions had to be reinforced, and a new one formed for Rosyth, and men had to be found for other naval and military stations. A further 988 were lost in this way. Though the paper strength of the force actually rose—in 1916 to 22,355, the highest figure in its history—the total available in London was reduced by the equivalent of several divisions, there being more than 3000 away on special duties in that same year, 1900 in the Army or Navy, and another 230 lent as drill instructors. With so much extra work to be done, the temporary suspension of rest days and the recall of one or two thousand pensioners did little to fill the gap; and in the early days of the War recourse was had on a large scale, and, as events were to prove, in permanency, to an expedient of considerable antiquity—the Special Constable.

Sir John Moylan points out that "the special constable of to-day may be regarded as the modern representative of the old parish constable."[1] The name has been in use since the reign of Charles II, and the office was regularized by the Special Constables Act of 1831, which empowered local justices to nominate special constables in an emergency, and rendered persons so nominated liable to punishment for refusal to serve. Service was demanded only for the duration of the emergency. When such an occasion arose volunteers always came forward in ample numbers, as during the Chartist troubles, the Fenian alarm in the 1860's, and one or two serious strikes, the last instance before the War being in 1911, when 8000 'specials' were sworn-in. It has been said earlier that the police system of this country has always rested on the theory that every male subject of the Crown is a potential policeman, and the Special Constabulary is simply this theory put into modern practice; but before 1914 the impermanence of this purely civilian adjunct to the regular force had dimmed popular comprehension of its functions and history. It was thought of as a temporary improvisation for special and rare circumstances.

It is now, as the Metropolitan Special Constabulary, a familiar constituent of the London scene. After returning from work scores of public-spirited men leave their homes again to do voluntary duty as policemen, wearing uniforms scarcely distinguishable from that of the regular force, except that all ranks wear a peaked cap instead of a helmet. Invaluable services during the First World War led to the continuance of a temporary measure; but from the first it was temporary in a sense different from that envisaged by the Act of 1831. The large force of special constables organized in August 1914 was not required because of riots, tumults, or disturbances, but to help the regular police in its normal duties, and a new Act was rapidly passed authorizing the

[1] Moylan, *op. cit.*

appointment of 'specials' irrespective of possible disorders and for an indefinite period. The force was under the command of a Chief of Staff, Colonel Sir Edward Ward, who had been Secretary of the War Office, and "that no better or more prescient organiser could well have been chosen is proved by the fact that both the War force of 'specials' and the post-war Reserve have been carried on with little or no change from the lines he laid down in the hurried days of August, 1914."[1] The Chief of Staff had, as he still has (though he is now styled Commandant-in-Chief), his headquarters at Scotland Yard, and his force was formed in divisions corresponding to those of the regular police, each with its own headquarters at a police station in the divisional area. A feature of the organization was that factories and other large businesses maintained their own sections of special constables for local protection, an idea adopted by the Home Guard in a later war. By the end of 1914 there were 31,300 'specials' in the Metropolitan Area, of whom 8700 performed their duties in privately owned premises. The Special Constabulary was, as it remains (with the exception of a few senior officers), a part-time force and unpaid; allowances were made to cover expenses, and serious injury incurred on duty entitled a member to pension or gratuity. The raising of this great civilian auxiliary force, the smooth working of its machinery, and its continuance because it has been found of permanent value are characteristic of the national genius for getting important things done in unorthodox and almost casual ways.

3

More unorthodox still, and startling to those who were elderly when the War began, was the insinuation of women into a police force. The word is chosen because for some time to come they were not recognized as policewomen; but they were the thin end of the wedge. Their permanent value as an adjunct to the force, like that of the special constables, was recognized before the War was over. As an organized body they sprang from committees formed to handle the swarm of refugees, chiefly Belgians, seeking refuge in England in August 1914. Miss Damer Dawson, an energetic and versatile woman who was in charge of the transport of the refugees to homes found for them, was struck by the need of some sort of sifting and policing of the crowds of her own sex arriving daily at the railway termini from the Continent. If scarcely Mata Haris, not a few were of a dubious type. From this idea sprang the Women Police Volunteers.

[1] Moylan, *op. cit.*

Though Henry, the Commissioner, was persuaded to authorize Miss Dawson to form such a body, it had then no other connexion with the regular police. It was a loose organization raised from among the members of the National Union of Women Workers and the Women's Auxiliary Service, a wartime creation. As the Volunteers proved their usefulness in spheres of action far removed from refugee problems, gaining the sympathy of magistrates, and even of Chief Constables, it had to be decided whether they should continue to work in isolation, or attach themselves, if permitted, to the regular custodians of law and order, the police. Many Suffragists had found an outlet for their energies in the Volunteers, and there was some doubt as to whether they would compromise with their principles. Patriotism, and possibly policy, won an overwhelming victory; with only two exceptions, the members voted for co-operation with men.

Henry being now wholly converted, in 1916 the Home Office approved his extending official recognition to a limited number of Volunteer patrols, to be known as the Women's Police Service. The members were not sworn-in as constables, and had, of course, no powers of arrest. A few weeks before the War ended a new Commissioner, Sir Nevil Macready, who had succeeded Henry in circumstances to be described, recognized the patrols as an integral part of the Metropolitan Police. They then numbered a hundred, under a superintendent. They still took no oath, however, and the arrangement was regarded as a temporary one. It was a threat of disbandment, four years later, on the ground of economy, that caused the question to be fought out in Parliament, with the result that a nucleus of the Women Police was absorbed in the force on a permanent basis. There were at first only twenty, but they were sworn in as constables and posted to divisions.

The Volunteers of 1914 wore a dark-blue uniform, and were issued with a broad-brimmed hat of hard felt, ugly but useful, not only as a protection against rain, but also against the attacks by rowdies, which, in these early days, were less uncommon than they are now. The modern policewoman has been given a more becoming peaked cap.[1]

4

The war-time counter-espionage work of the Special Branch remains in the obscurity which, for the same reasons, shrouds the similar

[1] For the origins and early years of the Women Police, see Commandant Mary S. Allen, O.B.E., *The Pioneer Policewoman* (Chatto, 1925).

machinations of Military Intelligence. Naval Intelligence is even less forthcoming than M.I.5; the recent release of the true story of certain stratagems seems to have been due to revelations, in the form of fiction, by an influential personage behind the scenes. In general, the Official Secrets Act blocks the curiosity of the historian—and no doubt rightly. It has been divulged that within a few hours of the outbreak of war in 1914 a score or more of German spies had been rounded up in London and at various ports; and tantalizing glimpses of a very efficient security system were obtained from time to time during judicial proceedings which usually ended with a firing-squad at the Tower—particularly in the course of the trial of Sir Roger Casement. The value of the work of the Special Branch in connexion with espionage caused it, towards the end of the War, to be so closely associated with Military Intelligence that it was virtually seconded from the C.I.D.; and in 1919 the experiment was tried of detaching it altogether. It became a separate department under an Assistant Commissioner who was styled Director of Intelligence. This arrangement, however, lasted for only a few years.[1]

A conspiracy of which more details than is usual were revealed was aimed at the life of the Prime Minister. Mrs Wheeldon, her two daughters, and the husband of the younger one, a retail chemist, were not foreign agents, and they were so foolish that no intelligent plotter could learn anything from their methods, except what not to do. These were publicly disclosed at a trial in which scientific evidence, supplied by Sir Bernard Spilsbury, was mingled with pure fantasy and medievalism. Two figures from the underground world of counter-espionage briefly emerged—one of them a person, known to the police for other reasons, who for the purposes of this case went by the name of "Gordon." The gullibility of the plotters (and their natural preference for committing crime by proxy) was shown when they invited the second agent, a man of a very different type from Gordon, to lurk among the bushes on Walton Heath and dispatch Mr Lloyd George, when playing golf there, by means of darts tipped with curare. Mr Arthur Henderson was also a prospective victim. There was a serious side to the affair, for alternative schemes involved the use of strychnine, of which the chemist casually sent through the post enough to exterminate the Cabinet; but the plotters themselves were unbalanced cranks, and their associates the jetsam thrown up by every war, conscientious objectors and the disgruntled of all kinds.

The incidence of major crime is little affected by such conditions,

[1] Moylan, *op. cit.*

and Londoners in these years had their minds taken off more wholesale slaughter by the murder of Mme Gerard in Soho and the trial of George Joseph Smith. The latter's technique of murder showed considerable ingenuity, not only in the use of the homely bath for lethal purposes, but in the choice of *locus crimini* far apart and of the end of the week for the deed itself, the victim's family learning of the inquest and burial when it was too late to attend either. Smith's crimes almost equalled those of Landru in Paris as a distraction from present discontents. The civil courts also continued on their deliberate way, and of possible interest to the police was a decision by the Lord Chief Justice and two brother judges that a winkle could be sold as a fish. If there was less minor crime than in normal times—apart from the internment of alien offenders, many native professionals had been absorbed in the fighting forces—circumstances offered novel opportunities to the enterprising. There was a small but regular trade in drugs which by their temporary effect enabled men to evade military service. Abortionists flourished. The replacement of gold coins by Treasury notes at first printed on inferior paper was an invitation to forgers; and before the arrest of a skilful gang was brought about by the no less skilful and patient work of the C.I.D., forged notes to the face-value of £60,000 were in circulation.

In March 1915 it was found possible to restore the force's weekly rest day. In that year it suffered its first casualties from bombing, a regular constable and a 'special' being killed. Henry was writing again to the Home Office about Chief-Inspector Thomas, still performing the duties of a superintendent of the C.I.D., with the help of only two other chief-inspectors. (One of these was Charles Stockley Collins, who had been made head of the Fingerprint Branch on its creation by Henry himself in 1901.) The capture of Vimy Ridge in April 1917 caused General Headquarters in France to indulge in the wildest hopes, the Cavalry Corps taking up miles of road while it waited to break through; and Scotland Yard was asked to provide six officers speaking good French for counter-espionage work in Lille—a city we were not to approach, still less enter, until the final weeks of the War. The officers, however, no doubt had a pleasant trip.

Things were not going so well with the force as a whole. More will be said of this in the next chapter; but back in 1915 internal problems had been causing the Commissioner serious anxiety. On the 5th of December that year he drew the attention of the Under-Secretary of State at the Home Office to a relatively minor injustice arising from the conditions of war. Men who had joined immediately after the Police

Act of 1890 had now completed twenty-five years' service, and would normally be retiring on pension. By the Police (Emergency Provisions) Act of 1915—one of a series of war-time enactments affecting the force—this right was temporarily withdrawn without the consent of the individuals concerned. So far from receiving compensation for being thus debarred from seeking other employment, the effect of the new Act, taking pension rights into account, was to reduce their pay, already insufficient to meet the increased costs of living, to a rate below what they should be drawing for the posts they filled. Henry ended his letter with some prophetic words: "There is serious unrest in the Force which must be allayed by all means in our power."

23

THE MUTINIES

In subservience to what is called the democratic idea, euphemisms designed to spare the feelings of everybody except those in authority have become common usage. Thus, though the refusal of a body of persons under discipline to obey orders is defined by the dictionary as mutiny, the police who so acted in 1890, 1918, and 1919 are now almost invariably described as "strikers." Since the passing of the Promissory Oaths Act of 1868 all who join a police force in this country have to make a Declaration in the following terms:

> I . . . being appointed a Constable of the Police Force of the . . . District, do solemnly, sincerely and truly declare and affirm that I will well and truly serve our Sovereign Lord the King (Queen) in the Office of Constable, and that I will act as a Constable for the preserving of peace and preventing robberies and other felonies, and apprehending offenders against the peace, and in all respects to the best of my skill and knowledge discharge all the duties of the said office faithfully according to law.[1]

Section 12 of the Promissory Oaths Act says explicitly, if in involved language, that "the making of a Declaration . . . instead of Oath shall in all respects have the same effect as the taking the oath for which such Declaration is substituted would have had if this Act had not passed." In short, police officers who refuse to obey orders are, like soldiers in similar case, guilty of mutiny. They have broken their oath.

Even in mutiny, however, there may be degrees of guilt. The two outbreaks now to be described differ considerably in their causes and intentions. The week-end outbreak in 1918, though confined to London, might at first sight appear the graver of the two, but extenuating circumstances were recognized by the authorities. The sequel, just over a year later, fell in a different category. It was flat mutiny; and the mutineers suffered accordingly.

[1] For some reason an abridged version of this Declaration is made by police officers attached to royal palaces.

2

During the labour troubles in the years immediately preceding the First World War the old question of a Police Union was revived. Among the trade-union leaders of the period there were some who aimed deliberately at obtaining control of the police. In the Metropolitan Force itself another old question, that of pay and pensions, was again to the fore, coupled with an agitation for what was termed "the right to confer." An outside organization with vague aims called the Police and Citizens Friendly Association gained a footing in the force, and, in 1913, became the Metropolitan Police Union. This, again, expanded a little later into the National Union of Police and Prison Officers, or N.U.P.P.O., an active figure in which was ex-Inspector John Syme. This body, generally known as the Police Union, never had official recognition; on the contrary, the Home Office and police authorities throughout the country made it clear that for a serving police officer to join the Union was an offence involving dismissal. Henry, still Commissioner, pointed out in Metropolitan Police Orders that membership of any such association was prohibited by Standing Orders. The membership of the Union, however, increased, the names of members being kept secret; it published its own journal, the *Police and Prison Officers' Magazine*, which constantly advocated recognition; and it became affiliated with outside trade-union organizations, such as Trades Councils and the Trades Union Congress.

Recognition of the Union, in the view of its advocates, meant recognition of the right of policemen to strike, a right implicitly denied by the constable's oath or declaration. If a policeman could strike, so could a soldier, who took a very similar oath. The Government felt that any appearance of recognition of the Union might have a mischievous effect on the Army. On the other hand, thoughtful people, including members of police forces who had no use for the Union, realized that the "right to confer" was a reasonable aspiration, and had something been done to satisfy it before the unsettling interlude of a great war, the outbreak of 1918 and its sequel would not have occurred.

But in these years before the War, in the Metropolitan Police, at any rate, there seems to have been complacency and apathy at the top. Labour unrest and very serious strikes had thrown the usual heavy strain on the force. The lower ranks were alive to certain genuine grievances, as well as to those manufactured by the agitators of the Union. A prolonged recruiting drive throughout England had introduced a strong element full of trade-union ideas, and some of these new men were prominent in the banned Police Union itself. The authorities at Scotland Yard had become rather out of touch with the feelings of the body they controlled. Henry himself was still a very popular head, with great influence, and it has been shown that he was well aware, after war came, of the growing discontent in the force; but even he did not realize how far this had gone, probably because, as has been suggested, he was not too well served by his staff.[1] The same may well be true of the period immediately before the War. Henry, who had reached the age of sixty, and whose health was affected by the wound received in 1912, was by then anxious to retire, but the Government, faced with internal troubles and the increasing possibility of war, could not spare him. The next administration was to forget how much he had done for the Metropolitan Police, and with the existing machinery his men remained ignorant of many of the efforts he made to the very end to improve the conditions of their service.

The War came; and the loss in four years of some 4000 trained men who joined the armed forces (nearly a thousand of them being killed or injured), and of another fifteen hundred sent to reinforce the small Dockyard divisions and on other special duties outside the London Area, could not be made good by young recruits, recalled pensioners, and predominently part-time special constables, however numerous and willing. War brought its own police problems and extra tasks, leave was restricted, and all the time the cost of living was rising. Allowances were increased, but such increases were no more than palliatives. Henry's successor, Sir Nevil Macready, writes of the state of things in 1918: "During my inquiries I came across cases of men with families who before the pay was increased were in a pitiable condition." Sir William Nott-Bower, then Commissioner of the City Police, which was to be involved in the troubles of that year, refers to instances "approximating to destitution" that came to his personal knowledge. "I well remember," he goes on, "Sir Edward Henry and myself, not very long before the crisis came, together *begging* for a very small increase of wages, and receiving the reply, 'Impossible, impossible.' "[2] At the moment of the crisis, in fact, these representations were at last bearing fruit. Before the men left duty they were told that a permanent increase of pay was under consideration. But the announcement came too late.

[1] Sir Charles Mallet, *Lord Cave: A Memoir* (Murray, 1931). The reference is to the months immediately preceding the events of August 1918.

[2] Sir Nevil Macready, *Annals of an Active Life* (Hutchinson, 1924); Nott-Bower, *op. cit.*

3

The secret of the action about to be taken by the majority of some 16,000 disciplined men was well kept. For knowledge of undercurrents of feeling in the force the Commissioner was virtually dependent upon reports from the twenty-one Divisional Superintendents, who met weekly at Scotland Yard for the purpose of discussing problems and exchanging views. In 1918 most of these officers were elderly men who had reached their rank by seniority. On account of the War some had stayed on after they would normally have retired. Upon all of them fresh duties and responsibilities had been piled, and it is scarcely surprising that after four years of strain and overwork the majority were no longer fit to handle large divisions numbering a thousand or more of all ranks. It is certain that their weekly reports gave altogether too rosy a picture of a situation that had for a long time been deteriorating.

There was, indeed, an intermediate link at Scotland Yard itself between the Commissioner's Office and the superintendents and their divisions. Henderson's District Superintendents had become Chief Constables,[1] but the original quartette had been reduced to three, who seem to have had little to do. According to Sir Nevil Macready, they spent most of their time on paper-work in their offices at Headquarters. There was also there an Executive Branch, but this is described by the same authority as an anomaly, and it was soon to be absorbed, as 'A.3,' in the department controlled by Assistant Commissioner 'A.' Like the Chief Constables, the Executive Branch appears to have led a life remote from realities, for knowledge of which it also relied on what the Divisional Superintendents had to tell.

How little this was worth the events of the last few days of August 1918 were to show. Portents had not been wanting; but alarms earlier in the year proved false. The conspirators of the council of the N.U.P.P.O. were biding their time. They perfected their plans so secretly that towards the end of August, after the third superintendents' meeting of the month, the Commissioner had no hesitation in going to Ireland on leave. In his absence one of the Assistant Commissioners, Sir Frederick Wodehouse, acted as Commissioner. On the 28th, a Wednesday, the Divisional Superintendents were again conferring at Scotland Yard. The activities of the Police Union were no doubt discussed, as were the increases of pay already decided upon and announced. Such proposals could not be put into effect by a stroke of

[1] Chapter XVI, p. 201

the pen, and a scheme for widows' pensions, pressed upon the authorities by Henry himself, had caused further procrastination and actuarial delays. Knowing that these remedies were in hand, the superintendents remained satisfied with outward appearances of calm in their divisions, and after their conference reported to the Acting Commissioner that all was well.

Yet only the day before there had been a conference of another sort, when representatives of these divisions were summoned by the Executive Committee of the Police Union to the Pimlico Mission Hall, by Ebury Bridge. The Committee had prepared an ultimatum demanding immediate recognition of the Union. The plan of action received its final touches, orders were issued, and the ultimatum was sent on its way to Scotland Yard, addressed to the Commissioner. That the time chosen was when he was out of the country, that a scheme for redressing genuine grievances was nearing completion, and that the tone and substance of the demand were such as must provoke instant rejection are factors which reveal the motives behind its dispatch. It must have been in Wodehouse's hands not long after the superintendents had dispersed from their meeting next day, the 28th; and it called for a reply before midnight on the 29th.

It met the fate expected and hoped for, and on Friday, the 30th, a number of police in several divisions failed to report for duty. The state of affairs on Saturday may be illustrated by one of a score of reports from divisions. The superintendent of M Division wrote that afternoon: "I beg to report that no uniform constables paraded at any Station in M Division for duty either at 8.45 A.M. or 9.45 A.M., 31st August, 1918. Six Constables, Assistant Warrant Officers and Assistant Gaolers employed at Tower Bridge Police Station, have abstained from coming on duty. No uniform constables on the streets since 10 A.M., 30th August. C.I.D. officers patrolled the streets." So it went everywhere; on that Saturday morning the Metropolis found itself almost without a regular police force. A total of 12,000 men—of whom very few, however, were above the rank of constable—was legally in a state of mutiny. The City Police were out too. Only the C.I.D. and the Special Branch were unaffected.

But if the Union could spring a surprise the authorities immediately concerned showed that they could react with speed and firmness. Fortunately only London was involved. The country was at war, and thousands of special constables were enrolled in the capital and available at short notice to take over patrol and traffic duties. King's Regulations provided for such an emergency, Regulation No. 956

placing troops at the call of the Commissioner or of an Assistant Commissioner "for the maintenance of the public peace." The Regulation had been invoked before, but never on such a scale as during these two days. Early on the Friday Wodehouse requested assistance from the G.O.C. London District; five justices, he said, were ready to proceed with the troops. A detachment of the Scots Guards marched to Scotland Yard, where the gates were closed; Grenadiers, in steel helmets, filled the quadrangle of the Foreign Office. On the Saturday two companies were there. Memories of 1890, perhaps, suggested that F Division was a dangerous area, and 100 Guardsmen drove in lorries from Wellington Barracks to Paddington Police Station. London District was now responsible for order throughout the Metropolitan Police Area, excepting Woolwich, where the Arsenal came under the Eastern Command.

To a bewildered public these martial precautions may have seemed a little excessive. London remained remarkably calm; traffic proceeded as usual, regulating itself; and the underworld, as surprised as the law-abiding, failed to take advantage of a unique but fleeting opportunity. Almost the only scenes of turbulence occurred in Whitehall, where patrols of the Guards marched to and fro on Friday night; on the Saturday the environs of Scotland Yard and the Ministries were packed with thousands of excited policemen in plain clothes, many wearing the red-and-white ribbon of the Police Union. There were one or two exhibitions of mass hysteria, startling to witnesses who had come to think that their friends in blue were far above such displays of emotion. Eminent persons were hustled; special constables were booed, and one was roughly handled, having his lips cut. A few soldiers on leave cried "Blacklegs!" But with the majority of the mutineers habits of discipline soon prevailed. They streamed away to a meeting in Smith Square, and from here marched off in an orderly manner, in fours, led by a piper, to Tower Hill. To the puzzled crowds they seemed to be in a very good humour. A constable of the City Police, defying his colleagues and the Union by parading for point duty, held up the traffic at Blackfriars for the procession to pass. On the whole it was all very British and restrained.

But if tempers could rise in Whitehall there was no knowing how far or how fast the infection might spread. There was, in the overworked phrase, a war on, and no one, at the end of August 1918, suspected how soon it would be over. London must not be left without a police force for a day longer than could be helped. In the circumstances it was necessary to have troops at hand, but only for strictly limited uses; the mutineers, or 'strikers,' as they preferred to be called, must be brought back to duty before the crisis could develop. That Saturday was a day of anxious conferences and hasty decisions—decisions too hasty, and too ill-defined, which sowed the seeds of more trouble in the future.

Henry, hastening back from Ireland, had found a section of the Cabinet, led by the Prime Minister, calling for his head. His immediate offer to resign was accepted with graceless alacrity. The Home Secretary, Sir George Cave, had also been out of London. Returning on the Friday, he too proffered his resignation, but was told by Mr Lloyd George that he was in no way to blame—he had been badly let down by Scotland Yard. "The worst time I had," he wrote to his wife, "was when I had my interview with Henry. . . . He was as delightful as usual. I was so sorry to part with him. We had always got on so well."[1] The precipitate actions of the Cabinet, in fact, had all the signs of panic. Henry, in his own words, having been jettisoned, the Adjutant-General, Sir Nevil Macready, was summoned from the War Office to take his place. An offer of mediation by General Smuts, then in London, being refused by the committee of the Police Union, the Prime Minister agreed to meet delegates from this body; and before the day was out the 'strike' was at an end. London, which had scarcely had time to realize that it should hold its breath, could breathe again. On Sunday thousands of the familiar men in blue were back on their beats, and by the Monday things were almost normal.

It was quick work, but not sound. There was soon disagreement over the terms of settlement. The Prime Minister, not for the first or the last time, had contrived to convey a wrong impression of what he afterwards said he meant to say. One of his predecessors, Mr Gladstone, having accused a Colonel Dopping of feloniously using a rifle, explained when brought to book that he had not said that the rifle was loaded. Endeavours had now to be made to correct Mr Lloyd George's errors of phrasing. When he told the delegates from the Police Union that this could not possibly be recognized "in war-time," he was very far from implying that recognition might follow at some future date. If the delegates failed to realize that they had been received, not as representatives of the Metropolitan Police, but merely as members of an unauthorized organization, the mistake was theirs. There were other misunderstandings seized upon by the malcontents, and if attempts to exploit them eventually failed, in spite of further mishandling of a delicate situation, it was because the police as a whole

[1] Mallett. *op. cit.*

were reasonable and patriotic men, whose just grievances had been met.

In the printing department at Scotland Yard, underneath the Receiver's Office in Scotland House, men and machines worked late that Saturday night; and Police Orders for Sunday, September 1, gave details of a revised scale of pay for all ranks. The increase was a flat rate of 13*s.* a week. A constable who had been drawing 30*s.*, rising to 40*s.*, would now receive 43*s.*, rising to 53*s.* Pensions were augmented accordingly, so that the constable's 53*s.*, to which were added war bonuses for himself and children averaging 17*s.*, entitled him after twenty-six years' service to a pension of 35*s.* 4*d.* Finally, the cause for which Henry had been fighting almost up to the moment of the mutiny, the plight of police officers' widows, was recognized by the grant of a non-contributory pension of 10*s.* a week to widows of all ranks.

To the reasonable members of the force, the great majority, these were the features of the settlement which mattered most. Next in importance to them was the concession of the "right to confer." A representative body was to be formed which could approach the Commissioner to discuss any matter not affecting discipline. To a minority, the agitators of the Union and their followers, this clause was no less important, because tactically it could be linked to another. Recognition of the Union itself was conceded to the extent that membership of it by serving officers was not forbidden provided that no claim or attempt was made to interfere with discipline, or to induce men to withhold their services. In this final clause of the settlement, No. 5, lay the most troublesome possibilities. It was vague, it was dangerous, and it was premature.

The men having returned to duty, there were no punishments. One of the grounds for the 'strike' was alleged to be the dismissal of a constable who had taken a prominent part in the management of the Union; he was reinstated. The Commissioner of the City Police, in consequence, felt compelled to reinstate two of his men who had been dismissed for rather similar though less flagrant offences. Both he and Henry had been altogether opposed to retrospective acts of clemency in such cases, because they might be (as they were) construed as weakness; but it does not appear that either of the Commissioners, or any other senior police official, was consulted before the Prime Minister made his final decision on this and more important matters.

Within a few hours of expressing his views on the case of Constable Thiel, Henry was no longer Commissioner. The eventual acceptance of his offer of resignation was no doubt inevitable, but it was done in an inexcusably hasty and shabby way. A scapegoat had to be found in even more of a hurry than usual. In the nature of things, he could make no public defence, but none was made for him. He had held his office for more than fifteen years, after nearly two as Assistant Commissioner, and during the long period "that he was the presiding genius, the force underwent the most rapid development it has known, and attained a very high standard of efficiency."[1] As Commissioner he was undoubtedly the most outstanding figure since Mayne. A reserved man of precise, scientific turn of mind, the achievements by which he is best known, and which gained him an international reputation, were on the practical side; but few Commissioners have been better liked or respected by the force at large, and few have done or attempted more for its welfare. A grant of a baronetcy was a belated recognition of his services, and, perhaps, of the fact that they entitled him to very different treatment at the crisis of his career than that which he received.

4

If new brooms could speak one and all no doubt would take a poor view of the conditions they were called in to rectify. Sir Nevil Macready was a man of the stamp of Warren, not of Henderson or Bradford or Henry. He was masterful and outspoken, with a sense of humour and the gift of getting on with people, and this was not the first or the last time he was to be called in to grapple with an emergency. A regular soldier, before the War he had shown his fitness for difficult jobs when commanding mixed bodies of troops and police during industrial troubles in South Wales and elsewhere. He was then earmarked to succeed Henry, but the latter's retirement was postponed, and Macready continued his military career, holding various administrative posts—he was a first-rate organizer—until 1918 found him Adjutant-General at the War Office. With the Army at war, this was his true *métier*, and in far happier circumstances he would now have been reluctant to become a policeman. For two hours on that famous Saturday afternoon the Cabinet argued with him. At last, in the interests of the country, he consented to take on an unpalatable piece of work which the fate of Henry and others suggested would also be a thankless one. Thus transferred, against his wishes and at a moment's notice, from one end of Whitehall to the other, it is not to be wondered at if his first impressions of conditions at Scotland Yard were blacker than the facts justified.

[1] Moylan, *op. cit.*

He found the atmosphere of the place lugubrious. It was full of hysteria and rumours. People tried to keep out of his way, and too many of them—*e.g.*, the Chief Constables—seemed to have too little to do. Though Sir Nevil, with his usual frankness, has committed these early impressions to print, no doubt he soon modified them, or at least realized that much of the atmosphere was the natural result of events. The organization had suffered a severe shock. Such a thing as mutiny on such a scale had never occurred before in the ninety years of the Metropolitan Police. It must have seemed inconceivable. In the midst of this cataclysm a long-known and respected chief had been swept out of office. And now, upon a headless and bewildered organism, had descended—what? Macready himself had given his own reputation as one of the main reasons for his reluctance to become Commissioner. After the Samuel Committee,[1] and what the newspapers had said about him, the police would think he had come to dragoon them. Whether or no such fears existed to any wide extent, at Scotland Yard itself, where every one, tired by the strain of war, was now thoroughly on edge, this vigorous iconoclast, striding along corridors, bursting into rooms, uttering trenchant sarcasms, may well at first have seemed the most bristly and unfeeling of new brooms.

Macready was so conscious of his rôle, and so different a type from Henry, that he seems never to have appreciated the great services of his predecessor, and criticisms which appeared to reflect adversely upon the latter were naturally resented. Senior officers who remained, however—for there were great changes, and a number went—revised many of their early judgments. The new Commissioner could be as likeable as he was bracing. With the force as a whole he went down well, after a difficult beginning; and that this was difficult was largely due to the Cabinet's over-hasty, if not panic-stricken, handling of the recent crisis.

Immediately after the settlement the Home Secretary met representatives of the two police forces concerned. Among memoranda agreed to, the most controversial—the question of pay and pensions being decided—were those dealing with the proposed Representative Board and with the right to join the Police Union. The Board, it was laid down, "shall be entirely within the Force and independent of and unassociated with any outside body." Its purpose was to provide machinery other than the Police Union for bringing grievances before the authorities. The terms of the settlement, however, permitted men to join the Union as well—a concession incompatible with the whole

[1] Select Committee of the House of Commons on National Expenditure, 1917–18.

idea of a representative body within the police. If men could belong to both, the Union's politics would inevitably influence the Board. The men themselves, indeed, or the more politically-minded among them, professed to believe that the Board was a temporary measure, pending full recognition of the Union. No proper attempt seems to have been made to disabuse their delegates of this notion. If the Prime Minister had appeared to imply anything of the kind he was speaking beyond his brief, for the truth was, in fact, the very opposite. As the new Commissioner pointed out in his first annual report, for 1918–19, it was the concession of conditional membership of the Union that was "experimental."

This meeting with Sir George Cave was followed, on the 3rd of September, by a conference summoned by the executive of the Union. A reporter from the *Morning Post* was present, and his impressions, submitted to the Commissioner, were filed for reference. The extremists made it clear that the question of pay was from their point of view almost a minor matter. It was only a beginning. Full recognition of the Union was their aim, and with it its corollary, the right to strike. The next essential was what they called demilitarization of the police. A civilian force should not be run on military lines, and there were already too many soldiers in high places at Scotland Yard; now it was rumoured that the new Commissioner, a soldier himself, was bringing in more—as, in fact, he was. It was significant, however, that the firebrands no longer had it all their own way. More sober opinions were aired. Speakers who emphasized the need for an authoritative body to present the men's views had the courage to say that a disciplined force could not be run on trade-union lines. Other subjects of legitimate interest were discussed, such as the system of reports on conduct, and the slow rate of advancement in the Metropolitan Police, which caused men to transfer to provincial forces.

It is probable that the extremists had never felt sure of their hold on the great mass of the men who came out, and therefore leaped at the loosely worded terms first offered them, because these could be interpreted in their own way. With signs of reaction so soon apparent, every possible use was made of the loopholes provided. The new Representative Board was elected on the 2nd of October, and great pressure was exerted to ensure that it was almost wholly made up of aggressive members of the Union. At its first meeting, held in the Commissioner's library on the 17th, Macready took the chair, made a short speech of welcome, and withdrew. He disapproved of the constitution of the Board, on which all ranks were represented; and after very little experience of its methods of deliberation he pronounced the existing arrangement quite unworkable. As he wrote in his first Annual Report, the Board "was dominated by certain men who, as time went on, hardly concealed their intention of governing the Force in all respects." Members of senior rank, with some sense of responsibility, were cowed by constables and sergeants, meetings took longer and longer, and all sorts of irrelevancies were dragged in. Attention being drawn in Police Orders to this wasteful procedure, the Board became truculent, refusing in writing to receive a statement from the Commissioner. It was thereupon informed that he would have no further dealings with those of its members who were also members of the Executive Committee of the Union.

It was March 1919 when this deadlock was reached. Macready's action was approved by the Home Secretary, now Mr Edward Shortt, who had succeeded Cave at the end of the old year. Events were moving to another crisis, of a more widespread but happily much less serious character than that of the past August. A committee under the chairmanship of Lord Desborough was making a general investigation of police affairs throughout England and Wales. The Cabinet, alarmed by the results of its own weakness, had stiffened its attitude, and a Police Bill was being drafted which, while granting the police the statutory "right to confer," flatly prohibited membership of any outside organization claiming to interfere in matters of pay and conditions of service. Macready's view of the Representative Board had been accepted, and it was to be replaced by separate Boards for different grades. The new system, under the title of the Police Federation, was to be common to all forces outside Scotland, each having its branch; and there was to be an advisory council of police authorities, chief officers, and representatives of the Federation itself. Clause 3 of the Bill made it an offence to cause disaffection in a police force.

The leaders of the Union, partly through their instrument the Representative Board, were well informed about the measures under consideration. Macready complained that there was a continual leakage of confidential information, some of which was used by the *Police and Prison Officers' Magazine*. He had a reliable intelligence service of his own, for he correctly estimated the still dissatisfied minority in the Metropolitan force at under 15 per cent.; these men, however, by their indiscipline and influence, were lowering the standard of work of the whole. Constables left their beats, or did not come on duty, and there was other evidence of a deliberate campaign of provocation of the authorities, and of intimidation of loyal men. The extremists sank so low as to attempt to limit testimonials on retirement to Union members. The committee of the Union was working hand in hand with the more extreme trade unionists, such as Tom Mann; and when, in February, the Government summoned a National Industrial Conference, the N.U.P.P.O. applied to the Ministry of Labour for cards of admission, and, whether by design or inadvertence, received two, under cover of a circular letter issued to elected trade unions—a lapse of which the Minister of Labour knew nothing until the president of the Union spoke at the conference, obtaining, by his own account, "a goodly measure of recognition."

The most was made of such small tactical successes, but the real struggle began in March. When Macready took a high hand with the Representative Board he knew that his scheme for a Federation had been adopted. Announced on the 8th of the month, it met with violent opposition from the Union, which tried to boycott the elections to the new graded Boards. From what was stated to be a reliable source came the report that "John Syme is telling people privately that a Police Strike is fixed for March 22nd"; but they knew better at Scotland Yard, where the new Assistant Commissioner 'A,' Brigadier-General Horwood (one of Macready's "military men"), dismissed the rumour with the note, "There is no truth in it." The Union, in fact, though only too willing to wound, was still afraid to strike, even when, on the 17th, it learnt from Police Orders that the Cabinet had decided against any sort of recognition. The only immediate reaction was an approach to the Home Secretary, who refused to meet a delegation.

At the end of the month a station representative on the Representative Board, Constable Spackman, was dismissed for gross insubordination. A meeting of protest in Trafalgar Square, attended by serving as well as civilian officers of the Union, was addressed by a Member of Parliament, Pemberton-Billing, of "Black Book" notoriety. Otherwise April, and then May, passed fairly quietly, though the Union, holding what professed to be a national ballot on the question of a 'strike,' announced the figures to be 44,539 in favour and only 4,324 against. The majority appears to have been in every sense a paper one; but great efforts were being made to rally the disaffected and disgruntled in provincial police forces, especially in the big cities, and the importance attached to this extension of the conspiracy may have been responsible for delays in taking action. The Union was well aware that in London it was losing ground every week.

Police Orders of the 29th of May quoted a further statement by the Home Secretary on the banning of Union membership; and on the

30th, anticipating a demonstration in Hyde Park on the 1st of June, a Sunday, Macready issued his Special Order No. 1. Referring to "a movement to again withdraw from duty," the Commissioner said he was confident that the great majority of the force had no such intention. But "after the events of August he must make it clear that any officer or man of whatever rank who fails to report for ordinary duty, or when called upon, will be forthwith dismissed, with loss of all service counting towards a pension. No excuses of intimidation will be accepted." Next day's Orders stated that this pronouncement had the full approval of the Government, and would be adhered to, as would the Cabinet's decision about the Union. Constable Spackman would not be reinstated. The force was then reminded that the Desborough Committee was at work on questions of pay, pensions, and conditions of service. The Metropolitan Police Provident Association, about which there had been complaints, was to be put on a sound footing by a prominent insurance company.

Sunday's noisy demonstration was as fallacious an indication of the real trend of events as are most of the gatherings with which Hyde Park is too familiar. Prominent among the speakers who did their best with a failing cause was Sergeant J. H. Hayes, of the Representative Board, who still represented the N.U.P.P.O. five years later when he was a Member of Parliament ("the policeman's M.P.") under the first short-lived Labour Government. Scotland Yard was scarcely interested, except to correct misconceptions in the Press about a few members of the voluntary Women's Police Service who were present, and who, though not members of the force, were described as uniformed Women Police. Macready had his own characteristic way of countering public mis-statements and downright lies; a few days later he was talking to 3000 police officers summoned to meet him at the Queen's Hall. It was a talk, not an address, and for the first time many of those present heard both sides of debatable questions clearly and humorously put. Of one of the most controversial, the new Representative Boards, the Commissioner put the case for grading, as against a mixture of ranks, in words that all could understand. "Suppose that a sergeant and a constable have a real good row across the Board table, and thoroughly lose their tempers, that sergeant would hardly be human if he clean forgot about it, and did not let it influence him in any way should he meet that man on duty." This unorthodox meeting ended with applause and cheers far more genuine and spontaneous than any heard in Hyde Park.

5

There was another lull, lasting into July. The Desborough Committee issued the first part of its Report, dealing with increases of pay and the constitution of the new Police Federation. The Bill to bring these and other recommendations into effect, afterwards known as the Police Act, was introduced on the 8th of July; and now the tension increased again. It was known, or reasonably conjectured, that when the Bill reached the report stage, probably at the end of the month, the Union would make its last throw by calling a national 'strike.' So far as the Metropolitan Police was concerned, this could be awaited with confidence.

In the meantime there was much paper-work to be done, in readiness for the Bill's passing; and the lighter side of the proceedings was seen when Scotland Yard got down to working out how ballots for the graded Boards of the Police Federation were to be conducted. An extremely efficient organization proved to be in some respects surprisingly innocent. There was to be a Board for constables, in the ratio of one per division, another for sergeants of all ranks, a third for sub-divisional and ordinary inspectors elected by districts, and a fourth small Board of five superintendents and chief inspectors. All these individuals had to be voted for. Every police station must therefore have a ballot-box, but there were two hundred stations in the Metropolitan Area, and hardly any ballot-boxes. Recourse was had to the local authorities, who agreed to provide boxes. This was relatively simple, but then came the question of ballot-papers. No one in Scotland Yard appeared to feel competent to devise one, and again the help of local authorities was invoked—this time not merely in London, but throughout Great Britain. Specimens of voting-papers poured in, from Dunfermline (which cannily sent a copy in pencil) to the Corfe Castle Division of Dorset and the Charles Dickens Ward of Portsmouth. Every sort of election was covered—to Borough Councils, County Councils, Urban District Councils, the Westminster City Council, and Parliament. Nothing was overlooked, and a Declaration of Secrecy (under the Ballot Act) was accompanied by one of Inability to Read. Much poring over and comparison of these evidences of sympathy with a sort of relation in difficulties brought forth a rather cumbersome form of ballot-paper which experience has reduced to the simplest terms on coloured slips about four inches square.

The expected crisis came on the 31st of July, the date foreseen as soon as it was known that the Police Bill would then reach the report stage. It was therefore no surprise, though, again, there was no warning from the Union beyond a manifesto issued at the last moment. Needful precautions had this time been put in hand well in advance; but in London they remained in abeyance, for the blow, when it fell, was so ineffectual there that the loyal police had little difficulty in handling the situation. In calling upon every man in the Metropolitan and City forces to come out, and to remain out until recognition of the Union itself was granted, the fomenters of the mutiny uttered brave words to conceal their misgivings; at Scotland Yard even the pessimists did not expect more than 3000 to leave duty. In the event, Macready's much more modest estimate of the proportion of real malcontents proved to be well above the mark. The first abstentions from duty were reported at the 9.45 P.M. parades on the 31st, a Thursday. A total of 240 men in nineteen divisions were known to be out that evening, when there was a meeting of serving Union members and their wives at the Central Hall in Commercial Road, at which the reading of fraternal messages from such bodies as the Bexhill Branch of the Workers' Union and the Hornsey Trades Council may have smacked of an anticlimax. More influential and active support was needed. Nor can the wives of the 240 have been comforted next morning by learning that their deluded husbands were no longer serving—they had been dismissed from the force. One wife, so the story goes, went on strike herself, locking her husband out of the house until he found another job.

In London, that Friday, the 1st of August, saw, to all intents and purposes, the end of the mutiny. The morning's parades found just over a thousand men absent; those not already dismissed were automatically thrown out, and by the evening some of them were openly hoping for reinstatement if they returned promptly to duty. It was a vain hope; both Macready and the Commissioner of the City Police, Sir William Nott-Bower, who had worked in close co-operation,[1] issuing their final warnings on the same date, had told the Home Secretary that if they were compelled to reinstate a single man they would resign; nor was the Cabinet now in an apprehensive or lenient mood. The Police Bill, as every man in the two forces knew, remedied the grievances which had caused earlier discontent. The new mutiny was purely subversive; and the course it took, for a few hours in

[1] In *Fifty-two Years a Policeman* Sir William Nott-Bower writes warmly of "the friendly and cordial co-operation of Sir Nevil Macready," who was "always ready to lend the help of the 'Big Brother' to the 'Little Brother' of the City." Probably Sir William never knew that on the 17th of September, 1919, Macready was writing to Sir Edward Troup, of the Home Office: "The sooner the City Police is amalgamated with the Metropolitan, the better." The Little Brother, however, still survives.

London, and for longer elsewhere, revealed the spirit behind it. There was none of the prevailing cheerfulness and good order of August. So soon was failure obvious that the hard core of extremists attempted violent measures almost from the first, welcoming the rowdy crowds which attached themselves to every procession or knot of mutineers. On the Thursday evening loyal men going on night duty were molested at King's Cross and City Road Stations. On Friday large mobs, each with its nucleus of discharged policemen, caused trouble in Old Street and at Islington Police Station, where 'strikers' and their friends tried to force their way in; and down in Shoreditch, next day, roughs attacked police on duty who endeavoured to arrest their late comrades for using violence in resisting orders to disperse.

But these scenes were almost the last flickers of the rebellion. Its result, in Macready's words, "was an undisguised blessing to the Force, as the extreme element disappeared, and from that moment the Force has steadily improved in efficiency and discipline." This extreme element, in his opinion, did not amount to more than 20 per cent. of the 1083 policemen—one inspector, one station sergeant, 32 sergeants, and 1049 constables—who withdrew from duty and were dismissed. The majority, he thought, "were led away through pure moral weakness"; and while adamant on the question of reinstatement, he afterwards did much to help them.[1]

Of 970 City Police, only 58 mutinied and suffered accordingly. As a national police revolution, of which the Union boasted, the conspiracy was a complete failure. It was confined to a few big cities, and in Liverpool, where half the force came out, and in Birkenhead, where 110 out of 180 refused duty, there was serious rioting and intimidation, and troops had to restore order. In Birmingham less than 10 per cent. of 1320 men were affected. There were 60,000 policemen in England and Wales; 2400 obeyed the orders of the Union, and 74 prison warders out of 2000. The same drastic but necessary measures were taken everywhere; and everywhere, within a week, all was quiet again. "We hereby challenge the Government," wrote the General Secretary of the Union in the *Police and Prison Officers' Magazine* of the 23rd of July, "and leave it to Father Time to prove that they have apparently misjudged the measure of our worth."[2] Father Time had answered promptly for once.

[1] George Dilnot, *The Story of Scotland Yard* (Bles, revised edition, 1930).
[2] Nott-Bower, *op. cit.*

24

PRESS ATTACKS AND THE GENERAL STRIKE

WITH the issue of the first part of the Desborough Committee's Report, the introduction of a Police Act embodying its recommendations, and the fiasco of the second mutiny, all of which events occurred within two months, June and July 1919, the police throughout the country knew where they stood. Part I of the Report, dealing with the urgent points at issue—pay and pensions, housing, certain questions of organization, and the "right to confer" has been called the Policeman's Charter (or by those with rather muddled ideas about history, Magna Carta), a catchword which had been used before, and will no doubt be used again. The police had indeed won much, and most of it was only their due. The resulting Act gave legal form to the scale of pay and pensions announced at the end of August 1918, as outlined in the previous chapter. The men had a promise of better living conditions, and they had their Federation and its Branch Boards. Though the so-called Police and Prison Officers Union was not dead, its subversive ambitions had been cast into the limbo of lost causes.

At Scotland Yard Macready could devote his time—he was not to have long—to reorganizing in his breezy way the affairs of the Metropolitan Police. He had already begun with his own office. Deputy Assistant Commissioners were appointed. The Secretariat rose temporarily in status with the promotion of the chief clerk to the new post of Secretary, and of the senior clerks in Departments 'B' (Traffic) and 'D' (Civil Business) to that of Assistant Secretary. Senior Assistant Secretaries were created in 1936. The quota of Chief Constables was made up, and the four, three of them new men, were sent out into the hard world to live and work in their respective districts, or sub-areas, as had been Henderson's intention when he created their predecessors, the District Superintendents, and as was laid down in Orders in 1886. It was impossible, said Macready, in forwarding his proposals to the Under-Secretary of State, for him to know twenty-eight divisions (this included the dockyards) and thirty-seven superintendents; the Chief Constables were to be in fact what latterly they had been only in theory, the direct link between the divisions and the Commissioner. To speed their work they were given cars instead of traps. The Commissioner's Office itself having no modern means of keeping in touch with outlying areas, the four Assistant Commissioners shared a car between them.

All this meant many new faces at Scotland Yard, and several of them, as the prophets of evil had foreseen, were military ones. Brigadier-General Horwood came in as Assistant Commissioner 'A,' Wodehouse retiring after twenty-eight years' service as A.C. with the City and Metropolitan forces; and Colonel Laurie, of the Scots Greys, was brought in as Deputy Assistant Commissioner to reorganize the Mounted Branch. Macready seems to have wished to have Army officers seconded for five years to act as Chief Constables, and Horwood actually functioned as one for three days, but so far as the four districts were concerned the posts remained in the hands of policemen, of whom Superintendent Olive was soon to become an Assistant Commissioner, and later Sir James Olive—the first man from the ranks to climb so high. Chief Constable Morgan, another promotion, had been one of the youngest superintendents. General Horwood presently got a brevet, when it was decided that A.C. 'A,' should in future be Deputy Commissioner in name as well as in practice. Later the post of Deputy Commissioner was to become distinct.

A separate appointment of this time is one for which every historian of the Metropolitan Police must be profoundly grateful. Mr (now Sir John) Moylan succeeded Mr G. H. Tripp as Receiver.

Most of these rearrangements took place between Macready's own appointment and the end of 1918. Early next year, when the Commissioner was having trouble with the new Representative Board, and even with the Special Constabulary, which force he thought needed disciplinary boards, he was pressing for a reform advocated by Henry—the creation of a separate Traffic Department. Partly as a result of the peace, which not only restored normal conditions in the motor industry and in public services, but foreshadowed the release of thousands of vehicles for private use, the traffic problem, hitherto manageable, loomed as a serious worry ahead, particularly in the London Area. Here the regulation of traffic was divided between the Public Carriage Branch at Scotland Yard and a Traffic Branch without executive powers at the Board of Trade. A Parliamentary Committee began to investigate the matter, and a Traffic Bill was introduced in April. The London Traffic Act was not to become law for another four years, but a Ministry of Transport and an Advisory Committee on

London's traffic were at once established, and traffic control became wholly the business of the Public Carriage Branch at Scotland Yard. Continually expanding, this was now in effect, if not in name, the Traffic Department, with an Assistant Secretary under its Assistant Commissioner. In 1923 the experiment was tried of appointing a Director of Traffic Services, with a status equivalent to that of Chief Constable; but three years later the appointment was allowed to lapse.[1]

The second oldest body of regular police in the Metropolis was little concerned with the internal-combustion engine, and Colonel Laurie was introducing new methods of training for the Mounted Branch, then numbering about three hundred and fifty, a total soon to be reduced. Imber Court, at Thames Ditton, was acquired, and in 1920 was opened as the Mounted Police Training Establishment, with excellent accommodation, indoor and outdoor riding schools, and a sports club. In many respects this establishment, starting from scratch, was in advance in its facilities for training and recreation of anything that could yet be provided for the mass of the force, and the Mounted Police were regarded in some quarters as rather pampered, and, with the advent of the motor-car, scarcely necessary. It has often been proved since 1920, however, that a trained man on a trained horse is still worth a dozen on foot when an unruly crowd has to be controlled. Three years after that date occurred the celebrated instance at Wembley, where the F.A. Cup Final was being played, and where a vast crowd which overran the ground was brought under control by a single constable on a white horse. One change in the equipment of the mounted policeman had long been overdue; his useless sword was now replaced by the more practical long baton.

Macready, as has been seen, incorporated the Women's Police Patrols in the regular force. Writing in later years, he claimed to have "invented" Women Police, and his ideas of the possibilities of a feminine constabulary were of the widest; had he remained at Scotland Yard he hoped to have turned over to the women "the entire work of checking immorality and prostitution."[2] Such notions and claims were characteristic of a vigorous and fertile mind which, if at times too contemptuous of things past, was at its best in a determination to cut through red tape and combat outworn tradition. Since Peel's day, to take one more example, Commissioners had put up with a stupid ruling which compelled them to obtain the formal approval of the

[1] A sign of the times was the introduction of motor-vans to replace the horse-drawn "Black Marias," the last of which went out of service in November 1924.

[2] Allen, *op. cit.* The scope of the work of the Women Police, and not only in the Metropolitan Area, has in fact greatly increased since his day.

Home Office of any promotion within the force. As a rule only a formality, it left an opening for such interference as had deprived the C.I.D. for several years, in Henry's time, of a senior officer of higher rank than chief inspector. It took a Macready to fight and win a battle over this archaic canon.

2

A man who is not afraid to accept responsibility can be very useful to a government. If he is a success those who employed him claim the credit; if he lands them in trouble it is because he has taken too much upon himself, and out he goes. Few such men can get themselves besieged in the middle of Africa, like General Gordon, and so compel exasperated Ministers to support them, even if too late. Past history of the Metropolitan Police suggests that Macready was fortunate in a different way. Once he had accomplished the immediate tasks he was brought in to do, it seems unlikely that he would have lasted long; so forceful and opinionated a Commissioner must soon have raised dust elsewhere than in New Scotland Yard. But the turmoil of his arrival there had barely settled when he was called away from a job he had taken on reluctantly, but was beginning to enjoy, to try to clear up another mess. He was given the command of 60,000 troops in Ireland. This was in April 1920, and he had been Commissioner for twenty months, one month longer than Monro.

Strong characters instinctively avoid choosing equally strong characters as subordinates. Hay was thrust upon Mayne, and Monro upon Warren. Macready had been given so free a hand that he brought with him to Scotland Yard the man whom he then intended should soon succeed him. General Horwood, beginning as Assistant Commissioner 'A,' was soon in status Deputy Commissioner. He was another regular soldier, who had been Provost-Marshal of the British Expeditionary Force in France. Eighteen months after his appointment as Commissioner differences of opinion led to the resignation of Sir Basil Thomson, then head of the C.I.D., and again the Army, in the person of Sir Wyndham Childs, a Major-General, filled the breach; and less than a year later Lieutenant-Colonel Carter became the third Deputy Assistant Commissioner to be appointed. Horwood's new responsibilities had come upon him suddenly, and much sooner than he can have expected, and, like Macready, he preferred to have about him men of his own profession, whose capabilities he knew. But, unlike Macready, he was an administrator, not an innovator; and as the reforming impetus slackened after the departure of the reformer, the Commissioner's Office, and the force in general, settled down—possibly with some sighs of relief—to something like the normal and humdrum existence of the days before the mutinies. The tempest had come and gone, leaving in its wake much tidying to be done in a quiet way. At this date, in 1920, the public and the police (which was a part of the public) were still living in a dream induced by certain effects of the war just over. It was "assumed that the piping times of War would be indefinitely prolonged, that Peace would bring in her train even more than the proverbial prosperity."[1] Sharing in this, the police could rest satisfied with their gains, and look contentedly to the future. A steady-going Commissioner, who was a good organizer and who watched after their welfare, but did not try disturbing experiments, was just the man for the times.

There were economists and others who realized that things were not what they seemed. Sir John Marriott, who has just been quoted, remarks that though the economic momentum of the War lasted for about two years after the Armistice, "towards the end of 1920 there were ominous signs that Peace and prosperity were not invariably associated." It was perhaps not to be expected that the annual reports of the Commissioner of the Metropolitan Police should reveal that the country was drifting towards catastrophe. These reports are domestic in character, and naturally on the whole make dull reading. Even relevant events which shake the country, like the mutinies, are treated briefly and with calculated detachment. Only now and then is the man who signs these reports of the type to impress his own personality on what has become a stereotyped document; Mayne, Warren, Macready, and, in the years to come, Lord Trenchard were not content with routine phraseology, and where they felt strongly took a wide survey and put into their own vigorous language what had been drafted for them by others. No one, however, reading the Commissioners' reports for the eventful decade after 1920 would suspect from these colourless annals that anything out of the ordinary was happening to a society of which the police formed a very sensitive part.

Discipline continued to improve. There having been a high rate of removals in 1919 and 1920—a tactful allusion to the 1083 mutineers and some other undesirables got rid of—in the latter year an intensive recruiting campaign was launched. An electric lantern superseded the old bull's-eye. In 1921 a new division, Z, was formed out of parts of W and P, to take in Croydon. Shooting outrages and arson were committed in the London Area by Irish terrorists; of a gang trying to

[1] Marriott, *op. cit.*

set fire to the depot of the Vacuum Oil Company at Wandsworth, four were arrested in the act; but the murderers of two men shot dead from what were called political motives were never found. The second of these murders was one of a peculiarly dastardly series of attempts simultaneously directed against the relatives of men serving with the R.I.C. or with the troops in Ireland. Whitley Councils were coming into being, and one was set up by the civil staff at Scotland Yard, and the provisions of the Pensions Act of 1918 were extended to cover the widows of pensioners, as well as those of serving officers.

Among ominous events beyond the ken of the Commissioner's reports was the appointment of a committee under Sir Eric Geddes to consider an immediate reduction of national expenditure. This, to start with, meant an end of recruiting drives; instead, the force was to be reduced by some 600 men, and by the close of 1922 the strength had fallen to 20,114 (18,692 in the Metropolitan Area), or nearly 900 below establishment. Though the Women's Patrols were disbanded, twenty women were taken into the force as an integral part of it. In this year patrol cars were fitted with wireless, and police information and requests were broadcast from 2LO. The Special Branch ceased to have a semi-independent existence, and resumed its place as a subdivision of the C.I.D. 'D' Department, whose civil business comprised such a mixed bag as legal questions, betting and gaming, intoxicating liquor laws, street collections, fire-alarms, and the registration of aliens, was renamed 'L.' In January it had extracted an apology from the *Daily Graphic* (published in Police Orders) for an allegation that gambling houses in London "can afford to bribe the Police to a certain extent." If there was no truth in this at the time there was soon to be an unhappy instance of gambling houses finding a weak spot in the organization watching over their activities.

In the meantime problems of national economy were becoming acute. The boom years were over, and the number of unemployed, which had been negligible in the autumn of 1920, leaped up in less than twelve months to the shocking total of two millions and a half. The war-time Coalition administration went out of office at the end of 1922; the Conservatives, under Bonar Law and then Baldwin, came and went in their turn, and the country's first Labour Government began its brief career in the early days of 1924. In these unsettled conditions, with money increasingly hard to come by, not much could be done for the police. They escaped a serious cut in pay threatened by the Geddes Axe, but though Horwood had the question of housing much at heart, no new building could be done until 1926, when quarters for married men were opened in Marylebone; and the reduced strength of the force was a continual worry to the Commissioner. It meant, as he said in his annual report for 1923, that beats were far too long; men were expected to cover such distances—twice, three times, and even four times as long as normal beats—that efficiency suffered. And they had to be on the look-out for as many things as ever; suspicious signals and balloons might have gone the way of iron hoops and fusees, but novelties were always cropping up in Police Orders, as when (December 3) to Paragraph 198 of General Orders (Dentists) instructions were added that itinerant vendors of drugs and others found extracting or offering to extract teeth in public places were to be warned, and have their names and addresses taken.

The effects of the 5-per-cent. reduction in strength caused by the Geddes Axe were again regretfully noted by the Commissioner in 1924. But discipline continued to improve, and better pay and amenities for training, education, and sport were resulting in a gratifying rise in the social status of recruits. On the surface all seemed to be going tolerably well. In Parliament, in this year, the Labour administration was induced to appoint a committee to consider the claims of the mutineers dismissed in 1919, whose supporters had ever since been demanding the men's reinstatement. Ex-Sergeant Hayes, now an M.P., made the most of the discrepancies between the hasty provisional settlement of 1918 and the subsequent Police Act; but there was a general feeling that what Mr Lloyd George had seemed to say at an informal meeting had best now be forgotten. A majority of the committee was emphatically against reinstatement, but with regard to other claims affected by the Police Pensions Act opinion was unanimous "that the matter ought not to be left where it is." The police authorities were recommended in their discretion to extend to this particular case a provision of the Act whereby dismissed officers might be refunded all or part of rateable deductions of their pay, a matter on the average of twenty pounds, for the benefit of their wives and children. The recommendation was honoured, though before the committee's report was issued in December 1924 the Government which had appointed that tribunal was swept away. Resigning after defeat on a division in the House, the Labour administration lost what chance it had at the polls through the timely publication by the Foreign Office of the Zinoviev Letter, the authenticity of which is now disputed. The Conservatives came in again with a large majority.

One of the Commissioner's worries was somewhat alleviated by the action of the Admiralty, which took in hand the reduction of Rosyth and Pembroke Dockyards to a state of care and maintenance, and at Deptford and others substituted its own watchmen for Metropolitan Police; and during 1925 and 1926 the release of these dockyard detachments helped materially to bring the strength of the force very nearly up to establishment once more. Overcrowding at Scotland Yard itself was relieved by the transference, in the winter of 1926–27, of both the Lost Property Office and the Public Carriage Branch to new quarters at Lambeth, across the river. A Press Bureau, formed by Macready was enlarged in the latter year. (The post of Public Information Officer was created in 1945.) The year 1927 also saw the passing of the Police (Appeals) Act, which entitles police officers dismissed or compelled to resign to appeal to the Home Secretary.

The Special Branch and the C.I.D. were engaged in 1927 in two cases which, in their different ways, made history. Early in the year War Office documents were discovered to be missing; and in May, under the direction of Sir Wyndham Childs, no fewer than 200 police raided the Moorgate premises of the All-Russian Co-operative Society, known as Arcos. For the offices of a simple trading concern these premises were equipped with a surprising number of safes, some hidden in the walls, and some so armoured that pneumatic drills had to be used to open them. The missing papers were not found, but others that were provided ample proof that Arcos was a clearing-house for subversive activities.

On September the 27th P.C. Gutteridge, of the Essex Constabulary, was shot dead while on night patrol near the village of Stapleford Abbots, a few miles outside the Metropolitan Police boundary. The murder was of a particularly brutal character, two of the four revolver bullets in the constable's head having been fired after he had fallen dead or dying to the ground. The C.I.D. was at once called in, and officers from the Central Office were on the spot within a few hours. If anything was required to inspire every policeman concerned in the case to special efforts, it was the killing of a fellow-officer in such an atrocious manner; and the ensuing hunt for the murderers, for there were two, has become a classic of patient detective work.

A stolen car, in which when found were bloodstains and a discharged cartridge-case, was an early and important clue. Though the case against the murderers was to rest on other and more conclusive evidence, it was the travels of this car, doubling in the dark at high speed through a network of narrow lanes, and traced with remarkable accuracy in the course of police visits to hundreds of houses scattered about the countryside, that drew attention to Frederick Guy Browne, a dangerous criminal known to carry firearms who at one time had covered dealings in stolen cars by running a garage and repair business in the Romford neighbourhood. His guilt had yet to be proved, however; and in spite of ceaseless routine inquiries and much publicity, including a reward of £2000 offered by a Sunday newspaper for information leading to the murderer's arrest, four months went by before an incident at the other end of England, of which Browne himself probably thought little at the time, finally led to his arrest at a garage he now had in Battersea. It was an instructive example of the value of thoroughness in police work. Having stolen a car in Tooting in November, Browne drove it to Sheffield, where he intended to sell it. Reckless driving in that city involved him in a collision with a van; the van-driver took the car's number; and an hour later it was stopped by a constable, who took the driver's name and address and noted that he had a passenger. The name and address proved to be false, but more routine inquiries by the Sheffield police, who then had no idea where they were to lead, eventually discovered the passenger. He was a man with a criminal record, but he was so frightened of Browne that for a long time he would say nothing. But there was the £2000 reward; and at the end of December, having written an anonymous letter in vague terms to Scotland Yard, he obtained an interview with the Chief Constable of Sheffield, Mr (now Sir) Percy Sillitoe, to whom he confessed that Browne was not only the driver of the car involved in the collision, but was the murderer of P.C. Gutteridge. He also named Browne's accomplice in that crime, Kennedy.

Police concealed in Browne's garage were able to arrest him before he could reach the firearms he possessed. Kennedy was later taken in Liverpool, his attempt to shoot his captor happily failing because he had forgotten to release the safety-catch of the revolver he was carrying. He did his best to save his neck at Browne's expense, but both were hanged on May the 31st, 1928. Of the conviction of this very dangerous pair of ruffians Sir John Moylan rightly points out that though scientific aids, such as ballistics, were the basis of the prosecution's case,

> science would have been of no avail, had it not been for the persistence and courage of the police. . . . It was almost by a miracle that the Liverpool detective escaped being shot dead by Kennedy, and, if Browne had been come upon suddenly, or without the most careful preparation being made to surprise him, sudden death might well have overtaken several of the officers concerned.[1]

[1] Moylan, *op. cit.*, which contains, as Appendix I, an excellent brief account of the Gutteridge case. Sir Percy Sillitoe deals with the Sheffield end of it in *Cloak without Dagger* (Cassell, 1955).

3

Long before the Gutteridge case, and the raid on Arcos, Horwood was being plagued by various domestic troubles. The short-lived experiment of altering the status of Assistant Commissioner 'C,' calling him Director of Intelligence, and giving him rather loosely defined powers of co-operation with the Home Office and other public departments in matters normally outside routine police work, did not prove altogether a success, and led to the Director's resignation and questions about his treatment in the House. The Home Secretary, then Arthur Henderson, was not, according to *The Times*, "seen at his best in this incident,"[1] and both the Commissioner and his late colleague had some cause to feel aggrieved. But in the meantime more serious cause for worry had arisen.

The attack on the police by the *Daily Graphic*, referred to above, heralded a newspaper campaign of abuse based on a series of incidents of which the worst that can be said of most of the officers concerned was that their actions were sometimes injudicious. Three constables were convicted of giving false evidence; but the majority of the cases which were to provoke an uproar between 1922 and 1928 fell in that very difficult and controversial class involving women who either are of doubtful reputation, or act in a highly indiscreet manner. Little, probably, would have been heard of them if it had not happened that among the men accused were several whose names were known to the public, while others were of established position. Newspapers, and their readers, being what they are, charges of indecency, or even drunkenness, when brought against an eminent archæologist, a major in the Indian Army, an ex-Crown official, an ex-police official of senior rank, and an ex-M.P. with a national reputation as an economist (these last three being knights), are bound to make bigger headlines than similar cases which are a commonplace of certain police courts. By such influences the populace was wrought up into one of its fits of self-righteousness. (1923, incidentally, was the year of the trial of Bywaters and Edith Thompson, at which the judge and jury appeared to confuse murder with immorality.) Anonymous letters poured into Scotland Yard, and there were the wildest accusations of venality and perjury by the police. Innocent people, according to the Press, were positively afraid to go out, lest they should be arrested. It was the 1850's or 1870's all over again. The police could do nothing right.

At the expense of strict chronology, this rather discreditable agitation

[1] Major Maurice Tomlin, *Police and Public* (Long, 1936).

may be followed here to its lame conclusion. The inevitable tribunals were set up to thrash out the rights and wrongs of some of the incidents. The first committee, meeting in 1927 under the chairmanship of Mr Hugh Macmillan, K.C., was appointed to consider how cases of the type in question were affected by law and practice. In a rather inconclusive report it did not deprecate popular sensitiveness in the matter, but it went on to say, "We regard it as unfortunate that when a mistake does occur it should be made the occasion of a general attack on the police." Nothing could be truer, but popular sensitiveness was much less concerned with this report than with that of a sub-committee to which the case of the Indian Army officer was referred. The sub-committee found that in this single instance the police had not acted with due care and judgment, and had not taken the proper steps proscribed by General Orders. This was News, and so was the fact that the sufferer considered an *ex gratia* compensation of £500 to be insufficient.

Horwood was called as a witness by the main tribunal, and had some forthright and pertinent things to say about club gossip and the difficulties of the police in handling this obnoxious type of case. No one, obviously, would be better pleased than the average police officer, who is a normal, decent citizen, if the control of such offences in streets and parks were handed over to vigilance committees made up of his critics. As things are, he has to carry out the law to the best of his judgment. If occasionally this fails him it is not surprising. In such a case, as a rule he may safely be left to the mercies of a disciplinary board, as happened to five officers after their conduct had been criticized in the main committee's report. Two of them were reprimanded.

A new and noisier hue and cry after police culprits had been raised in the meantime. In May 1928, while the Macmillan committee was drafting its report, a Labour Member of Parliament gave a harrowing account in the House of the treatment meted out to Miss Irene Savidge, who, with Sir Leo Chiozza Money, the writer on finance and economics, had been arrested after nightfall in Hyde Park. A magistrate had dismissed the case, awarding costs against the police, whose sworn evidence he refused to accept. Other officers, one of them a woman inspector, had then been sent, on the instructions of the Director of Public Prosecutions, to obtain a statement from Miss Savidge, with a view to possible further proceedings. Miss Savidge was invited to make this statement at Scotland Yard. That was all there was to it, except that Miss Savidge's version of what happened there, and of the state of her mind and health when she was allowed to return home, was at variance with that of the senior police officers who interviewed her, and, indeed, of other quite disinterested persons. But not all were disinterested; not only were sentimentalists now up in arms, but here was another stick with which to beat the police, and, through them, to harass the Government. The Home Secretary, Joynson-Hicks, in yielding to political clamour for another Committee of Inquiry, pointed out that a thorough investigation was certainly desirable in fairness to the police, who were as much entitled to justice as other members of the public. This was not at all the view of some of those who pressed for the inquiry.

Sir John Eldon Bankes, a former Lord Justice of Appeal, presided over the new committee, his colleagues being two Members of Parliament, a Conservative and a Socialist. The only question to be decided was the treatment of Miss Savidge; was her account of it to be believed, or that of the police? Had she been bullied for five hours in a sinister chamber at Scotland Yard, and reduced to a state of terror and exhaustion, or had she met with tact and friendliness? Two members of the committee, the Chairman and the Conservative M.P., had no difficulty in coming to the latter conclusion. In the majority report they compared the chief interlocutors at the famous interview:

> On the one hand, Chief Inspector Collins, a man beyond middle age, married and with a family, possessing an unblemished record of thirty-two years' service during which he has been commended by judges upon ninety-three occasions for skill and ability in the performance of his duties and for rendering public service, and, on the other hand, Miss Savidge, a young woman of twenty-two years of age, intelligent, of quick perception and of considerable acuteness, quite capable of taking care of herself, though highly strung.

Without trying to read too much between these lines, it would appear that the third member of the committee, Mr Lees Smith, the Labour M.P., who in a minority report disagreed with every word of them, was a poor judge of character; for it is no disparagement of Miss Savidge to say that though the majority report also spoke of her "youthful and childlike manner," its earlier summing up of her qualities suggests that she was not the "simple and somewhat childlike witness" whom he saw. She was, in fact, a self-possessed young woman, and, like most people, probably much preferred to be thought intelligent and acute than simple.

Though the majority report was tactfully phrased, it completely exonerated the police. For this reason the inquiry was valuable; but it is a question whether as a rule committees of this kind, whose terms of reference are strictly limited, are really worth while. Cases involving the arrest of couples are cordially disliked by the normal policeman, and, usually, therefore, he does not, as his detractors profess to believe, rush in on the spur of the moment to arrest any couple whom he happens to see sitting together after dark. He much prefers, if he feels he must do something about it, to warn them and move them on. If he does take stronger action it is most probably because he has been instructed to do so. Either he is engaged in one of the periodical 'sweeps,' to use a naval term, in Hyde Park or Paddington or wherever it may be (they appear to be as useless as some committees), or he has been on the watch for some particular couple, or for one of them, again on instructions. In other words, behind some of these squalid cases there is much that can never be made public, and if the police are accused of mishandling them they may have to defend themselves with one arm, as it were, tied behind their backs. Committees who investigate their conduct may be equally shackled. Among others whom the shoe pinches are newspaper editors, who also must often know far more than they can tell, but this does not always deter them from joining in the hunt for a scapegoat.

There was a sequel to Miss Savidge's adventures. Not long afterwards Sir Leo Chiozza Money was convicted of molesting a young woman in a railway carriage. There being no opening here for an attack upon the police, no fuss whatever was made.

4

As General Horwood approached sixty, and the date of his retirement, he may sometimes have wished that he had resigned, as he once talked of doing, some years earlier. Hopes of a quiet time, organizing and ministering to what had been a somewhat unsettled police force, a task for which he was eminently fitted, had scarcely been realized. There was little or no trouble within the force, but few of the Commissioner's eight years in office were without very serious problems and worries affecting it, none of which could be foreseen in 1920.

Horwood had been less than three years at Scotland Yard, and the series of incidents in Hyde Park and elsewhere had already begun, when he had a very narrow escape from death. 1922 was the year of the Armstrong trial. The little solicitor was originally charged with poisoning a fellow-lawyer, and at his trial for the murder of his wife it was suggested that he had made an earlier attempt to get rid of his local rival by means of arsenic injected into chocolates. This may well have put the idea into the demented brain of a man named Tatam, who in November that year tried to poison several senior police officials in London by the same method and the same poison. Of his intended victims only the Commissioner ate any of the sweets. Most unluckily for himself, Horwood had just had a birthday, and was expecting a box of chocolates.

He had barely recovered from an illness that was nearly fatal when throughout the country the effects of the industrial depression became acute. Governments came and went, and the police had to get used to three new Home Secretaries in two years. More distasteful arrests of well-known personages drew disproportionate attention to that side of police work; and then, in the middle of all this, came the stoppage of work known as the General Strike.

This began at midnight on May the 3rd, 1926, and it was over in a week. So far as its declared objects were concerned, it was a complete failure; but during that week conditions in London and other big cities were very strange. For the first day or two there was hardly any public transport. The few newspapers that appeared shrank to the size of the old news-sheets. Millions of people, who could not get lifts in cars, were walking to their places of business, while other millions, who were not working, stood about in rather dejected-looking groups, watching the results of obedience to orders which many of them were reluctant to obey. Factory fires were out, and only once before in recent times, during the coal strike of 1911, had skies been so clear and visibility so good. By the 5th, however, the unprecedented situation was seen to be well in hand. Volunteers, including thousands of the unemployed, were helping to run trains, omnibuses, and trams. Strikers were drifting back to work. It was already obvious that the strike was doomed, unless the trade-union leaders were prepared to counsel more drastic action, and from this they shrank, or were too sensible even to consider it.

It was, in fact, creditable to almost all concerned that throughout this week order was on the whole maintained, people were fed, and transport for normal purposes was found. The authorities were prepared, the mass of the populace reacted as one man against intimidation, and the strikers themselves, few of whom were of the stuff of which revolutionaries are made, behaved in general with sense and decorum. But the situation was full of dangerous possibilities; and that serious trouble was averted was very largely due to the restraint and tact shown by the police. Theirs was perhaps the most responsible job of all. When the strike was over *The Times* raised a very large sum in contributions from grateful citizens, to be administered as a fund for the benefit of the police forces of the country. With the Savidge case and others of its kind due in the near future, the London policeman who thus found himself a hero was soon to have cause again to reflect on the fickleness of popular favour.

Among the weapons upon which the trade-union leaders had chiefly relied was a complete paralysis of the Press. This was not achieved even for one day; but to ensure the dissemination of news the Government produced its own *British Gazette*, No. 1 coming out on May the 5th. Scotland Yard was even earlier in the field with a daily summary of events which was distributed to police stations throughout the Metropolitan Area. If these sheets naturally took a rosy view from the first, this was proved to be justified; and they gave the London police, in compact form, information of every aspect of the strike.

During the critical first days there was no disorder except in the docks area; 8000 of the original special constables and 3000 recruits had enrolled at once, and more were coming in in large numbers; by the 5th of May *The Times* and *Daily Mirror* were being published as single sheets, independent omnibuses were on the streets, and even some of those owned by the London General Omnibus Company, and the Great Western Railway was running a hundred trains. Altogether more than five hundred were running. On the 6th the police learnt that Ramsay MacDonald, Smith, Cook, and other Labour leaders were already trying to find a way out. An omnibus had been put out of action at Hammersmith, and windows had been broken in Old Rectory Road, down Stepney way. Two hundred ex-cavalrymen and polo-players under Major-General Vaughan had been added to the Mounted Police; naval ratings were guarding sixteen vital points in the London District, the Scots Guards were at Deptford, and two destroyers were lying in the Thames. More daily papers were coming out. While on the 7th the rioters were being sentenced at the Old Street and West London courts for assaults upon the police, foot and mounted men were having to clear the East India Dock Road; but police preparations caused a proposed demonstration in the West End to be abandoned. Two hundred R.A.C. motor-cyclist scouts were attached to divisions, and the Underground Railway was running again. The police were reminded that it was a criminal offence to spread alarmist rumours: they must take action against transgressors; among the rumours being circulated were such fables as mutinies in the Army and by the whole of the Liverpool police.

As the failure of the strike became every day more obvious, and men streamed back to work, extremists, roughs, and criminals became more troublesome. On May the 9th thirty-seven arrests were made in the Harrow Road, where omnibuses were stoned, and there was window-smashing in Camden Town. The police showed great tact and forbearance in dealing with attempts to intimidate drivers of food convoys. There was some nasty work near Nine Elms goods yard in Battersea, where a sergeant of L Division was attacked with a hammer, a special constable was stabbed, and twenty-one other policemen were slightly injured. Patrols of the Mounted Constabulary Reserve were used, and made an excellent impression. Twenty-five men of R Division were rushed in a tender to Charlton, near Woolwich, where an attempt was being made to set fire to the Midway Oil Storage Company's depot; the twenty-five made a baton charge and dispersed a crowd of 800. Metropolitan Police magistrates were giving rioters heavier sentences, and the strike leaders were now so alarmed by the conduct of paid Communists and hooligans, which they should have foreseen, that they were urging the better-behaved strikers to wear war medals. On that day, the 9th, 3000 trains were running, but some people were still walking twenty or thirty miles to work. The Special Constabulary had now reached something like double its war-time strength, and Sir Nevil Macready had come back to his old friends as Chief Staff Officer to the Commandant.

The strike was almost over. It came officially to an end on Wednesday, May the 12th. The last issue of Scotland Yard's daily summary quoted admiring comments, especially from America, on the way in which the British police, armed only with batons, which were seldom used, had controlled a national upheaval. "I have seen," wrote a Washington correspondent then on the spot, "more fighting in one night of a local steel strike in Pittsburg than there has been in all England this week." However peaceable the intentions of the great mass of the strikers, many of them were embittered men, and things might have gone very differently had they been handled in a less tolerant way; and nowhere was this more clearly the case than in the capital.

25

LORD BYNG

It was soon after the Savidge case burst upon the public that Lord Horwood announced his intention to retire on his sixtieth birthday, but the decision had been made some time before. The public did not know until he had gone that his last six months at Scotland Yard were clouded by an authentic scandal in the force which during the early part of his Commissionership he had done much to steady and improve. It must have been without regret that he left the unsavoury case of Sergeant Goddard to be cleared up by his successor.

In general 1928 was a year of misleading calm. Half a million more were at work than in the previous year. January saw the disastrous Thames floods, which caused the deaths of fourteen people trapped in basements along the London riverside, a tragedy that would have been averted had there been any one authority, instead of half a dozen, to give early warning. A sub-committee set up by the Ministry of Health reached the obvious conclusion that when such danger impended the police must receive instant information and instructions to pass it on. A belated precaution taken was the strengthening of the Embankment wall. The Savidge case led to the appointment in August of a Royal Commission, under Lord Lee of Fareham, to consider police powers and procedure.

Early in the year anonymous letters began to come to Scotland Yard accusing the police of taking bribes from owners of night clubs and disorderly houses in the Soho region of London. The division concerned was C, and a woman signing herself "Richette" named Sergeant Goddard, a station sergeant at Vine Street Police Station, as the principal culprit. Goddard had been employed for six years on the duty of suppressing brothels and gambling dens, and keeping an eye on the activities of ostensibly reputable night clubs which were, in fact, constantly infringing liquor and other regulations. He had an excellent record in the force, but the matter had to be inquired into; and as early as May Chief Constable Wensley, of the C.I.D., was instructed to investigate the case. Without Goddard's fore-knowledge the 43 Club in Gerrard Street was raided, with the result that its proprietor, Mrs

Meyrick, a well-known character of the time, received a sentence of six months' imprisonment; but nothing directly incriminating Goddard himself was brought to light. More stories about him, however, were coming in, and he appeared to be living in a style as a rule unattainable by police sergeants. Wensley now turned his staff to unravelling Goddard's financial position.

All this had to be done very cautiously, and it took time. How much Goddard suspected can only be conjectured. September had come, and Mrs Meyrick was out of prison and had opened another club, when the Commissioner received an anonymous letter neatly typed on the headed paper of a celebrated West End store. The writer offered to reveal his name and come forward as a witness if necessary, and he appeared to be so well informed about Goddard's actions that Horwood sent a message by hand to the secretary of the store to arrange an immediate interview. Whatever came of this, the investigation of the sergeant's finances simultaneously reached the stage when he could be asked to throw some light upon them. It was now known that he had deposit accounts totalling £2700 at two different banks, a house worth £2000, and a valuable car; he was also renting safes from two safe-deposit companies. He told a story of successful betting transactions and speculations in the shares of a music publisher's, but, confronted with Wensley's knowledge of the safes, he broke down. He was found to have hidden away in this manner upward of £12,000 in notes.

All was up with him now; on October the 23rd he was suspended, and on the 29th he came before a disciplinary board and pleaded guilty to discreditable conduct in gambling with undesirable characters and to neglect of duty in failing to account for sums of money he had received when directed to do so. Dismissed from the force with forfeiture of all pension rights, he was arrested and charged at Bow Street, on December the 18th, with conspiring with Mrs Meyrick, Luigi Ribuffi, and Mrs Gadda to pervert the course of justice. With Mrs Meyrick and Ribuffi, Mrs Gadda having fled the country, he stood in the dock at the Central Criminal Court at the end of January 1929. The judge was Avory. Goddard was sentenced to eighteen months' hard labour, fined £2000, and made to pay the costs of the prosecution. Avory very rightly passed sentences almost as heavy—fifteen months' hard labour—on both Mrs Meyrick and Ribuffi.

An important witness against the accused was a detective constable who had worked regularly under Goddard, and had received gifts from him. The use of this evidence raised a delicate question. In order to obtain it the man was promised immunity from punishment, but obviously he could not remain in the force. To dismiss him, however, would in such circumstances normally have meant the forfeiture of his pension. But this would be a punishment, and it was contrived that he should retain his pension rights, a solution that caused questions to be asked in Parliament.

Moylan comments on this case that "it was widely and justly remarked, as a reassuring feature, that it was the police themselves who brought the facts so fully to light."[1] And the whole facts, though they do not exculpate Goddard, suggest that he may perhaps be regarded as one of many victims of a most unhealthy aspect of the social life of London during this period between two great wars. At any time such duties as his include association with the most dubious characters, many of them foreigners of the lowest type. When Goddard's own financial transactions were traced, among the names of persons who had bribed him or who had changed the notes of small denomination he received into banknotes of £5, £50, or £100, only one, Mrs Meyrick's, was English. During the investigation a Dutchman, a Roumanian, a Belgian, Italians, French men and women, and several foreign Jews emerged momentarily from the sordid obscurity in which they carried on their usually discreditable occupations. This type, as often as not, has a foot in both camps; those who themselves run brothels or illegal clubs act as informants against their rivals. In this demoralizing atmosphere, with money flowing like water, police officers, not ever well paid, have to keep their heads and their integrity; and never have there been bigger temptations than when Sergeant Goddard himself was tempted and fell. Side by side with millions of unemployed, and amid talk of national bankruptcy, a small group of people with more money than sense was making vice so profitable that Mrs Meyrick and her like could afford bribes for protection on a scale unknown before or since. It was the heyday of the drug traffic; fantastic sums were paid for pinches of cocaine, Brilliant Chang, with his Chinese restaurant in Regent Street, was making a fortune, and unhappy drug addicts, young girls like Billie Carlton and Freda Kempton—an habitué of Mrs Meyrick's 43 Club—were killing themselves from depression or despair. In 1920 it was found necessary to pass a Dangerous Drugs Act to strengthen Home Office regulations, and in 1923, when there were 295 prosecutions under it, to increase the penalties it imposed. A drug pedlar sentenced to three years' penal servitude had opium worth £9000 in his possession.[2] The traffic was got under

[1] Moylan, *op. cit.*
[2] Troup, *op. cit.*

some control, but other deleterious conditions of this side of London life were to outlast Sergeant Goddard's professional career.

2

This state of things was symptomatic of a national malaise, a phase of anxiety and shiftlessness affecting every class of the community, and therefore affecting the police themselves. Like the rest of his countrymen, the police officer saw the future, which a few years ago had seemed secure, becoming problematical and even menacing. His guaranteed scale of pay had been threatened, and the threat still hung over him. In 1926, indeed, the doubling by statute of the superannuation deduction from that pay came to the same thing as a cut in it. Uncertainties and misgivings to which we have grown accustomed were unpleasant novelties in the 1920's, and the policeman—especially if he was a London policeman—found himself a sort of permanent butt for prevailing scepticism. In ten years ten inquisitive tribunals—a Royal Commission, Parliamentary and departmental committees and sub-committees, and other bodies—had been probing into his affairs. Apart from the recommendations of the Desborough Committee, little concrete help had emerged, while in general these inquiries implied a readiness in high quarters to listen to any adverse criticism. Most of it was directed at the Metropolitan Police. Ten years of this would unsettle any force, at any time; and, with the times themselves out of joint, it was doubly mischievous.

A Commissioner who had seemed just the right man at the hopeful beginning of this period perhaps lacked the qualities increasingly necessary as the situation deteriorated. The Government, at any rate, outlining the requisites looked for in Horwood's successor, used such terms as "idealism" and "re-inspiration." What was wanted, said the Home Secretary, Herbert Samuel, was "a man who would restore to the police and the public that confidence which I have been told on both sides of the House—particularly by the late Home Secretary—has been missing for a time." Inspiring leaders should not be rare in English public life; and it was another symptom of an unhappy period—it cannot have been altogether coincidence—that it proved unusually difficult to fill a post which confers considerable distinction. For the first time, on such a scale, there were excuses and refusals. No one appeared to want the job. The Government turned at last to a man who had almost every qualification, but whose age and ill-health fully entitled him to rest on laurels won in many quarters of the globe. The one argument he could not question was brought forward; it was a call of duty; and Lord Byng became the twelfth Commissioner of the Metropolitan Police.

He was a remarkable man—perhaps, considering his whole career, with two exceptions the most remarkable of the series. Before commanding the Third Army in France he had commanded the Canadian Corps, not an easy position for a regular British officer, set in his ways, to fill successfully. Byng was so popular with his Canadians that his appointment, in 1921, as Governor-General of Canada was hailed there with acclamation, and in the Dominion he was better liked than ever. This was his secret; he had "a genius for friendship,"[1] without which, and the simplicity that went with it, his other great gifts could not have fulfilled themselves as they did. Because, however, he was another soldier, with no experience of police work, hackneyed cries were raised when it was announced that he was going to Scotland Yard. The force was to be "disciplined," there was to be more militarization, and all the rest of it. Byng's character being by then so well known, this outcry was more foolish than usual. The party to which those who made it belonged was in power again within eight months of his appointment, and, characteristically, he went at once to the Home Secretary, Clynes, with an offer to resign. "I am the most readily 'sack-able' person in the world, so please don't hesitate." Ministers having learnt more than some of their supporters, he was told that the Government had complete confidence in him; and it was to be said of his short Commissionership that "it had passed as had all other appointments held by Lord Byng; with comfort and pleasure in their duties by those serving under him, and with good results from the point of view of the public."[2]

It was inevitable that his term would be short. He had fought at El Teb and Tamai in 1884, he was now sixty-six—by which age almost every previous Commissioner had retired—and for some time his heart had been causing anxiety. These were the only cogent reasons advanced against his appointment to the post. Obviously he could not hold it long. But Governments—there was to be yet another, the sixth in nine years, before he did retire—were living from day to day. "The problem of national finance overshadowed all others. Each successive Government since the War had shirked its plain duty in this matter."[3] By 1928 things had reached the stage when Ministers, of whatever party, felt that every year without a major crisis was a gain. The worst might be averted if, for a little while longer, a troubled

[1] Captain Cyril Falls, in the *Dictionary of National Biography*.
[2] Tomlin, *op. cit.* [3] Marriott, *op. cit.*

society could be kept steady. The police were an important element, especially in the capital, and the Metropolitan force was not happy. To steady it, and "re-inspire"* it, was Byng's task.

A major crisis, however, was at hand. By 1929 Great Britain felt the full effect of financial disaster abroad. The total of unemployed was approaching 3,000,000, and the consequent debt to the State of the Insurance Fund was £115,000,000. This alone threatened national bankruptcy. The crash of the Hatry group did not reassure a nervous City. In this year King George V was ill, and the weather was more freakish than usual, with cold so intense in February that there was a shortage of water, and a temperature of 88 degrees in London in September, followed by gales which ripped away roofs, hoardings, and shop-fronts. The Thames rose dangerously again. These varied portents were the background against which, on May the 27th, the Metropolitan Police celebrated its centenary. A force of 10,000 men paraded in Hyde Park. Two months earlier the Lee Commission on powers and procedure, a thoroughly representative body, had issued its report. Its terms of reference covered the work of every police force in England and Wales, and the report, apart from some rather unpractical proposals, ran on lines that might have been expected. Among 60,000 men there were bound to be occasional cases of misconduct. The majority had never been better behaved, and the public was well protected against the actions of the rare exceptions. As a whole the police were competent and highly efficient. It had all been said before.

3

Byng found the force he was to command some 250 below its establishment of 20,029. The establishment varies from year to year, according to internal adjustments; in 1929, when it was augmented by 250, the deficiency had fallen to 94. With so much unemployment, there was no shortage of would-be recruits, but the standard of physique and education required was too often higher than that of the applicants. Indifferent education was often the stumbling-block; "in 1928, for example, more than 30 per cent. of the applicants who were satisfactory so far as regards character and physique had to be rejected as being too illiterate."[1] To look a little ahead, in 1931, the blackest of all these black years, when the Metropolitan Police alone had the

[1] Moylan, *op. cit.* H. M. Howgrave-Graham, in *Light and Shade at Scotland Yard*, gives the following reply to a question in a general-knowledge paper: "The Battle of Trafalgar was fought in 1066, on and around the ground which is now called Trafalgar Square. It was a victory for the English against Oliver Cromwell and his men."

record number of 42,000 applications—70 per cent. over the total for 1930—only 30 per cent. of the applicants had been to secondary schools.

Byng's character and reputation, and his way with men, were his greatest assets as a steadier and inspirer of the force. He was also essentially a practical man, and his three years' Commissionership is notable for the number of reforms, designed to increase efficiency, which he introduced or fostered. At Scotland Yard itself, where a decade had passed since the last vigorous new broom had swept through its corridors and obscure little rooms, Macready's new men had in their turn grown elderly, and perhaps, under Horwood's less stimulating rule, rather hide-bound. Byng retired several senior officers, replacing them with fresh blood. He instituted the Information Room; and it was in his time that Superintendent Battley, the head of the Fingerprint Department, put the finishing touch to Henry's work by creating the Single Fingerprint Collection. To trace the duplicate of a single casual print in a Main Fingerprint Collection containing one or two million sets of ten prints was, in Goss's words, "almost an insuperable task." Battley, with the assistance of Inspector Cherrill (as he then was), devised a further classification of Henry's formulæ by which, using a special lens, it became as easy to turn up a wanted single print as it already was to find a complete set.

While tightening discipline, the new Commissioner, by his introduction and encouragement of innovations, made routine police duty more interesting as well as more efficient, with corresponding benefit to the public. He reorganized beats, doing away with the traditional regularity which criminals had only to study to know when the coast would be clear. The man on the beat, for his part, now had a fresh incentive to keep his eyes open. In the meantime traffic patrols, and the replacement of fixed points by automatic signals, first permanently set up in Oxford Street in July 1931, released men and eased the ever-increasing work of the Traffic Department. A Road Traffic Act passed in 1930 had introduced pedestrian crossings and the Highway Code.

There was a greatly increased use of cars. These vehicles, squad cars, area cars, and 'Q' cars (so called because car and crew are disguised in the manner of 'Q' ships), kept in touch by wireless with the Information Room at Scotland Yard, where before long another novelty, the '999' dialling system, increased at a bound the percentage of immediate arrests. In particular, this system has proved its value to the Flying Squad in connexion with smash-and-grab raids, to counter which the Squad had originally been formed in Macready's time. It then consisted of nothing more than two vans per division, used to speed the arrival of C.I.D. officers at the scene of a raid. From this small and utilitarian beginning the Squad rapidly expanded, both in means and methods, and it had been on an established basis a decade before the '999' system greatly enhanced its usefulness.

Byng's adaptability in a rapidly changing world, unusual in a man of his profession who had been born during the American Civil War, is shown by his ready adoption of so many new things; but it must not be thought that he, or Scotland Yard, always led the way in applying scientific innovations to police work. Almost every Continental capital had a police laboratory, and by Byng's time some English provincial forces had small laboratories of their own; the Metropolitan Police was still without one. Police telephone-boxes in this country were introduced by a Chief Constable of Sunderland, and automatic traffic signals were first tried in the provinces—among other places, at Brighton, where in 1933 another enterprising Chief Constable was to equip his officers with pocket radio-sets. About this time the Lancashire Constabulary was experimenting with a teleprinter.[1] The larger county and borough forces had long been out of leading-strings, and with their own scientists and efficient detective departments were relying less and less, in cases of serious crime, on help from the Metropolitan C.I.D.

In this connexion it may be noted that in 1930 the first was heard of a scheme which, in a modified but more controversial form, was soon to cause a considerable to-do. This was the creation of a national police college. The Police Council, an *ad hoc* body representing the higher authorities and the central committees of the Police Federation, set up a committee to consider the proposal; but national problems of a much graver kind were now moving so fast and so far that the scheme got no further than discussion.

4

In the autumn of 1931 the long-feared financial crisis arrived with shattering effect. A National Government was formed in August, and within a month the Bank of England warned the Prime Minister, Ramsay MacDonald, that £200,000,000 in gold had been withdrawn by foreign investors, that the drain was continuing, that a credit raised in August was exhausted, and that something must be done about it at once. On September the 21st, a day of gloom, the Stock Exchange was closed, and gold payments were suspended.

The immediate cause of the crisis was the issue, on July the 31st,

[1] E. H. Glover, *The English Police* (1934).

of the report of a committee set up in February, under Sir George May, to consider how the country could economize. If the report caused alarm abroad, it raised a howl at home. Its proposals, if carried out, would affect everybody; and while everybody professed to see the need for economy, it must be at some one else's expense. Ministers and judges kept silence in face of a threatened cut in salaries of from 10 per cent. to 20 per cent., but teachers, who were expected to lose 15 per cent., were infuriated, and, most ominous of all, proposed deductions from the pay of the services and the police had immediate and serious repercussions. It had been thought that, when all else failed, the Navy could be trusted; but the Atlantic Fleet, assembled for autumn manœuvres at Invergordon, was shaken by a mutiny. It was on a minor scale, but it caused the exercises to be abandoned. The police, perhaps, had had enough of mutinies, and, through their Federation, they now had constitutional means of making their resentment felt. They did not, however, neglect more spectacular methods, though these, again, were employed in a constitutional manner.

In their case the cut in pay originally proposed by the May Commission was 12½ per cent. This was amended to 10 per cent., half to be deducted immediately and half in a year's time. It was felt that, apart from the financial loss, the reduction ran counter to the recommendations of the Desborough Committee and the Police Act of 1919, which every policeman in the country regarded as permanently establishing his status and rights. To bring this grievance before the public, permission was obtained from the Home Secretary for a mass meeting at the Albert Hall. It was attended by 12,000 delegates from every part of the kingdom, and the proceedings were carried to an end in a perfectly orderly manner.

As probably was foreseen, this form of protest failed to influence the Government. Legislation to enforce the cuts was hurried through, and the first deduction of 5 per cent. then came into force, together with the other economies laid down. But though the Cabinet was determined, it was extremely anxious about the possible outcome of these steps. In especial, how would the police react—particularly the Metropolitan force, which from its numbers and its prominence could powerfully influence the attitude of the whole? Byng had done much to pull it together after the unsettling experiences of the mutinies and the later troubles, but at this very time it was under fire again, the annual criminal statistics for 1930 having shown a serious increase in crime. This was not unconnected with unemployment and the general national malaise, but the police were blamed, and those of the capital, with its national Press and its population of 8,000,000—more than a fifth of the total for England and Wales—as usual attracted a disproportionate share of censure, or at least of attention. The Goddard case and the series of inquiries into police conduct and discipline were very recent. There had been laxity, and not only in the instances that became public knowledge; and it was not realized how great an improvement had been brought about by three years of strong but benevolent rule. On the other hand, the authorities knew that a longer time was needed fully to restore the force to contentment and stability. And now, instead of allowing it a further breathing-space, fresh trouble and resentment must be stirred up by an encroachment on what 20,000 men regarded as their guaranteed rights.

Such was the situation when Byng, on medical advice, felt compelled to retire. In addition to his weak heart, he suffered from what he called his "old tubes," and he had to spend the worst part of every winter in South Africa or the South of France. "It is a good indication," says one who knew him well, "of the extent to which his services were valued that even when this disability became apparent, the authorities pressed him not to retire, as he was perfectly ready to do at any time."[1] He is reported to have said that he was called in to Scotland Yard as a soothing influence; and one of his first questions on his appointment was, "Are they a happy family there?" Informed that they were not altogether happy, he remarked that this must be attended to; it was important. But he was much more than a soothing influence. He was a very active force for good. He travelled about the divisions to get to know his men, and if he met them casually would talk to them in the most informal way, and few Commissioners have gained so much real affection. He shared with his successor, Lord Trenchard, a dislike of paper-work, especially of the stereotyped official kind, his usual word for which was "garbage" (Trenchard employed a stronger one). His encouragement of new inventions was inspired by a practical sense of what was useful, and therefore should be used[2]—but not by himself; he detested scientific mechanisms, and only with difficulty was persuaded to use his telephone. A strong preference for doing things, instead of writing about them, may have sprung from an instinctive knowledge of the value of his own personality, not the least important factor of which was a sense of the comic unusual in high places. During his three years, as during the three which were to follow, the rather arid

[1] Howgrave-Graham, *op. cit.*

[2] In the 1914–18 War he was the only Army Commander who from the first believed in tanks.

annals of Commissioners' sayings were much lightened by humour, often directed at official solemnity and routine waste of time, but just as often some spontaneous piece of absurdity. Mr Howgrave-Graham, whose book, already quoted, is full of good stories of the police, tells two characteristic ones of Byng. The latter drew his secretary to the window and pointed at "a very old and disreputable rag-and-bone man who was trundling a barrow slowly along the side of the road. 'Do you see that man with the barrow? I think it is one of my nephews. It's certainly very like him. Would you find out, please?'" It was after Byng had retired from Scotland Yard, and not long before his death, at the age of seventy-three, in 1935, that he was rather belatedly created a Field-Marshal. His grandfather, the first Earl of Stafford, who had commanded a brigade at Waterloo, had held this rank, and it was an honour the grandson prized above all others. But, however deeply Byng's feelings were concerned, he never lost his lightness of touch. To a congratulatory letter he replied: "My pleasure at being made a Marshal is nothing to my Lady's delight in becoming a Snelgrove."

Byng was appointed Commissioner at a critical time in the history of the force; and an early instance of his reliance on the personal factor, in other words, on his own personality, was his handling of the Press. The publicity given to the Savidge case and others of its kind, and then to the Goddard scandal, was by exaggerated presentation having a very bad effect on a ruffled and unsettled police. Byng's remedy was to approach Lord Riddell, the Chairman of the Newspaper Proprietors' Association, and address a meeting of that powerful body, with the best possible effects. For two or three years—a long period of editorial restraint—the doings of the Metropolitan Police almost ceased to be news.[1] Retirement came at the height of another crisis, of national dimensions. The police, in addition to having their pay cut, felt that they were being unjustly blamed for the increase of crime. With Byng's departure from Scotland Yard becoming imminent, much of the ground he had regained was once more lost, and the Government was faced with the new difficulty of finding some one fit to take his place.

[1] Howgrave-Graham, *op. cit.*

26

LORD TRENCHARD

SUCCESSFUL experiments are usually repeated; and again a Commissioner was found who had spent all his life with the armed forces, who had no experience of police work, and who had passed middle age. In 1931 Lord Trenchard was fifty-eight. A Major-General in 1916, when he had never piloted an aircraft, by 1919 he was Chief of the Air Staff, and in 1927 Marshal of the Royal Air Force, which in the interim he had more or less created. He is known as the "Father" of the R.A.F., and he shares with the reigning monarch the distinction of having his birthday annually commemorated by the force. As a soldier his military and administrative experience included the command of Imperial Yeomanry, the Bushman Corps, the Canadian Scouts, the Southern Nigeria Regiment, and the West African Frontier Force, and all this before the war in Europe provided him with his great opportunity. The Government, anxious about the spirit of the Metropolitan Police in the existing crisis, and seeking another strong character in which the gift of getting on with men was combined with organizing ability and driving-power, turned to Lord Trenchard; and after considerable pressure he was induced, as Byng had been, to take up fresh duties.

He is still very well remembered at Scotland Yard. Like Byng and Macready, he left the stamp of his vigorous personality on every department. It has been remarked that he had Byng's dislike of paperwork. He hated writing letters or anything else. Everything was dictated, while he strode about the room. But it was no ordinary dictation—as with Marshal Foch, clipped, cryptic sentences had to be interpreted, and this could be done only by some one who had come to know him well. Sometimes there had to be conferences to decide what he really did mean. References to people were complicated by his inability to get their names right. The correct name of the Secretary, whom he saw daily, defeated him for a long time, and he always spoke of another old friend as Sir John "Moylam." He showed even less patience than Byng with what he thought was unnecessary scribbling; rude epithets would be scrawled over portentous documents, and some junior clerk might suddenly find the immensely tall figure looming over him, and hear a voice rumbling, "Why are you writing that letter?" The nervous writer would try to explain. "Yes, but why? *Why?*" Only when the Commissioner had left the room, and the subject of this visitation had been able to pull himself together, would it dawn on him that the whole sacred business of drafting and minuting and form-filling had been called in question. There were some who after four years never understood what Lord Trenchard was driving at; but it was all immensely stimulating.

He became Commissioner in November 1931. The first annual report he signed being for that year, it dealt almost exclusively with events with which he was in no way connected, but he must have agreed in deprecating public alarm about increase of crime. The report pointed out that this was not altogether justified. The statistical method used made things appear worse than they were, and economic conditions had much to do with what increase there was. A rather disturbing feature, for which the police were blamed, the number of cases of crime in which no arrest, or no prompt arrest, was made, was largely due to a factor less generally appreciated then than it is now—the use of stolen cars as a means of escape. An inquiry into the whole question had been started in 1930, and the results of a reorganization and redistribution of resources, and of the introduction of new methods, to be continued by the new Commissioner, were already apparent.

But it was not chiefly to deal with increase of crime that Trenchard had been pressed into service. The effect of economic conditions on the force itself was the immediate danger. Behind the decorum of meetings at the Albert Hall lay a deep sense of grievance, and the malcontent element which can never be eradicated from any large organized body of men was once more gaining ground. Having a definite aim, and being energetic, this small minority was always trying to push its way into the councils of the Police Federation. Even after the clean-up in 1919, and the reorganization of the Boards, Macready had found that the latter were sometimes inclined to take too much upon themselves; under Horwood this tendency had grown, and now, with political support, Parliament being bitterly divided over the question of national economy, the extremists' influence had increased, was increasing, and had to be diminished. During 1932, while Trenchard was considering and drafting his famous second annual report, he was keeping a close watch on these activities; and in December he issued a sharp warning in Police Orders. "Metropolitan Police Branch Board. An instance has come to the Commissioner's notice of a Divisional

Committee of Constables passing a vote of censure on a Constable in connection with his work in the Force. Action of this character must altogether cease. Any further case with be severely dealt with."

In the process of scraping the barrel all sorts of economies were considered, and this year saw the issue of the report of a select committee which had been inquiring into the whole police system of England and Wales. It must have come as a surprise to many people to learn that there were 182 separate police forces south of the Tweed. Some had an authorized establishment of twenty-five men or less. Eighty-six altogether had establishments of a hundred or under. One county and one borough force served districts with populations of less than 10,000. The purpose of the select committee was to work out a scheme for amalgamating these small forces with larger units, which would mean a saving of money and an increase of efficiency. The Metropolitan Police was, of course, not affected. There may have been an ulterior motive behind obvious reasons of economy; it was thought at the time that the Home Office was feeling its way towards the creation of a National Police Force, a plan which Peel had been compelled to forgo a hundred years earlier.

2

A member of the general public, asked to specify Lord Trenchard's "reforms," might very likely remember only one—the Police College and its products, "Trenchard's Young Men." His short-service system might perhaps also be recalled. These two experiments, and what was called an attack on the Police Federation, were the features of his second annual report, for the year 1932, and of the subsequent White Paper, upon which Press and public seized with indignation or approval according to the point of view. Parliamentary debates further riveted attention on them. Certainly it is little realized to-day, outside the Metropolitan Police, how many other reforms of lasting value Lord Trenchard accomplished in his short term of office.

Not all these reforms were proposed in the Commissioner's second report, which concentrated on the more controversial items. The first was discipline, with special reference to interference by the Police Federation, and it was inevitable that a small section of the force, and its supporters outside, should talk of attacks and misrepresentation. It was a partisan matter, and few can now doubt the essential justice of Trenchard's comments on the behaviour of a faction in the Federation, already alluded to. Like the increase of crime, the revival of discontented elements was a sign of the times. The Commissioner gave chapter and verse for his charges of deliberate attempts to stir up trouble. Insubordinate notices had been pinned up at police stations. A constable had been censured by a committee for a perfectly proper action. The training of 'specials' was misrepresented, and the Federation had been distributing mischievous propaganda. It was a recrudescence, if on a small scale, of the portents before the mutinies, and it was no news to the Government, which had called in Trenchard expressly to deal with it, among other things.

The report went on to discuss, in language which, whether dictated or interpreted, was Trenchard's own, the wide question of conditions in the force. The Police Act of 1919, based on the recommendations of the Desborough Committee, had not made much change in the type of men joining the Metropolitan Police, or in the life they led there. The standard of education was no better: the proportion of entrants who had not gone beyond the elementary stage remained far too high, 80 or 90 per cent., yet there were now four times as many boys with secondary-school education as there had been in 1919. This type was not attracted in sufficient numbers to the police. Then came the crux of the Commissioner's argument: there had been throughout the history of the force too rigid an adherence to Peel's doctrine that the force should be filled up from below, the material for higher ranks being supplied exclusively by the lower ranks. This was too narrow a view for modern times and circumstances. The 1929 Committee on Police Powers and Procedure had emphasized the great importance of selecting superior officers who could exercise a high standard of influence and example; but how were such officers to be found? Long experience and good service in the lower ranks were not the most important qualifications for high position.

There was nothing new in this. The same points had been made by the committee set up in 1930 by the Police Council to discuss the formation of a Police College, referred to in the previous chapter. This committee had included representatives of the Home Office, Scotland Yard, the Inspectors of Constabulary, and the chief officers of provincial forces. It noted that as far back as 1868 it had been suggested that Peel's system of promotion, adequate for a force of 3000 men, was not suitable for one of 8000; it was still less applicable to one of 20,000 sixty years later. Policemen work alone, and an inspector had not the opportunities of an officer in the Army of gauging the capabilities of his men. Inspectors themselves had as a rule served for at least seven years, and often much longer, as constables and sergeants. Desirable though it was that the higher posts should be filled by men with police experience, duties in the lower ranks, as things were, did not foster a broad outlook or gifts of leadership.

The 1930 committee's scheme for tackling the problem by means of a Police College, to provide higher and specialized training for selected officers from all the police forces in the country, remained in abeyance. Trenchard now adapted it to the needs of the Metropolitan Police, and included some novel propositions of his own. It was over these that heated controversy arose. They were amplified in a White Paper published in May 1933. It was imperative, said this document,[1] that the basis of recruitment should be broadened to adapt the Metropolitan force to modern requirements. The existing system had never yet produced a Commissioner, or (with one exception) a Deputy or Assistant Commissioner. All but a few of the Chief Constables had been brought in from outside. In general, young and active control was required, with a directing and supervising staff of many types, having good education and wide outlook. Constables with the requisite education, character, and personality had insufficient opportunities of advancement, because the preponderance of lower ranks made promotion slow; and knowledge of this deterred many such men from joining the force. It was therefore proposed, said the White Paper, to create a Police College for the Metropolitan Police. The entrants to this college would be chosen by competitive selection not only from the younger elements in the force—that is, from constables—but also from candidates from public and elementary schools and the universities. There was to be approximately two years' training at the college, with two (or three) examinations on Civil Service lines, from which, however, candidates from outside the force might be exempted if they had already reached an adequate educational standard. All candidates on passing out would be promoted to the new grade of Junior Station Inspector, and sent direct to divisions. There was one list for the uniform branch and the C.I.D. The White Paper gave reasons for the limitation of this experiment to the Metropolitan Police. Apart from its size, this has its own large-scale problems, besides having as its statutory authority the Home Secretary, not a committee, as is the case with county and borough forces.

Following as it did on the annual report, with its "attack" on the Police Federation, it could be taken for granted that the proposal to introduce outsiders, and educated ones at that, would cause a bitter outcry. Whatever the merits or demerits of the scheme, "seldom," to

[1] *Memorandum on the Subject of Certain Changes in the Organisation and Administration of the Metropolitan Police* (H.M.S.O., 1933).

quote Mr Howgrave-Graham, "has so much wrong-headed nonsense been talked on a serious subject."[1] Nonsense was to be expected, but this was particularly wrong-headed because, either deliberately or from ignorance, Trenchard's motives were grossly misrepresented. If he wished to create an "officer class"—largely, incidentally, from within the force—it was with the sole aim of increasing efficiency and *esprit de corps*, a seriously felt want. It was, of course, called militarization, and it was even suggested that the Commissioner and the Government, in wishing to raise the educational standard of a section of the force, were laying a deep plot to divide it, in order to render it more amenable in times of industrial unrest—a typical example of a type of outlook which still, after the experience of a hundred and twenty years, professes to regard our thoroughly civilian police as a potential enemy of the rest of the public. A mere glance at reports of the debates in the House of Commons on the legislation introduced to carry the White Paper's proposals into effect amply bears out the comment of Mr Howgrave-Graham, who, as Secretary, had to listen to them. With the exception of a few newspapers which would naturally be hostile, Press opinion was favourable to the idea of higher education for policemen, with reservations on the wisdom of bringing in outsiders.

The attitude of the force itself had yet to be learnt. The small vocal element, the extremists of the Federation, was, of course, against the whole thing. The Federation as a whole not unnaturally took a poor view of separate proposals in the White Paper and the Bill to restrict its scope. Higher-grade inspectors, for instance, were to be excluded from membership. Here, however, the grumblers were on weak ground; the junior representatives on Branch Boards had been getting out of hand again, and owing to their preponderance, as had happened with the old Representative Board, on which ranks were mixed, they exerted an unfortunate influence on senior and more sober members. With regard to the Police College, and the introduction, on however limited a scale, of outsiders, it cannot be pretended that these reforms were welcomed by more than a small minority in the force, and in retrospect they are still unpopular; but they never had a fair trial.

Parliament, Press, and public were on the whole less interested in this domestic matter than in the second of Trenchard's controversial proposals, incorporated in the Bill—that of a short-service system. This was, however, merely another form of approach to the same problem. Twenty-five years' service, with a slow system of promotion, but with a pension at the end of it, produced a type of policeman who

[1] *Op. cit.*

was content to plod along, doing his bare duty, but little more. If he showed initiative it might get him into trouble; there had been many widely publicized instances of this; inaction was safer, and less bother. The attitude has been heard of in other forms of public service to which pensions are attached. Trenchard's idea was to recruit a proportion of the force, about half, on a ten-year basis. Thus would be formed a body of young and active constables prepared to take responsibility. At the end of their ten years these men would receive a gratuity. The Commissioner fully realized the obvious weaknesses of the scheme, which he admitted was experimental; and as it was soon abandoned little need be said about it. The two systems of long and short service, running side by side, were incompatible; of the latter, it was at once pointed out that since it takes ten years to make a good policeman, it was a pity to get rid of a man just when he had learnt his job. A further result of the experiment became apparent only after it had been put into force; a number of the short-service recruits used their training at the London ratepayers' expense to obtain good posts in provincial forces. The abandonment of the scheme restored the *status quo ante*, with all its own imperfections, and no other alternative to this has yet been found.[1]

All this was in the future in 1933; the Bill passed, and the short-service system and the Police College came into being. For the latter a large house and its grounds near Hendon were taken over. The premises had been a country club, and then a factory. In a few years "Trenchard's Young Men," the Junior Station Inspectors, were finding their feet in a highly critical if not hostile atmosphere. As a body, together with the short-service system, they had a brief career, the College being closed in 1939, to be converted to other uses. A handful of individual graduates remain in the Metropolitan Police, but the rank of Junior Station Inspector has died out.

It must remain conjectural whether, in different circumstances, the original purpose of the College could have been achieved. When Lord Trenchard was at Scotland Yard he used to apply to himself the phrase used of Gladstone by Lord Randolph Churchill—"an old man in a hurry." He was not an old man, as men go nowadays; but he was in a hurry. It had never been his nature to make haste slowly, and, besides, he had taken on the Commissionership only on the understanding that he was to give it up in three or four years. He even then had his eye on the man who was to succeed him, and who was intended to carry on his plans to completion. If he himself had stayed on to attempt this it

[1] Howgrave-Graham, *op. cit.*; Glover, *op. cit.*

is at least possible that his character, energy, and popularity would have overcome the hostility which the Police College, alone among his many reforms, aroused both inside and outside the force. This, at any rate, is one view held; against it is a strong conviction that not even he could have made his ideal of a class of trained leaders, jumped up from nothing, palatable to the mass of the men they were to lead. The prejudice in the police against his "young men," and not merely against the outsiders, ran very deep, being based on common human instincts. It was, and is, supported by the old and reasonable argument that only fully trained policemen make good policemen; that only many years of general duty, not two of intensive training, can make a man fit for promotion. That they may not make him fit to "lead," in Trenchard's sense, is naturally not generally admitted, whatever committees may say.

Conceding the existence of the problem, it is not only an important one; it is of historic interest, because it involves an ideal—the democratic origins of regular constabulary forces in the British Isles. During the controversy about Trenchard's "young men" the argument was put forward that since the Army has what is termed an officer class, the police should have no objection to one. But there is no real analogy between the two cases. Military officers have for centuries been drawn from a certain section of society, and until recently there were very few men in the ranks who even thought themselves fit to lead. A very old tradition has thus stamped itself on regular troops. The police also have a tradition of respectable antiquity; and it is diametrically opposed to the military one. Every policeman inherits, by training and associations, Peel's doctrine of filling up the force from below. The least enterprising constable is, by this inheritance and the solitary nature of his duties, in his way an individualist. He is also, and he never really forgets it, a civilian. With one thing and another, it looks as though any officer class for the police will have to be found from its own resources. As to this, the ideas of the Police Council's committee of 1930 have now been realized, and there is a Police College at Ryton-on-Dunsmore which serves all the police forces in the country. Besides, however, being limited in its scope, this college is too new for any judgment to be formed as to its future influence on the question of leadership.

3

His two outstanding proposals apart, Lord Trenchard's reforms make an impressive list. To take them in the order arranged by Mr Howgrave-Graham, who was Secretary to the Metropolitan Police from 1927 to 1946, the next three are the Scientific Laboratory, the Driving School, and the Wireless School. All were given what was intended to be a temporary home at the Hendon Police College.

Only a few years before this was opened Sir John Moylan could write: "English criminal procedure and rules of evidence are not favourable to some of the scientific proofs which continental experts can produce, and English courts and juries are distrustful of them."[1] The fact that Scotland Yard was in the capital tended to prolong reliance on casual help from the best brains in science and pathology congregated there, a system against which Sir Bernard Spilsbury, among others, had protested. Things have moved fast since Trenchard decided that in certain respects the Metropolitan Police had lagged too long behind some of the provincial forces, to say nothing of what was happening abroad; and courts and juries now everywhere accept the most abstruse testimony, on the word and reputation of those who give it, without a blink. The Metropolitan Police Laboratory itself is in the forefront of its kind.

After an early trial of a legal adviser, which did not prove to be a workable solution,[2] a firm of solicitors, Messrs Wontner, was appointed to handle all such matters on behalf of the Metropolitan Police. Trenchard decided to alter this arrangement, a delicate business, as Mr Howgrave-Graham remarks, considering Wontner's long and valuable service. In their stead a Legal Department was created at Scotland Yard. It took the name of 'L' Department, and 'D' Department was revived. There being constant legal work and Wontner's office being in the Holborn district, one effect of this move was to save time, and it was really part of a general reorganization of Headquarters effected by the Commissioner with this end, among others, in view. Simplification was always Trenchard's aim, and at the same time he caused duties throughout the force to be so rearranged that the concentration was on essential work.

The use of wireless greatly enhanced the resources of Byng's Information Room; fifty-two Wireless Areas were created, a car with a receiver operating in each, and 2000 arrests were made by this means in the first year. The appointment of a Wireless Officer at Scotland Yard, and of Transport and Welfare Officers, improved supervision, and each district was given a superintendent, and each division a C.I.D. chief

[1] *Op. cit.*

[2] Inspector Whicher, it will be remembered, complained that he was hampered at the proceedings against Constance Kent before the magistrates at Road because the police were not legally represented, while the accused was defended by counsel.

inspector. Certain divisional boundaries were altered, and the police-box system, started in Byng's time, was extended. The whole statistical system was overhauled. Map-rooms were introduced at Scotland Yard and in districts and divisions, and what is now the daily crime report from divisions began life as the Daily Crime Telegram.

All these things formed only one aspect of Trenchard's campaign to increase efficiency. Recreation and comfort were no less important than laboratories and police-boxes. Before he came there was only one athletic ground for the four districts; each now has its own, partly supported by regular weekly subscriptions by the men, partly by what was called the Commissioner's Fund. A problem which has recently become acute was there in his time, and long before, and an ambitious programme was drawn up to provide better police stations and more as well as better married quarters and section houses for single men. The Commissioner looked ahead; they must build, he said, for 1980. War came to interrupt this process, and it is only now gathering way again.

Many years earlier Warren had said much the same thing about New Scotland Yard itself; it should have been designed, not for 1890, but for 1930. Scotland House went up, and was soon overcrowded too, and extensions across the river failed to keep up with the demand for space. Trenchard took in hand the second enlargement of New Scotland Yard. New Scotland Yard (North), or the North Building, was designed to house the whole C.I.D.; the new laboratory, the Fingerprint Department and the photographic studios, and the Criminal Record Office. It was in use, though not quite completed, a few months before the outbreak of war in 1939, and was then soon requisitioned by authorities who thought that their need was greater than that of the police. "Combined Operations" were there from 1940 to 1945. Linked by a bridge to the original New Scotland Yard, the North Building is inharmonious with that structure and its twin, the old Scotland House; but Norman Shaw is out of fashion, and it was planned by what was then the Office of Works as part of a scheme of riverside development for growing ministries.

The Commissioner's Fund has been mentioned. In Trenchard's second report he made some incisive observations on the "gratuity" system—that is, the employment and direct payment of police by private persons—which, he said, had again reached "startling proportions." He coupled with it the equally long-established custom of ticket-selling, house-to-house visitations not only by constables, but by sergeants, inspectors, and C.I.D. men, to induce the public to buy tickets for football-matches, bazaars, concerts, sales, and other recreational activities of the force. This custom obviously lent itself to abuse, because, however decorously carried out, and however worthy the object, it could become a form of compulsion, like every other kind of legalized begging, and more compelling than most. In every community there would be people who did not wish to subscribe, but had a vague idea that it was well to keep in with the police. Both ticket-selling and employment on gratuity were naturally limited to hours between turns of duty; but the police were paid as a full-time force, and off-duty hours were necessary for rest and recreation. If ticket-selling was not exhausting, a man who was employed at a wedding or a reception might well not be at his best immediately afterwards. It is surprising that these rather deleterious anachronisms had been authorized for so long. Trenchard abolished them, and in their place established the system of subscriptions referred to, and also a special Commissioner's Fund, to provide an income for athletics and charities. In connexion with employment on gratuity, it need scarcely be pointed out that no ruling can prevent a policeman earning extra money in his spare time, but he is less likely to overdo it if he knows that he is committing a serious irregularity.

In line with the sweeping away of these usages was the Commissioner's reform of what was known as the Metropolitan Police Provident Fund. This was neither provident nor a fund; springing from so-called "burial funds," it had become, though voluntary in theory, a compulsory levy on every man in the force to raise a sum of money when a fellow-officer retired, or for his widow on his death. As the money was collected only when occasion arose, there was no reserve, and the system worked very unfairly. However, it was another tradition, and the men liked it, and more than one attempt to put the "fund" on a proper actuarial basis had come to nothing. Trenchard took it in hand also; a committee of police officials had the advice of an insurance company; and, help from the Police Fund being guaranteed, the Metropolitan Police Provident Association was formed, with trustees, investments, and an income. Since everybody contributed a few pennies to the old scheme, its benefits had varied according to the strength of the force and the generosity of the givers; the new scheme fixed the contribution by all ranks at a weekly sum of *1s. 6d.*, and members secured fixed benefits—in the case of a constable with more than four years' completed service, for example, at the rate of £160 on death during service, £80 on retirement, and another £80 if death occurred within six months of this.

4

Enough has been said to show over how wide a field Lord Trenchard's energies ranged—from higher education to building, and from methods of recruitment to minor details of organization within the force. Of this last feature much has been omitted, but it may be added that in his term of office a fifth Assistant Commissioner was appointed (one of the five is now Deputy Commissioner), and four Deputy A.C.'s were put in charge of the four Police districts, over the Chief Constables. (Holders of these positions have since been renamed Commanders and Deputy Commanders.) The numbers of the higher ranks, particularly that of chief inspector, were increased; and the C.I.D. took on its first policewoman. Beside all this—and it was all done in four years—the general history of the force takes a secondary place. Events to be noted are the 1938 Committee on Detective Work and Procedure, which clarified a detective officer's powers, and the taking over by the Admiralty of the policing of the remaining dockyards which had employed small Metropolitan Police divisions since 1841. This process was completed by 1936. The establishment of the London Passenger Transport Board in 1933 clarified much of the work of the Traffic Department, by eliminating, together with the London General Omnibus Company, rival 'pirate' concerns less efficient and less easy to control. The 8000 cabs on the streets of London still included a handful of horsed four-wheelers and two hansoms.

It is not given to every reformer to earn, while still in office, the thanks of those who only a year or two before had disagreed violently with him. When, in 1935, Lord Trenchard retired from Scotland Yard it was to be expected that newspapers like *The Times* would praise him; but what may have given him more satisfaction was that even the ranks of Tuscany could scarce forbear to cheer. "Lord Trenchard's reign at Scotland Yard," said the *Daily Herald*, at one time his bitter opponent, "has left an indelible mark on the police organization of London. . . . He brought it to such a pitch that it began to work with the sureness of a machine." Going on to enumerate some of the things that had been done in four years, the *Herald* ended: " 'Give him a job,' it was once said of him, 'and he never lets go.' " The only serious complaint made against him at the time of his retirement was that he had let go, by retiring when he did; but his Commissionership was to him an interlude in another job, and he returned to what long before had become his real life's work, the welfare of the Royal Air Force.

27

THE SECOND WORLD WAR

During the next four years events which foreshadowed the Second World War, and others which affected Great Britain alone, were a distraction—except, perhaps to more than two million unemployed—from the financial situation. Though some sort of equilibrium was restored, this was still precarious; and those who, like the police, had suffered cuts in their pay, may have felt that Members of Parliament, who had imposed these cuts, chose the wrong time to raise their own salaries. This was in 1937; already King George V had died, King Edward VIII had reigned and abdicated, and King George VI and Queen Elizabeth had been crowned. Italy had invaded Abyssinia, Germany reoccupied the Rhineland and repudiated the Locarno Treaty, and there was civil war in Spain. A London landmark, the Crystal Palace, was gutted by fire. Of the domestic occasions, the Royal Funeral and the Coronation caused considerable anxiety at Scotland Yard. The lesson of the funeral of King Edward VII in 1910, when the crowds were thought enormous, was forgotten—or perhaps it would be truer to say that what was overlooked in 1936 was twenty-five years' increase in the means by which the populace of the capital could converge from the extremities upon the centre. There were some very nasty moments during the passing of King George V's funeral procession; a year later, when King George VI was crowned, everything went off well, the police having introduced a precautionary measure which has become a regular feature of ceremonial displays in London. Very stout, tall barriers, fixed in sockets in the road, blocked the ends of all side-streets on the procession's route. Many people having been frightened by the previous year's scenes, the Coronation crowds were not, in fact, as large as had been expected, and superior persons were scornful of these formidable barricades, but they had come to stay.

Sir Philip Game was now Commissioner of the Metropolitan Police. As an Air Vice-Marshal he had been with Lord Trenchard at the Air Ministry, where he stood to the latter roughly in the relationship of Horwood to Macready when they had been in the Army together. He was a sort of Chief of Staff. Like Mr Belloc's Lord Lundy, he was then sent out to govern New South Wales, from which post he was recalled to succeed his old chief and friend at Scotland Yard. Trained to read Trenchard's mind, and to interpret his plans and his language, he was another of the administrative type. Where Trenchard liked to have a finger in every pie, Sir Philip believed in delegating powers, and a system of decentralization during the War allowed great latitude to officers in charge of districts, divisions, and even sub-divisions. He was patient, imperturbable, and kind-hearted, and he positively enjoyed writing letters, which were very good ones; he could even inject a flash of humour into an annual report. His patience and good-nature were probably an asset in his relations with the Branch Boards of the Police Federation, members of which tend to be very talkative and easily ruffled. They had been badly ruffled by Trenchard's frank expression of his views upon the Federation's behaviour, however well justified these were. When long-winded deputations came to see Sir Philip Game he sat and listened to them courteously, saying little himself. If he was bored, as he must often have been, he was the last man to show it; some Commissioners, perhaps, have been less sympathetic. He seldom committed himself to an opinion on the spot, so that "if, as occasionally happened, he felt that the Board's suggestion was quite obviously impossible and said so, the deputation was so surprised that they made no attempt at argument or resistance."[1]

In short, once more the brief transit of a vigorous influence for reform and change was succeeded by what is usually referred to as a period of consolidation. The machine slowed down. The international situation apart, things were remarkably quiet, in spite of unemployment and privation; but the police had to handle a new sort of trouble caused by the Nazis' ridiculous imitators in this country, Sir Oswald Mosley's British Union of Fascists, which provoked scuffles with communists in the East End. At Scotland Yard the post of Senior Assistant Secretary, a temporary creation of Macready's, became a permanent appointment; there were until recently two of these civilian officials, for administration and traffic. In the next year, 1937, the '999' dialling scheme was introduced in London, with immediate success. Abroad, with the absorption of Austria in the Reich, and the abandonment of Czechoslovakia by her friends and allies, events were moving rapidly towards a new crisis, in sympathy with which the I.R.A., for a long time quiescent in this country, started a fresh campaign of bomb outrages in London. There were explosions in the West End, at King's

[1] Howgrave-Graham, *op. cit.*

Cross, Victoria, and elsewhere. The last few months of peace saw a reform approved by the Home Office which affected the police; the number of London coroners' districts was reduced from five to four. About the same time, in that fine summer of 1939, the departments of the C.I.D. began to leave their cramped, congested quarters in New Scotland Yard for the large, well-lighted offices behind the white façade of the North Building.

It was on Christmas Eve, 1938, that a murderer, like Franz Müller three-quarters of a century earlier, left his hat on the scene of his crime, the back-room of a jeweller's shop in Surbiton. The hat was a bowler, and Dr Eric Gardner, then County Pathologist for Surrey, deduced from it the size of the murderer's head and the fact that he was red-haired. London newspapers made a feature of this relatively simple piece of detective work, and a more garbled story presently appearing in a Berlin daily attributed almost magic arts to the pathologist. The German police do not neglect the occult, and Scotland Yard received a request for information about "the clairvoyant, Erich Gardner," from the *Reichkriminalpolizeiamt* in Berlin.

2

Within a very short time of the declaration of war against Germany on September the 3rd, 1939, the strength of the Metropolitan Police was doubled by the calling-up of pensioners, war reservists, and full-time special constables, almost all of whom had reported by the end of forty-eight hours. By the end of the year, when recruiting, except for these auxiliaries, had been stopped, the regular establishment was 19,465 and the strength 18,805; there were also on duty 18,868 war reservists, 5380 full-time 'specials,' and 2737 pensioners, making up a formidable force of 45,790 full-time police, of whom 228 were mounted and 136 women. Thousands of part-time 'specials' were enrolled as before. That previous occasion had provided some indication of the conditions London would now have to face; bombing on a large scale was a certainty, but as it was still supposed that hostile aircraft would always have to cross the North Sea, stories that began to come in from Poland were somewhat discounted. Raids on the capital, however, were expected to begin at once; and one of the first war-time jobs of the police was to help with the evacuation of tens of thousands of children, often accompanied by their mothers, to safer rural districts. It was feared that this dispersion would infect an idyllic countryside with all sorts of evils, disease in particular, but most of these alarms proved to be groundless. There were no epidemics, and an anxious inquiry from the Home Office about an alleged marked increase of drunkenness among persons evacuated to reception areas does not seem to have disclosed any very unusual tendency to escape boredom by this means. London children, however, were thought to be excessively destructive.

Among precautions taken by the Metropolitan Police on their own account were the provision of an alternative headquarters to Scotland Yard, and the leasing by the Receiver of a large school near Wimbledon Common for the overflow of an increased Headquarters staff. There seemed to be no likelihood of a second refugee problem in London on a large scale, but the Special Branch was augmented, and promotions enabled forty inspectors to be detailed for duty on war emergency measures. The Civil Defence organizations relieved the police of many tasks, notably the enforcement of the rigid blackout regulations. On the other hand, the system of air-raid warnings by sirens, of which many were fixed on police stations, at first required the services of a considerable number of men. These useful but hideous instruments were soon synchronized, so that 500 could be sounded within two minutes; and methods of operating them by switches at sub-divisional stations and at divisional headquarters had, by 1943, released 680 officers.

The British are often caught unprepared, but much forethought and planning had gone towards giving London protection against air raids. What had occurred to nobody was that for the best part of a year there would be no raids on the capital. The deceptive lull in hostilities on land, once Poland was wiped off the map, encouraged evacuated families to drift back, in spite of warnings. Time was given, however, for the development and perfection of Civil Defence methods. The Commissioner extended his decentralizing policy, with good effects when the raids did begin and communications were interrupted. From the twenty-two land divisions and the Thames Division eighty-five sub-district officers were appointed early in 1940 to consider conditions during bombing in districts as different as the West End and Stepney, or Kensington and Sunbury. A great deal of responsibility was delegated down to sub-divisions; directives issued were on general lines, and when the need for action came officers in charge of areas, who understood local problems, were not hampered by interference from above.[1] There were better ways in which the Commissioner could make his influence felt, and it must have given him great satisfaction to be able to announce in Police Orders, in January that year, that the 5-per-cent. cut in pay had been restored.

[1] Howgrave-Graham, *op. cit.*

The nine months' lull was broken, so far as London was concerned (for a further contribution by the I.R.A. scarcely counted), by the daylight raids of August 1940; and for the next year the capital was to be in the forefront of the battle. In proportion to the numbers of the police, the Fire Service, and the Civil Defence organization, losses in personnel continuously exposed to danger were not perhaps excessive, but they were high enough. The last half of this period was the worst, and between January 1 and July 28, 1941, seventy-eight raids caused 714 casualties in the Metropolitan Police and its auxiliaries. Sixty-seven men were killed and 389 seriously injured. Senior officers, from the Commissioner downward, made a point of being out and about during raids, especially at night. A number of police stations and section houses were hit, and on the 11th of May a bomb struck the south-east turret of New Scotland Yard, penetrating several floors and putting fifteen rooms out of action, including that of the Commissioner, whose table was buried beneath a cascade of filing cabinets and cards from the Registry under the roof. No one was even injured; Sir Philip Game himself was out, as usual, among his men. The people most upset appear to have been the Registry clerks, and the Secretary, called at 8 A.M. from the bed into which he had just crawled, found two young women searching a pile of rubble on the Embankment, with shaken bricks and masonry overhanging them "in a most threatening manner," for some of the million index-cards that had come fluttering down. This particular index, as it happened, needed overhauling.

At this time the possibility of invasion was still taken seriously. (Some fear of it was to be revived much later, as a last desperate throw by the enemy.) The Local Defence Volunteers had become the Home Guard, based administratively in the Metropolis on police divisions, and squads of sixty stood ready nightly in each sub-division. Iron and emergency rations had been issued to the police themselves, and when the Lease and Lend Bill was signed by the President of the United States on March the 11th the force indented under it for 25,000 revolvers and 300,000 rounds of ammunition. As this source, and factories at home, began to provide weapons for the expanding Army, instructors and recruits of high standard were needed, and a ban on policemen volunteering for the forces was lifted. Out of 833 of the Metropolitan force released, 758 joined the R.A.F. Of a large number of applicants from the war reserve and the other auxiliaries, nearly 500 were passed as fit for active service.[1]

[1] Nearly 200 Metropolitan policemen were decorated for war service. 86 won D.F.C.'s, 4 D.S.O.'s, 5 M.C.'s, 7 D.S.C.'s, and one a D.C.M.

3

After another lull of close on three years the second and in some ways the most nerve-racking mass attack on the London Area began in July 1944 with the arrival of the first batch of flying bombs. It might have been disastrous but for the retaliatory raids on launching sites by the Royal Air Force, and the unreliability of the jet-propelled missiles themselves. As it was, some 11,000 people were killed or gravely injured within three weeks.

In the early evening of September the 8th a new and even more damaging projectile struck the capital; the first rocket, the V2, exploded in a quiet residential street in Chiswick, demolishing several houses. The pretence that a gas-main had blown up could not be long maintained. The fall of more than a thousand of these huge rockets, each containing a ton of explosive, caused some shocking incidents, but quite failed in the effect intended; like the Parisians under an earlier infliction of miscalculated ingenuity, the shells of "Big Bertha," Londoners refused to be demoralized, comforting themselves with the reflection that if one heard the explosion one was all right, and arguing gravely about the respective demerits of V1 and V2. The Commissioner thought it worth while to draw attention in his annual report to this general attitude of phlegmatic good humour, instancing the lorry-driver who chalked on his van, "When Doodles dawdle duck."

These few months, however, almost trebled police casualties, and when the 1050th and final rocket fell at Orpington in March 1945, and the last of 640 alerts was sounded, eighty-four regular officers of the Metropolitan Police, and 116 auxiliaries, had lost their lives by enemy action, and just over 2000 of all kinds had been wounded. Provincial forces in safe areas were prompt in offering the most valued help by finding homes for 400 wives and children of their comrades in the Metropolis.

It should be superfluous to say that the police in London, as everywhere else, showed great gallantry in rescue work. The conditions in which this was carried on, partly in the night-time with bombs still falling—the tunnelling for buried victims amid toppling buildings and a hellish noise, fights for time against fire and fumes and burst gas- and water-mains—these were part and parcel of the Metropolitan and City policeman's life for months on end, a strain they shared with firemen and the Civil Defence squads. Inevitably many acts of courage went unnoticed or unreported. A high standard was taken for granted, and recommendations for awards were scrutinized by a national committee. Examples of exceptional devotion to duty earned for the Metropolitan force 150 medals (the King's Police Medal, the George Medal, and the British Empire Medal), and upward of a hundred commendations.[1]

The equally high standard of courage and endurance shown by the mass of ordinary London citizens was scarcely lowered by the less creditable conduct of a minority. There were a few panics, and the foreign element in some districts was a constant trial to its guardians. Panic caused one of the worst catastrophes, which could scarcely have been averted. An air-raid warning set a crowd of people fighting to find shelter in a Tube station; a woman fell on the short stairway, others tripped over her, and pressure behind piled bodies in scores on the stairs. The dead, almost all victims of suffocation, numbered 173.

4

For everybody in London the year 1945 fell into two halves. During the first war was still raging and V2's were raining on the capital; the second half was filled with what have proved to be rather premature jubilations, processions, and parades, a State Opening of Parliament, and a General Election. The Metropolitan Police, like the rest, had to readjust themselves to a relatively normal life. Homes had to be repaired; sixty-seven sets of married quarters and twelve section houses were more or less damaged. Owing largely to the stoppage of recruitment, the force was 4000 under strength; recruiting began again, and 1700 men were released from the armed services and given a three weeks' refresher course. A swarm of British and foreign deserters, without ration-books or papers, found refuge in the capital, where bombed premises were easy of access for unlawful purposes and made good hiding-places as well, and it was quite like old times to have the newspapers blaming the police for a 24·2-per-cent. increase in crime. The Fingerprint Department's annual intake of forms jumped by 10,000 above the figure for 1944, and the Main Collection passed the million. The Black Market, which had become a topic of the day during the last phase of the War, flourished exceedingly.

But in most ways the old times were gone. A second world conflict would seem to have finished a process which the first had begun, and the year 1945 has proved a turning-point in the history of nations and races all over the globe, down to every constituent of society. After so violent an upheaval the immediate necessity was reconstruction, in the

[1] Howgrave-Graham, *op. cit.*

widest sense, and in many countries this was the case in the most literal meaning of the word. Large parts of London, for instance, would have to be rebuilt; and this undertaking gave opportunity for radical reforms never seriously considered since the Great Fire, but now most urgently needed, and far beyond the limits of the City. About certain aspects of the problem, particularly facilities for traffic, there was no better authority than the police, and when, with unusual foresight, in the middle of the War, the authorities took thought for the future, the planners of a new Greater London, Sir Patrick Abercrombie and Mr J. H. Forshaw, sought advice from Scotland Yard.

No doubt they also sought it from the City Police. It is a long time since this body was on any but the friendliest terms with the Metropolitan force; but in a history of the latter it may be remarked that in the general sphere of City *versus* Metropolis, where antagonism has so often caused difficulty in the past, something of the spirit of old times seems to survive, after all. Replanning and rebuilding of Greater London is at least in hand; but a decade after victory celebrations the ruins and old narrow lanes of the City still stand where they did, and the worst traffic headache for both police forces appears to be no nearer cure.

The Metropolitan policeman, like everybody else, has been affected by another sort of planning which is a feature of the turning-point in Great Britain. The General Election of 1945 brought in a Socialist administration with a very large majority. Its ideas, as these concern police affairs, will be touched upon in the Epilogue. An immediate change at Scotland Yard was a symptom of the new order of things. Sir Philip Game retired from the Commissionership, which he had held for ten years. As Monro and Henry, both Civil Servants, were seconded for police work before they came to Scotland Yard, Game's successor, Sir Harold Scott, another Civil Servant, may be described as the first civilian to occupy the post since Sir Richard Mayne.

EPILOGUE

WITH the eviction of Combined Operations from New Scotland Yard (North), the headquarters of the Metropolitan Police was able to begin to set its three central houses in order. The release of the North Building, however, emphasized the fact that requirements were still outgrowing accommodation. Additional quarters, and not very handy ones, have had to be taken over for certain sub-divisions of the Secretariat, and new offices are going up above Cannon Row Police Station. It would seem that a great opportunity was lost when Ministries were allowed to lay hands upon the site of Buccleuch House and Henry VIII's wine-cellar; a police headquarters worthy of the capital, including every department, could have been fitted compactly into the furlong or two between Bridge Street and the Banqueting House. The Ministries could have had the Lost Property Office and the rest at Lambeth.

Norman Shaw's New Scotland Yard now houses a large part of the administrative staff—the Commissioner himself, the Deputy Commissioner, four Assistant Commissioners, and the Secretary (who has the status of a fifth A.C.), the Senior Assistant Secretary, some of the Assistant Secretaries, the Commanders and some of the subordinate senior officers of the departments, the Chief Superintendent and the two Superintendents of the Women Police, some of the Principal Executive Officers, and several hundred other officials of the police and civil staffs. There have been recent rearrangements of personnel; and one familiar rank has gone, replaced by a new one. Chief Constables of provincial forces, commanding perhaps a thousand or two thousand men, and in their way so many Commissioners responsible only to their local authorities, have never been too happy about the confusion arising from their having the same designation as officers who were second in command of Metropolitan police districts, or third in the hierarchy of the C.I.D. at Scotland Yard. For other reasons a change was thought desirable, and in the Metropolitan force the rank of Commander has been introduced, and that of Chief Constable abolished, not only in the districts and in the C.I.D. but in the headquarters staff. In the districts Commanders and Deputy Commanders have replaced Deputy Assistant Commissioners and Chief Constables. The four Police Departments at Scotland Yard, A (Administration), B (Traffic), C (Crime), and D (Organization), now have Commanders under their Assistant Commissioners, a reform which has involved the disappearance of one of the two Senior Assistant Secretaries of the old order, who had been allotted to Traffic. Headquarters also include two civil departments, the Secretariat (S) and L for legal business.

The Central Building is not entirely given over to the administrative staff. The Information Room is connected with all telephone-boxes and telephone pillars, and by two-way wireless with the area cars, 'Q' cars, motor-cycle patrols,[1] Traffic and Accident Group cars, and the launches of the Thames Division. On four glass-topped tables in the Information Room are large-scale maps of the four Metropolitan Police districts; objects resembling counters, of different shapes and colours, representing police cars and launches on duty, are moved about as the crews from time to time report their position by wireless, or are themselves moved, by the same means, on instructions from the Information Room, often because some citizen has dialled '999.' These calls come in at one end of the room, and police information and messages are handled by microphone at the other end. The Map Room (which is in the basement), as now arranged, is relatively new; it contains an enormous upright map of the London Area on a scale of sixty inches to the mile, on which thousands of pins with heads of different colours, sometimes with little flags attached, indicate the location of current crimes, from murders to pocket-picking. Colours and flags vary according to the type of crime, and in certain areas, such as big shopping streets, flags are clustered as thickly as swarms of bees. A second big vertical map, on the more normal scale of twenty-five inches to the mile, is perhaps even more interesting; it is devoted entirely to the flourishing industry of car-stealing. It may be possible to trace the route taken by a stolen vehicle for a considerable distance, and these routes are shown on the map by coloured threads—in the literal sense, clues—which will often be seen to converge towards some particular district of the capital, where, presumably, a hiding-place exists for conversion and disguise.

Across the courtyard and right of way from the Central Building, in what was Scotland House, are some of the offices of the Receiver and his staff, the architects' department in the upper floors and attics, and

[1] At the time of writing the M.P. is the only police force in the world with wireless-equipped motor-cycles.

in the basement the printing office. Some of the staff of the Traffic Department now occupy the rooms over Cannon Row Police Station, the headquarters of A Division.

Though a few departments of the Criminal Investigation Department remain in the Central Building, most of the C.I.D. has moved back into the quarters built for it before the last War, New Scotland Yard (North), the North Building. In the well-lighted upper floors are the Fingerprint Department, with its Main and Single Fingerprint Collections, the Criminal Record Office, and the photographic studios and the laboratories, these last having been moved from their original home in Hendon Police College. Here also is housed the Special Branch.

Except for the Public Carriage Office and the Lost Property Office, across the river in Lambeth, the Aliens' Registration Office, Beak Street (Recruiting), Ramillies Place (Pensions and Firearms, etc.), and Walton Street (Pay and Accounts, Records, etc.), Scotland Yard stands, as it has always stood, in A Division. A Division is in No. 1 District, and a historical link is preserved by the District's headquarters, which is in Great Scotland Yard, opposite the site of the first station-house converted from the servants' quarters of No. 4 Whitehall Place in 1829.

If the Frenchman referred to in the opening paragraph of this book had been able to read English his confused ideas about Scotland Yard might well have remained unclarified. In descriptions of these Headquarters buildings and of the work that goes on in them the epithet 'grim' is constantly applied. Almost the only department to receive serious attention is the C.I.D. If the Metropolitan Police were up to establishment the proportionate strength of the C.I.D. would be little more than a twentieth. Crime plays a relatively small part in the day-to-day work of the police force of a modern capital, especially when it is responsible for an area the size of Greater London. Outside the specialized North Building, any topic under the sun except crime may come up for discussion or inquiry at any moment. Within a few minutes the Reference Library will be answering queries about the latest amendments to the Explosives Act, the rate of widows' pensions before the Act of 1921, the spelling of Popocatapetl, and precedents for the letting off of fireworks in cinemas. Throughout the world, indeed, Scotland Yard appears to be regarded as guide, philosopher, and friend, for the request for Sherlock Holmes's autograph, or the letter from a Canadian lumberman who enclosed a dollar bill for a bottle of a particular "embrokation" once bought by him in the Strand, are merely among the rather special oddities in the volume of wishful correspondence which pours into the Commissioner's Office. Every such letter, it may be added, is replied to, and very possibly the lumberman obtained his embrocation. It still seems to be a fairly universal belief that our London police are wonderful.

It was the man on the beat, the adviser of the bewildered stranger, the controller of traffic, who first won for the force this enviable reputation. In one respect, unfortunately, times, though not the men, have changed for the worse, and the prophet is too often without honour in his own country. For this the motor-car and the rules and regulations concerning it are largely responsible. The car-owning public, which will gratefully acknowledge the courage and devotion to duty of the unarmed constable who tackles a desperado brandishing a pistol, takes a very different view of the same officer if he is compelled by his instructions to report a parking offence, or to trap a driver exceeding the speed limit. These opposed attitudes of mind are fully appreciated by police authorities everywhere. In modern traffic conditions the problem is serious, as well as difficult of solution. The authority of a civilian police force rests wholly on public approval; and with a constant increase in the number of car-owners and -drivers, leading inevitably to more and more of what too often they regard as pettifogging interference, causes of friction are multiplying. In such a state of affairs there is no place for the type of policeman or magistrate out to secure conviction for conviction's sake, a type not uncommon in the early days of motoring. Probably it is all but extinct; nowadays, indeed, so far as the police are concerned, the trend is the other way, and the lesson is enforced of the need for tact and good manners in handling minor offences of this class. Among the first to stress the importance of this factor was Lord Trenchard. The experiment of giving polite warning, instead of taking immediate action, having been tested officially with good results, the Metropolitan Police, among the rest, now has its courtesy cops to exemplify its general high standards of behaviour. But the social problem remains.

To return to the headquarters where it is always under consideration, 'grim' is the least suitable of words for the atmosphere, whatever the functions, of the various departments of Scotland Yard. As an institution this may take itself a little seriously, but as an organization it is like any other Government office (and more human than some) or any large business concern. The constable's helmet is no longer an appropriate symbol for headquarters, since the civil staff, including detached sections at Lambeth and elsewhere, numbers nearly 1500.

Women form a considerable proportion; the Commissioner and other senior persons have women secretaries on their staffs, women act as maids of all work, doing different jobs at different times and being very well informed about them all, and there are many girl typists. A mixed staff of seventy deals, among other things, with the daily flow of documents sent up to be registered and filed away. It was perhaps the women who introduced tea at the usual office hours, and large uniformed but bareheaded policemen carrying small cups along the passages somehow look particularly homely. At certain times of day the first impression the awestruck visitor receives of the 'grim' Central Building, where there are two canteens with which ventilation fails to cope—Norman Shaw never thought of canteens—is of a rather overpowering smell of food.

Also concentrated at the Metropolitan Police Office—the old style of 1829 is still in official use—are the senior representatives of the other services which make the force a self-sufficient whole: doctors and dentists (at Lambeth), engineers, and the rest. A Reception Officer looks after authorized visitors, while a Public Information Officer deals with the Press, and supplies suitable information to all who seek it. In a police force this is a very important task, and had such an official existed in earlier and more troubled days much of the misunderstanding between police and public in the Metropolis might have been avoided. Even more important, perhaps, is the internal work of the Welfare Officer, to whom all ranks can come for sympathetic advice or practical help in difficulties of every kind, from matters domestic or financial to the merely trivial.

It may be added that two public houses, virtually within the precincts, have almost acquired official status.

2

The Metropolitan Police ended the late War 4000 below establishment, recruiting having been suspended. To illustrate the Commissioner's chief anxiety during the post-war period it will be enough to say that nine years later the strength was still 4000 short of what it should be. "The position," says the Commissioner's Report for 1952,

> is really far more serious than the overall percentage shortage would suggest, for when other duties have been provided for, and they have increased greatly in recent years, it is in the men available for beat and patrol duty that the shortage is really felt. Whereas in 1932 87·6 per cent. of the men required for beat and patrol duty were available, the percentage available last year was only 44·6.

The picture presented by these startling figures is rendered the graver by a further recent increase (in 1947) in the Metropolitan Police Area, and by what the Report describes as the growth of "whole new towns" in that area. Since 1932 over a thousand extra miles of road have required patrolling.

The almost stationary discrepancy, during nine years, between strength and establishment is easily accounted for. To find a remedy is another matter. The policeman works a six-day week. He is on shift duty; and that duty covers every hour of the twenty-four. When his turn comes he is out at night and during week-ends. The Welfare State seems to have helped him little, and, indeed, has rather aggravated his discontents, for while he is doing all this his friends in industry are earning more money for a five-day week, knocking off every day in time to go to the pictures, and, if they choose to work overtime, getting very well paid for it. Moreover, what used to be an attraction in police work, privileges such as medical attention and dental treatment, are no longer privileges, since, in return for a moderate contribution, they are enjoyed by all. The policeman still has advantages peculiar to his job, particularly in the matter of pensions and generous housing allowances, but, being human, he does not always think of them. When all the various factors, pro and con a policeman's lot, are considered and whittled down, two grievances stand out—pay and housing. A third old cause of dissatisfaction among the lower ranks, the poor prospects of promotion, is still to the fore.

These problems are, of course, common, in different degrees, to all police forces in the country, but it is recognized that the Metropolitan Police has its peculiar duties and difficulties which give it special claim to consideration. Before finally touching upon official inquiries, and suggested remedies, a few events within the framework of the Metropolitan force, and one or two others of national police significance, call to be noticed.

In 1948 the Criminal Justice Bill suggested the suspension of capital punishment, and it was accordingly held in abeyance pending a Parliamentary vote. A Socialist majority in the House of Commons, against the advice of the Government, passed a vote in favour of suspension for five years; the Lords took a less sentimental view of murderers, and the clause was dropped. Seventeen convicted murderers had in the meantime been reprieved. The first to be executed after this seven-months interlude was Peter Griffiths, for the murder of a child named June Devaney in Blackburn in May of that year. The case is otherwise notable for the mass fingerprinting of the entire adult male population of Blackburn and others, to the number of more than 46,000 persons; and in this tremendous work, with its spectacular justification of the fingerprint system, C.I.D. officers from Scotland Yard played a prominent part; but to the local forces, the Blackburn Borough Police and the Lancashire Constabulary, chief credit is due for the success of an investigation that may well remain unique.

In this year also, following the deferred amalgamation of certain borough police forces, to the number of forty-five, another recommendation of the pre-war Police Council was carried into effect. A National Police College for the higher training of officers from all over the country was opened at Ryton-on-Dunsmore, in Warwickshire, appropriately almost in the centre of England. And in 1948, again, was set up the Oaksey Committee, to inquire into police conditions of service throughout Great Britain.

The Metropolitan force's own training college, now officially known as Peel House II, but universally called "Hendon," ended its short career in its original form in 1939, when Lord Trenchard's scheme for recruiting for the higher ranks from outside the force was abandoned, together with his short-service system. The disappearance of junior station inspectors has been followed by a reduction in the numbers of the much older rank of station sergeant, and there have been other alterations since the War in the senior ranks of the Metropolitan Police. Superintendents have become Chief Superintendents; chief inspectors and first-class and Sub-divisional Inspectors have become Superintendents. The present chief inspector is a new grade, having pay and responsibilities placing him on an equality with chief inspectors in provincial forces. During this period the London policeman's uniform has also undergone modification, whether solely in the interests of comfort, or to emphasize afresh his civilian character, may be conjectural. Like the soldier, he now wears a shirt with a collar and tie, blue in colour, an open-necked jacket having replaced the old tunic with its high collar. His overcoat is open-necked, and instead of the long-familiar heavy glazed waterproof cape he has a belted mackintosh of rather flimsy and insignificant appearance. Time will no doubt accustom Londoners to sartorial changes which at present seem somehow to detract from the dignity of its guardians in blue. These changes have not been universally approved in the force itself, which is nothing if not traditionalist; and a proposal to replace the helmet by a peaked cap came to nothing after a vote was taken on the question and found to be equally divided between the alternatives.

A very interesting feature of the last decade, amid much that is disappointing, or at least causing anxiety, has been the increasing popularity and success of the Women Police. Their rôle has gradually been extended to cover many of the duties which Macready, in advance of his time, foresaw for them. This is the case not only in the Metropolitan force; all provincial forces now have women police, and many their women detectives in the C.I. Branch. After the original small establishment in the Metropolitan Police began to be augmented, in the 1930's, recruiting for a time fell off; but in 1952 it was found possible and desirable to raise the establishment to over 400, which the strength very nearly reached. The establishment is now, in 1954, 524, and the strength 466. There are plenty of applicants, if not all of them attain the standard of fitness and education required. If only women did not wish to get married and set up a home and family there would seem to be no reason why the Women Police should not be always up to strength.

During Sir Harold Scott's Commissionership a number of innovations of a practical nature were introduced. Such is the small Research and Planning Branch (a recommendation of the Dixon Committee), which, under the Deputy Commissioner, from time to time reviews the organization and considers new ideas. A Traffic and Accident Group has been formed, consisting of cars and motor-cycles which can be called by wireless to the scene of a serious hold-up of traffic. The whole problem of London's traffic, constantly increasing in complexity, is always under review, and further experiments have been made in the use of one-way streets and of unilateral parking, a system already adopted in the provinces. School crossings and road surfaces are among the many other aspects of this question which come within the purview of the Traffic Department.

Civil Defence and a great influx of aliens are among the legacies of the last War which especially concern the police of the capital. The enormous increase of civil aviation has thrown a new strain on the Special Branch, which now has to keep a watch at aerodromes as well as at ports. Technical advances, however, are also at the service of the police; the Metropolitan force has considered making use of helicopters, and there is talk of a Police Air Arm. Scotland Yard employs television, and is now in communication by wireless not only with certain provincial police headquarters, but with those on the Continent. On the other hand, a very ancient device for tracking suspected criminals, once frowned upon at Scotland Yard, has again proved its value. Police dogs, mostly Alsatians, now have their own training quarters at West Wickham.

On this technical side something should be said about the great strides made in recent years by the Photographic Department. For reasons undisclosed this is still no more than a branch of the Fingerprint Department, and only with the recent upgrading of ranks has the officer in charge of it been given that of superintendent; yet its activities now cover a very wide field, and its equipment is correspondingly specialized. The cameras in normal use range from the tiny 35 mm. to the half-plate. Enlargement is carried out in the studio on the sixth floor of the North Building. The photographing of fingerprints, or of scenes of crime or of traffic accidents, is routine work; of far greater interest and ingenuity are the means now employed to detect documentary forgeries and the like. Ultra-violet and infra-red rays bring up writing apparently obliterated by chemicals, or hidden beneath paint or some other substance. The busy industry of car-stealing entails much forging of licences and registration cards; it is enough to put one of these fabricated documents under a lamp for the original writing to appear. The Heat and Chemical Process similarly brings up in a miraculous manner engine-numbers which even under a strong magnifying-glass seem to have been filed completely away. Colour photography, as an aid to criminal detection, has been found of special use to pathologists. On the educational side the Department makes its own films for training purposes.

3

The multiplicity of Select Committees, Special Committees, Royal Commissions, and other inquisitive bodies which for a century and a quarter have concerned themselves with the affairs of the police suggests that some simple numerical formula by which to distinguish one from another would be of great use. But there have been a few of these tribunals whose work has been so memorable that they will always be known, at any rate in police history, by a name—generally that of the Chairman. Such was the Desborough Committee. Another is the Oaksey Committee, referred to above, which issued its report, in two parts, in 1949. To those interested in police administration the Oaksey Reports are mentioned with respect approaching veneration.

It was the disturbing failure to keep police forces at their proper strength that brought the Oaksey Committee into being. Its task was to consider conditions of service in every police force in the country, with a view to making those conditions more attractive. For some years before 1949 the Home Office had been attacking the problem of shortage of recruits in the Metropolitan Police from a different angle; what is called a working party, under the chairmanship of Sir Arthur Dixon, has undertaken a survey of the employment and distribution of strength in that force. The aim of the survey is to discover the most efficient and economical use of manpower. It has considered, for instance, the further replacement of policemen by civilians in office duties. This step would result in the releasing of a considerable number of officers in the whole Metropolitan Area for purely police duty. But a hundred or two hundred so released represents only a drop in the ocean. The business of the Oaksey Committee was to get down to the root of the matter, the causes of the decline in recruitment, and to propose remedies.

The Committee's two reports comprise over two hundred pages of text and statistics. Recommendations for reforms of one sort or another number over ninety. The members of the Committee travelled all over England, Wales, and Scotland. It is impossible in a book of this kind to give even a précis of the views expressed and the suggestions put forward, for there has never been anything like these reports before, whether in respect of ground covered or of minute scrutiny of detail and weighing of evidence. But, as has been observed above, two factors, out of all the ninety-odd recommendations, obviously predominate—pay and housing.

Pay can be increased, almost overnight, by administrative action, as was shown in 1918; and the improved scale for constables and sergeants recommended by the Committee was immediately adopted. The pay of constables rose to £330 a year on appointment, and to £420 a year after twenty-two years' service; that of sergeants now began at £445 a year, and of station sergeants at £495. The Committee made the interesting point that "it would be more in keeping with the status of the police as a profession, and with sums of these dimensions, for constables and sergeants to be paid an annual salary rather than a weekly wage"—a suggestion which in theory has also been adopted. These increases affected every police force in the country. A later inquiry into their comparison with further rises in the cost of living, conducted by a new committee under Sir Malcolm Trustram Eve, has again led to slight augmentations of pay.

"All our witnesses," the Oaksey Committee reported, "said that housing difficulties had been one of the chief obstacles to the recruitment and retention of men." There were then, in 1949, at least 7000 out of some 56,000 married policemen without homes of their own, and a tenth of these were separated from their wives. Many of the houses in police occupation were unsatisfactory. With regard to the Metropolitan Police, which it was again recognized had its special problems, the Committee thought that more might have been done by the Commissioner and the Receiver, or, "in the last resort," by the Home Secretary, as the supreme police authority. This comment appears to have been unfair to the Commissioner, who for years pressed in vain for a higher allocation of labour and materials. The Committee, it would seem with greater justice, animadverted more severely on the conduct of planning and housing authorities, in particular on that of "practically all housing authorities in London." Few people pause to wonder how or where policemen live, and at this time the Welfare State was probably, like Martha, too busy about many other things to consider the question at all.

There has been a marked improvement in the last four or five years. Sir Harold Scott was able to report of 1952 that the Metropolitan Police had then fifty-three section houses capable of accommodating 2773 single men, of which, owing to shortage of strength, only forty were in use. It was therefore possible to concentrate on married quarters. The Commissioner obtained approval for a programme of 5000; by the end of the year 2466 of these quarters were in occupation, and another 1400 were under construction or in the planning stage. Older premises were being modernized, and there was a further proportion purchased or rented by the Receiver. There were then nearly 1500 men waiting for official accommodation, of whom 214 were living apart from their families. Local authorities were still proving unhelpful on the whole; only five, the Commissioner observed, were letting houses or flats to the Receiver. At any rate, Lord Trenchard's comprehensive and far-seeing scheme of rebuilding is again gathering way; in 1954 Sir Harold Scott was able to write: "The housing problem, I am glad to say, is in sight of solution."[1]

When first section houses were built expressly for the purpose of housing single policemen, they were small buildings. It was Trenchard who told the architects at Scotland Yard that they must build for 1980, not for their own times, and it was then that there began to rise the big police hostels of to-day. It is said that many men disliked them, preferring the old cramped and often inconvenient quarters because they were more homely. There are now section houses going up with space about them and accommodation and amenities that make for homeliness, whatever the scale. The new married quarters completed or being completed, blocks of flats with two or perhaps three bedrooms,

[1] Sir Harold Scott, *Scotland Yard* (Deutsch, 1954).

will bear comparison with any other buildings of the kind, and are, indeed, better than many for which high rents are charged. The housing problem, which has plagued the Metropolitan force since Wray went hunting among the old watch-houses of the 1820's, is at last not only in sight of solution, but being tackled in the right way.

In line with the national recommendations of the Oaksey Committee is a very recent reorganization (in 1954) of the Police Council. It is, in fact, more than a reorganization; a new Police Council has been created to supersede the old, in co-operation with which it is already functioning, pending legislation to regularize its position. The old Council will then disappear. The new body has an independent chairman appointed for three years by the Prime Minister and eligible for reappointment. Under him are three panels to deal with matters affecting respectively (*a*) police officers above the rank of Chief Superintendent, (*b*) Chief Superintendents and superintendents, and (*c*) the federated ranks—inspectors and below. Questions of discipline and promotion affecting individuals are outside the purview of the Council; otherwise it has power, through its panels, to negotiate on such matters as pay, expenses, allowances, hours of duty, and leave, while it may also advise the Secretaries of State on pensions and any other questions, not negotiable, which may be referred to it. The Council and its panels are organized in two sides, staff and official, the latter comprising representatives of the Home Office, the Scottish Home Department, and the associations representing local authorities in both countries and in Wales. On the staff side are delegates of the senior police grades (including the Women Police), the Police Federation of England and Wales, and the Scottish Police.

It was while the Oaksey Committee was sitting that the national problem of manning the police was attacked from a new direction by certain provincial forces; and in 1949, in which year the Committee issued its report, the early results of these forces' experiments with police cadets were announced by the Inspectors of Constabulary. A total of 741 cadets was then undergoing training, a total which within a few years was nearly doubled. In the meantime the Metropolitan Police had adopted the scheme, an establishment of 160 cadets being authorized for the Metropolitan Area in May 1951. There was a rush of applicants, over a thousand coming forward in the first fortnight, and by the end of the year 2300 names had been on the roll for examination. Of these, 525 applicants were considered suitable, and, the establishment being raised to 175, the remainder were put on a waiting-list.

These youths, from the age of sixteen, were given two years' training. Divided into six groups, they went to Peel House II, otherwise Hendon, for four weeks, and were then distributed among Metropolitan Police districts and divisions, where they gained practical experience in clerical work or in garages and elsewhere, as well as a general insight into the whole machinery of a modern police force. Put into uniform, they received pay—£3 or £4 a week, according to age.

The scheme seemed so successful that in 1952 the establishment of the cadets was raised by stages to 500. Twelve months later the first entrants, having completed their training as cadets, were called up for national service. Police cadets are now, however, exempt from national service provided they join the police force and remain in it until they are twenty-six years of age.

4

The present Metropolitan Police Area reaches out some fifteen miles from Charing Cross—from Thames-side Dagenham and Erith on the east to Staines and Cobham on the west, and along the north–south axis from Cheshunt and Elstree to Orpington and Walton-on-the-Hill. The whole is divided into eleven small central police divisions, eleven large outer ones, and the Thames Division—the police afloat. According to the size of the division, the Chief Superintendent in charge has under him three or four superintendents of sub-divisions. Each of the four districts in which the twenty-three divisions are grouped is controlled by a Commander and his Deputy Commander.

The core of this structure is A Division, in which Scotland Yard stands, and which is curiously shaped, being virtually in two parts, joined by a narrow neck at Hyde Park Corner. Westward of this neck the divisional area consists of open space—Hyde Park and Kensington Gardens. These are Crown property, as are St James's Park, in the other half of the division, and Green Park which is also in A, and for a time all four were policed by the Metropolitan force; but all except Hyde Park have now been returned to the charge of park-keepers under the authority of the Royal Parks Division of the Ministry of Works, which also meets the cost of the pleasantly embowered police station in Hyde Park itself, with its considerable staff and its tiny sub-stations in the attics of Marble Arch and the Wellington Arch at the top of Constitution Hill.[1] The eastern part of A Division forms a striking contrast to such rural scenes, for it contains packed within it all that goes to make up the heart of the nation, the Commonwealth,

[1] Other parks and gardens in London are the responsibility of public authorities, including the L.C.C.

and the Empire. The peculiar functions of the division thus include the safeguarding of the Royal Family and of two royal palaces, of the Ministries and their Ministers and the Houses of Parliament and their Members, and of embassies, diplomats, and every sort of V.I.P. Its position and experience has also made the division pre-eminent, even in the Metropolitan Police, in the technique of handling crowds. The Festival of Britain and the Coronation of Queen Elizabeth II have launched a revival of ceremonial occasions, and with ample transport the public habit of streaming into the centre of London on the slightest excuse is making crowd control in this area a periodical problem.

Every one of the twenty-two other divisions has problems of its own—crowds, generally in the form of political meetings, among them, though from this factor the Thames Division is happily exempt. Such necessities are reflected in the concentration of police in a given area. The most highly policed divisions, for their size, are those in the centre of the Metropolis, A, C, D, and E, which together cover little more than four square miles. The small but densely crowded Whitechapel Division (H) also has a high establishment, and other East End divisions run it close, for the same reason—density of population, sometimes very mixed. With the outer ring conditions are reversed, divisional areas jumping from a square mile or so to thirty, fifty, and in two cases, S and X, to more than eighty square miles. Excluding the C.I.D., police on special employment, and the Thames Division, a very small one, the average authorized establishment of a division is rather more than 800, but this, in present conditions, is a paper strength.

The Metropolitan Police District, represented by the large outer divisions, has made considerable encroachments upon what are generally known as the Home Counties—Hertfordshire, Essex, Kent, and Surrey. (Two more, Middlesex and the County of London—excluding the City—have been swallowed whole.) To the bigger houses, with their estates, which have for centuries fringed the capital, the suburban spread has added many more of some size. Usually the homes of well-to-do or wealthy business men, and often rather isolated, these residences are an invitation to enterprising cracksmen equipped with cars, and a long series of successful country-house robberies round London has led very recently to the formation of the Home Counties Crime Branch of the C.I.D., with its Country House squads. The result of consultations between the Commissioner (Sir Harold Scott) and the Chief Constables of the counties concerned, this new measure entails police co-operation of a novel kind. Though the Country House squads are in the charge of a Metropolitan detective superintendent, Grade I, who takes his orders from the Assistant Commissioner (C), they are mixed bodies of Metropolitan and provincial police officers, who work together as a unit, instead of in the fortuitous combinations hitherto employed. The outcome of this experiment, which dates only from 1954, will be watched with interest—especially by the potential victims of the specialists in large-scale rural felonies.

In this connexion it may be emphasized here that the Metropolitan Police has been so successful as a prototype and teacher that it no longer occupies the unique position, with respect to other police forces in the country, which it held for a century or more. The constabularies of large provincial boroughs and counties have attained an equally high stage of efficiency, and, as has been mentioned, have sometimes taken the lead in the introduction of improved technical equipment. It has also been pointed out that in consequence Scotland Yard, in the form of the Metropolitan C.I.D., is nowadays far less often 'called in' to investigate cases of major crime than was the rule (if sometimes acted upon rather belatedly) until recent times. The National Police College at Ryton seems likely to further this process. On the technical side the provinces not only possess first-class forensic laboratories (some antedating that originally established at Hendon), but they have their own fingerprint bureaux, one for the Midlands and one for the northern districts. These bureaux, however, while serving the local forces and forming their own fingerprint collections, send duplicates of every print or set of prints taken to Scotland Yard, where the Fingerprint Department still contains the only national collection. Also still national in their scope are the Criminal Record Office at Scotland Yard and C.6, otherwise the Fraud Squad. Within the last few years chief inspectors and detective constables of this sub-department have been lent to Board of Trade organizations all over the country to help in unravelling a conspiracy to divert china for export to the home market.[1] C.6 now works in close co-operation with the City Police.

Though a gradual levelling process may be changing certain scales of value at home, the international reputation of "Scotland Yard" remains as high as ever, and not only in the valley of the Isère. Dominion and Colonial officers attend courses at the Metropolitan Police Detective Training School, and study Metropolitan Police methods in general. Foreign countries send police representatives for the same purpose; and senior officers from Scotland Yard, seconded to the

[1] Sir Harold Scott, *op. cit.*

Foreign and Colonial Offices, are sent overseas to organize or command police forces in lands as differently circumstanced as Western Germany and Austria, Trieste, Greece, Kenya, and Malaya.

In this international sphere an event of incalculable importance in police history has to a great extent realized the dreams of Juan Vucetich, the Dalmatian Director of the Fingerprint Bureau in Buenos Aires fifty years ago. Far ahead of his time, Vucetich recommended the establishment of inter-continental bureaux of criminal identification, one to be in North America, one in South America, and one in Europe. Before the last World War there came into being the International Criminal Police Commission, now revived, with its Headquarters and General Secretariat in Paris, in the Boulevard Gouvion-Saint-Cyr. In this building information about criminals of all nationalities is hourly being pooled, collated, and passed on to interested members of the organization—that is to say, to every country in Europe except those under Russian control, to certain South American states, and to such a newcomer as Israel. For physical reasons, among others, the Metropolitan C.I.D. works in very close contact with the Commission Internationale de Police Criminelle, and the names and personalities of certain prominent officials at Scotland Yard are as well known in the Boulevard Gouvion-Saint-Cyr as they are in Westminster.

In Westminster itself a still more recent innovation rounds off appropriately, and perhaps significantly, one hundred and twenty-five years of Metropolitan Police history. Between Sir Richard Mayne and Sir Harold Scott only one civilian, Monro, has been appointed to the office of Commissioner; and the long list of distinguished men holding this post during a century and a quarter contains the name of only one policeman, and during the greater part of Sir Edward Henry's career in India he was in the Civil Service. Sir Harold Scott's successor is a policeman not only by training, but by inheritance. Sir William Nott-Bower, having been Chief Constable of Liverpool, was Commissioner of the City Police at the time of the Sidney Street battle and the mutinies; his son, now Sir John Nott-Bower, was then in the Indian Police. He came to Scotland Yard in 1933 as Deputy Assistant Commissioner, became Assistant Commissioner (A) in 1940, and Deputy Commissioner six years later. He succeeded Sir Harold Scott as Commissioner in August 1953. This appointment of a man who has, if only in a limited sense, risen from below, and who for more than twenty years has held the King's Police Medal, should gratify the shade of Robert Peel.

SELECT BIBLIOGRAPHY

ALLEN, L. B.: *Brief Considerations on the Present State of the Police of the Metropolis* (1821).
ALLEN, M. S.: *The Pioneer Policewoman* (Chatto and Windus, 1925).
ANON: *Fatal Effects of Gambling* (1824).
Annual Register, The.
ARMITAGE, GILBERT: *The History of the Bow Street Runners*, 1729–1829 (Wishart, 1932).
AYDELOTTE, FRANK: *Elizabethan Rogues and Vagabonds* (Clarendon Press, 1913).
"BRITANNICUS": *A Letter to the Honourable House of Commons*, etc. (1750).
CLARKSON, C. T., and RICHARDSON, J. H.: *Police!* (1889).
COLQUHOUN, PATRICK: *A Treatise on the Police of the Metropolis* (sixth edition, 1800).
CREW, ALBERT: *The Old Bailey* (Nicholson and Watson, 1933).
"CUSTOS": *The Police Force of the Metropolis in* 1868 (1868).
DILNOT, GEORGE: *Scotland Yard* (Bles, 1929).
——: *The Trial of the Detectives* (Bles, 1928).
FIELDING, JOHN: *A Plan for Preventing Robberies* (1755). *An Account of the Origin and Effects of a Police set on Foot by His Grace the Duke of Newcastle in the Year* 1753, *upon a Plan presented to His Grace by the Late Henry Fielding* (1758).
FOWLE, T. W.: *The Poor Law* (1881).
GLOVER, E. H.: *The English Police* (Police Chronicle, 1934).
GURNEY, W. B.: *The Trials of Joseph Merceron* (1819).
HART, J. M.: *The British Police* (Allen and Unwin, 1951).
HAWORTH, PETER: *Before Scotland Yard* (Blackwell, 1927).
HOBHOUSE, HENRY: *Diary* (Home and Van Thal, 1947).
HOLLOWAY, ROBERT: *The Rat Trap* (1773).
HOWGRAVE-GRAHAM, H. M.: *Light and Shade at Scotland Yard* (Murray, 1948).
INDERWICK, F. A.: *The King's Peace* (1895).
IRVING, JOSEPH: *The Annals of Our Time* (1880).
JAYNE, E. EVERETT: *Jonas Hanway* (Epworth Press, 1929).
JONES, B. M.: *Henry Fielding* (Allen and Unwin, 1929).
LAWRENCE, FREDERICK: *The Life of Henry Fielding* (1855).
LEE, W. L. MELVILLE: *A History of Police in England* (Methuen, 1901).

LESLIE-MELVILLE, R.: *The Life and Work of Sir John Fielding* (Lincoln Williams, 1934).

LOCKIE, JOHN: *Topography of London* (1810).

MACFARLANE, CHARLES, and ARCHER, THOMAS: *The Popular History of England* (1886).

MACNAGHTEN, MELVILLE L.: *Days of My Years* (E. Arnold, 1914).

MACREADY, NEVIL: *Annals of an Active Life* (Hutchinson, 1925).

MALLET, C. E.: *Lord Cave: A Memoir* (Murray, 1931).

MARRIOTT, J. A. R.: *Modern England: 1885–1932* (Methuen, 1934).

MARTIENSSON, A. K.: *Crime and the Police* (Secker and Warburg, 1951).

MILDMAY, WILLIAM: *The Police of France* (1763).

"MORNING HERALD": *The Punishment of Death* (1836–37).

MOYLAN, JOHN F.: *Scotland Yard and the Metropolitan Police* (Putnam, 1929).

NOTT-BOWER, WILLIAM: *Fifty-two Years a Policeman* (E. Arnold, 1926).

POLICE, METROPOLITAN: *Case of the City considered* (1839).

RADZINOWITZ, L.: *A History of English Criminal Law*, vol. i (Stevens, 1948).

REITH, CHARLES: *The Police Idea* (Oxford University Press, 1938).

——: *The British Police and the Democratic Ideal* (Oxford University Press, 1943).

SCOTT, HAROLD R.: *Scotland Yard* (Deutsch, 1954).

SOLMES, ALWYN: *The English Policeman* (Allen and Unwin, 1935).

THOMSON, BASIL: *The Story of Scotland Yard* (Grayson, 1936).

TOMLIN, MAURICE: *Police and Public* (Long, 1936).

TROUP, EDWARD: *The Home Office* (Putnam, 1925).

DE VEIL: *Life and Times of Sir Thomas de Veil* (1748). (Anonymous.)

VOLTAIRE: *An Essay on Crimes and Punishments, with a Commentary attributed to Mons. de Voltaire* (1770).

WALLAS, GRAHAM: *Life of Francis Place* (Allen and Unwin, 1925).

WELCH, SAUNDERS: *An Essay on the Office of Constable* (1758).

WHITE, W.: *The Police Spy* (1838).

Annual Reports of the Commissioners of the Police of the Metropolis; Minutes of Evidence, House of Commons Select Committee, 1816; Report of the Committee on Police Conditions of Service (the Oaksey Report), 1949; reports of Parliamentary and Home Office Committees and Royal Commissions; *The Police Journal*; etc.

INDEX